Hidden Job Market 1994

A Job Seeker's Guide to America's 2,000 Little-Known, Fastest-Growing High-Tech Companies

**Selected from the
Corporate Technology Database
Compiled by CorpTech
(Woburn, Massachusetts)**

Peterson's Guides
Princeton, New Jersey

ISSN 1064-1769
ISBN 1-56079-316-3

Composition and design by Peterson's Guides

Printed in the United States of America

10 9 8 7 6 5 4 3 2 1

Contents

Competing for Jobs in the Information Age

Richard A. Shinton
Director of Human Resources
Exabyte Corporation

Welcome to the information age. We live in a fascinating new world, one in which the workplace has changed forever. As we approach the on-ramp to an information superhighway leading who knows where, there's a PC on every desk, and now almost all of those PCs are connected to a network. High-tech used to mean the computer industry—not anymore. High-tech has reached into every job, every company. It is simply a way of business life.

Today's job seekers face the challenge of adapting to and excelling in a world that never slows its pace. Daunting? Yes. But the information revolution has spawned more creative opportunities than ever before in the American workplace. Entire industries—biotechnology, for example—spring to life seemingly overnight. Entrepreneurs spin off companies that grow, thrive, and vanish like summer thunderstorms.

We live in an economic world that was unimaginable just a few decades ago. Industry has changed. The workforce has changed. You are being asked to bring greater capabilities to jobs—even entry-level personnel must know several word-processing packages. And, ironically, these jobs are inherently less secure, but that's just the nature of the high-tech environment. What all of this does is place the responsibility for a successful career back where I believe it has belonged all along: on you, the employee.

The idea of remaining with one company all the way to retirement is fading fast, as it should. It's a fallacy that any company can determine what is best for you as a person. And while this instability and demand for employee responsibility can create some difficulties, I believe the benefits are far greater. Employees now find themselves in jobs that allow for continuous learning, even at the higher levels of management. Although I've been a human resources professional for more than fifteen years, every day I come into contact with a new software package or create a flexible benefits package to reflect the diverse nature of today's corporate payroll—from single mothers to head-of-household fathers. One size no longer fits all. This means that life in the company will never be as easy as it once was.

Or as stifling.

Put Technology to Work for You—But Don't Forget ...

So how do you keep up? You work with these changes, and you uncover opportunities. You make technology work for you. Start with the job search itself. The world is smaller now. You're not limited by geographic concerns. Your resume can be in a distant human resources office in just seconds, thanks to the fax machine and the modem. Master these modern-day tools. Harness them and use them in your search. If you have a PC at home, use it to learn software packages that will prove helpful in the industries you've targeted. Keep expanding.

Apply technology to show creativity even as part of your job-search process. I've seen graphic artists include diskettes with a brief software slide show of their work. Confirm receipt of your resume through the use of electronic mail. Show that you know how to put technology to work for you. Use it to separate yourself from the pack—that's exactly what employers want. But, as always, be careful to avoid gimmickry. Sell yourself the same way you would sell one of your ideas on the job.

You must also be aware that today's employers are often looking beyond your specific skill set. As someone who has overseen hiring through periods of tremendous growth, I know we can't afford to bypass creative, dynamic people just because they lack experience in one certain area. We look for people who show confidence that they can learn whatever they need to learn. You can demonstrate this confidence by familiarizing yourself—familiarizing, not necessarily becoming an expert—with the tools of business. Show that you understand the concepts of word-processing, database, and spreadsheet software, that you have an idea about how these packages help make a business more effective. Skill is nothing but the implementation of talent. I believe that we're all born with the same amount of talent and that we have an unlimited capacity to learn. Take the talent you were born with, and turn it into something employers can use. And let them know about it.

But don't let your view get too sidetracked by technology. In the end we always come back to the basics, even in the high-tech arena. There's no substitute for hard work. You may dazzle prospective employers with your application of technology, but their interest will only last as far as a phone call if you haven't build a reputation as a quality contributor to the teams you've worked with in the past. You need to be reliable. Go to work on time. Go to work every day. And once you're there, accept responsibilities. You're not going to get ahead by picking and choosing projects. Take charge of what needs to be done and *do it*. That's how you build a name as an effective person. Does that mean harder work and more hours? Probably so. Does it mean you'll always get real-time rewards for your efforts? Probably not. But in the end you'll come out ahead because that reputation as a make-it-happen player will precede you wherever you go.

What it boils down to is this: the same thing that made people successful in the 1920s makes people successful in the 1990s. There's no substitute for getting the job done.

Employees and Employers: A New Relationship

No other time in history has given the job seeker so many options. And the high-tech world takes those options to the extreme. Do you want to be part of a startup team, or are you looking for something more established? Do you want a loosely structured environment where you essentially manage yourself, or do you prefer a solid chain of command where you work closely with managers and supervisors? There's something out there for everyone. The first step to finding a position that's right for you is recognizing that you have some power and responsibility in the job-search process.

Determine what it is you want. Not just from a job, but from your life. You need to go through some sort of self-examination before throwing yourself into the market. Figure out what is important to you personally, because work isn't all that different. I'll often ask people, "What do you have fun doing? What is the most fun you ever had at work?" It's vital that you *know* these things, not just that you have an answer.

Then learn about the companies with which you hope to work. This comes back to putting technology to work for you—it's easy to find basic information about companies. Look at the information you uncover from two sides. First, does this company fit your desired profile, whether through its financial outlook, management styles, or kinds of jobs and growth opportunities? You'll find yourself much more effective when you are competing for a position you truly desire. Second, know what the company actually does. Human resources personnel don't expect you to be a walking encyclopedia about their company, but if you've taken the time to send in a resume, you should at least know what business they're in. By not knowing the basics, you paint an all-too-real—at not very appealing—picture of the kind of employee you will be.

This book is called *The Hidden Job Market*. I like that, because there are markets—especially today—that you must uncover for yourself. We've come through a difficult time in American business recently. People have been through layoffs and have gotten caught in downsizing. But once again, every crisis creates opportunity. Don't base your strategy on panic, saying "I've got to find a job right now." Instead, think about the options. You could work for a temporary agency while you plan your job search. Many companies now use consultants and contract groups. Take care of your physical needs, and put some time into building a plan that works for you.

Finally, never let yourself become complacent, even when you've won the perfect job. It comes back to taking responsibility for your life. You can be loyal to your employer and, at the same time, think about your future. Understand the high-technology trade-off: excitement and creativity for traditional security. You always have to have a plan. It's your own insurance policy.

Communicate, Communicate, Communicate

To get what you want from a job, you need to let people know exactly what you want. Make it clear during the interviewing process, during the negotiation process, and, most of all, once the work has commenced. The "hidden" job usually isn't very far from a job you already have.

Some companies, like Exabyte, sponsor employee-education programs on everything from software packages to personality dynamics. If you find something that interests you, learn all you can about it, and let your enthusiasm shine through in your work, your resume, and your interviews. The best positions are those that are created. Play a role in that process. Sell yourself and your talent/ skills package. Innovation is the crux of all high-tech industries. Make yourself and your work visible. Make your voice heard. Drive your ideas into every part of your professional life.

One of the most exciting aspects of today's corporations is their focus on team building and teamwork. More and more companies are forming Total Quality Management programs or employee-action teams as a way of empowering employees. Volunteer for teams focusing on areas in which you're interested. These teams often report directly to the president or to other executives in the corporation. One of the best ways to tap into unseen opportunity is to make yourself visible to those at the top levels. Never turn down a chance to do this.

At Exabyte, we've tried to give every employee an opportunity to be heard by holding a monthly breakfast where a group of 10 or so employees meets with the CEO. Don't view such events as useless gestures. The reason management does this is because they *really do* want to hear what's on your mind. Tell them! Let someone know if your job has become less challenging than you would like. Propose a project of your own design and offer to lead it. Make it happen and see what transpires. *The job you've always wanted just may be the one you already have.*

Follow the time-proven methods of networking. Join professional organizations and make yourself available to serve on event or program committees. You'll meet countless people who have made it to where you're trying to go. Knock them out with your energy and creativity. Be open to all possibilities. Who knows what could transpire through a casual contact?

Finally, throughout my years of experience I have found that all successful people share one trait, and it's something that anyone can master: *learn to change ideas into action.* By doing this you become more than an asset. You become a vital force—a hot commodity, so to speak. This trait will come out in interviews. It will come out in your current job. It will come out in any conversation where your name arises.

In today's competitive and high-tech world, you just don't have the option of showing up every day for forty years and then collecting a gold watch and a pension. You've got to carve your own niche. You've got to meet management on its own level, with your hand extended and your grip firm. Find the ways to do this, and you'll find all the opportunities you once thought were hidden.

Richard A. Shinton heads the human resources department at Exabyte Corporation. He was the first member of this department in 1988, when Exabyte had just a handful of employees. Now he oversees the department, maintaining responsibility for more than 1,100 employees.

Exabyte Corporation of Boulder, Colorado, designs, manufactures, and markets tape backup subsystems to a worldwide customer base. Founded in 1985, the company has shipped nearly half a million subsystems to date. Exabyte reported more than $287 million in revenue in 1992.

The Thriving Technology Industry

Andrew Campbell
President
CorpTech Information Services, Inc.

Manufacturers and developers of technology products constitute the most successful business segment in the country today, the one major area that has expanded consistently over the past decade. With every facet of industry, commerce, and government looking to them to solve problems of productivity and competitiveness, technology companies are creating our tomorrow, and many analysts anticipate that this will be the sector that leads the economy back to prosperity.

Although many large technology manufacturers are experiencing considerable difficulty, small and midsize companies have been better able to adapt to changing demands and consequently have been riding a steady wave of expansion. Technology manufacturers with under 1,000 employees now represent over 20 percent of durable goods manufacturing employment, and, in 1992, this was the strongest sector of the economy:

- Overall employment expanded by 3.3 percent.
- More than one firm in eight expanded by over 25 percent.

In contrast, during 1992, the U.S. Department of Labor reported a net reduction of 1.7 percent in durable goods manufacturing.

The next year promises to be even more exciting. Between March and May 1993 CorpTech surveyed 2,129 emerging technology manufacturers with under 1,000 employees. These firms projected a combined job growth rate of 5.6 percent during the following year, with one in five expecting to grow at over 25 percent. The graph on the next page gives the growth projections broken down by industry.

Over 90,000 Jobs Created

The 2,000 firms listed in *The Hidden Job Market* were selected from a unique database of 35,000 technology manufacturers and developers created by Corporate Technology Information Services, Inc. (CorpTech), one of the country's leading suppliers of information on

Projected Job Growth in Emerging Technology Manufacturers

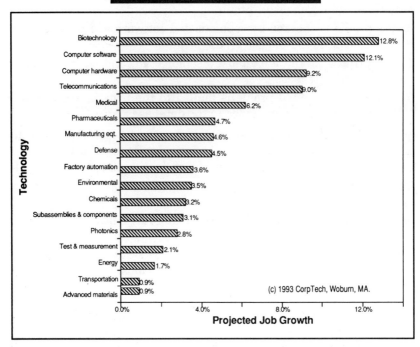

Technology	Projected Job Growth
Biotechnology	12.8%
Computer software	12.1%
Computer hardware	9.2%
Telecommunications	9.0%
Medical	6.2%
Pharmaceuticals	4.7%
Manufacturing eqt.	4.6%
Defense	4.5%
Factory automation	3.6%
Environmental	3.5%
Chemicals	3.2%
Subassemblies & components	3.1%
Photonics	2.8%
Test & measurement	2.1%
Energy	1.7%
Transportation	0.9%
Advanced materials	0.9%

(c) 1993 CorpTech, Woburn, MA.

the high-tech industry. These are the firms with under 1,000 employees that added the most employees during the survey year. In fact, these 2,000 companies expanded their combined work force by 28 percent in the past year, creating over 90,000 new jobs!

These are not just technical jobs that are being created. Expanding firms need people in all areas and at all levels of experience—from sales to clerical, from manufacturing to accounting, and from entry level to senior management. This is the hidden job market.

How Does CorpTech Collect Its Information?

CorpTech has assembled the country's most comprehensive source of information about technology companies. It tracks over 35,000 technology manufacturers and developers with a unique five-stage research and checking process:

1. New and emerging firms are identified through local economic development groups, trade associations, the trade press, and other technology companies. Each is then entered into a central database.

2. Each new company is interviewed by phone for information on over 100 data elements, which are then entered into the database to form a comprehensive profile.
3. The profile is checked by sophisticated software and printed. Any errors detected are flagged on the printout.
4. The printed profile is edited by senior staff, and corrections are made to the database.
5. A copy of the edited profile is mailed to the firm for verification, and any corrections are added to the database.

Steps 2 through 5 are repeated each year for each company to ensure the currency and accuracy of the database, which has been continuously refined for nine years at an investment of over $4 million.

What Information Can You Find in This Book?

The companies listed in this book are arranged alphabetically by state and by telephone area code within the state. (See the map of area codes immediately following this article.) Most profiles include:

- Company name and address
- Year the company was founded
- Number of employees
- Annual sales revenue in the survey year
- The technology industries in which the company is active
- Number of employees added in the year prior to CorpTech's latest interview
- Percentage of growth, based on the previous year's employee number
- Contact name and title (usually the executive responsible for the personnel function or the chief executive officer)
- Telephone and fax numbers

The company listings are followed by two indexes. The **Industry Index** lists the companies in this book according to the industry or industries in which they are active, along with their state and the page number of their profile. The eighteen categories of technology industry used are as follows:

- Advanced Materials
- Biotechnology
- Chemicals
- Computer Hardware
- Computer Software
- Defense
- Energy
- Environmental

- Factory Automation
- Holding Companies
- Manufacturing Equipment
- Medical
- Pharmaceuticals

- Photonics
- Subassemblies and Components
- Telecommunications
- Test and Measurement
- Transportation

The **Company Index** lists companies alphabetically, giving their state and the page number on which their detailed information appears.

Using the Book to Your Advantage

This book has been developed to assist in all three phases of the job-hunting process:

1. Identifying potential employers
2. Persuading a potential employer that you are a good applicant
3. Convincing a potential employer that you would be a good employee

Identifying Potential Employers

For a company to be regarded as a potential employer, it must currently be hiring new staff, be in a location where you wish to work, and be an employer of people with your skills at your income level. No approach will guarantee success, but the following steps will help you identify potential employers.

1. *Concentrate on growing companies.* Simply by using this book, you have an advantage over other job seekers. The 2,000 firms profiled are those that have added the most new jobs in the past year in the most dynamic sector of the country's economy.
2. *Find companies in your area.* Turn to your state in the book and find your telephone area code. The companies in that area code are listed alphabetically by name. Scan the profiles for organizations in cities that are close to you.
3. *Find companies active in your industry.* If your job skills are specific to a particular industry, turn to the **Industry Index**. Firms active in specific areas of industry are listed alphabetically, with a page number directing you to their detailed description.
4. *Use the press.* Read the business section of your local paper and the regional and national business press. Look for stories about firms that are doing well. Notice which companies have just won a major contract, opened a new manufacturing plant, or are simply growing rapidly. When you find one that sounds interesting, look for it

in the **Company Index**; if it is listed, the index will direct you to its profile.

Once you have found a firm that you would like to approach, call its sales department and request company literature. When this arrives, scan it to gain an overview of the company's products, noting questions that occur to you. If you are still interested, memorize the main facts—number of employees, growth, annual sales, and industries in which the company is active. (For the firms listed in *The Hidden Job Market 1994,* all of this information is featured.) Now you are ready to make contact.

Persuading a Potential Employer That You Are a Good Applicant

Remember that companies receive job applications every day. Your task is to make your application stand out from the pack so that you get an interview. The good news it that 95 percent of job applications are poorly prepared, and yours won't be among them if you take this advice:

- Don't mail out a form letter to dozens of firms.
- Don't enclose a poorly copied resume—in fact, don't enclose a resume at all. The task at this phase is to get in the door, not to get hired. The more you say about yourself, the more reasons the employer will have to cross you off the list before ever meeting you.
- Don't apply to a company unless you can think of several reasons you would be of value. Consider the job for which you are applying, and write down the skills and experience it requires. Then note your own skills and experience as they relate to the employer's needs. If your skills and experience are strong, make sure you communicate this to the company. If they are not, think about another job. If *you* can't think of some good reasons why you should be hired, it is certain the company won't either!

On the positive side, there are a number of things you can do to advance your application:

- Make a personal approach to a named executive, not just to a department. (The listings in this book usually give the name of the personnel director or CEO.)
- Make your initial contact a telephone call rather than a letter.
- Make sure you are sufficiently prepared *before* making your approach.
- Explain in as few words as possible what you have to offer the company, emphasizing your past accomplishments rather than fu-

ture goals. The world is full of dreamers with goals, but companies hire people to do a job, and your list of actual accomplishments is your best selling tool. Even if you are looking for your first job, you should be able to cite accomplishments in community or leisure activities that demonstrate your ability to define a goal and work to achieve it.

- If you choose to approach the executive in writing, call first to double-check his or her name, title, and address and make sure that the person is still in the same position. Make your letter brief, and design it to get yourself in the door only. There must be no typing or spelling errors. The letter should be perfect and attractively laid out. Use a word processor with a good printer if you have them, or enlist the aid of a friend or professional who does. You will be judged by the impression the letter makes.

- If you phone as suggested, rehearse your technique with a friend until you know without thinking what you will say to a variety of responses, from "He's not in" to "We aren't hiring" to "Put your resume in the mail" to "Why should I see you?"

- Whether you call or write, use your knowledge of the firm's products to explain why you think that you would be of value to the company, and request an interview.

Convincing a Potential Employer That You Would Be a Good Employee

Take the sales literature you received to the interview together with the list of questions you compiled. Make a point of asking your questions as early in the interview as possible, showing the interviewer that you are serious and interested. Refer to the job analysis you made, and ask if this accurately defines the skills and experience required—this demonstrates that you have made an effort to see the job from the employer's perspective, a valuable quality. The answers you receive to these questions will allow you to present yourself in a way that is relevant to the company's needs.

In interviewing hundreds of job applicants over many years, I have found that most interviewees have little or no knowledge of the companies to which they apply. This comes across as a lack of interest. Those few who take the modest amount of time needed to do the kind of research described stand out head and shoulders above the rest. They are not simply *claiming* competence, they are *demonstrating* it! And remember that the interviewer has a hard job—to choose the best applicant. Make that job easier by showing exactly what you have to offer in terms of accomplishments and a proven willingness to work hard.

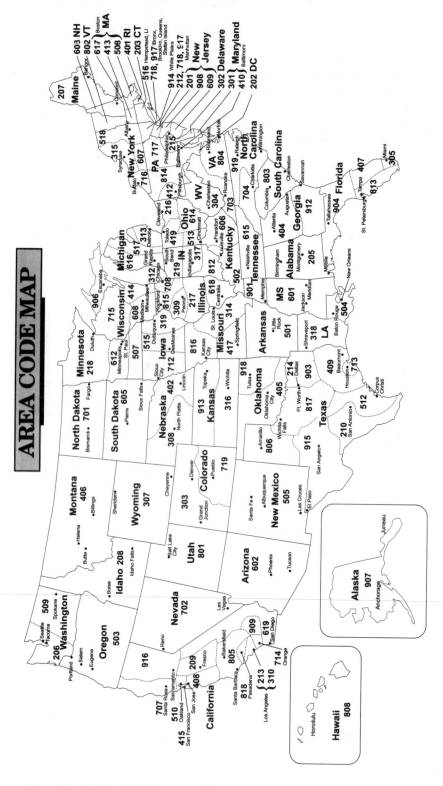

AREA CODE MAP

The 2,000 Fastest-Growing High-Tech Companies in the United States

Alabama

■ **205 Area Code**

Adtran, Inc.
901 Explorer Blvd.
Huntsville, AL 35806

Founded 1986
Total employees 340
Annual sales $60 million
Industry Telecommunications
Growth Openings in past year 90; percentage growth 36%
Contact Mark Smith, President
Tel 205-971-8000
Fax 205-937-8699

Applied Research, Inc.
6700 Odyssey Dr.
Huntsville, AL 35806

Founded 1980
Total employees 265
Industry Defense
Growth Openings in past year 65; percentage growth 32%
Contact Keith Frost, Personnel Manager
Tel 205-922-8600
Fax 205-922-8601

BioCryst Pharmaceuticals, Inc.
2190 Parkway Lake Dr.
Birmingham, AL 35244

Founded 1986
Total employees 25
Industry Biotechnology
Growth Openings in past year 16; percentage growth 177%
Contact Frederick J. Dechow, Ph.D., President/CEO
Tel 205-444-4600
Fax 205-444-4640

CAS, Inc.
PO Box 11190
Huntsville, AL 35814

Founded 1979
Total employees 500
Industry Defense
Contact William H. Stender, Jr., Chief Executive Officer
Tel 205-895-8600
Fax 205-895-8668

CFD Research Corp.
3325 Triana Blvd. Southwest, Suite D
Huntsville, AL 35805

Founded 1987
Total employees 45
Industries Chemicals, Computer Software, Defense, Energy

Growth Openings in past year 9; percentage growth 25%
Contact Dr. Ashok K. Singhal, President/Technical Director
Tel 205-536-6576
Fax 205-536-6590

CMS Research Corp.
200 Chase Park South, Suite 100
Birmingham, AL 35244

Founded 1986
Total employees 41
Industry Environmental
Growth Openings in past year 16; percentage growth 64%
Contact Gary Sides, President
Tel 205-733-6900
Fax 205-733-6919

Command Data, Incorporated
2204 Lake Shore Dr., Suite 206
Birmingham, AL 35209

Founded 1976
Total employees 125
Annual sales $11 million
Industries Computer Software, Holding Companies

Growth Openings in past year 25; percentage growth 25%
Contact Ms. Betty Todd, Controller
Tel 205-879-3282
Fax 205-870-1405

Cybex Corp.
2800 H. Bob Wallace Ave.
Huntsville, AL 35805

Founded 1981
Total employees 75
Annual sales $5.3 million
Industry Computer Hardware
Growth Openings in past year 25; percentage growth 50%
Contact Steven F. Thornton, President
Tel 205-534-0011
Fax 205-534-0010

DP Associates, Inc.
4900 Century St.
Huntsville, AL 35816

Founded 1970
Total employees 450
Annual sales $10 million
Industries Computer Hardware, Computer Software
Growth Openings in past year 120; percentage growth 36%
Contact Ms. Sandra Lankford, Manager of Human Resources
Tel 205-837-8300
Fax 205-837-8454

Dynetics, Inc.
PO Drawer B
Huntsville, AL 35814

Founded 1974
Total employees 290
Annual sales $29 million
Industries Computer Software, Defense, Manufacturing Equipment

Growth Openings in past year 3; percentage growth 1%
Contact Dr. Marcus J. Bendickson, President/CEO
Tel 205-922-9230
Fax 205-922-9255

Eaton Corp., Controls Division
200 East Elm St.
Athens, AL 35611

Founded 1911
Total employees 320
Annual sales $25 million
Industries Subassemblies and Components, Test and Measurement
Growth Openings in past year 170; percentage growth 113%
Contact Bob Robillard, Plant Manager
Tel 205-232-8300
Fax 205-233-4336

Electro Design Manufacturing, Inc.
Hwy. 31 South, PO Box 2208
Decatur, AL 35609

Founded 1985
Total employees 285
Industries Manufacturing Equipment, Subassemblies and Components
Growth Openings in past year 19; percentage growth 7%
Contact Rick Stephenson, President
Tel 205-353-3855
Fax 205-353-3979

EMCO, Inc.
PO Box 2193
Gadsden, AL 35903

Founded 1967
Total employees 700
Annual sales $75 million
Industry Defense

Growth Openings in past year 249; percentage growth 55%
Contact Jerry Weaver, President
Tel 205-492-8890
Fax 205-492-7657

Life-Guard, Inc.
18 Grimes Dr., PO Box 1039
Guntersville, AL 35976

Founded 1987
Total employees 100
Industry Test and Measurement
Growth Openings in past year 35; percentage growth 53%
Contact Rodney Kreps, CEO/President
Tel 205-582-0011
Fax 205-582-7327

Mevatech Corporation
1525 Perimeter Pkwy., Suite 500
Huntsville, AL 35806

Founded 1985
Total employees 85
Annual sales $9.1 million
Industry Defense
Growth Openings in past year 30; percentage growth 54%
Contact Ms. Nancy Archuleta, President/CEO
Tel 205-890-8000

Prattville Manufacturing, Inc.
101 Echlin Blvd.
Prattville, AL 36067

Founded 1924
Total employees 350
Annual sales $34 million
Industry Subassemblies and Components
Growth Openings in past year 49; percentage growth 16%
Contact Thomas Barthel, Personnel Manager
Tel 205-365-2145
Fax 205-365-2258

Research Genetics
2310 South Memorial
  Pkwy.
Huntsville, AL 35801

Founded 1986
Total employees 28
Industry Biotechnology
Growth Openings in past
  year 12; percentage
  growth 75%
Contact James Hudson,
  President
Tel 205-533-4363
Fax 205-536-9016

Teledyne Industries, Inc., Teledyne Power Systems Division
1975 Michigan Ave.
Mobile, AL 36605

Founded 1991
Total employees 300
Annual sales $23 million
Industry Subassemblies
  and Components
Growth Openings in past
  year 50; percentage
  growth 20%
Contact C.E. McGill,
  President
Tel 205-433-4848
Fax 205-432-8575

Industries Factory
  Automation,
  Manufacturing
  Equipment,
  Subassemblies and
  Components
Growth Openings in past
  year 23; percentage
  growth 7%
Contact Ms. Sue
  Knowles,
  Manager of Human
  Resources
Tel 602-437-1405
Fax 602-437-1403

Sigmatech, Inc.
4810 Bradford Blvd.
  Northwest
Huntsville, AL 35805

Founded 1986
Total employees 60
Annual sales $6 million
Industry Defense
Growth Openings in past
  year 10; percentage
  growth 20%
Contact Dr. Gurmej
  Sandhu,
  President
Tel 205-721-1188
Fax 205-830-1394

VME Microsystems International Corp.
12090 South Memorial
  Pkwy.
Huntsville, AL 35803

Founded 1983
Total employees 130
Annual sales $21 million
Industries Computer
  Hardware,
  Telecommunications
Growth Openings in past
  year 40; percentage
  growth 44%
Contact Ms. Faye
  Robinson,
  Human Resources
  Administrator
Tel 205-880-0444
Fax 205-882-0859

Anasazi, Inc.
7500 North Dreamy Draw
  Dr., Suite 120
Phoenix, AZ 85020

Founded 1980
Total employees 120
Annual sales $13 million
Industries Computer
  Software,
  Telecommunications
Growth Openings in past
  year 15; percentage
  growth 14%
Contact Tom Castleberry,
  President
Tel 602-870-3330
Fax 602-861-7687

Stamped Products, Inc.
PO Box 5175
Gadsden, AL 35905

Founded 1983
Total employees 45
Annual sales $4.9 million
Industry Manufacturing
  Equipment
Growth Openings in past
  year 13; percentage
  growth 40%
Contact Fred
  Scheidweiler,
  General Manager
Tel 205-492-2919
Fax 205-494-0015

Arizona

■ 602 Area Code

Advanced Semiconductor Materials America, Inc.
4302 East Broadway
Phoenix, AZ 85040

Founded 1976
Total employees 350
Annual sales $60 million

Antenna Technology Corp.
1140 East Greenway St.,
  Suite 2
Mesa, AZ 85203

Founded 1979
Total employees 40
Annual sales $10 million
Industry
  Telecommunications
Growth Openings in past
  year 21; percentage
  growth 110%
Contact Gary S. Hatch,
  President
Tel 602-264-7275
Fax 602-898-7667

Arizona Instrument Corp.
PO Box 1930
Tempe, AZ 85280

Founded 1987
Total employees 105
Annual sales $10 million
Industries Factory
Automation, Test and
Measurement
Growth Openings in past
year 30; percentage
growth 40%
Contact Ms. Sue Berry,
Corporate Secretary
Tel 602-731-3400
Fax 602-731-3434

Continental Circuits Corp.
3502 East Roeser Rd.
Phoenix, AZ 85040

Founded 1973
Total employees 850
Annual sales $65 million
Industry Subassemblies
and Components
Growth Openings in past
year 49; percentage
growth 6%
Contact Bob Lutz,
President
Tel 602-268-3461
Fax 602-268-0208

EFData Corp.
2105 West 5th Pl.
Tempe, AZ 85281

Founded 1985
Total employees 200
Annual sales $30 million
Industries Energy,
Subassemblies and
Components,
Telecommunications
Growth Openings in past
year 25; percentage
growth 14%
Contact Robert Fitting,
Chief Executive Officer
Tel 602-968-0447
Fax 602-921-9012

Artisoft, Inc.
691 East River Rd.
Tucson, AZ 85704

Founded 1982
Total employees 400
Annual sales $51.1 million
Industries Computer
Hardware, Computer
Software,
Subassemblies and
Components,
Telecommunications
Growth Openings in past
year 175; percentage
growth 77%
Contact Ms. Margaret
Bundy,
Human Resources
Manager
Tel 602-293-4000
Fax 602-293-8065

Dataforth Corp.
2731 East Elvira Rd.,
Suite 171
Tucson, AZ 85706

Founded 1984
Total employees 30
Annual sales $3 million
Industries Computer
Hardware, Photonics,
Telecommunications
Growth Openings in past
year 15; percentage
growth 100%
Contact Lee Payne,
President
Tel 602-741-1404
Fax 602-741-0762

ESH, Inc.
3020 South Park Dr.
Tempe, AZ 85282

Founded 1983
Total employees 75
Annual sales $5.5 million
Industry Factory
Automation
Growth Openings in past
year 15; percentage
growth 25%
Contact Dennis Gauthier,
President
Tel 602-438-1112
Fax 602-431-9633

GTE Health Systems
2510 West Dunlap Ave.,
Suite 600
Phoenix, AZ 85021

Founded 1984
Total employees 175
Annual sales $22 million
Industries Computer
Hardware, Computer
Software
Growth Openings in past
year 25; percentage
growth 16%
Contact Jan Michael
Norton,
Director of Finance and
Administration
Tel 602-678-6000
Fax 602-678-6332

Dynaco West Corp.
1000 South Priest Dr.
Tempe, AZ 85283

Founded 1989
Total employees 130
Annual sales $12 million
Industry Subassemblies
and Components
Growth Openings in past
year 20; percentage
growth 18%
Contact John Carr,
General Manager/Vice
President
Tel 602-968-2000
Fax 602-921-9830

ASM Lithography
2315 West Fairmont Dr.
Tempe, AZ 85282

Founded 1984
Total employees 600
Industry Manufacturing
Equipment
Growth Openings in past
year 100; percentage
growth 20%
Contact Doug Marsh,
President
Tel 602-438-0559
Fax 602-438-0793

Hybridyne, Inc.
2155 North Forbes Blvd.
Tucson, AZ 85745

Founded 1987
Total employees 68
Annual sales $4.0 million
Industries Advanced
Materials,
Subassemblies and
Components
Growth Openings in past
year 13; percentage
growth 23%
Contact Ms. Wendy
Rawlings,
Product Manager
Tel 602-629-0001
Fax 602-791-3899

Microtest, Inc.
4747 North 22nd Str.
Phoenix, AZ 85016

Founded 1984
Total employees 160
Annual sales $2.7 million
Industries Factory
Automation,
Telecommunications
Growth Openings in past
year 50; percentage
growth 45%
Contact David C. Bolles,
Chief Executive Officer
Tel 602-942-6400
Fax 602-952-6604

Photometrics, Ltd.
3440 East Britannia Dr.,
Suite 100
Tucson, AZ 85706

Founded 1979
Total employees 120
Annual sales $10 million
Industry Factory
Automation
Growth Openings in past
year 20; percentage
growth 20%
Contact Keith Niccum,
Human Resources
Manager
Tel 602-889-9933
Fax 602-573-1944

Integrated Technology Corp.
1228 North Stadem Dr.
Tempe, AZ 85281

Founded 1975
Total employees 75
Industries Factory
Automation,
Manufacturing
Equipment,
Subassemblies and
Components
Growth Openings in past
year 20; percentage
growth 36%
Contact Gary Orman,
President
Tel 602-968-3459
Fax 602-968-3099

Modular Mining Systems, Inc.
3289 East Hemisphere
Loop
Tucson, AZ 85706

Founded 1979
Total employees 96
Annual sales $6 million
Industries Computer
Hardware, Energy
Growth Openings in past
year 21; percentage
growth 28%
Contact Michael J.
Arnold,
President
Tel 602-746-9127
Fax 602-889-5790

Simula, Inc.
10016 South 51st St.
Phoenix, AZ 85044

Founded 1975
Total employees 200
Annual sales $23 million
Industries Advanced
Materials, Manufacturing
Equipment,
Transportation
Growth Openings in past
year 30; percentage
growth 17%
Contact Ms. Linda
Burson,
Personnel Manager
Tel 602-893-7533
Fax 602-893-8643

Microsemi Corp., Scottsdale Division
8700 East Thomas Rd.,
PO Box 1390
Scottsdale, AZ 85252

Founded 1982
Total employees 330
Annual sales $21.4 million
Industry Subassemblies
and Components
Growth Openings in past
year 13; percentage
growth 4%
Contact Ms. Lorraine
Greager,
Personnel Manager
Tel 602-941-6300
Fax 602-947-1503

Pacific Scientific Co., Energy Systems Division
7073 West Willis Dr., Box
5002
Chandler, AZ 85226

Founded 1975
Total employees 100
Annual sales $9 million
Industry Defense
Growth Openings in past
year 30; percentage
growth 42%
Contact Robert Day,
Vice President/General
Manager
Tel 602-796-1100
Fax 602-796-0754

Slate Corp.
15035 North 73rd St.
Scottsdale, AZ 85260

Founded 1989
Total employees 45
Industry Computer
Software
Growth Openings in past
year 15; percentage
growth 50%
Contact Vern Raburn,
COB/CEO
Tel 602-443-7322
Fax 602-443-7325

Steris Laboratories
620 North 51st Ave., PO
Box 23160
Phoenix, AZ 85063

Founded 1931
Total employees 550
Industry Pharmaceuticals
Growth Openings in past
year 149; percentage
growth 37%
Contact James McGee,
President
Tel 602-278-1400
Fax 602-269-7468

**Sunquest Information
Systems, Inc.**
4801 East Broadway
Tucson, AZ 85711

Founded 1979
Total employees 456
Annual sales $60 million
Industry Computer
Software
Growth Openings in past
year 106; percentage
growth 30%
Contact Jeff Grant,
VP of Human Resources
Tel 602-570-2000
Fax 602-570-2492

Three-Five Systems, Inc.
10230 South 50th Pl.
Phoenix, AZ 85044

Founded 1985
Total employees 400
Annual sales $18.7 million
Industries Computer
Hardware, Photonics
Growth Openings in past
year 100; percentage
growth 33%
Contact David R.
Buchanan,
COB/President/CEO/
Treasurer
Tel 602-496-0035
Fax 602-496-0168

Viasoft, Inc.
3033 North 44th St., Suite
101
Phoenix, AZ 85018

Founded 1983
Total employees 160
Annual sales $18 million
Industry Computer
Software
Growth Openings in past
year 70; percentage
growth 77%
Contact LeRoy Ellison,
President/CEO
Tel 602-952-0050
Fax 602-840-4068

Westech Systems, Inc.
3502 East Atlanta Ave.
Phoenix, AZ 85040

Founded 1973
Total employees 180
Industries Factory
Automation,
Manufacturing
Equipment
Growth Openings in past
year 55; percentage
growth 44%
Contact Donald M.
Jackson,
CEO/President
Tel 602-276-4261
Fax 602-268-8807

Arkansas

■ **501 Area Code**

**American Fuel Cell and
Coated Fabrics Co.**
PO Box 887
Magnolia, AR 71753

Founded 1983
Total employees 725
Annual sales $50 million
Industries Environmental,
Transportation
Growth Openings in past
year 121; percentage
growth 20%
Contact M. Cain,
VP of Human Resources
Tel 501-234-3381
Fax 501-235-7270

Arkansas Systems, Inc.
8901 Kanis Rd.
Little Rock, AR 72205

Founded 1975
Total employees 115
Annual sales $6.8 million
Industry Computer
Software
Growth Openings in past
year 15; percentage
growth 15%
Contact Dr. James K.
Hendren,
President
Tel 501-227-8471
Fax 501-227-5436

**Babcock & Wilcox,
Struthers Thermo-Flood**
8900 Fourche Dam Pike
Little Rock, AR 72206

Founded 1971
Total employees 210
Annual sales $28 million
Industries Energy,
Subassemblies and
Components
Growth Openings in past
year 80; percentage
growth 61%
Contact Arthur Young,
President
Tel 501-490-2424
Fax 501-490-1414

California

■ **209 Area Code**

Dantel, Inc.
2991 North Argyle Ave.
Fresno, CA 93727

Founded 1971
Total employees 275
Industries Manufacturing
Equipment,
Subassemblies and
Components,
Telecommunications
Growth Openings in past
year 25; percentage
growth 10%
Contact Ms. Chris Greco,
Personnel Administrator
Tel 209-292-1111
Fax 209-292-9355

Duncan Enterprises, Inc.
5683 East Shields
Fresno, CA 93727

Founded 1948
Total employees 400
Industries Advanced
Materials, Factory
Automation,
Manufacturing
Equipment
Growth Openings in past
year 50; percentage
growth 14%
Contact Larry Duncan,
President
Tel 209-291-4444
Fax 209-291-9444

Fisher Research Laboratory, Inc.
200 West Willmott Rd.
Los Banos, CA 93635

Founded 1931
Total employees 93
Industries Factory
Automation, Test and
Measurement
Growth Openings in past
year 18; percentage
growth 24%
Contact Ms. Delia
Esquivel,
Assistant Controller
Tel 209-826-3292
Fax 209-826-0416

Sunrise Medical Inc., Quickie Designs
2842 Business Park Ave.
Fresno, CA 93727

Founded 1983
Total employees 408
Annual sales $44 million
Industry Medical
Growth Openings in past
year 31; percentage
growth 8%
Contact Dave Lauger,
Director of Human
Resources
Tel 209-292-2171
Fax 209-292-7412

■ 213 Area Code

IDB Communications Group, Inc.
10525 West Washington
Blvd.
Culver City, CA 90232

Founded 1983
Total employees 460
Annual sales $104 million
Industries Holding
Companies,
Telecommunications
Growth Openings in past
year 134; percentage
growth 41%
Contact Ms. Carrie
Armenta,
Director of Personnel
Tel 213-870-9000
Fax 213-870-3400

Robert M. Hadley Co., Inc.
750 West 51st St.
Los Angeles, CA 90037

Founded 1929
Total employees 130
Annual sales $5 million
Industry Subassemblies
and Components
Growth Openings in past
year 20; percentage
growth 18%
Contact Ms. Jeanne
Hadley,
Director of Personnel
Tel 213-234-9091
Fax 213-234-2779

■ 310 Area Code

Activision, Inc.
11440 San Vicente Blvd.,
Suite 300
Los Angeles, CA 90049

Founded 1979
Total employees 65
Annual sales $20.3 million
Industry Computer
Software

Growth Openings in past
year 35; percentage
growth 116%
Contact Robert Kotick,
COB/CEO
Tel 310-207-4500
Fax 310-820-6131

Aura Systems, Inc.
2335 Alaska Ave.
El Segundo, CA 90245

Founded 1987
Total employees 175
Annual sales $13 million
Industry Holding
Companies
Growth Openings in past
year 55; percentage
growth 45%
Contact Harry Kurtzman,
President
Tel 310-643-5300
Fax 310-643-8719

Automated Design Centers, Inc.
1149 West 190th St.,
Suite 1004
Gardena, CA 90248

Founded 1979
Total employees 44
Annual sales $3 million
Industries Computer
Hardware, Computer
Software, Factory
Automation
Growth Openings in past
year 12; percentage
growth 37%
Contact Bruce Denning,
VP of Engineering
Services
Tel 310-327-7744
Fax 310-217-8196

Busak & Shamban, Inc.
2951 28th St., Suite 2010
Santa Monica, CA 90405

Founded 1952
Total employees 526
Industry Holding
Companies

Growth Openings in past year 125; percentage growth 31%
Contact Henning Skou Jensen, President
Tel 310-450-0020
Fax 310-450-7031

Growth Openings in past year 14; percentage growth 28%
Contact Robert Stuckleman, Chief Executive Officer
Tel 310-643-5106
Fax 310-536-6128

Growth Openings in past year 15; percentage growth 42%
Contact Andrew Skow, President
Tel 310-326-8228
Fax 310-326-9358

Evernet Systems, Inc.
5777 West Century Blvd., Suite 1680
Los Angeles, CA 90045

Certron Corp.
1545 Sawtelle Blvd., Suite 34
Los Angeles, CA 90025

Founded 1967
Total employees 400
Annual sales $17.69 million
Industries Computer Hardware, Telecommunications
Growth Openings in past year 62; percentage growth 18%
Contact Marshall I. Kass, COB/CEO/COO
Tel 310-914-0300
Fax 310-914-0310

Davidson & Associates, Inc.
19840 Pioneer Ave., PO Box 2961
Torrance, CA 90503

Founded 1984
Total employees 150
Annual sales $17 million
Industry Computer Software
Growth Openings in past year 45; percentage growth 42%
Contact Ms. Jan Davidson, President
Tel 310-793-0600
Fax 310-793-0601

Founded 1989
Total employees 270
Annual sales $44 million
Industry Computer Hardware
Growth Openings in past year 49; percentage growth 22%
Contact Luther J. Nussbaum, COB/CEO
Tel 310-649-5900
Fax 310-649-2755

Industrial Dynamics Co., Ltd.
2927 Lomita Blvd.
Torrance, CA 90505

Clarion Corp. of America
661 West Redondo Beach Blvd.
Gardena, CA 90247

Founded 1964
Total employees 270
Annual sales $180 million
Industry Telecommunications
Growth Openings in past year 20; percentage growth 8%
Contact Ms. P.P. Garcias, Manager of Personnel and Administration
Tel 310-327-9100
Fax 310-327-1999

Digitalk, Inc.
9841 Airport Blvd.
Los Angeles, CA 90045

Founded 1983
Total employees 65
Annual sales $7.5 million
Industry Computer Software
Growth Openings in past year 30; percentage growth 85%
Contact Douglas Wride, Vice President/CFO
Tel 310-645-1082
Fax 310-645-1306

Founded 1960
Total employees 320
Industry Factory Automation
Growth Openings in past year 70; percentage growth 28%
Contact Ms. Kris Booz, Personnel Manager
Tel 310-325-5633
Fax 310-530-1000

Integrated Decision Systems, Inc.
1950 Sawtelle, Suite 255
Los Angeles, CA 90025

Founded 1981
Total employees 54
Industry Computer Software
Growth Openings in past year 19; percentage growth 54%
Contact Gerald Jackrel, President
Tel 310-478-4015
Fax 310-473-4352

CompuMed, Inc.
1230 Rosecrans Ave.
Manhattan Beach, CA 90266

Founded 1979
Total employees 64
Annual sales $5 million
Industry Medical

Eidetics International, Inc.
3415 Lomita Blvd.
Torrance, CA 90505

Founded 1982
Total employees 50
Annual sales $6 million
Industries Defense, Transportation

IntelligenceWare, Inc.
5933 West Century Blvd.
Los Angeles, CA 90045
Founded 1984
Total employees 50
Annual sales $10 million
Industry Computer
Software
Growth Openings in past
year 20; percentage
growth 66%
Contact Dr. Kamran
Parsaye,
President
Tel 310-216-6177
Fax 310-417-8897

Mega Drive Systems, Inc.
489 South Robertson
Blvd.
Beverly Hills, CA 90211
Founded 1988
Total employees 45
Industry Computer
Hardware
Growth Openings in past
year 20; percentage
growth 80%
Contact Alex Bouzari,
President
Tel 310-247-0006
Fax 310-247-8118

Pacific Industrial Service Corp.
925 West Esther St.
Long Beach, CA 90813
Founded 1976
Total employees 300
Industry Environmental
Growth Openings in past
year 100; percentage
growth 50%
Contact Ms. Rita Crow,
Personnel Manager
Tel 310-590-8626
Fax 310-435-9203

Lear Astronics Corp.
3400 Airport Ave.
Santa Monica, CA 90406
Founded 1948
Total employees 870
Annual sales $88 million
Industry Transportation
Growth Openings in past
year 18; percentage
growth 2%
Contact Bern Lefson,
VP of Human Resources
Tel 310-915-6881
Fax 310-915-8384

Modular Devices, Inc.
4115 Spencer St.
Torrance, CA 90503
Founded 1963
Total employees 255
Annual sales $14 million
Industry Subassemblies
and Components
Growth Openings in past
year 95; percentage
growth 59%
Contact Ms. Thelma
Javier,
Personnel Manager
Tel 310-542-8561
Fax 310-371-6331

Quarterdeck Office Systems, Inc.
1901 Main St.
Santa Monica, CA 90405
Founded 1982
Total employees 190
Annual sales $48.0 million
Industry Computer
Software
Growth Openings in past
year 101; percentage
growth 113%
Contact Ms. Therese E.
Myers,
President/CEO/CFO
Tel 310-392-9851
Fax 310-314-4218

Longshine Microsystems, Inc.
10400-9 Pioneer Blvd.
Santa Fe Springs, CA
90670
Founded 1985
Total employees 30
Annual sales $18 million
Industry Computer
Hardware
Growth Openings in past
year 15; percentage
growth 100%
Contact C.Y. Huang,
President
Tel 310-903-0899
Fax 310-944-2201

NDE Environmental Corp.
20000 Mariner Ave., Suite
500
Torrance, CA 90503
Founded 1981
Total employees 85
Annual sales $6.1 million
Industries Energy,
Environmental,
Transportation
Growth Openings in past
year 40; percentage
growth 88%
Contact J. Chaffee,
President/CEO
Tel 310-542-4342
Fax 310-542-6657

Retix, Inc.
2401 Colorado Ave.
Santa Monica, CA 90404
Founded 1985
Total employees 430
Annual sales $60.45
million
Industries Computer
Hardware, Computer
Software,
Telecommunications
Growth Openings in past
year 180; percentage
growth 72%
Contact Steven Frankel,
President
Tel 310-828-3400
Fax 310-828-2255

SCS Engineers, Inc.
3711 Long Beach Blvd.
Long Beach, CA 90807

Founded 1970
Total employees 375
Annual sales $40 million
Industry Environmental
Growth Openings in past
year 75; percentage
growth 25%
Contact Robert Stearns,
President
Tel 310-426-9544
Fax 310-427-0805

Trident Data Systems, Inc.
5933 West Century Blvd.,
Suite 700
Los Angeles, CA 90045

Founded 1975
Total employees 480
Industries Computer
Hardware, Computer
Software
Growth Openings in past
year 70; percentage
growth 17%
Contact Ms. Scherri
Pearson,
Personnel Manager
Tel 310-645-6483
Fax 310-670-5121

Tri-Star Electronics International, Inc.
2201 Rosecrans Ave.
El Segundo, CA 90245

Founded 1975
Total employees 300
Industries Factory
Automation,
Subassemblies and
Components
Growth Openings in past
year 100; percentage
growth 50%
Contact John Schnepf,
President/CEO
Tel 310-536-0444
Fax 310-536-9322

U.S. Magnetics Corp.
2041 West 139th St.
Gardena, CA 90249

Founded 1975
Total employees 150
Annual sales $24 million
Industry Computer
Hardware
Growth Openings in past
year 30; percentage
growth 25%
Contact C. Paul Kim,
President
Tel 310-329-0970
Fax 310-643-9886

■ **408 Area Code**

Accolade, Inc.
5300 Stevens Creek
Blvd., Suite 500
San Jose, CA 95129

Founded 1984
Total employees 85
Annual sales $9.8 million
Industry Computer
Software
Growth Openings in past
year 15; percentage
growth 21%
Contact Alan R. Miller,
COB/President/CEO
Tel 408-985-1700
Fax 408-246-1282

ACTEL Corp.
955 East Arques Ave.
Sunnyvale, CA 94086

Founded 1985
Total employees 150
Industry Subassemblies
and Components
Growth Openings in past
year 30; percentage
growth 25%
Contact Rich Mora,
VP of Finance
Tel 408-739-1010
Fax 408-739-1540

ADAC Laboratories
540 Alder Dr.
Milpitas, CA 95035

Founded 1970
Total employees 480
Annual sales $101.3
million
Industries Computer
Hardware, Medical
Growth Openings in past
year 80; percentage
growth 20%
Contact Stanley D.
Czerwinski,
COB/CEO
Tel 408-945-2990
Fax 408-945-1516

Adeza Biomedical Corp.
1240 Elko Dr.
Sunnyvale, CA 94089

Founded 1985
Total employees 50
Annual sales $4.8 million
Industries Biotechnology,
Medical
Growth Openings in past
year 15; percentage
growth 42%
Contact Ms. Susan Dube,
Chief Operating Officer
Tel 408-745-0975
Fax 408-745-0968

ADI Systems, Inc.
2121 Ringwood Ave.
San Jose, CA 95131

Founded 1984
Total employees 60
Annual sales $12 million
Industries Computer
Hardware,
Telecommunications
Growth Openings in past
year 20; percentage
growth 50%
Contact Raymond Hou,
Vice President
Tel 408-944-0100

AG Associates
1325 Borregas Ave.
Sunnyvale, CA 94089

Founded 1981
Total employees 180
Annual sales $25 million

Industry Manufacturing Equipment
Growth Openings in past year 20; percentage growth 12%
Contact Ms. Anita Lazare, Director of Human Resources
Tel 408-745-1791
Fax 408-747-0902

Aitech International Corp.
830 Hillview Ct., Suite 145
Milpitas, CA 95035

Founded 1987
Total employees 51
Annual sales $6 million
Industry Computer Hardware
Growth Openings in past year 21; percentage growth 70%
Contact Dr. Michael Chen, COB/CEO/President
Tel 408-946-3291
Fax 408-946-6901

Akashic Memories Corporation
305 West Tasman Dr.
San Jose, CA 95134

Founded 1982
Total employees 900
Industry Computer Hardware
Growth Openings in past year 248; percentage growth 38%
Contact Yoshiki Takemura, President/CEO
Tel 408-944-9080
Fax 408-944-9150

Altera Corp.
2610 Orchard Pkwy.
San Jose, CA 95134

Founded 1983
Total employees 450
Annual sales $107 million
Industries Computer Software, Subassemblies and Components

Growth Openings in past year 49; percentage growth 12%
Contact Ms. Sandy Scarsella, VP of Human Resources
Tel 408-984-2800
Fax 408-248-6924

Anelva Corp.
1745 Fox Dr.
San Jose, CA 95131

Founded 1980
Total employees 25
Annual sales $2.7 million
Industry Manufacturing Equipment
Growth Openings in past year 13; percentage growth 108%
Contact K. Ojiro, General Manager
Tel 408-436-8311
Fax 408-436-1924

Answer Computer, Inc.
1263 Oakmead Pkwy.
Sunnyvale, CA 94086

Founded 1988
Total employees 50
Annual sales $3.5 million
Industry Computer Software
Growth Openings in past year 12; percentage growth 31%
Contact Curtis C. Hare, President/CEO
Tel 408-739-6130
Fax 408-739-2455

Applied Signal Technology, Inc.
160 Sobrante Way
Sunnyvale, CA 94086

Founded 1984
Total employees 385
Annual sales $41.6 million
Industries Defense, Telecommunications

Growth Openings in past year 54; percentage growth 16%
Contact Ms. Diane Cusano, Human Resources Director
Tel 408-749-1888
Fax 408-738-1928

Asante Technologies, Inc.
821 Fox Ln.
San Jose, CA 95131

Founded 1988
Total employees 140
Annual sales $19 million
Industry Telecommunications
Growth Openings in past year 100; percentage growth 250%
Contact Wilson Wong, President
Tel 408-435-8388
Fax 408-734-4864

Ashtech, Inc.
1170 Kifer Rd.
Sunnyvale, CA 94086

Founded 1987
Total employees 108
Annual sales $36 million
Industries Telecommunications, Transportation
Growth Openings in past year 21; percentage growth 24%
Contact Javad Ashjaee, President
Tel 408-737-2400
Fax 408-524-1500

ASP Computer Products, Inc.
160 San Gabriel Dr.
Sunnyvale, CA 94086

Founded 1987
Total employees 100
Annual sales $16 million
Industries Computer Hardware, Telecommunications

Growth Openings in past year 70; percentage growth 233%
Contact Amnon Evan-Kesef,
President/CEO
Tel 408-746-2965
Fax 408-746-2803

Aspect Telecommunications Corp.
1730 Fox Dr.
San Jose, CA 95131

Founded 1985
Total employees 351
Annual sales $61 million
Industry
Telecommunications
Growth Openings in past year 17; percentage growth 5%
Contact Ms. Shelley Brown,
VP of Human Resources
Tel 408-441-2200
Fax 408-441-2260

Auspex Systems, Inc.
2952 Bunker Hill Ln.
Santa Clara, CA 95054

Founded 1987
Total employees 180
Annual sales $50 million
Industry
Telecommunications
Growth Openings in past year 75; percentage growth 71%
Contact Laurence B. Boucher,
President
Tel 408-492-0900
Fax 408-492-0909

Becton Dickinson Immunocytometry Systems
2350 Qume Dr.
San Jose, CA 95131

Founded 1972
Total employees 610
Annual sales $58 million
Industries Biotechnology, Chemicals

Growth Openings in past year 56; percentage growth 10%
Contact Bob Phelps,
Director of Personnel
Tel 408-432-9475
Fax 408-954-2009

BusLogic, Inc.
4151 Burton Dr.
Santa Clara, CA 95054

Founded 1988
Total employees 95
Annual sales $15 million
Industries Computer Hardware, Computer Software
Growth Openings in past year 45; percentage growth 90%
Contact Jesse Chen,
President
Tel 408-492-9090
Fax 408-492-1542

Calera Recognition Systems, Inc.
475 Potrero Ave.
Sunnyvale, CA 94086

Founded 1982
Total employees 100
Annual sales $16 million
Industries Computer Hardware, Computer Software
Growth Openings in past year 20; percentage growth 25%
Contact Steven Hayden,
President
Tel 408-720-8300
Fax 408-720-1330

California Micro Devices Corp.
215 Topaz St.
Milpitas, CA 95035

Founded 1980
Total employees 400
Annual sales $22.8 million

Industries Computer Hardware, Holding Companies, Subassemblies and Components
Contact Chan Desaigoudar,
COB/CEO
Tel 408-263-3214
Fax 408-263-7846

Casady & Greene, Inc.
22734 Portola Dr.
Salinas, CA 93908

Founded 1984
Total employees 30
Industry Computer Software
Growth Openings in past year 15; percentage growth 100%
Contact Michael Greene,
President
Tel 408-484-9228
Fax 408-484-9218

C-Cube Microsystems Corp.
1778 McCarthy Blvd.
Milpitas, CA 95035

Founded 1988
Total employees 80
Annual sales $13 million
Industry Computer Hardware
Growth Openings in past year 20; percentage growth 33%
Contact Bill O'Meara,
President/CEO
Tel 408-944-6300
Fax 408-944-6314

Celeritek, Inc.
617 River Oaks Pkwy.
San Jose, CA 95134

Founded 1985
Total employees 275
Annual sales $26 million
Industry Subassemblies and Components

Growth Openings in past year 130; percentage growth 89%
Contact John W. Beman, VP of Human Resources
Tel 408-433-0335
Fax 408-433-0991

Chaplet Systems USA, Inc.
252 North Wolfe Rd.
Sunnyvale, CA 94086

Founded 1986
Total employees 350
Annual sales $98 million
Industry Computer Hardware
Growth Openings in past year 54; percentage growth 18%
Contact Ms. Ceceilia Chang, President
Tel 408-732-7950
Fax 408-732-6050

ChemTrack, Inc.
929 East Arques Ave.
Sunnyvale, CA 94086

Founded 1985
Total employees 120
Annual sales $6.7 million
Industry Medical
Growth Openings in past year 30; percentage growth 33%
Contact Dr. Prithipal Singh, Chief Executive Officer
Tel 408-773-8156
Fax 408-773-1651

Claris Corp.
5201 Patrick Henry Dr.
Santa Clara, CA 95052

Founded 1987
Total employees 550
Industry Computer Software
Growth Openings in past year 100; percentage growth 22%
Contact Daniel Eilers, President/CEO
Tel 408-987-7000

Compression Labs, Inc.
2860 Junction Ave.
San Jose, CA 95134

Founded 1976
Total employees 340
Annual sales $10.9 million
Industry Telecommunications
Growth Openings in past year 60; percentage growth 21%
Contact Ms. Bonnie Nunke, VP of Human Resources
Tel 408-435-3000
Fax 408-922-5429

Condor Systems, Inc.
2133 Samaritan Dr.
San Jose, CA 95124

Founded 1981
Total employees 330
Annual sales $38.4 million
Industries Defense, Telecommunications, Transportation
Growth Openings in past year 80; percentage growth 32%
Contact Thomas R. Mulcahy, COB/CEO
Tel 408-371-9580
Fax 408-371-9589

Cylink Corp.
310 North Mary Ave.
Sunnyvale, CA 94086

Founded 1984
Total employees 150
Annual sales $20 million
Industries Subassemblies and Components, Telecommunications
Growth Openings in past year 25; percentage growth 20%
Contact Lewis Morris, President/CEO
Tel 408-735-5800
Fax 408-720-8294

Data Circuit Systems, Inc.
335 Turtle Creek Ct.
San Jose, CA 95125

Founded 1978
Total employees 106
Annual sales $8 million
Industry Subassemblies and Components
Growth Openings in past year 16; percentage growth 17%
Contact Don Burns, President
Tel 408-280-0422
Fax 408-280-0641

Delfin Systems
3000 Patrick Henry Dr.
Santa Clara, CA 94089

Founded 1984
Total employees 156
Industries Computer Hardware, Computer Software, Holding Companies
Growth Openings in past year 41; percentage growth 35%
Contact Ms. Pat Yanez, VP of Human Resources and Administration
Tel 408-748-1200
Fax 408-748-1140

Diamond Computer Systems, Inc.
1130 East Arques Ave.
Sunnyvale, CA 94086

Founded 1981
Total employees 80
Annual sales $70 million
Industry Computer Hardware
Growth Openings in past year 15; percentage growth 23%
Contact Chong-Moon Lee, President/CEO
Tel 408-736-2000
Fax 408-730-5750

Digicom Systems, Inc.
188 Topaz St.
Milpitas, CA 95035

Founded 1987
Total employees 85
Annual sales $10 million
Industry
  Telecommunications
Growth Openings in past
  year 15; percentage
  growth 21%
Contact Gwong Lee,
  President
Tel 408-262-1277
Fax 408-262-1390

Digimedics Corp.
280 Technology Cir.
Scotts Valley, CA 95066

Founded 1976
Total employees 50
Industry Computer
  Software
Growth Openings in past
  year 18; percentage
  growth 56%
Contact John Frieberg,
  CEO/CFO
Tel 408-438-4735
Fax 408-438-8422

Digital Tools, Inc.
18900 Stevens Creek
  Blvd.
Cupertino, CA 95014

Founded 1989
Total employees 45
Annual sales $6 million
Industry Computer
  Software
Growth Openings in past
  year 25; percentage
  growth 125%
Contact Mohan Uttarwar,
  President
Tel 408-366-6920
Fax 408-446-2140

Dolch American Instruments, Inc.
372 Turquoise St.
Milpitas, CA 95035

Founded 1979
Total employees 65

Industries Computer
  Hardware,
  Telecommunications
Growth Openings in past
  year 15; percentage
  growth 30%
Contact Volker Dolch,
  COB/President
Tel 408-957-6575
Fax 408-263-6305

Emerson Electric Co., Rosemount Analytical Division
3240 Scott Blvd.
Santa Clara, CA 95054

Founded 1959
Total employees 110
Annual sales $10 million
Industries Environmental,
  Test and Measurement
Growth Openings in past
  year 15; percentage
  growth 15%
Contact Ms. Lynn
  Bourquet,
  Human Resources
  Manager
Tel 408-727-6000
Fax 408-727-1601

E-Tek Dynamics, Inc.
1885 Lundy Ave.
San Jose, CA 95131

Founded 1983
Total employees 58
Annual sales $6.2 million
Industry Photonics
Growth Openings in past
  year 28; percentage
  growth 93%
Contact Ms. Teresa Pan,
  President
Tel 408-432-6300
Fax 408-432-8550

Exicom Technologies, Inc.
355 East Trimble Rd.
San Jose, CA 95131

Founded 1979
Total employees 250
Annual sales $24 million
Industry Subassemblies
  and Components

Growth Openings in past
  year 25; percentage
  growth 11%
Contact Ms. Margie Lotz,
  Personnel Manager
Tel 408-954-8977

Expertware, Inc.
3235 Kifer Rd., Suite 220
Santa Clara, CA 95051

Founded 1981
Total employees 30
Annual sales $3.4 million
Industry Computer
  Software
Growth Openings in past
  year 15; percentage
  growth 100%
Contact Dale Darnley,
  President
Tel 408-746-0706
Fax 408-746-0331

Frame Technology Corp.
1010 Rincon Cir.
San Jose, CA 95131

Founded 1986
Total employees 321
Annual sales $36.4 million
Industries Computer
  Software, Holding
  Companies
Growth Openings in past
  year 21; percentage
  growth 7%
Contact Paul Robichaux,
  CEO/COB
Tel 408-433-3311
Fax 408-433-1928

Hoya Electronics Corp.
960 Rincon Cir.
San Jose, CA 95131

Founded 1980
Total employees 95
Industries Computer
  Hardware,
  Manufacturing
  Equipment,
  Subassemblies and
  Components

Growth Openings in past year 25; percentage growth 35%
Contact Kyung Kim, President
Tel 408-435-1450
Fax 408-435-1536

Indala Corp.
711 Charcot Ave.
San Jose, CA 95131

Founded 1985
Total employees 75
Industry Computer Hardware
Contact Ms. Marie Regan, Personnel Manager
Tel 408-434-7010
Fax 408-434-7057

Insite Peripherals, Inc.
4433 Fortran Dr.
San Jose, CA 95134

Founded 1987
Total employees 80
Industry Computer Hardware
Growth Openings in past year 20; percentage growth 33%
Contact William P. Sousa, President/CEO
Tel 408-946-8080
Fax 408-946-4403

Integrated Silicon Solution, Inc.
680 Almanor Ave.
Sunnyvale, CA 94086

Founded 1988
Total employees 40
Annual sales $10 million
Industry Computer Hardware
Growth Openings in past year 14; percentage growth 53%
Contact Jimmy Lee, COB/President
Tel 408-733-4774
Fax 408-245-4774

Integrated Systems, Inc.
3260 Jay St.
Santa Clara, CA 95054

Founded 1980
Total employees 196
Annual sales $25.3 million
Industry Computer Software
Growth Openings in past year 61; percentage growth 45%
Contact Scott C. McDonald, VP of Finance and Administration/CFO
Tel 408-980-1500
Fax 408-980-0400

Inventa Corp.
2620 Augustine Dr., Suite 225
Santa Clara, CA 95054

Founded 1988
Total employees 50
Industry Computer Software
Growth Openings in past year 15; percentage growth 42%
Contact Ashok Santhanam, President
Tel 408-987-0220

Kalpana, Inc.
3100 Patrick Henry Dr.
Santa Clara, CA 95054

Founded 1987
Total employees 50
Industry Telecommunications
Growth Openings in past year 30; percentage growth 150%
Contact Jim Jordan, President/CEO
Tel 408-988-1600
Fax 408-988-1361

Linear Technology Corp.
1630 McCarthy Blvd.
Milpitas, CA 95035

Founded 1981
Total employees 800
Annual sales $107 million

Industries Subassemblies and Components, Test and Measurement, Telecommunications
Growth Openings in past year 150; percentage growth 23%
Contact Paul Coghlan, VP of Finance/CFO
Tel 408-432-1900
Fax 408-434-0507

LJL Biosystems, Inc.
404 Tasman Dr.
Sunnyvale, CA 94089

Founded 1984
Total employees 25
Annual sales $2.2 million
Industries Biotechnology, Manufacturing Equipment
Growth Openings in past year 15; percentage growth 150%
Contact Lev Leytes, President/CEO
Tel 408-541-8787

Lynx Real-Time Systems, Inc.
16780 Lark Ave.
Los Gatos, CA 95030

Founded 1985
Total employees 65
Annual sales $7.5 million
Industry Computer Software
Growth Openings in past year 25; percentage growth 62%
Contact Dr. Inder Mohan Singh, President
Tel 408-354-7770
Fax 408-354-7085

MasPar Computer Corp.
749 North Mary Ave.
Sunnyvale, CA 94086

Founded 1988
Total employees 170
Annual sales $18 million
Industry Computer Hardware

Growth Openings in past year 40; percentage growth 30%
Contact Jack Moyer, VP of Human Resources
Tel 408-736-3300
Fax 408-736-9560

Maxim Integrated Products, Inc.
120 San Gabriel Dr.
Sunnyvale, CA 94086

Founded 1983
Total employees 586
Annual sales $86.9 million
Industry Subassemblies and Components
Growth Openings in past year 86; percentage growth 17%
Contact Jack Gifford, President/CEO
Tel 408-737-7600
Fax 408-737-7194

Megatest Corp.
880 Fox Ln.
San Jose, CA 95131

Founded 1975
Total employees 400
Annual sales $50 million
Industry Factory Automation
Growth Openings in past year 50; percentage growth 14%
Contact Jack Halter, President
Tel 408-437-9700
Fax 408-453-8729

Meta-Software, Inc.
1300 White Oaks Rd.
Campbell, CA 95008

Founded 1977
Total employees 52
Annual sales $7 million
Industries Computer Software, Factory Automation
Growth Openings in past year 17; percentage growth 48%
Contact Shawn Hailey, President
Tel 408-371-5100
Fax 408-371-5638

Micro Linear Corp.
2092 Concourse Dr.
San Jose, CA 95151

Founded 1983
Total employees 250
Annual sales $24 million
Industry Subassemblies and Components
Growth Openings in past year 40; percentage growth 19%
Contact Phil Russell, VP of Finance and Administration
Tel 408-433-5200
Fax 408-432-0295

Microtec Research, Inc.
2350 Mission College Blvd., Suite 500
Santa Clara, CA 95054

Founded 1975
Total employees 165
Annual sales $19 million
Industry Computer Software
Growth Openings in past year 24; percentage growth 17%
Contact Ms. Mary Heeney, Human Resources Manager
Tel 408-980-1300
Fax 408-982-8266

MiLAN Technology, Inc.
894 Ross Dr., Suite 101
Sunnyvale, CA 94089

Founded 1990
Total employees 25
Annual sales $3.4 million
Industries Computer Hardware, Photonics, Telecommunications
Growth Openings in past year 20; percentage growth 400%
Contact Michael Conrad, President
Tel 408-752-2770
Fax 408-752-2790

Molecular Dynamics
880 East Arques Ave.
Sunnyvale, CA 94086

Founded 1987
Total employees 135
Annual sales $20 million
Industries Medical, Test and Measurement, Telecommunications
Growth Openings in past year 25; percentage growth 22%
Contact John Gordon, VP of Human Relations
Tel 408-773-1222
Fax 408-773-8343

Navigation Technologies
740 East Arques Ave.
Sunnyvale, CA 94086

Founded 1985
Total employees 146
Industry Computer Software
Growth Openings in past year 100; percentage growth 217%
Contact Ms. Barbara LeCompte, Support Services Administrator
Tel 408-737-3200
Fax 408-736-3734

Nycomed Salutar, Inc.
428 Oakmead Pkwy.
Sunnyvale, CA 94086

Founded 1983
Total employees 70
Industries Chemicals, Medical
Growth Openings in past year 20; percentage growth 40%
Contact Ms. Anne Jeannette Reed, Personnel Manager
Tel 408-732-1771
Fax 408-738-0998

Oak Technology
139 Kifer Ct.
Sunnyvale, CA 94086

Founded 1987
Total employees 100
Annual sales $50 million

Industries Computer
Hardware,
Subassemblies and
Components
Growth Openings in past
year 20; percentage
growth 25%
Contact David Tsang,
President
Tel 408-737-0888
Fax 408-737-3838

On Command Video, Inc.
1135 Kern Ave.
Sunnyvale, CA 94086

Founded 1986
Total employees 45
Industry
Telecommunications
Growth Openings in past
year 20; percentage
growth 80%
Contact Dr. Bob Fenwick,
Chief Executive Officer
Tel 408-738-1138

Pacific Monolithics, Inc.
245 Santa Ana Ct.
Sunnyvale, CA 94086

Founded 1984
Total employees 110
Industries Subassemblies
and Components,
Telecommunications
Growth Openings in past
year 27; percentage
growth 32%
Contact Christopher J.
Weseloh,
President/CEO
Tel 408-732-8000
Fax 408-732-3413

ParcPlace Systems, Inc.
999 East Arques Ave.
Sunnyvale, CA 94086

Founded 1988
Total employees 110
Annual sales $12 million
Industry Computer
Software

Growth Openings in past
year 50; percentage
growth 83%
Contact William Lyons,
President/CEO
Tel 408-481-9090
Fax 408-481-9095

Plantronics, Inc.
337 Encinal St.
Santa Cruz, CA 95060

Founded 1952
Total employees 900
Annual sales $120 million
Industry Holding
Companies
Growth Openings in past
year 398; percentage
growth 79%
Contact Robert Cecil,
President/CEO
Tel 408-426-6066
Fax 408-425-5198

PROMIS Systems Corp.
1731 Technology Dr.
San Jose, CA 95110

Founded 1980
Total employees 160
Annual sales $18 million
Industry Computer
Software
Growth Openings in past
year 35; percentage
growth 28%
Contact Eliot
Wassarman,
President
Tel 408-441-9090
Fax 408-441-9099

Radionics, Inc.
1800 Abbott St.
Salinas, CA 93901

Founded 1975
Total employees 400
Annual sales $50 million
Industries Computer
Hardware, Test and
Measurement
Growth Openings in past
year 50; percentage
growth 14%
Contact Glen Greer,
President
Tel 408-757-8877
Fax 408-757-8877 X334

Rational
3320 Scott Blvd.
Santa Clara, CA 95054

Founded 1981
Total employees 320
Annual sales $40 million
Industry Computer
Software
Growth Openings in past
year 45; percentage
growth 16%
Contact James Barth,
Vice President/CFO
Tel 408-496-3600
Fax 408-496-3636

**Recognition
International, Inc.,
Software Division**
1310 Chesapeake
Terrace
Sunnyvale, CA 94089

Founded 1980
Total employees 150
Industry Computer
Software
Growth Openings in past
year 50; percentage
growth 50%
Contact Ms. Joanne
Anderson,
Human Resources
Manager
Tel 408-747-1210
Fax 408-747-1245

Recom Technologies, Inc.
1245 South Winchester
Blvd., Suite 201
San Jose, CA 95128

Founded 1980
Total employees 210
Annual sales $24 million
Industry Computer
Software
Growth Openings in past
year 70; percentage
growth 50%
Contact Jack G. Lee,
President
Tel 408-261-7688
Fax 408-261-7699

Resumix, Inc.
2953 Bunker Hill Ln., 3rd
Floor
Santa Clara, CA 95054

Founded 1988
Total employees 70
Annual sales $2 million
Industry Computer
Software
Growth Openings in past
year 20; percentage
growth 40%
Contact Steve Leung,
President
Tel 408-764-9204
Fax 408-727-9893

RFI Enterprises, Inc.
360 Turtle Creek Ct.
San Jose, CA 95125

Founded 1979
Total employees 190
Annual sales $24 million
Industry Holding
Companies
Growth Openings in past
year 40; percentage
growth 26%
Contact Lawrence L.
Reece,
President
Tel 408-298-5400
Fax 408-275-0156

Rhetorex, Inc.
200 East Hacienda Ave.
Campbell, CA 95008

Founded 1988
Total employees 55
Industry Computer
Hardware
Growth Openings in past
year 25; percentage
growth 83%
Contact Allan Wokas,
President
Tel 408-370-0881
Fax 408-370-1171

Sanmina Corp.
2121 O'Toole Ave.
San Jose, CA 95131

Founded 1980
Total employees 525
Annual sales $48 million

Industries Computer
Hardware, Holding
Companies,
Subassemblies and
Components
Growth Openings in past
year 21; percentage
growth 4%
Contact Jure Sola,
President
Tel 408-435-8444
Fax 408-435-0716

SATO America, Inc.
545 Weddell Dr.
Sunnyvale, CA 94089

Founded 1940
Total employees 20
Annual sales $3 million
Industry Computer
Hardware
Growth Openings in past
year 12; percentage
growth 150%
Contact Dennis Stevens,
Vice President
Tel 408-745-1300
Fax 408-745-1309

Sherpa Corp.
611 River Oaks Pkwy.
San Jose, CA 95134

Founded 1984
Total employees 120
Annual sales $13 million
Industry Computer
Software
Growth Openings in past
year 35; percentage
growth 41%
Contact Al Castleman,
VP of Finance/CFO
Tel 408-433-0455
Fax 408-943-9507

**Sierra Semiconductor
Corp.**
2075 North Capital Ave.
San Jose, CA 95132

Founded 1984
Total employees 330
Annual sales $86 million
Industry Subassemblies
and Components

Growth Openings in past
year 69; percentage
growth 26%
Contact James V. Diller,
President
Tel 408-263-9300
Fax 408-263-3337

S-MOS Systems, Inc.
2460 North First St.
San Jose, CA 95131

Founded 1983
Total employees 230
Annual sales $150 million
Industries Computer
Hardware,
Subassemblies and
Components
Growth Openings in past
year 19; percentage
growth 9%
Contact Dan Hauer,
President
Tel 408-922-0200
Fax 408-922-0238

Solitec, Inc.
3901 Burton Dr.
Santa Clara, CA 95054

Founded 1970
Total employees 75
Annual sales $25 million
Industry Holding
Companies
Growth Openings in past
year 25; percentage
growth 50%
Contact Ms. Marcella
Wells,
Director of Human
Resources
Tel 408-980-1355
Fax 408-980-9230

**Strategic Simulations,
Inc.**
675 Almanor Ave., Suite
201
Sunnyvale, CA 94086

Founded 1979
Total employees 110
Annual sales $14 million
Industry Computer
Software

Growth Openings in past year 35; percentage growth 46%
Contact Ms. Roberta Gibbons,
VP of Human Resources
Tel 408-737-6800
Fax 408-737-6814

Structural Integrity Associates, Inc.
3150 Almaden Expwy., Suite 145
San Jose, CA 95118

Founded 1983
Total employees 50
Annual sales $7 million
Industries Computer Software, Energy
Growth Openings in past year 18; percentage growth 56%
Contact Peter Riccardella,
President
Tel 408-978-8200

SunDisk Corp.
3270 Jay St.
Santa Clara, CA 95054

Founded 1988
Total employees 120
Annual sales $22 million
Industry Computer Hardware
Growth Openings in past year 20; percentage growth 20%
Contact Eli Harari,
CEO/President
Tel 408-562-0500
Fax 408-980-8607

Synergy Semiconductor Corp.
3450 Central Expwy.
Santa Clara, CA 95051

Founded 1987
Total employees 130
Annual sales $12 million
Industry Subassemblies and Components

Growth Openings in past year 30; percentage growth 30%
Contact Thomas D. Mino,
President/CEO
Tel 408-730-1313
Fax 408-737-0831

Systems Chemistry, Inc.
370 Montague Expwy.
Milpitas, CA 95035

Founded 1985
Total employees 40
Annual sales $12 million
Industries Chemicals, Factory Automation
Growth Openings in past year 15; percentage growth 60%
Contact John Traub,
President
Tel 408-263-5200
Fax 408-263-9411

Tanon Manufacturing, Inc.
337 Trade Zone Blvd.
Milpitas, CA 95035

Founded 1982
Total employees 335
Industry Subassemblies and Components
Growth Openings in past year 34; percentage growth 11%
Contact Ms. Sherry Inselman,
Personnel Manager
Tel 408-945-0400
Fax 408-263-3750

Telebit Corp.
1315 Chesapeake Terr.
Sunnyvale, CA 94089

Founded 1984
Total employees 225
Annual sales $64 million
Industry Telecommunications
Growth Openings in past year 30; percentage growth 15%
Contact Jamed D. Narrod,
Chairman of the Board
Tel 408-734-4333
Fax 408-734-3333

Ultratech Stepper
3230 Scott Blvd.
Santa Clara, CA 95054

Founded 1981
Total employees 350
Annual sales $38 million
Industry Manufacturing Equipment
Growth Openings in past year 100; percentage growth 40%
Contact Robert Weston,
VP of Human Resources
Tel 408-727-4930
Fax 408-748-9474

UMAX Technologies, Inc.
3170 Coronado Dr.
Santa Clara, CA 95054

Founded 1989
Total employees 20
Industry Computer Hardware
Growth Openings in past year 15; percentage growth 300%
Contact Dao Wu,
President
Tel 408-982-0771
Fax 408-982-0776

Vertex Semiconductor Corp.
1060 Rincon Cir.
San Jose, CA 95131

Founded 1984
Total employees 100
Annual sales $7.7 million
Industry Subassemblies and Components
Growth Openings in past year 20; percentage growth 25%
Contact Bruce Bourbon,
President/CEO
Tel 408-456-8900
Fax 408-456-8910

VISX, Inc.
3400 Centeral Expwy.
Santa Clara, CA 95051

Founded 1987
Total employees 120
Annual sales $20.3 million

Industries Holding
Companies, Medical
Growth Openings in past
year 50; percentage
growth 71%
Contact Dr. Charles R.
Munnerlyn,
COB/CEO
Tel 408-733-2020
Fax 408-733-0227

VMX, Inc.
2115 O'Nel Dr.
San Jose, CA 95131

Founded 1978
Total employees 480
Annual sales $71 million
Industry
Telecommunications
Growth Openings in past
year 80; percentage
growth 20%
Contact Patrick S.
Howard,
President/CEO
Tel 408-441-1144
Fax 408-441-7026

**Western Digital Corp.,
Drive Engineering
Division**
6201 San Ignacio
San Jose, CA 95119

Founded 1970
Total employees 350
Annual sales $57 million
Industry Computer
Hardware
Growth Openings in past
year 150; percentage
growth 75%
Contact Ms. Denise
McCarney,
Human Resources
Manager
Tel 408-365-1190

Xilinx, Inc.
2100 Logic Dr.
San Jose, CA 95124

Founded 1984
Total employees 482
Annual sales $178 million

Industries Computer
Software, Holding
Companies,
Subassemblies and
Components
Growth Openings in past
year 145; percentage
growth 43%
Contact Ray Madorin,
VP of Human Resources
Tel 408-559-7778
Fax 408-559-7114

Zoran Corp.
1705 Wyatt Dr.
Santa Clara, CA 95054

Founded 1983
Total employees 45
Annual sales $4.3 million
Industry Subassemblies
and Components
Growth Openings in past
year 15; percentage
growth 50%
Contact Levi Gerzberg,
President
Tel 408-986-1314
Fax 408-986-1240

■ **415 Area Code**

Adobe Systems, Inc.
1585 Charleston Rd.
Mountain View, CA 94039

Founded 1982
Total employees 887
Annual sales $265.9
million
Industry Computer
Software
Growth Openings in past
year 184; percentage
growth 26%
Contact Ms. Rebecca
Guerra,
Director of Human
Resources
Tel 415-961-4400
Fax 415-961-3761

Advent Software, Inc.
512 Second St.
San Francisco, CA 94107

Founded 1983
Total employees 90
Annual sales $10 million

Industry Computer
Software
Growth Openings in past
year 40; percentage
growth 80%
Contact Ms. Stephanie
DiMarco,
President
Tel 415-543-7696
Fax 415-543-5070

Aehr Test Systems
1667 Plymouth St.
Mountain View, CA 94043

Founded 1977
Total employees 210
Annual sales $40 million
Industries Factory
Automation, Holding
Companies,
Manufacturing
Equipment
Growth Openings in past
year 50; percentage
growth 31%
Contact Bob Morgan,
Human Resources
Manager
Tel 415-691-9400
Fax 415-691-9300

Allied Telesis, Inc.
575 East Middlefield Rd.
Mountain View, CA 94043

Founded 1988
Total employees 250
Annual sales $61 million
Industry
Telecommunications
Growth Openings in past
year 130; percentage
growth 108%
Contact Ms. Beth Haba,
Manager of Human
Resources
Tel 415-964-2771
Fax 415-964-0944

**AMP Incorporated,
Kaptron**
2525 East Bay Shore Rd.
Palo Alto, CA 94303

Founded 1973
Total employees 50
Industries Photonics,
Test and Measurement,
Telecommunications

Growth Openings in past year 15; percentage growth 42%
Contact Dr. Narinder Kapany, Ph.D., President
Tel 415-493-8008
Fax 415-493-8924

Application Group, Inc.
200 Pine St., Suite 800
San Francisco, CA 94104

Founded 1978
Total employees 200
Annual sales $25 million
Industries Computer Hardware, Computer Software
Growth Openings in past year 90; percentage growth 81%
Contact Ms. Peggy Negus, Personnel Manager
Tel 415-421-1627
Fax 415-765-5200

Applied Immune Sciences, Inc.
200 Constitution Dr.
Menlo Park, CA 94025

Founded 1984
Total employees 100
Industry Medical
Growth Openings in past year 30; percentage growth 42%
Contact Dr. Thomas Okarma, President/CEO
Tel 415-326-7302
Fax 415-326-0923

Aspect Development, Inc.
4410 El Camino Real, Suite 208
Los Altos, CA 94022

Founded 1991
Total employees 25
Industry Computer Software

Growth Openings in past year 13; percentage growth 108%
Contact Dr. Romesh Wadhwani, Ph.D., COB/President
Tel 415-961-2525
Fax 415-941-9757

Athena Neurosciences, Inc.
800 Gateway Blvd.
South San Francisco, CA 94080

Founded 1986
Total employees 124
Industry Pharmaceuticals
Growth Openings in past year 59; percentage growth 90%
Contact John Groom, President
Tel 415-877-0900
Fax 415-877-8370

Bell Atlantic Healthcare Systems, Inc.
100 Drakes Landing, Suite 100
Greenbrae, CA 94904

Founded 1984
Total employees 100
Industry Telecommunications
Growth Openings in past year 50; percentage growth 100%
Contact Donald Simborg, President
Tel 415-925-0121
Fax 415-925-0273

Biotrack, Inc.
1058 Huff Ave.
Mountain View, CA 94043

Founded 1984
Total employees 125
Annual sales $13 million
Industry Medical
Growth Openings in past year 25; percentage growth 25%
Contact Bill Dippel, President
Tel 415-965-7400
Fax 415-965-0439

Broderbund Software, Inc.
500 Redwood Blvd., PO Box 6121
Novato, CA 94948

Founded 1980
Total employees 300
Annual sales $55.8 million
Industry Computer Software
Growth Openings in past year 30; percentage growth 11%
Contact Doug Carlston, COB/CEO
Tel 415-382-4400
Fax 415-382-4665

Cardiometrics, Inc.
645 Clyde Ave.
Mountain View, CA 94043

Founded 1985
Total employees 70
Industry Medical
Growth Openings in past year 15; percentage growth 27%
Contact Meno Nassi, President/CEO
Tel 415-961-6993
Fax 415-961-8753

Cell Genesys, Inc.
322 Lakeside Dr.
Foster City, CA 94404

Founded 1988
Total employees 73
Industry Biotechnology
Growth Openings in past year 29; percentage growth 65%
Contact Stephen A. Sherwin, MD, President/CEO
Tel 415-358-9600
Fax 415-358-0803

Cisco Systems, Inc.
1525 O'Brien Dr.
Menlo Park, CA 94025

Founded 1984
Total employees 882
Annual sales $339.62 million
Industry Telecommunications

California

Growth Openings in past
year 381; percentage
growth 76%
Contact John Morgridge,
Chief Executive Officer
Tel 415-326-1941
Fax 415-326-1989

Growth Openings in past
year 35; percentage
growth 58%
Contact James Dao,
President/CEO/COB
Tel 415-802-7888
Fax 415-802-7777

Growth Openings in past
year 15; percentage
growth 15%
Contact Gibson
Anderson,
Director of Human
Resources
Tel 415-855-7400
Fax 415-856-6153

**CLONTECH
Laboratories, Inc.**
4030 Fabian Way
Palo Alto, CA 94303

Founded 1984
Total employees 80
Annual sales $7 million
Industries Biotechnology,
Chemicals, Computer
Software
Growth Openings in past
year 15; percentage
growth 23%
Contact Ms. Hensl Lise,
Personnel Manager
Tel 415-424-8222
Fax 415-424-1064

**Devices for Vascular
Intervention, Inc.**
595 Penobscot Dr.
Redwood City, CA 94063

Founded 1984
Total employees 320
Annual sales $25 million
Industry Medical
Growth Openings in past
year 140; percentage
growth 77%
Contact Alan Will,
President
Tel 415-361-1444
Fax 415-364-2889

**Electric Power Research
Institute**
PO Box 10412
Palo Alto, CA 94304

Founded 1973
Total employees 780
Industry Energy
Growth Openings in past
year 45; percentage
growth 6%
Contact Dr. Richard
Balzhiser,
President
Tel 415-855-2000
Fax 415-855-2954

Comdisco Systems, Inc.
919 East Hillsdale Blvd.
Foster City, CA 94404

Founded 1969
Total employees 90
Annual sales $9.9 million
Industry Computer
Software
Growth Openings in past
year 15; percentage
growth 20%
Contact Vincent Ricci,
President
Tel 415-574-5800
Fax 415-358-3601

Digidesign, Inc.
1360 Willow Rd., Suite
101
Menlo Park, CA 94025

Founded 1983
Total employees 130
Industries Computer
Hardware, Computer
Software,
Telecommunications
Growth Openings in past
year 50; percentage
growth 62%
Contact Peter Gotcher,
CEO/President/Founder
Tel 415-688-0600
Fax 415-327-0777

**Electronics for Imaging,
Inc.**
2855 Campus Dr.
San Mateo, CA 94403

Founded 1989
Total employees 154
Annual sales $53.7 million
Industry Computer
Software
Growth Openings in past
year 28; percentage
growth 22%
Contact Efi Arazi,
President
Tel 415-286-8600
Fax 415-286-8686

**Communication
Intelligence Corp.**
275 Shoreline Dr., 6th Fl.
Redwood Shores, CA
94065

Founded 1981
Total employees 95
Industries Computer
Hardware, Computer
Software

Echelon Corp.
4015 Miranda Ave.
Palo Alto, CA 94304

Founded 1988
Total employees 110
Annual sales $15 million
Industries Computer
Software,
Telecommunications

Etak, Inc.
1430 O'Brien Dr.
Menlo Park, CA 94025

Founded 1983
Total employees 286
Industries Computer
Hardware, Computer
Software, Transportation

Growth Openings in past year 86; percentage growth 43%
Contact Ms. Elaine Montaine, Personnel Manager
Tel 415-328-3825
Fax 415-328-3148

Growth Openings in past year 40; percentage growth 66%
Contact Ms. Linda A. Fitzpatrick, Director of Human Resources
Tel 415-574-3000
Fax 415-578-9264

Growth Openings in past year 20; percentage growth 14%
Contact Mike Killeen, Director of Human Resources
Tel 415-321-9500
Fax 415-321-5471

Focus Graphics, Inc.
1191 Chess Dr., Suite B
Foster City, CA 94404

Founded 1984
Total employees 30
Industries Photonics, Telecommunications
Growth Openings in past year 14; percentage growth 87%
Contact Johan Brag, President
Tel 415-377-0596
Fax 415-377-0598

Global Village Communications, Inc.
685 East Middlefield Rd.
Mountain View, CA 94043

Founded 1989
Total employees 100
Industry Telecommunications
Growth Openings in past year 90; percentage growth 900%
Contact Neil Selvin, CEO/President
Tel 415-329-0700
Fax 415-390-8282

Harris Corp., Digital Telephone Systems Division
300 Bel Marin Keys Blvd.
Novato, CA 94949

Founded 1968
Total employees 300
Annual sales $60 million
Industry Telecommunications
Growth Openings in past year 50; percentage growth 20%
Contact Harry Roberts, Director of Human Resources
Tel 415-382-5000
Fax 415-883-1626

GCH Systems, Inc.
777 East Middlefield
Mountain View, CA 94043

Founded 1984
Total employees 150
Annual sales $45 million
Industries Computer Hardware, Subassemblies and Components, Telecommunications
Growth Openings in past year 30; percentage growth 25%
Contact George Huang, President
Tel 415-968-3400
Fax 415-960-0594

GO Corp.
919 East Hillsdale Blvd., Suite 400
Foster City, CA 94404

Founded 1987
Total employees 185
Industry Computer Software
Growth Openings in past year 55; percentage growth 42%
Contact Bill Campbell, President/CEO
Tel 415-345-7400
Fax 415-345-9833

HSQ Technology
1435 Huntington Ave.
South San Francisco, CA 94080

Founded 1979
Total employees 100
Annual sales $17 million
Industries Energy, Factory Automation, Test and Measurement
Growth Openings in past year 20; percentage growth 25%
Contact Henry D. Hoge, President
Tel 415-952-4310
Fax 415-952-7206

Gupta Technologies, Inc.
1060 Marsh Rd.
Menlo Park, CA 94025

Founded 1984
Total employees 160
Annual sales $21 million
Industry Computer Software

Gilead Sciences, Inc.
344-346 Lakeside Dr.
Foster City, CA 94404

Founded 1987
Total employees 100
Industry Pharmaceuticals

Imatron, Inc.
389 Oyster Point Blvd.
South San Francisco, CA 94080

Founded 1983
Total employees 140
Annual sales $22.9 million
Industry Medical

Growth Openings in past year 30; percentage growth 27%
Contact Ms. Gina Caruso, Manager of Human Resources
Tel 415-583-9964
Fax 415-871-0418

Growth Openings in past year 30; percentage growth 30%
Contact Don Gallagher, Executive VP of Sales and Marketing
Tel 415-694-7600
Fax 415-964-5434

Growth Openings in past year 101; percentage growth 25%
Contact Scott Cook, President
Tel 415-322-0573
Fax 415-322-1013

Indus Group
60 Spear St.
San Francisco, CA 94133

Founded 1987
Total employees 180
Annual sales $20 million
Industry Computer Software
Growth Openings in past year 55; percentage growth 44%
Contact Bob Felton, President
Tel 415-904-5000
Fax 415-904-4949

Interactive Development Environments, Inc.
595 Market St., 10th Fl.
San Francisco, CA 94105

Founded 1983
Total employees 200
Annual sales $23 million
Industry Computer Software
Growth Openings in past year 50; percentage growth 33%
Contact Anthony Wasserman, President
Tel 415-543-0900
Fax 415-543-3716

Island Graphics Corp.
4000 Civic Center Dr.
San Rafael, CA 94903

Founded 1982
Total employees 150
Industry Computer Software
Growth Openings in past year 15; percentage growth 11%
Contact Daniel Remer, President
Tel 415-491-1000
Fax 415-491-0402

Keller and Gannon
1453 Mission St., PO Box 422430
San Francisco, CA 94142

Founded 1941
Total employees 75
Annual sales $6 million
Industries Defense, Manufacturing Equipment
Growth Openings in past year 15; percentage growth 25%
Contact Thomas Reinarts, President
Tel 415-621-1199
Fax 415-864-3681

Inforite Corp.
1670 South Amphlett Blvd., Suite 100
San Mateo, CA 94402

Founded 1983
Total employees 70
Annual sales $20 million
Industry Computer Hardware
Growth Openings in past year 55; percentage growth 366%
Contact K. Kato, President
Tel 415-571-8766
Fax 415-571-7547

Interactive Network, Inc.
1991 Landings Dr.
Mountain View, CA 94043

Founded 1988
Total employees 80
Industry Telecommunications
Growth Openings in past year 19; percentage growth 31%
Contact David B. Lockton, Chief Executive Officer
Tel 415-960-1000
Fax 415-960-3331

Insignia Solutions, Inc.
526 Clyde Ave.
Mountain View, CA 94043

Founded 1986
Total employees 130
Annual sales $19 million
Industry Computer Software

Intuit, Inc.
PO Box 3014
Menlo Park, CA 94026

Founded 1983
Total employees 503
Annual sales $83.79 million
Industry Computer Software

Kensington Microware, Ltd.
2855 Campus Dr.
San Mateo, CA 94403

Founded 1982
Total employees 50
Annual sales $4.8 million
Industries Computer Hardware, Energy, Subassemblies and Components

Growth Openings in past year 16; percentage growth 47%
Contact Peter DuPont, President/CEO
Tel 415-572-2700
Fax 415-572-9675

Kentex International, Inc.
1718 Broadway
Redwood City, CA 94063

Founded 1978
Total employees 25
Annual sales $5 million
Industries Computer Hardware, Energy, Factory Automation
Growth Openings in past year 14; percentage growth 127%
Contact Ms. Rosa Ho, Office Manager
Tel 415-365-0111
Fax 415-365-2523

Knowledge Data Systems, Inc.
80 East Sir Francis Drake Blvd.
Larkspur, CA 94939

Founded 1964
Total employees 98
Annual sales $13 million
Industry Computer Software
Growth Openings in past year 14; percentage growth 16%
Contact Joe Sullivan, Chief Executive Officer
Tel 415-461-5374

Legato Systems, Inc.
260 Sheridan Ave.
Palo Alto, CA 94306

Founded 1988
Total employees 50
Annual sales $5.8 million
Industries Computer Hardware, Computer Software

Growth Openings in past year 15; percentage growth 42%
Contact Louis Cole, President/CEO
Tel 415-329-7880
Fax 415-329-8898

Liposome Technology, Inc.
1050 Hamilton Ct.
Menlo Park, CA 94025

Founded 1981
Total employees 85
Industry Biotechnology
Growth Openings in past year 25; percentage growth 41%
Contact Michael K. Ullman, President/COO
Tel 415-323-9011
Fax 415-323-9106

Lotus Development Corp., cc:Mail Division
2141 Landings Dr.
Mountain View, CA 94043

Founded 1983
Total employees 150
Annual sales $50 million
Industry Computer Software
Growth Openings in past year 90; percentage growth 150%
Contact Rex Cardinale, Vice President/General Manager
Tel 415-961-8800
Fax 415-961-8400

Macrovision, Inc.
700 El Camino Real East
Mountain View, CA 94040

Founded 1983
Total employees 50
Industry Telecommunications
Growth Openings in past year 15; percentage growth 42%
Contact Joeseph F. Swyt, President
Tel 415-691-2900
Fax 415-691-2999

Make Systems, Inc.
201 San Antonio Cir., Suite 225
Mountain View, CA 94040

Founded 1987
Total employees 60
Annual sales $6.9 million
Industry Computer Software
Growth Openings in past year 30; percentage growth 100%
Contact Steven Howard, President
Tel 415-944-9800
Fax 415-941-5856

Micro Focus, Inc.
2465 East Bayshore Rd., Suite 400
Palo Alto, CA 94303

Founded 1976
Total employees 575
Annual sales $98 million
Industry Computer Software
Growth Openings in past year 173; percentage growth 43%
Contact Richard Butts, Human Resources Manager
Tel 415-856-4161
Fax 415-856-6134

Mozart Systems Corp.
1350 Bayshore Hwy., Suite 630
Burlingame, CA 94010

Founded 1985
Total employees 35
Annual sales $2 million
Industry Computer Software
Growth Openings in past year 20; percentage growth 133%
Contact Alan P. Parnass, President
Tel 415-340-1588
Fax 415-340-1648

Netra Corp.
185 East Dana St.
Mountain View, CA 94041

Founded 1967
Total employees 40
Industries Advanced
Materials, Photonics,
Subassemblies and
Components
Growth Openings in past
year 15; percentage
growth 60%
Contact William Harry,
President
Tel 415-964-1230
Fax 415-968-3115

Parallan Computers, Inc.
1310 Villa St.
Mountain View, CA 94041

Founded 1988
Total employees 90
Industry Computer
Software
Growth Openings in past
year 45; percentage
growth 100%
Contact Gianluca
Rattazzi,
President/CEO
Tel 415-960-0288
Fax 415-962-8141

Resound Corp.
220 Saginow Dr.
Redwood City, CA 94063

Founded 1984
Total employees 104
Annual sales $7.9 million
Industry Medical
Growth Openings in past
year 25; percentage
growth 31%
Contact Jim Gallogly,
Chief Executive Officer
Tel 415-780-7800
Fax 415-367-0675

Network General Corp.
4200 Bohannon Dr.
Menlo Park, CA 94025

Founded 1986
Total employees 300
Annual sales $63.1 million
Industries Computer
Software, Test and
Measurement,
Telecommunications
Growth Openings in past
year 100; percentage
growth 50%
Contact Harry J. Saal,
COB/President/CEO
Tel 415-688-2700
Fax 415-321-0855

Peninsula Engineering Group, Inc.
1091 Industrial Rd.
San Carlos, CA 94070

Founded 1983
Total employees 90
Annual sales $12 million
Industry
Telecommunications
Growth Openings in past
year 30; percentage
growth 50%
Contact Edward
Sherman,
President
Tel 415-593-2400
Fax 415-591-1624

Ross Systems, Inc.
555 Twin Dolphin Dr.
Redwood City, CA 94065

Founded 1972
Total employees 640
Annual sales $75.85
million
Industries Computer
Hardware, Computer
Software, Holding
Companies
Growth Openings in past
year 53; percentage
growth 9%
Contact Selby Little,
CFO/Secretary/VP of
Finance and Administ
Tel 415-593-2500
Fax 415-592-9364

Panamax
150 Mitchell Blvd.
San Rafael, CA 94903

Founded 1979
Total employees 100
Annual sales $15 million
Industries Energy,
Subassemblies and
Components
Growth Openings in past
year 22; percentage
growth 28%
Contact Henry Moody,
President
Tel 415-499-3900
Fax 415-472-5540

Precision Navigation, Inc.
1350 Pear Ave., Suite A
Mountain View, CA 94043

Founded 1987
Total employees 30
Industries Defense, Test
and Measurement,
Transportation
Growth Openings in past
year 25; percentage
growth 500%
Contact George Hsu,
President
Tel 415-962-8777
Fax 415-962-8776

RSA Data Security, Inc.
100 Marine Pkwy.
Redwood City, CA 94065

Founded 1982
Total employees 25
Annual sales $10 million
Industry Computer
Software
Growth Openings in past
year 13; percentage
growth 108%
Contact D. James
Bidzos,
Chief Executive Officer
Tel 415-595-8782
Fax 415-595-1873

Software Toolworks, Inc.
60 Leveroni Ct.
Novato, CA 94949

Founded 1986
Total employees 350
Annual sales $102.6 million
Industry Computer Software
Growth Openings in past year 81; percentage growth 30%
Contact Robert E. Lloyd, President/COO
Tel 415-883-3000
Fax 415-883-3303

Systems Applications International, Inc.
101 Lucas Valley Rd.
San Rafael, CA 94903

Founded 1968
Total employees 120
Annual sales $13 million
Industry Computer Software
Growth Openings in past year 20; percentage growth 20%
Contact Thomas Brown, Controller
Tel 415-507-7100
Fax 415-507-7177

Verity, Inc.
1550 Plymouth St.
Mountain View, CA 94043

Founded 1988
Total employees 110
Annual sales $14.7 million
Industry Computer Software
Growth Openings in past year 25; percentage growth 29%
Contact Ms. Sarah Whitely, Manager of Human Resources
Tel 415-960-7600
Fax 415-960-7698

SunSoft, Inc.
2550 Garcia Ave.
Mountain View, CA 94043

Founded 1977
Total employees 800
Annual sales $92 million
Industry Computer Software
Growth Openings in past year 99; percentage growth 14%
Contact Ed Zander, President
Tel 415-960-3200
Fax 415-961-6070

Tencor Instruments
2400 Charleston Rd.
Mountain View, CA 94043

Founded 1976
Total employees 375
Annual sales $58 million
Industry Factory Automation
Growth Openings in past year 25; percentage growth 7%
Contact Ms. Cynthia Dooley, Manager of Human Resources
Tel 415-969-6767
Fax 415-969-6371

VoiceCom Systems, Inc.
222 Kearny, Suite 308
San Francisco, CA 94108

Founded 1984
Total employees 150
Annual sales $30 million
Industry Telecommunications
Growth Openings in past year 50; percentage growth 50%
Contact Ms. Gail Conely, CFO/VP of Finance
Tel 415-397-1900
Fax 415-398-1518

Synopsys, Inc.
700 East Middlefield Rd.
Mountain View, CA 94043

Founded 1986
Total employees 400
Annual sales $40.5 million
Industry Computer Software
Growth Openings in past year 175; percentage growth 77%
Contact Ms. Tricia Tomlinson, Director of Human Resources
Tel 415-962-5000
Fax 415-965-8637

Terrapin Technologies, Inc.
750-H Gateway Blvd.
South San Francisco, CA 94080

Founded 1986
Total employees 28
Industries Biotechnology, Medical
Growth Openings in past year 16; percentage growth 133%
Contact Renaldo Gomez, President/CEO
Tel 415-244-9303
Fax 415-244-9388

Wollongong Group, Inc.
1129 San Antonio Rd., PO Box 51860
Palo Alto, CA 94303

Founded 1980
Total employees 190
Industry Computer Software
Growth Openings in past year 19; percentage growth 11%
Contact Noel O. Kile, COB/CEO
Tel 415-962-7100
Fax 415-969-5547

California

■ 510 Area Code

Action Technologies, Inc.
1301 Marina Village Pkwy., Suite 100
Alameda, CA 94501

Founded 1983
Total employees 75
Annual sales $8.7 million
Industries Computer Hardware, Computer Software
Growth Openings in past year 30; percentage growth 66%
Contact Tom White, President/CEO
Tel 510-521-6190
Fax 510-769-0596

Amax Engineering Corp.
47315 Mission Falls Ct.
Fremont, CA 94539

Founded 1980
Total employees 130
Annual sales $55 million
Industries Computer Hardware, Subassemblies and Components, Telecommunications
Growth Openings in past year 30; percentage growth 30%
Contact Ms. Jean Shih, VP of Operations
Tel 510-651-8886
Fax 510-651-3720

American Mitac Corp.
48571 Milmont Dr.
Fremont, CA 94538

Founded 1981
Total employees 80
Annual sales $80 million
Industry Computer Hardware
Growth Openings in past year 20; percentage growth 33%
Contact Ms. C.C. Hu, Personnel Manager
Tel 510-623-5300

AuraVision Corp.
47885 Fremont Blvd.
Fremont, CA 94538

Founded 1992
Total employees 30
Industry Subassemblies and Components
Growth Openings in past year 15; percentage growth 100%
Contact Steve Chan, Chief Executive Officer
Tel 510-440-7180
Fax 510-438-9350

Banner Blue Software, Inc.
PO Box 7865
Fremont, CA 94537

Founded 1985
Total employees 30
Annual sales $3.4 million
Industry Computer Software
Growth Openings in past year 15; percentage growth 100%
Contact Ken Hess, President
Tel 510-794-6850
Fax 510-794-9152

Baxter Healthcare Corp., Novacor Division
7799 Pardee Ln.
Oakland, CA 94621

Founded 1979
Total employees 160
Annual sales $14 million
Industry Medical
Growth Openings in past year 35; percentage growth 28%
Contact Ms. Marian Sticht, VP of Human Resources
Tel 510-568-8338
Fax 510-633-1057

Berkeley Systems, Inc.
2095 Rose St.
Berkeley, CA 94709

Founded 1985
Total employees 49
Industry Computer Software

Growth Openings in past year 27; percentage growth 122%
Contact Wesley Boyd, President
Tel 510-540-5535

BioGenex Laboratories, Inc.
4600 Norris Canyon Rd.
San Ramon, CA 94583

Founded 1981
Total employees 100
Annual sales $9.6 million
Industries Biotechnology, Chemicals, Medical
Growth Openings in past year 30; percentage growth 42%
Contact Krishan L. Kalra, Ph.D., President/CEO
Tel 510-275-0550
Fax 510-275-0580

Bit Software, Inc.
57987 Fremont Blvd.
Fremont, CA 94538

Founded 1983
Total employees 50
Annual sales $5.8 million
Industry Computer Software
Growth Openings in past year 15; percentage growth 42%
Contact Jon Wan, President
Tel 510-490-2928
Fax 510-490-9490

Cirrus Logic, Inc.
3100 West Warren Ave.
Fremont, CA 94538

Founded 1984
Total employees 750
Annual sales $171 million
Industries Holding Companies, Subassemblies and Components

Growth Openings in past year 247; percentage growth 49%
Contact William Bennett, VP of Human Resources
Tel 510-623-8300
Fax 510-226-2180

Growth Openings in past year 20; percentage growth 35%
Contact Ms. Janine Suing, Personnel Administrator
Tel 510-657-7555
Fax 510-657-7576

Growth Openings in past year 16; percentage growth 80%
Contact Dennis Row, President
Tel 510-848-7080
Fax 510-486-1245

Davis Liquid Crystals, Inc.
14722 Wicks Blvd.
San Leandro, CA 94577

Founded 1981
Total employees 27
Annual sales $3.2 million
Industries Factory Automation, Medical, Photonics, Test and Measurement
Growth Openings in past year 12; percentage growth 80%
Contact Fred Davis, President
Tel 510-351-2295
Fax 510-351-2328

DisCopyLabs, Inc.
48641 Milmont Dr.
Fremont, CA 94538

Founded 1982
Total employees 200
Annual sales $23 million
Industries Computer Software, Telecommunications
Growth Openings in past year 100; percentage growth 100%
Contact Norman Tu, President
Tel 510-651-5100
Fax 510-651-2261

DSP Technology Inc.
48500 Kato Rd.
Fremont, CA 94538

Founded 1985
Total employees 77
Annual sales $10 million
Industries Holding Companies, Test and Measurement

Elamet Technologies, Inc.
25932 Eden Landing Rd.
Hayward, CA 94540

Founded 1985
Total employees 290
Annual sales $43 million
Industry Advanced Materials
Growth Openings in past year 49; percentage growth 20%
Contact John Fulton, Director of Human Resources
Tel 510-782-1052
Fax 510-782-2158

Endosonics Corp.
6616 Owens Dr.
Pleasanton, CA 94588

Founded 1984
Total employees 90
Annual sales $9.9 million
Industry Medical
Growth Openings in past year 50; percentage growth 125%
Contact Michael Henson, President/CEO
Tel 510-734-0464
Fax 510-734-0465

Engineering Design Automation
1930 Shattuck Ave.
Berkeley, CA 94704

Founded 1991
Total employees 36
Annual sales $4.1 million
Industry Computer Software

ESS Technology, Inc.
46107 Lending Pkwy.
Fremont, CA 94538

Founded 1984
Total employees 50
Annual sales $25 million
Industries Computer Hardware, Computer Software, Subassemblies and Components
Growth Openings in past year 25; percentage growth 100%
Contact Fred Chan, President
Tel 510-226-1088

Farallon Computing, Inc.
2000 Powell St., Suite 600
Emeryville, CA 94608

Founded 1986
Total employees 250
Industries Computer Software, Subassemblies and Components, Telecommunications
Growth Openings in past year 50; percentage growth 25%
Contact Alan Lefkof, President
Tel 510-596-9100
Fax 510-596-9020

First International Computer of America, Inc.
30077 Ahern Ave.
Union City, CA 94587

Founded 1991
Total employees 56
Annual sales $35 million
Industry Computer Hardware

Growth Openings in past year 40; percentage growth 250%
Contact Peter Ow, President
Tel 510-475-7885
Fax 510-475-5333

Fresenius U.S.A., Inc.
2637 Shadelands Dr.
Walnut Creek, CA 94598

Founded 1974
Total employees 880
Annual sales $129 million
Industry Medical
Growth Openings in past year 204; percentage growth 30%
Contact Ben Lipps, President
Tel 510-295-0200

Friden Neopost
30955 Huntwood Ave.
Hayward, CA 94544

Founded 1977
Total employees 300
Annual sales $57 million
Industry Computer Hardware
Growth Openings in past year 50; percentage growth 20%
Contact Neil Malhstead, President
Tel 510-489-6800
Fax 510-487-6704

Gatan, Inc.
6678 Owens Dr.
Pleasanton, CA 94588

Founded 1960
Total employees 165
Annual sales $17 million
Industry Photonics
Growth Openings in past year 15; percentage growth 10%
Contact Ms. Betty Harris, Personnel Manager
Tel 510-463-0200
Fax 510-463-0204

General Parametrics Corp.
1250 Ninth St.
Berkeley, CA 94710

Founded 1981
Total employees 90
Annual sales $14 million
Industries Computer Hardware, Computer Software, Photonics, Telecommunications
Growth Openings in past year 20; percentage growth 28%
Contact Herbert Baskin, President
Tel 510-524-3950
Fax 510-524-9954

Giga-tronics, Inc.
2495 Estand Way, PO Box 232015
Pleasant Hill, CA 94523

Founded 1980
Total employees 200
Annual sales $16.18 million
Industries Energy, Factory Automation, Holding Companies, Subassemblies and Components
Growth Openings in past year 60; percentage growth 42%
Contact Donald F. Bogue, President/CEO
Tel 510-680-8160
Fax 510-680-7736

Innovative Interfaces, Inc.
2344 Sixth St.
Berkeley, CA 94710

Founded 1978
Total employees 100
Industry Computer Software
Growth Openings in past year 40; percentage growth 66%
Contact Gerald Kline, President
Tel 510-644-3600
Fax 510-644-3650

Kaiser Aerotech
PO Box 1678
San Leandro, CA 94577

Founded 1948
Total employees 251
Annual sales $52 million
Industries Defense, Manufacturing Equipment, Transportation
Growth Openings in past year 23; percentage growth 10%
Contact Ms. Maryanne Giles, Personnel Manager
Tel 510-562-2456
Fax 510-568-6420

Learning Co.
6493 Kaiser Dr.
Fremont, CA 94555

Founded 1979
Total employees 130
Annual sales $19.59 million
Industry Computer Software
Growth Openings in past year 19; percentage growth 17%
Contact Les Schmidt, Chief Financial Officer
Tel 510-792-2101
Fax 510-792-9628

Logistix
48021 Warm Springs Blvd.
Fremont, CA 94539

Founded 1974
Total employees 200
Annual sales $27 million
Industries Computer Hardware, Computer Software, Telecommunications
Growth Openings in past year 50; percentage growth 33%
Contact Stephen Weinstein, President
Tel 510-498-7000
Fax 510-438-9486

Media Vision, Inc.
3185 Laurel View Ct.
Fremont, CA 94538

Founded 1991
Total employees 200
Annual sales $68.91
million
Industries Computer
Hardware,
Telecommunications
Growth Openings in past
year 100; percentage
growth 100%
Contact Paul Jain,
President/CEO
Tel 510-770-8600
Fax 510-770-9592

Molecular Design, Ltd.
2132 Farallon Dr.
San Leandro, CA 94577

Founded 1978
Total employees 300
Annual sales $34 million
Industry Computer
Software
Growth Openings in past
year 20; percentage
growth 7%
Contact Dan Kingman,
VP of Human Resources
Tel 510-895-1313
Fax 510-352-2870

Optical Specialties, Inc.
4281 Technology Dr.
Fremont, CA 94538

Founded 1978
Total employees 100
Annual sales $10 million
Industry Factory
Automation
Growth Openings in past
year 25; percentage
growth 33%
Contact Levon Billups,
VP of Operations
Tel 510-490-6400
Fax 510-490-1748

PeopleSoft, Inc.
1331 North California
Blvd.
Walnut Creek, CA 94596

Founded 1987
Total employees 173
Annual sales $31.5 million
Industry Computer
Software
Growth Openings in past
year 43; percentage
growth 33%
Contact David Duffield,
President/CEO
Tel 510-946-9460

Peripheral Land, Inc.
47421 Bayside Pkwy.
Fremont, CA 94538

Founded 1984
Total employees 120
Annual sales $35 million
Industries Computer
Hardware, Computer
Software
Growth Openings in past
year 35; percentage
growth 41%
Contact Leo Berenguel,
President
Tel 510-657-2211
Fax 510-683-9713

RPC Industries, Inc.
21325 Cabot Blvd.
Hayward, CA 94545

Founded 1980
Total employees 75
Industries Factory
Automation,
Manufacturing
Equipment
Growth Openings in past
year 15; percentage
growth 25%
Contact Dr. Alan Klein,
President
Tel 510-785-8040
Fax 510-785-1518

SCITEC Communications Systems, Inc.
48025 Fremont Blvd.
Fremont, CA 94538

Founded 1979
Total employees 25
Annual sales $7 million
Industry
Telecommunications
Growth Openings in past
year 19; percentage
growth 316%
Contact Joe Younane,
President
Tel 510-226-1818
Fax 510-226-1820

Siemens Medical Laboratories, Inc.
4040 Nelson Ave.
Concord, CA 94520

Founded 1974
Total employees 340
Annual sales $39 million
Industries Computer
Software, Medical, Test
and Measurement
Growth Openings in past
year 50; percentage
growth 17%
Contact Karl Haug,
Executive VP of Finance
and Business Adm
Tel 510-246-8200
Fax 510-246-8204

Somatix Therapy Corporation
850 Marina Village Pkwy.
Alameda, CA 94501

Founded 1981
Total employees 80
Industries Biotechnology,
Medical
Growth Openings in past
year 13; percentage
growth 19%
Contact Ms. Arlene
Jordan-Levy,
Director of Human
Resources
Tel 510-748-3000
Fax 510-769-8533

TRW Financial Systems, Inc.
2001 Center St.
Berkeley, CA 94704

Founded 1977
Total employees 425
Annual sales $70 million
Industries Computer
Hardware, Computer
Software
Growth Openings in past
year 124; percentage
growth 41%
Contact Phillip Trapp,
President
Tel 510-704-3000
Fax 510-486-1376

Vantage Analysis Systems, Inc.
42808 Christy St., Suite 200
Fremont, CA 94538

Founded 1986
Total employees 60
Annual sales $8 million
Industry Computer
Software
Growth Openings in past
year 25; percentage
growth 71%
Contact Ron Abelman,
President
Tel 510-659-0901
Fax 510-659-0129

ViewStar Corp.
5820 Shellmound St.
Emeryville, CA 94608

Founded 1986
Total employees 130
Annual sales $15 million
Industry Computer
Software
Growth Openings in past
year 40; percentage
growth 44%
Contact Phil Johnston,
VP of Personnel
Tel 510-652-7827
Fax 510-653-9926

Wellex Corp.
44141 South Grimmer Blvd.
Fremont, CA 94538

Founded 1982
Total employees 350
Annual sales $34 million
Industry Subassemblies
and Components
Growth Openings in past
year 49; percentage
growth 16%
Contact Mrs. Rey Lisu,
Personnel Manager
Tel 510-490-3263
Fax 510-651-5047

West Coast Information Systems, Inc.
1901 Olympic Blvd.
Walnut Creek, CA 94596

Founded 1986
Total employees 100
Annual sales $10 million
Industries Computer
Hardware,
Manufacturing
Equipment
Growth Openings in past
year 30; percentage
growth 42%
Contact Charles R.
Adams,
President
Tel 510-930-7700
Fax 510-930-9316

Zycad Corp.
47100 Bayside Pkwy.
Fremont, CA 94538

Founded 1979
Total employees 240
Annual sales $43.5 million
Industries Computer
Software, Factory
Automation, Holding
Companies
Growth Openings in past
year 70; percentage
growth 41%
Contact Phillips W. Smith,
President/CEO
Tel 510-623-4400
Fax 510-623-4550

■ 619 Area Code

Academic Press, Inc.
1250 6th Ave.
San Diego, CA 92101

Founded 1949
Total employees 300
Industry Computer
Software
Growth Openings in past
year 100; percentage
growth 50%
Contact Pieter Bolman,
President
Tel 619-699-6345
Fax 800-336-7377

Action Instruments, Inc.
8601 Aero Dr.
San Diego, CA 92123

Founded 1971
Total employees 200
Annual sales $30 million
Industries Computer
Hardware, Computer
Software, Factory
Automation,
Subassemblies and
Components, Test and
Measurement
Growth Openings in past
year 30; percentage
growth 17%
Contact Scott Wall,
Personnel Manager
Tel 619-279-5726
Fax 619-279-2103

Advanced Processing Laboratories
6215 Ferris Sq., Suite 260
San Diego, CA 92121

Founded 1985
Total employees 35
Annual sales $5 million
Industry Computer
Hardware
Growth Openings in past
year 12; percentage
growth 52%
Contact Doug E. Giese,
President
Tel 619-546-8626
Fax 619-546-0278

Advanced Tissue Sciences, Inc.
10933 North Torrey Pines Rd.
La Jolla, CA 92037

Founded 1986
Total employees 115
Industry Medical
Growth Openings in past year 45; percentage growth 64%
Contact Arthur J. Benvenuto, COB/President/CEO
Tel 619-450-5730
Fax 619-450-5703

Alliance Pharmaceutical Corp.
3040 Science Park Rd.
San Diego, CA 92121

Founded 1983
Total employees 122
Annual sales $1.81 million
Industries Advanced Materials, Chemicals, Pharmaceuticals
Growth Openings in past year 42; percentage growth 52%
Contact Duane Roth, President/COB/CEO
Tel 619-558-4300
Fax 619-558-3625

Applied Digital Access, Inc.
6175 Lusk Blvd.
San Diego, CA 92121

Founded 1987
Total employees 80
Industry Telecommunications
Growth Openings in past year 30; percentage growth 60%
Contact Peter Savage, President
Tel 619-535-6595
Fax 619-535-6596

AGE Logic, Inc.
9985 Pacific Heights Blvd., Suite 200
San Diego, CA 92121

Founded 1984
Total employees 50
Annual sales $5.8 million
Industry Computer Software
Growth Openings in past year 25; percentage growth 100%
Contact Peter Shaw, President
Tel 619-455-8600
Fax 619-597-6030

American Precision Industries, Inc., Rapidsyn Division
3229 Roymar Rd.
Oceanside, CA 92054

Founded 1984
Total employees 60
Annual sales $5 million
Industry Subassemblies and Components
Growth Openings in past year 15; percentage growth 33%
Contact Dave Wegner, Personnel Manager
Tel 619-439-7500
Fax 619-722-5428

Autosplice, Inc.
10121 Barnes Canyon Rd.
San Diego, CA 92121

Founded 1958
Total employees 150
Annual sales $20 million
Industries Factory Automation, Subassemblies and Components
Growth Openings in past year 25; percentage growth 20%
Contact Irwin Zahn, President
Tel 619-535-0077
Fax 619-535-0130

Agouron Pharmaceuticals, Inc.
3565 General Atomics Ct.
San Diego, CA 92121

Founded 1984
Total employees 130
Industries Biotechnology, Pharmaceuticals
Growth Openings in past year 32; percentage growth 32%
Contact Ms. Pat Moses, Associate Director of Human Resources
Tel 619-622-3000
Fax 619-622-3298

Analytical Technologies, Inc.
5550 Morehouse Dr.
San Diego, CA 92121

Founded 1984
Total employees 350
Annual sales $45 million
Industries Chemicals, Environmental
Growth Openings in past year 150; percentage growth 75%
Contact John H. Taylor, Jr., President/General Manager
Tel 619-458-9141
Fax 619-558-2389

Biosym Technologies, Inc.
9685 Scranton Rd.
San Diego, CA 92121

Founded 1984
Total employees 210
Annual sales $34 million
Industry Computer Software
Growth Openings in past year 40; percentage growth 23%
Contact Ms. Kim McCullough, Director of Personnel
Tel 619-458-9990
Fax 619-458-0136

Bird Medical Technologies, Inc.
1100 Bird Center Dr.
Palm Springs, CA 92262

Founded 1984
Total employees 421
Annual sales $43.86 million
Industry Holding Companies
Growth Openings in past year 146; percentage growth 53%
Contact Felix 'Phil' T. Troilo,
COB/CEO
Tel 619-778-7200
Fax 619-778-7269

CBS Scientific Co.
PO Box 856
Del Mar, CA 92014

Founded 1976
Total employees 40
Annual sales $2 million
Industries Medical, Test and Measurement
Growth Openings in past year 20; percentage growth 100%
Contact Dr. Charles B. Scott, Ph.D.,
President
Tel 619-755-4959
Fax 619-755-0733

Cytel Corp.
3525 John Hopkins Ct.
San Diego, CA 92121

Founded 1987
Total employees 165
Annual sales $9.6 million
Industry Biotechnology
Growth Openings in past year 40; percentage growth 32%
Contact Ms. Sheryl Leyton,
Human Resources Administrator
Tel 619-552-3000
Fax 619-552-8801

Brooktree Corp.
9950 Barnes Canyon Rd.
San Diego, CA 92121

Founded 1981
Total employees 550
Annual sales $42.41 million
Industry Subassemblies and Components
Growth Openings in past year 88; percentage growth 19%
Contact Robert W. Zabaronick,
VP of Human Resources
Tel 619-452-7580
Fax 619-452-2104

Chipsoft, Inc.
6330 Nancy Ridge Rd., Suite 400
San Diego, CA 92122

Founded 1984
Total employees 320
Annual sales $32 million
Industry Computer Software
Growth Openings in past year 140; percentage growth 77%
Contact Lance Daly, Director of Human Resources
Tel 619-453-4446
Fax 619-453-1367

Dura Pharmaceuticals, Inc.
11175 FlintKote Ave., Suite F
San Diego, CA 92121

Founded 1981
Total employees 150
Annual sales $5.5 million
Industries Medical, Pharmaceuticals
Growth Openings in past year 65; percentage growth 76%
Contact Rich Everett, Human Resources Director
Tel 619-457-2553
Fax 619-452-7524

California Jamar, Inc.
3956 Sorrento Valley Blvd., Suite D
San Diego, CA 92121

Founded 1987
Total employees 70
Annual sales $2.57 million
Industries Defense, Holding Companies, Medical, Photonics
Growth Openings in past year 35; percentage growth 100%
Contact Dr. John S. Martinez,
COB/CEO
Tel 619-535-1706
Fax 619-535-1835

Cohu, Inc.
PO Box 85623
San Diego, CA 92186

Founded 1957
Total employees 521
Annual sales $54.3 million
Industry Holding Companies
Growth Openings in past year 21; percentage growth 4%
Contact Ms. Linda Jacobson,
Personnel Manager
Tel 619-277-6700
Fax 619-277-0221

Elgar Corp.
9250 Brown Deer Rd.
San Diego, CA 92121

Founded 1965
Total employees 250
Annual sales $27 million
Industries Energy, Subassemblies and Components
Growth Openings in past year 25; percentage growth 11%
Contact Thomas Erickson,
VP of Human Resources and Administration
Tel 619-450-0085
Fax 619-458-0267

ENCAD, Inc.
7710 Kenamar Ct.
San Diego, CA 92121

Founded 1981
Total employees 85
Annual sales $20 million
Industry Computer
Hardware
Growth Openings in past
year 30; percentage
growth 54%
Contact David Purcell,
President
Tel 619-578-4070
Fax 619-578-4613

Gen-Probe, Inc.
9880 Campus Point Dr.
San Diego, CA 92121

Founded 1983
Total employees 250
Industry Medical
Growth Openings in past
year 69; percentage
growth 38%
Contact Ms. Robin
Vedova,
VP of Human Resources
Tel 619-546-8000
Fax 619-452-5845

Gensia Pharmaceuticals, Inc.
11025 Roselle St.
San Diego, CA 92121

Founded 1986
Total employees 450
Annual sales $19.74
million
Industries Holding
Companies,
Pharmaceuticals
Growth Openings in past
year 150; percentage
growth 50%
Contact David Hale,
COB/President/CEO
Tel 619-546-8300
Fax 619-453-0095

Genta, Inc.
3550 General Atomics Ct.
San Diego, CA 92121

Founded 1989
Total employees 45
Annual sales $2.57 million

Industries Biotechnology,
Holding Companies,
Pharmaceuticals
Growth Openings in past
year 16; percentage
growth 55%
Contact Thomas H.
Adams, Ph.D.,
COB/CEO
Tel 619-455-2700
Fax 619-455-2712

Georgens Industries, Inc.
3346 Industrial Ct.
San Diego, CA 92121

Founded 1985
Total employees 30
Annual sales $2.5 million
Industry Computer
Hardware
Growth Openings in past
year 12; percentage
growth 66%
Contact Harold H.
Georgens,
COB/CEO
Tel 619-481-8114
Fax 619-481-6913

Hallmark Circuits, Inc.
5330 Eastgate Mall Rd.
San Diego, CA 92121

Founded 1970
Total employees 180
Annual sales $15 million
Industry Subassemblies
and Components
Growth Openings in past
year 15; percentage
growth 9%
Contact Donald
Beiwenga,
President
Tel 619-453-7800
Fax 619-453-1409

I-Bus PC Technologies
9596 Chesapeake Dr.
San Diego, CA 92123

Founded 1983
Total employees 100
Annual sales $16 million
Industries Computer
Hardware, Factory
Automation

Growth Openings in past
year 25; percentage
growth 33%
Contact Richard Eppel,
President/CEO
Tel 619-569-0646
Fax 619-268-7863

Immune Response Corp.
5935 Darwin Ct.
Carlsbad, CA 92008

Founded 1986
Total employees 75
Industries Biotechnology,
Pharmaceuticals
Growth Openings in past
year 26; percentage
growth 53%
Contact Ms. Paula Baxter
Atkins,
VP of Administration
Tel 619-431-7080
Fax 619-431-8636

International Business Associates, Inc.
4180 Russian Rd., Suite
190
San Diego, CA 92123

Founded 1980
Total employees 110
Industry Computer
Software
Growth Openings in past
year 30; percentage
growth 37%
Contact Dr. William
Shaw,
President
Tel 619-560-8584
Fax 619-560-7528

Mediashare, Inc.
2035 Corte Del Nogale,
Suite 200
Carlsbad, CA 92009

Founded 1990
Total employees 90
Industry Computer
Software
Growth Openings in past
year 15; percentage
growth 20%
Contact Greg Bestick,
President
Tel 619-931-7171
Fax 619-931-5752

**Medtronic, Inc.,
Interventional Vascular
Business**
9410 Carroll Park Dr.
San Diego, CA 92121

Founded 1984
Total employees 300
Annual sales $33 million
Industry Medical
Growth Openings in past
year 199; percentage
growth 197%
Contact Ms. Kerri-Jo
Cooper,
Director of Human
Resources
Tel 619-458-6400
Fax 619-453-0637

**QUALCOMM,
Incorporated**
10555 Sorrento Valley Rd.
San Diego, CA 92121

Founded 1985
Total employees 850
Annual sales $90.1 million
Industries Subassemblies
and Components,
Telecommunications
Growth Openings in past
year 98; percentage
growth 13%
Contact Dan Sullivan,
VP of Human Resources
Tel 619-587-1121
Fax 619-452-9096

**Remote Control
International, Inc.**
5928 Pascal Ct., Suite
150
Carlsbad, CA 92008

Founded 1985
Total employees 70
Industry Computer
Software
Growth Openings in past
year 30; percentage
growth 75%
Contact Michael
McCafferty,
President
Tel 619-431-4000
Fax 619-431-4006

Schumacher Co.
1969 Palomar Oak Way
Carlsbad, CA 92009

Founded 1972
Total employees 175
Annual sales $22 million
Industries Chemicals,
Test and Measurement
Growth Openings in past
year 60; percentage
growth 52%
Contact Joseph Quince,
Manager of Human
Resources
Tel 619-931-9555
Fax 619-931-7819

**Pacific Communication
Sciences, Inc.**
10075 Barnes Canyon Rd.
San Diego, CA 92121

Founded 1987
Total employees 200
Annual sales $27 million
Industries Computer
Software,
Telecommunications
Growth Openings in past
year 50; percentage
growth 33%
Contact Dr. David L.
Lyon,
President/CEO
Tel 619-535-9500
Fax 619-535-9235

Quantum Design, Inc.
11578 Sorrento Valley
Rd., Suite 30
San Diego, CA 92121

Founded 1982
Industries Holding
Companies, Test and
Measurement
Contact William B.
Lindgren,
President
Tel 619-481-4400
Fax 619-481-7410

Quantum Magnetics
11578 Sorrento Valley
Rd., Suite 30
San Diego, CA 92121

Founded 1982
Total employees 77
Industries Manufacturing
Equipment, Medical,
Test and Measurement
Growth Openings in past
year 27; percentage
growth 54%
Contact Dr. Lowell
Burnett, Ph.D.,
President
Tel 619-481-4400
Fax 619-481-7410

Stac Electronics, Inc.
5993 Avenida Encinas,
Suite 101
Carlsbad, CA 92008

Founded 1983
Total employees 200
Annual sales $33.36
million
Industries Computer
Hardware, Computer
Software,
Subassemblies and
Components
Growth Openings in past
year 135; percentage
growth 207%
Contact John Witzel,
VP of Finance and
Operations
Tel 619-431-7474
Fax 619-431-0880

Pharmingen, Inc.
11555 Sorrento Valley Rd.
San Diego, CA 92121

Founded 1987
Total employees 54
Industry Biotechnology
Growth Openings in past
year 18; percentage
growth 50%
Contact Dr. Ernest
Huang, Ph.D.,
President
Tel 619-792-5730
Fax 619-792-5238

Sutter Corporation
9425 Chesapeake Dr.
San Diego, CA 92123

Founded 1980
Total employees 200
Annual sales $22 million
Industry Medical
Growth Openings in past
year 25; percentage
growth 14%
Contact Timothy
Wollaeger,
President/CEO
Tel 619-569-8148
Fax 619-279-8249

Thermoscan, Inc.
6295 Ferris Square, Suite
G
San Diego, CA 92121

Founded 1984
Total employees 60
Annual sales $6.6 million
Industry Medical
Growth Openings in past
year 30; percentage
growth 100%
Contact John Trenary,
President
Tel 619-535-9600
Fax 619-535-9784

Viagene, Inc.
11075 Roselle St.
San Diego, CA 92121

Founded 1987
Total employees 100
Industry Biotechnology
Growth Openings in past
year 50; percentage
growth 100%
Contact Ms. Lucy Babbitt,
Human Resources
Coordinator
Tel 619-452-1288
Fax 619-452-2616

Xscribe Corp.
6285 Nancy Ridge Dr.
San Diego, CA 92121

Founded 1978
Total employees 50
Annual sales $8 million
Industries Computer
Software, Holding
Companies

Growth Openings in past
year 20; percentage
growth 66%
Contact Suren G. Dutia,
President/CEO
Tel 619-457-5091
Fax 619-457-3928

■ 707 Area Code

ASK Group, Data 3 Systems
1375 Corporate Center
Pkwy.
Santa Rosa, CA 95407

Founded 1980
Total employees 170
Annual sales $19 million
Industry Computer
Software
Growth Openings in past
year 20; percentage
growth 13%
Contact Ms. Jerry Smith,
Human Resources
Manager
Tel 707-528-6560
Fax 707-542-3114

■ 714 Area Code

Almatron Electronics, Inc.
644 East Young St.
Santa Ana, CA 92705

Founded 1983
Total employees 45
Annual sales $4.3 million
Industry Subassemblies
and Components
Growth Openings in past
year 21; percentage
growth 87%
Contact Ms. Eileen
Hathaway,
Human Resources
Manager
Tel 714-557-6000
Fax 714-557-6799

Alpha Systems Lab, Inc.
2361 McGaw Ave.
Irvine, CA 92714

Founded 1990
Total employees 70

Industry Computer
Hardware
Growth Openings in past
year 40; percentage
growth 133%
Contact Ms. Rose
Hwang,
President
Tel 714-252-0117
Fax 714-252-0887

Alton Geoscience, Inc.
25-A Technology Dr.
Irvine, CA 92718

Founded 1981
Total employees 170
Annual sales $17 million
Industry Environmental
Growth Openings in past
year 20; percentage
growth 13%
Contact Trueman Hiller,
President
Tel 714-753-0101
Fax 714-753-0111

Anacom General Corp.
1335 South Claudina St.
Anaheim, CA 92805

Founded 1970
Total employees 110
Annual sales $10 million
Industries Computer
Hardware, Computer
Software, Holding
Companies,
Subassemblies and
Components
Growth Openings in past
year 20; percentage
growth 22%
Contact William K.
Haines,
President
Tel 714-774-8080
Fax 714-774-7388

Arlon, Inc., Adhesives & Films Division
2811 South Harbor Blvd.
Santa Ana, CA 92704

Founded 1990
Total employees 210
Annual sales $40 million
Industries Advanced
Materials, Manufacturing
Equipment

Growth Openings in past
year 35; percentage
growth 20%
Contact Ms. Kathleen
Kasfa,
Director of Human
Resources
Tel 714-540-2811
Fax 714-754-8272

**Bio-Rad Laboratories,
Inc., ECS Division**
3726 East Miraloma Ave.
Anaheim, CA 92806

Founded 1957
Total employees 105
Annual sales $17 million
Industries Chemicals,
Medical
Growth Openings in past
year 20; percentage
growth 23%
Contact Ms. Marilyn
LaCharite,
Personnel Administrator
Tel 714-630-6400
Fax 714-666-1383

**Birtcher Medical
Systems**
50 Technology Dr.
Irvine, CA 92718

Founded 1937
Total employees 203
Annual sales $50.2 million
Industry Medical
Growth Openings in past
year 38; percentage
growth 23%
Contact Ms. Elizabeth
O'Hare,
Human Resources
Manager
Tel 714-753-9400
Fax 714-753-9174

Camintonn Corporation
22 Morgan St.
Irvine, CA 92718

Founded 1979
Total employees 45
Annual sales $7.4 million
Industry Computer
Hardware

Growth Openings in past
year 13; percentage
growth 40%
Contact Ms. Amy
Okayama,
Personnel Manager
Tel 714-454-1500
Fax 714-454-6500

Catalina Marketing Corp.
721 East Ball Rd.
Anaheim, CA 92805

Founded 1983
Total employees 285
Annual sales $51.71
million
Industries Computer
Hardware, Computer
Software
Growth Openings in past
year 114; percentage
growth 66%
Contact Tommy Greer,
Chief Executive Officer
Tel 714-956-6600

Cerplex, Inc.
3332 East La Palma Ave.
Anaheim, CA 92806

Founded 1990
Total employees 180
Annual sales $12 million
Industries Computer
Hardware, Medical
Growth Openings in past
year 88; percentage
growth 95%
Contact Ted Wisniewski,
President
Tel 714-632-2600
Fax 714-632-2619

**Cherokee International,
Inc.**
2841 Dow Ave.
Tustin, CA 92680

Founded 1979
Total employees 400
Industry Subassemblies
and Components
Growth Openings in past
year 50; percentage
growth 14%
Contact Ganpat I. Patel,
President
Tel 714-544-6665
Fax 714-838-4742

CMD Technology, Inc.
1 Vanderbilt
Irvine, CA 92718

Founded 1986
Total employees 80
Annual sales $10 million
Industry Computer
Hardware
Growth Openings in past
year 40; percentage
growth 100%
Contact Simon Huang,
President
Tel 714-454-0800
Fax 714-455-1656

**Control Components
Inc.**
22591 Avenida Empresa
Rancho Santa Margarita,
CA 92688

Founded 1961
Total employees 250
Annual sales $24 million
Industry Subassemblies
and Components
Growth Openings in past
year 65; percentage
growth 35%
Contact Stuart Carson,
President
Tel 714-858-1877
Fax 714-858-1878

**Dainippon Screen
Engineering of America,
Inc.**
3700 West Segerstrom St.
Santa Ana, CA 92704

Founded 1943
Total employees 40
Annual sales $6.5 million
Industries Computer
Hardware,
Manufacturing
Equipment, Photonics
Growth Openings in past
year 15; percentage
growth 60%
Contact H. Miwa,
President
Tel 714-546-9491
Fax 714-751-7826

Disc Manufacturing, Inc.
1120 Cosby Way
Anaheim, CA 92806

Founded 1979
Total employees 140
Annual sales $19 million
Industry
  Telecommunications
Growth Openings in past
  year 70; percentage
  growth 100%
Contact Ram Reddy
  Nomula,
  President of
  Manufacturing
  Operations
Tel 714-630-6700
Fax 714-630-1025

Environmental Forensics
6073 Nauru St.
Cypress, CA 90630

Founded 1978
Total employees 27
Industry Environmental
Growth Openings in past
  year 26; percentage
  growth 2600%
Contact Dr. Alan C. Buck,
  Ph.D.,
  President
Tel 714-898-4797

Information Management Associates
17550 New Hope St.,
  Suite A
Fountain Valley, CA
  92708

Founded 1983
Total employees 107
Annual sales $12 million
Industry Computer
  Software
Growth Openings in past
  year 27; percentage
  growth 33%
Contact AL Subbloie,
  President
Tel 714-549-3068
Fax 714-641-0689

Disposable Waste Systems, Inc.
16802 Aston St., Suite
  200
Irvine, CA 92714

Founded 1976
Total employees 140
Annual sales $14 million
Industries Environmental,
  Factory Automation
Growth Openings in past
  year 20; percentage
  growth 16%
Contact Ms. Judy Harris,
  Director of Human
  Resources
Tel 714-833-3888
Fax 714-833-8858

EPE Technologies, Inc.
1660 Scenic Ave.
Costa Mesa, CA 92626

Founded 1971
Total employees 400
Industries Energy,
  Factory Automation,
  Subassemblies and
  Components, Test and
  Measurement
Growth Openings in past
  year 50; percentage
  growth 14%
Contact Ms. Andrea
  Bortner,
  VP of Human Resources
Tel 714-557-1636
Fax 714-957-1103

KOR Electronics, Inc.
11958 Monarch St.
Garden Grove, CA 92641

Founded 1986
Total employees 60
Annual sales $8 million
Industries Defense,
  Transportation
Growth Openings in past
  year 15; percentage
  growth 33%
Contact Lou Greenbaum,
  CEO/President
Tel 714-898-8200
Fax 714-895-7526

D-Link Systems, Inc.
5 Musick
Irvine, CA 92718

Founded 1980
Total employees 330
Annual sales $50 million
Industries Computer
  Software,
  Subassemblies and
  Components,
  Telecommunications
Growth Openings in past
  year 120; percentage
  growth 57%
Contact Roger Kao,
  President
Tel 714-455-1688
Fax 714-455-2521

Flojet Corp.
12 Morgan
Irvine, CA 92718

Founded 1975
Total employees 230
Annual sales $25 million
Industry Subassemblies
  and Components
Growth Openings in past
  year 100; percentage
  growth 76%
Contact Benjamin Du,
  President
Tel 714-859-4945
Fax 714-859-1153

Label-Aire, Inc.
550 Burning Tree Rd.
Fullerton, CA 92633

Founded 1968
Total employees 150
Annual sales $18 million
Industry Factory
  Automation
Growth Openings in past
  year 50; percentage
  growth 50%
Contact Ms. Stella
  Rodriguez,
  Personnel Manager
Tel 714-441-0700
Fax 714-526-0300

LAIS Advanced Interventional Systems, Inc.
9 Parker
Irvine, CA 92718

Founded 1986
Total employees 140
Annual sales $3 million
Industries Holding
  Companies, Medical
Growth Openings in past
  year 18; percentage
  growth 14%
Contact Robert E. Wall,
  COB/CEO
  Tel 714-586-1342
  Fax 714-586-8515

Lucas Western, Inc., Electrosystems Division
610 Neptune Ave.
Brea, CA 92622

Founded 1986
Total employees 220
Industries Subassemblies
  and Components,
  Transportation
Growth Openings in past
  year 20; percentage
  growth 10%
Contact Tom Yearian,
  General Manager
  Tel 714-671-4500
  Fax 714-671-4503

Med-Tek Healthcare Products
1335 South Claudina St.
Anaheim, CA 92805

Founded 1970
Total employees 95
Annual sales $3 million
Industry Medical
Growth Openings in past
  year 30; percentage
  growth 46%
Contact Carter Lowry,
  Controller
  Tel 714-774-8484
  Fax 714-774-7388

Medtronic, Inc., Cardiopulmonary Business
4633 East La Palma Ave.
Anaheim, CA 92807

Founded 1987
Total employees 500
Annual sales $55 million
Industry Medical
Growth Openings in past
  year 100; percentage
  growth 25%
Contact Willard Lewis,
  President
  Tel 714-779-3700
  Fax 714-779-3618

Micro Technology, Inc.
5065 East Hunter Ave.
Anaheim, CA 92807

Founded 1979
Total employees 530
Annual sales $105 million
Industries Computer
  Hardware, Computer
  Software,
  Telecommunications
Growth Openings in past
  year 110; percentage
  growth 26%
Contact Steven J.
  Hamerslag,
  President
  Tel 714-970-0300
  Fax 714-970-5413

Nano Pulse Industries, Inc.
440 Nibus St., PO Box
  9398
Brea, CA 92621

Founded 1972
Total employees 800
Annual sales $9 million
Industries Subassemblies
  and Components,
  Telecommunications
Growth Openings in past
  year 199; percentage
  growth 33%
Contact Jay A. Harman,
  President
  Tel 714-529-2600
  Fax 714-671-7919

New Horizons Computer Learning Center
1231 East Dyer Rd., Suite
  140
Santa Ana, CA 92705

Founded 1982
Total employees 120
Industry Computer
  Hardware
Growth Openings in past
  year 45; percentage
  growth 60%
Contact Mike Brinda,
  Owner
  Tel 714-556-1220
  Fax 714-556-4612

Newport Systems Solutions, Inc.
4019 Westerly Pl., Suite
  103
Newport Beach, CA
  92660

Founded 1988
Total employees 25
Annual sales $3.4 million
Industry
  Telecommunications
Growth Openings in past
  year 13; percentage
  growth 108%
Contact Larry J.
  Stephenson,
  President/CEO
  Tel 714-752-1511
  Fax 714-752-8389

Nichols Institute Diagnostics
33608 Ortega Hwy.
San Juan Capistrano, CA
  92690

Founded 1974
Total employees 125
Annual sales $13 million
Industry Medical
Growth Openings in past
  year 30; percentage
  growth 31%
Contact Frank E. Taylor,
  President/COO
  Tel 714-661-8000

PDA Engineering
2975 Redhill Ave.
Costa Mesa, CA 92626

Founded 1972
Total employees 250
Annual sales $38 million
Industry Holding
Companies
Growth Openings in past
year 19; percentage
growth 8%
Contact Ms. Linda Baker
Sherman,
Personnel Director
Tel 714-540-8900
Fax 714-979-2990

Phoenician Faire
3545 Cadillac Ave.
Costa Mesa, CA 92626

Founded 1982
Total employees 40
Industry Computer
Hardware
Growth Openings in past
year 20; percentage
growth 100%
Contact Camael Faire,
President
Tel 714-549-4669

Pinnacle Micro, Inc.
19 Technology
Irvine, CA 92718

Founded 1987
Total employees 50
Industry Computer
Hardware
Growth Openings in past
year 20; percentage
growth 66%
Contact William F. Blum,
President
Tel 714-727-3300
Fax 714-727-1913

Quality Systems, Inc.
17822 East 17th St.
Tustin, CA 92680

Founded 1975
Total employees 150
Annual sales $13.13
million
Industry Computer
Software

Growth Openings in past
year 15; percentage
growth 11%
Contact S. Razin,
COB/President/CEO
Tel 714-731-7171
Fax 714-731-9494

Rainbow Technologies, Inc.
9292 Jeronimo Rd.
Irvine, CA 92718

Founded 1983
Total employees 95
Annual sales $18.9 million
Industries Computer
Hardware, Computer
Software
Growth Openings in past
year 35; percentage
growth 58%
Contact Walter Straub,
President
Tel 714-454-2100
Fax 714-454-8557

Satellite Technology Management, Inc.
3530 Highland Ave.
Costa Mesa, CA 92626

Founded 1982
Total employees 70
Annual sales $12.4 million
Industry
Telecommunications
Growth Openings in past
year 25; percentage
growth 55%
Contact Emil
Youssefzadeh,
President
Tel 714-557-2400
Fax 714-557-4239

SHURflo
12650 Westminster Ave.
Santa Ana, CA 92706

Founded 1970
Total employees 325
Annual sales $31 million
Industry Subassemblies
and Components

Growth Openings in past
year 25; percentage
growth 8%
Contact John Casey,
President
Tel 714-554-7709
Fax 714-554-4721

Simon Hydro-Search, Inc.
5882 Bolsa Ave.
Huntington Beach, CA
92649

Founded 1971
Total employees 175
Annual sales $12 million
Industry Environmental
Growth Openings in past
year 75; percentage
growth 75%
Contact Craig Eisen,
President
Tel 714-891-7446
Fax 714-891-9009

Simulation Sciences Inc.
1051 West Bastanchury
Rd.
Fullerton, CA 92633

Founded 1967
Total employees 170
Annual sales $19 million
Industry Computer
Software
Growth Openings in past
year 23; percentage
growth 15%
Contact Ms. Joan
Wolfsen,
Manager of Human
Resources and
Administr
Tel 714-879-9180
Fax 714-447-4107

Smith Micro Software, Inc.
51 Columbia
Aliso Viejo, CA 92656

Founded 1983
Total employees 29
Annual sales $5 million
Industry Computer
Software

Growth Openings in past year 14; percentage growth 93%
Contact William W. Smith, Jr., President
Tel 714-964-0412
Fax 714-968-0777

State Of The Art, Inc.
56 Technology Dr.
Irvine, CA 92718

Founded 1981
Total employees 215
Annual sales $21.6 million
Industry Computer Software
Growth Openings in past year 65; percentage growth 43%
Contact David S. Samuels, President/CEO
Tel 714-753-1222
Fax 714-753-0374

TCI Corp.
1211 East Dyer Rd., Suite 110
Santa Ana, CA 92705

Founded 1974
Total employees 40
Annual sales $6 million
Industry Computer Software
Growth Openings in past year 13; percentage growth 48%
Contact Richard Knopf, Partner/President
Tel 714-432-0600
Fax 714-432-0161

Tone Software Corp.
1735 South Brookhurst St.
Anaheim, CA 92804

Founded 1974
Total employees 60
Annual sales $5 million
Industry Computer Software

Growth Openings in past year 20; percentage growth 50%
Contact John Hutchinson, President/CEO
Tel 714-991-9460
Fax 714-991-1831

Toshiba Information Systems, Inc., Disk Products Division
9740 Irvine Blvd.
Irvine, CA 92718

Founded 1985
Total employees 430
Annual sales $70 million
Industries Computer Hardware, Subassemblies and Components
Growth Openings in past year 244; percentage growth 131%
Contact Duane Bazzette, VP of General Administration
Tel 714-583-3000
Fax 714-583-3133

Triconex Corp.
15091 Bake Pkwy.
Irvine, CA 92718

Founded 1983
Total employees 125
Annual sales $22.31 million
Industry Factory Automation
Growth Openings in past year 36; percentage growth 40%
Contact William Barkovitz, President/COB
Tel 714-768-3709
Fax 714-768-6601

UltraStor Corp.
15 Hammond, Suite 310
Irvine, CA 92718

Founded 1988
Total employees 53
Annual sales $13 million
Industries Computer Hardware, Subassemblies and Components

Growth Openings in past year 19; percentage growth 55%
Contact Steve Roberts, President/CEO
Tel 714-581-4100
Fax 714-581-0826

Unisyn Technologies, Inc.
14272 Franklin Ave.
Tustin, CA 92680

Founded 1990
Total employees 40
Annual sales $2.5 million
Industries Biotechnology, Test and Measurement
Growth Openings in past year 20; percentage growth 100%
Contact Stan Yakatan, Chief Executive Officer
Tel 714-544-4035
Fax 714-544-0322

UVC Corp.
16800 Aston St.
Irvine, CA 92714

Founded 1986
Total employees 45
Annual sales $6.2 million
Industry Telecommunications
Growth Openings in past year 20; percentage growth 80%
Contact John Looney, President/CEO
Tel 714-261-5336
Fax 714-261-1677

Verteq, Inc., Process Systems Division
1432 South Allec St., PO Box 3640
Anaheim, CA 92803

Founded 1985
Total employees 120
Annual sales $13 million
Industry Manufacturing Equipment

Growth Openings in past year 20; percentage growth 20%
Contact Mel Simmons, President
Tel 714-956-7330
Fax 714-758-1022

Virgin Games, Inc.
18061 Fitch Ave.
Irvine, CA 92714

Founded 1983
Total employees 100
Industry Computer Software
Growth Openings in past year 62; percentage growth 163%
Contact Martin Alper, President
Tel 714-833-8710
Fax 714-833-8717

Wonderware Software Development Corp.
16 Technology Dr., Suite 154
Irvine, CA 92718

Founded 1987
Total employees 46
Annual sales $5.1 million
Industry Computer Software
Growth Openings in past year 20; percentage growth 76%
Contact Dennis Morin, COB/CEO/President
Tel 714-727-3200
Fax 714-727-3270

■ **805 Area Code**

Advanced Compression Technology, Inc.
685 A East Cochran St.
Simi Valley, CA 93065

Founded 1987
Total employees 40
Annual sales $5 million
Industries Computer Hardware, Telecommunications

Growth Openings in past year 13; percentage growth 48%
Contact Martin Shum, President/CEO
Tel 805-527-2281
Fax 805-520-8099

Advanced Photonix, Inc.
1240 Avenida Acaso
Camarillo, CA 93012

Founded 1977
Total employees 90
Annual sales $2 million
Industry Photonics
Growth Openings in past year 30; percentage growth 50%
Contact Ms. Dena Coelho, Chief Financial Officer
Tel 805-484-2884
Fax 805-484-9935

Amber Engineering, Inc.
5756 Thornwood Dr.
Goleta, CA 93117

Founded 1980
Total employees 140
Industries Photonics, Test and Measurement
Growth Openings in past year 28; percentage growth 25%
Contact Art Lockwood, President
Tel 805-683-6621
Fax 805-964-2185

California Amplifier, Inc.
460 Calle San Pablo
Camarillo, CA 93012

Founded 1981
Total employees 250
Annual sales $20.63 million
Industries Subassemblies and Components, Telecommunications
Growth Openings in past year 150; percentage growth 150%
Contact Ms. Jackie Sheehan, Personnel Director
Tel 805-987-9000
Fax 805-987-8359

Circon Corp.
460 Ward Dr.
Santa Barbara, CA 93111

Founded 1957
Total employees 781
Annual sales $69 million
Industries Holding Companies, Medical, Photonics, Telecommunications
Growth Openings in past year 131; percentage growth 20%
Contact Jon D. St. Clair, VP of Human Resources
Tel 805-967-0404
Fax 805-967-5035

Core-Vent Bioengineering, Inc.
1170 Avenida Acaso
Camarillo, CA 93012

Founded 1989
Total employees 120
Annual sales $13 million
Industry Medical
Growth Openings in past year 30; percentage growth 33%
Contact Ms. Patricia Jacobs, VP of Human Resources
Tel 805-388-2690
Fax 805-388-2716

CU Services Corp.
2450 Tapo St.
Simi Valley, CA 93063

Founded 1974
Total employees 90
Annual sales $10 million
Industry Computer Software
Growth Openings in past year 45; percentage growth 100%
Contact Ed Harris, President
Tel 805-527-4066
Fax 805-526-7839

Executive Systems, Inc.
4115 Broad St., Bldg. 1
San Luis Obispo, CA
93401

Founded 1978
Total employees 80
Annual sales $9.2 million
Industry Computer
Software
Growth Openings in past
year 30; percentage
growth 60%
Contact King R. Lee,
President/CEO
Tel 805-541-0604
Fax 805-541-8053

Gaiser Tool Co.
4544 McGrath St.
Ventura, CA 93003

Founded 1962
Total employees 140
Annual sales $15 million
Industry Manufacturing
Equipment
Growth Openings in past
year 15; percentage
growth 12%
Contact Dennis Gaiser,
President
Tel 805-644-5583
Fax 805-644-2013

Industrial Tools, Inc.
201 Bryant St.
Ojai, CA 93023

Founded 1961
Total employees 150
Annual sales $20 million
Industry Factory
Automation
Growth Openings in past
year 50; percentage
growth 50%
Contact Eric Nielsen,
President
Tel 805-646-5561
Fax 805-646-5566

**Information
Presentation
Technologies, Inc.**
PO Box 12607
San Luis Obispo, CA
93406

Founded 1983
Total employees 40
Annual sales $5.2 million
Industries Computer
Hardware, Computer
Software
Growth Openings in past
year 20; percentage
growth 100%
Contact Jon Simonds,
President
Tel 805-541-3000
Fax 805-541-3037

McGhan NuSil Corp.
1150 Mark Ave.
Carpinteria, CA 93013

Founded 1980
Total employees 58
Annual sales $8.6 million
Industry Advanced
Materials
Growth Openings in past
year 13; percentage
growth 28%
Contact Richard
Compton,
President/COB
Tel 805-684-8780
Fax 805-684-2365

Mentor Corp.
5425 Hollister Ave.
Santa Barbara, CA 93111

Founded 1969
Total employees 860
Annual sales $89.42
million
Industries Holding
Companies, Medical
Growth Openings in past
year 26; percentage
growth 3%
Contact Christopher J.
Conway,
COB/CEO
Tel 805-681-6000
Fax 805-964-2712

qad.inc
6450 Via Real
Carpinteria, CA 93013

Founded 1979
Total employees 210
Industry Computer
Software
Growth Openings in past
year 90; percentage
growth 75%
Contact Ms. Pamela
Lopker,
President
Tel 805-684-6614
Fax 805-684-1890

**Siemens Solar
Industries**
4650 Adohr Ln.
Camarillo, CA 93010

Founded 1977
Total employees 500
Annual sales $67 million
Industry Energy
Growth Openings in past
year 50; percentage
growth 11%
Contact Dr. Charles Gay,
President/CEO
Tel 805-482-6800
Fax 805-388-6395

SMTEK, Inc.
2151 Anchor Ct.
Newbury Park, CA 91320

Founded 1986
Total employees 100
Annual sales $12 million
Industries Manufacturing
Equipment,
Subassemblies and
Components, Test and
Measurement
Growth Openings in past
year 25; percentage
growth 33%
Contact Ms. Andrea
Murchinson,
Human Resources
Manager
Tel 805-376-2595
Fax 805-376-2686

Spar Communications Group
PO Box 6005
Santa Maria, CA 93456

Founded 1978
Total employees 90
Annual sales $12 million
Industry
Telecommunications
Growth Openings in past
year 12; percentage
growth 15%
Contact Ms. Linda
Grieme,
Personnel Administrator
Tel 805-928-2581
Fax 805-925-2540

Vitesse Semiconductor Corporation
741 Calle Plano
Camarillo, CA 93012

Founded 1984
Total employees 315
Annual sales $37.3 million
Industry Subassemblies
and Components
Growth Openings in past
year 65; percentage
growth 26%
Contact Dr. Lou R.
Tomasetta,
President
Tel 805-388-3700
Fax 805-987-5896

Western Filter Corp.
26235 Technology Dr.
Valencia, CA 91355

Founded 1958
Total employees 120
Annual sales $12 million
Industries Subassemblies
and Components, Test
and Measurement,
Transportation
Growth Openings in past
year 20; percentage
growth 20%
Contact Paul Akian,
President
Tel 805-295-0800
Fax 805-295-0801

Whittaker Electronics Systems
1785 Voyager Ave.
Simi Valley, CA 93063

Founded 1968
Total employees 500
Annual sales $65 million
Industries Computer
Software, Defense,
Telecommunications
Growth Openings in past
year 50; percentage
growth 11%
Contact Ms. Sherida
Simmons,
Director of Human
Resources
Tel 805-584-8200
Fax 805-527-8332

■ 818 Area Code

Amperif Corp.
9232 Eton Ave.
Chatsworth, CA 91311

Founded 1971
Total employees 300
Annual sales $50 million
Industries Computer
Hardware, Holding
Companies
Growth Openings in past
year 35; percentage
growth 13%
Contact Tom Bates,
VP of Human Resources
Tel 818-998-7666
Fax 818-998-8129

Apex Voice Communications, Inc.
14900 Ventura Blvd.
Sherman Oaks, CA 91403

Founded 1987
Total employees 20
Industry Computer
Software
Growth Openings in past
year 12; percentage
growth 150%
Contact Ms. Lisa-Marie
Elton,
Corporate
Communications
Manager
Tel 818-379-8400
Fax 818-379-8410

Caching Technology Corp.
1312 John Reed Ct.
City of Industry, CA 91745

Founded 1987
Total employees 25
Annual sales $4 million
Industry Computer
Hardware
Growth Openings in past
year 13; percentage
growth 108%
Contact Danny Song,
General Manager
Tel 818-961-9688
Fax 818-961-5288

CAF Technologies, Inc.
1315 Johnson Dr.
City of Industry, CA 91745

Founded 1986
Total employees 35
Industry Computer
Hardware
Growth Openings in past
year 15; percentage
growth 75%
Contact Earl Yang,
President
Tel 818-369-3690
Fax 818-369-3692

Chalco Industries, Inc.
20130 Sunburst St.
Chatsworth, CA 91311

Founded 1951
Total employees 110
Annual sales $14 million
Industry Holding
Companies
Growth Openings in past
year 18; percentage
growth 19%
Contact Jan Hiszpansk,
President
Tel 818-882-6773
Fax 818-998-0810

CI Systems, Inc.
5137 Clareton Dr., Suite
220
Agoura Hills, CA 91301

Founded 1978
Total employees 150
Annual sales $16 million

Industries Photonics,
Test and Measurement
Growth Openings in past
year 50; percentage
growth 50%
Contact Dr. Robert
Buckwald,
President
Tel 818-865-0402
Fax 818-865-0403

Compact Video, Inc.
2813 West Alameda Ave.
Burbank, CA 91505

Founded 1973
Total employees 325
Annual sales $44 million
Industry
Telecommunications
Growth Openings in past
year 75; percentage
growth 30%
Contact Ms. Kristie
Klechner,
Corporate Office
Manager
Tel 818-840-7000
Fax 818-846-5197

**Computrend Systems,
Inc.**
1306 John Reed Ct.
City of Industry, CA 91745

Founded 1989
Total employees 200
Annual sales $70 million
Industry Computer
Hardware
Growth Openings in past
year 30; percentage
growth 17%
Contact Tom Tsao,
President
Tel 818-333-5121
Fax 818-369-6803

**Converse Professional
Group, Inc.**
3393 East Foothill Blvd.
Pasadena, CA 91107

Founded 1950
Total employees 400
Annual sales $40 million
Industry Holding
Companies

Growth Openings in past
year 199; percentage
growth 99%
Contact Cree L. Kofford,
Chairman of the Board
Tel 818-351-4741

**Delphi Information
Systems, Inc.**
31416 Agoura Rd.
Westlake Village, CA
91361

Founded 1976
Total employees 400
Annual sales $50 million
Industries Computer
Software, Holding
Companies
Growth Openings in past
year 50; percentage
growth 14%
Contact David J.
Torrence,
President
Tel 818-706-8989
Fax 818-991-6469

**Dexter Corp., Dexter
Electronic Materials
Division**
15051 East Don Julian
Rd.
City of Industry, CA 91746

Founded 1767
Total employees 480
Annual sales $71 million
Industries Advanced
Materials,
Subassemblies and
Components
Growth Openings in past
year 40; percentage
growth 9%
Contact Ronald Benham,
President
Tel 818-968-6511
Fax 818-336-0526

**Ensign-Bickford Optical
Technologies, Inc.**
6737 Valjean Ave.
Van Nuys, CA 91406

Founded 1980
Total employees 39
Annual sales $1.9 million

Industries Advanced
Materials, Photonics
Growth Openings in past
year 32; percentage
growth 457%
Contact William B. Beck,
President
Tel 818-786-7873
Fax 818-785-8951

Executive Software, Inc.
701 North Brand Blvd.
Glendale, CA 91203

Founded 1981
Total employees 140
Annual sales $15 million
Industry Computer
Software
Growth Openings in past
year 22; percentage
growth 18%
Contact Craig Jensen,
COB/CEO
Tel 818-547-2050
Fax 818-545-8808

Fibermux Corp.
9310 Topanga Canyon
Blvd.
Chatsworth, CA 91311

Founded 1986
Total employees 335
Annual sales $36 million
Industries Photonics,
Telecommunications
Growth Openings in past
year 89; percentage
growth 36%
Contact Ms. Cheryl
Tatangelo,
Personnel Director
Tel 818-709-6000
Fax 818-709-1556

Glenair, Inc.
1211 Air Way
Glendale, CA 91201

Founded 1958
Total employees 520
Annual sales $25 million
Industries Factory
Automation, Holding
Companies,
Subassemblies and
Components

Growth Openings in past year 20; percentage growth 4%
Contact Orlando Bernal, Personnel Manager
Tel 818-247-6000
Fax 818-500-9912

Incomnet, Inc.
21031 Ventura Blvd., Suite 1100
Woodland Hills, CA 91364

Founded 1974
Total employees 35
Annual sales $6 million
Industries Computer Software, Telecommunications
Growth Openings in past year 5; percentage growth 16%
Contact Sam Schwartz, President
Tel 818-887-3400
Fax 818-587-5697

J&L Information Systems, Inc.
9238 Deering Ave.
Chatsworth, CA 91311

Founded 1988
Total employees 50
Annual sales $10 million
Industry Telecommunications
Growth Openings in past year 25; percentage growth 100%
Contact Chuck Lubash, President
Tel 818-709-1778
Fax 818-882-9134

JMR Electronics, Inc.
19320 Londelius St.
Northridge, CA 91324

Founded 1982
Total employees 180
Annual sales $14 million
Industries Computer Hardware, Factory Automation, Subassemblies and Components

Growth Openings in past year 70; percentage growth 63%
Contact Josef Rabinovitz, President
Tel 818-993-4801
Fax 818-993-9173

Johanson Dielectrics, Inc.
15191 Bledsoe St.
Sylmar, CA 91342

Founded 1956
Total employees 425
Industry Subassemblies and Components
Growth Openings in past year 49; percentage growth 13%
Contact Robert Belter, President
Tel 818-364-9800
Fax 818-364-6100

Kinemetrics, Inc.
222 Vista Ave.
Pasadena, CA 91107

Founded 1969
Total employees 70
Annual sales $8.3 million
Industry Test and Measurement
Growth Openings in past year 40; percentage growth 133%
Contact Bilip Patel, Controller
Tel 818-795-2220
Fax 818-795-0868

Multi-Pure Corp.
21339 Nordhoff St.
Chatsworth, CA 91311

Founded 1970
Total employees 170
Annual sales $30 million
Industry Environmental
Growth Openings in past year 20; percentage growth 13%
Contact H. Allen Rice, Chief Executive Officer
Tel 818-341-7577
Fax 818-341-5275

Senior Systems Technology, Inc.
20150 Sunburst St.
Chatsworth, CA 91311

Founded 1984
Total employees 260
Annual sales $22 million
Industries Manufacturing Equipment, Subassemblies and Components
Growth Openings in past year 40; percentage growth 18%
Contact Joseph Candella, President
Tel 818-998-1818
Fax 818-998-0664

Sercomp Corp.
21050 Lassen St.
Chatsworth, CA 91311

Founded 1978
Total employees 170
Industry Computer Hardware
Growth Openings in past year 20; percentage growth 13%
Contact Ms. Marie Gonzales, Human Resources Manager
Tel 818-341-1680
Fax 818-341-9587

Sierracin Corp., Harrison Division
3020 Empire Ave.
Burbank, CA 91504

Founded 1975
Total employees 93
Annual sales $9.5 million
Industries Factory Automation, Subassemblies and Components
Growth Openings in past year 27; percentage growth 40%
Contact Dick Paul, President
Tel 818-842-2131
Fax 818-842-6042

Spectrolab, Inc.
12500 Gladstone Ave.
Sylmar, CA 91342

Founded 1959
Total employees 225
Annual sales $30 million
Industries Energy,
Factory Automation,
Photonics
Growth Openings in past
year 25; percentage
growth 12%
Contact D.K. Zemmrich,
President/CEO
Tel 818-365-4611
Fax 818-361-5102

Sterling Software, Inc., Dylakor Division
9340 Owensmouth Ave.
Chatsworth, CA 91311

Founded 1968
Total employees 235
Annual sales $27 million
Industries Computer
Hardware, Computer
Software
Growth Openings in past
year 20; percentage
growth 9%
Contact Ms. Carole
Morton,
President
Tel 818-718-8877
Fax 818-998-2171

SunGard Financial Systems, Inc.
22134 Sherman Way
Canoga Park, CA 91303

Founded 1978
Total employees 400
Annual sales $65 million
Industry Computer
Software
Growth Openings in past
year 50; percentage
growth 14%
Contact David Wismer,
Chief Executive Officer
Tel 818-884-5515
Fax 818-346-5044

Talandic Research Corp.
6042 North Irwindale Ave.
Irwindale, CA 91706

Founded 1973
Total employees 40
Annual sales $1.9 million
Industries Photonics,
Test and Measurement,
Telecommunications
Growth Openings in past
year 15; percentage
growth 60%
Contact Ms. Alice Reld,
Personnel Manager
Tel 818-334-3000
Fax 818-334-7551

Tekelec
26580 West Agoura Rd.
Calabasas, CA 91302

Founded 1979
Total employees 330
Annual sales $52 million
Industry Factory
Automation
Growth Openings in past
year 19; percentage
growth 6%
Contact Peter N. Vicars,
President/CEO
Tel 818-880-5656
Fax 818-880-6993

Teradyne, Inc., Semiconductor Test Division
30801 Agoura Rd.
Agoura Hills, CA 91301

Founded 1970
Total employees 650
Industry Factory
Automation
Growth Openings in past
year 19; percentage
growth 3%
Contact Jerry Cellner,
Personnel Manager
Tel 818-991-2900

Tetra Tech, Inc.
670 North Rosemead
Blvd.
Pasadena, CA 91107

Founded 1966
Total employees 570
Annual sales $65 million

Industries Environmental,
Holding Companies
Growth Openings in past
year 38; percentage
growth 7%
Contact Rich Lemmon,
Personnel Manager
Tel 818-449-6400
Fax 818-351-8126

UVP, Inc.
5100 Walnut Grove Ave.,
PO Box 1501
San Gabriel, CA 91778

Founded 1932
Total employees 70
Annual sales $7.5 million
Industries Photonics,
Test and Measurement
Growth Openings in past
year 20; percentage
growth 40%
Contact Paul Warren,
COB/President
Tel 818-285-3123
Fax 818-285-2940

Xontech, Inc.
6862 Hayvenhurst Ave.
Van Nuys, CA 91406

Founded 1970
Total employees 275
Industries Defense,
Environmental
Growth Openings in past
year 25; percentage
growth 10%
Contact Kenneth Schultz,
President
Tel 818-787-7380
Fax 818-786-4275

■ 909 Area Code

Bio Clinic Corp.
4083 East Airport Dr.
Ontario, CA 91761

Founded 1968
Total employees 350
Annual sales $50 million
Industry Medical

Growth Openings in past
year 64; percentage
growth 22%
Contact Ms. Karen
Gongaware,
Human Resource
Manager
Tel 909-391-0041
Fax 909-391-0063

Growth Openings in past
year 100; percentage
growth 18%
Contact Chuck Becker,
Personnel Director
Tel 909-793-2853
Fax 909-793-5953

Growth Openings in past
year 40; percentage
growth 14%
Contact Tony Liu,
Director of Finance and
Administration
Tel 909-923-3510
Fax 909-923-1461

BW/IP International, Inc./Seal Division
27455 Tierra Alta Way
Temecula, CA 92390

Founded 1973
Total employees 190
Annual sales $18 million
Industry Subassemblies
and Components
Growth Openings in past
year 65; percentage
growth 52%
Contact Dave Mulvihill,
Human Resources
Manager
Tel 909-676-5662
Fax 909-699-4157

Keypoint Technology Corp.
20480 Business Pkwy.
Walnut, CA 91789

Founded 1987
Total employees 90
Industries Computer
Hardware, Holding
Companies,
Subassemblies and
Components
Growth Openings in past
year 40; percentage
growth 80%
Contact James Chu,
President
Tel 909-944-3041
Fax 909-869-7958

Magellan Systems Corp.
960 Overland Ct.
San Dimas, CA 91773

Founded 1986
Total employees 160
Annual sales $30 million
Industries Test and
Measurement,
Transportation
Growth Openings in past
year 50; percentage
growth 45%
Contact Randy Hoffman,
President
Tel 909-394-5000
Fax 909-394-7050

Electro Pneumatic Corp.
3016 Kansas Ave.
Riverside, CA 92507

Founded 1970
Total employees 135
Annual sales $15 million
Industry Transportation
Growth Openings in past
year 24; percentage
growth 21%
Contact Ms. Karen
Whiteside,
Human Resources
Manager
Tel 909-784-0410

Kinetics Technology International Corp.
650 Cienega Ave.
San Dimas, CA 91773

Founded 1963
Total employees 225
Annual sales $60 million
Industries Chemicals,
Manufacturing
Equipment
Growth Openings in past
year 55; percentage
growth 32%
Contact David Baker,
President
Tel 909-592-4455
Fax 909-592-3399

Micro-Frame Technologies, Inc.
2151 East D St., Suite
201C
Ontario, CA 91764

Founded 1985
Total employees 80
Annual sales $8 million
Industry Computer
Software
Growth Openings in past
year 46; percentage
growth 135%
Contact John O'Neil, Jr.,
President
Tel 909-983-2711
Fax 909-984-5382

Environmental Systems Research Institute, Inc.
380 New York St.
Redlands, CA 92373

Founded 1969
Total employees 650
Industry Computer
Software

KYE International Corp.
2605 East Cedar St.
Ontario, CA 91761

Founded 1987
Total employees 320
Annual sales $50 million
Industry Computer
Hardware

Vestar, Inc.
650 Cliffside Dr.
San Dimas, CA 91773

Founded 1981
Total employees 100
Annual sales $14.8 million
Industries Biotechnology,
Pharmaceuticals

Growth Openings in past year 15; percentage growth 17%
Contact Dr. Roger J. Crossley, President
Tel 909-394-4000
Fax 909-592-8530

■ **916 Area Code**

Access Health Marketing, Inc.
11020 White Rock Rd.
Rancho Cordova, CA 95670

Founded 1988
Total employees 130
Annual sales $10 million
Industry Computer Software
Growth Openings in past year 40; percentage growth 44%
Contact Ken Plumlee, President
Tel 916-722-2100
Fax 916-725-0866

ALLDATA Corp.
9412 Big Horn Blvd.
Elk Grove, CA 95758

Founded 1986
Total employees 250
Annual sales $19.17 million
Industry Computer Software
Growth Openings in past year 80; percentage growth 47%
Contact Rod Georgiu, President
Tel 916-684-5200
Fax 916-684-5225

Data Image Systems Corporation
3054 Fite Cir., Suite 108
Sacramento, CA 95827
Founded 1958
Total employees 180

Industry Computer Software
Contact Merlin Shoemaker, Chief Executive Officer
Tel 916-364-7372
Fax 916-362-1273

Diamond Flower Instruments, Inc.
1355 Main Ave.
Sacramento, CA 95838

Founded 1986
Total employees 120
Industry Computer Hardware
Growth Openings in past year 50; percentage growth 71%
Contact Rocky Liu, Chief Executive Officer
Tel 916-568-1234
Fax 916-568-1233

Guided Wave, Inc.
5190 Golden Foothill Pkwy.
El Dorado Hills, CA 95630

Founded 1983
Total employees 46
Annual sales $5 million
Industries Photonics, Test and Measurement
Growth Openings in past year 12; percentage growth 35%
Contact David A. LeFebre, CEO/Chief Engineer
Tel 916-939-4300
Fax 916-939-4307

J&W Scientific
91 Blue Ravine Rd.
Folsom, CA 95630

Founded 1974
Total employees 150
Annual sales $17 million
Industry Test and Measurement

Growth Openings in past year 20; percentage growth 15%
Contact Ms. Nancy Kwiecien, Human Resources Manager
Tel 916-985-7888
Fax 916-985-1101

Jones Futurex, Inc.
3715 Atherton Rd.
Rocklin, CA 95675

Founded 1981
Total employees 60
Annual sales $6.5 million
Industries Computer Hardware, Subassemblies and Components, Telecommunications
Growth Openings in past year 25; percentage growth 71%
Contact James J. Krejci, President
Tel 916-635-3972
Fax 916-632-3445

Moller International, Inc.
1222 Research Park Dr.
Davis, CA 95616

Founded 1971
Total employees 40
Industries Defense, Transportation
Growth Openings in past year 18; percentage growth 81%
Contact Dr. Paul Moller, Ph.D., President
Tel 916-756-5086
Fax 916-756-5179

Ophthalmic Imaging Systems
221 Lathrop Way, Suite I
Sacramento, CA 95815

Founded 1986
Total employees 25
Annual sales $2.7 million
Industries Computer Software, Medical

Growth Openings in past year 12; percentage growth 92%
Contact Ms. Diana Brock, Office Manager
Tel 916-646-2020
Fax 916-646-0207

Growth Openings in past year 35; percentage growth 70%
Contact William T. Manak, President/CEO
Tel 916-852-1528
Fax 916-635-2655

Growth Openings in past year 20; percentage growth 30%
Contact Ms. Rogene Rivale, Personnel Manager
Tel 303-443-9660
Fax 303-442-4916

Prodata, Inc.
6929 Sunrise Blvd., Suite 105
Citrus Heights, CA 95610

Founded 1981
Total employees 250
Annual sales $14 million
Industries Computer Hardware, Computer Software
Growth Openings in past year 50; percentage growth 25%
Contact Bill Basham, President
Tel 916-969-3064
Fax 916-722-6042

Unify Corp.
3901 Lennane Dr.
Sacramento, CA 95834

Founded 1980
Total employees 273
Annual sales $43 million
Industry Computer Software
Growth Openings in past year 18; percentage growth 7%
Contact Ms. Doreen Paige, Human Resource Manager
Tel 916-928-6400
Fax 916-928-6401

3Net Systems, Inc.
3235 Sunrise Blvd, Suite B
Rancho Cordova, CA 95742

Founded 1979
Total employees 85
Annual sales $3.11 million
Industry Computer Software

Colorado

■ **303 Area Code**

Aguirre Engineers, Inc.
13276 East Fremont Pl.
Englewood, CO 80112

Founded 1977
Total employees 100
Annual sales $2.5 million
Industries Advanced Materials, Environmental
Growth Openings in past year 75; percentage growth 300%
Contact Vukoslav Aguirre, President
Tel 303-799-8378
Fax 303-799-8392

Chen-Northern, Inc.
96 South Zuni St.
Denver, CO 80223

Founded 1988
Total employees 404
Annual sales $43 million
Industries Advanced Materials, Environmental
Growth Openings in past year 23; percentage growth 6%
Contact Tom S. Ramsey, President
Tel 303-744-7105
Fax 303-744-0210

CliniCom, Inc.
4720 Walnut St., Suite 106
Boulder, CO 80301

Founded 1985
Total employees 85
Annual sales $7.08 million
Industries Computer Hardware, Computer Software, Medical

CN Geotech, Inc.
PO Box 14000
Grand Junction, CO 81502

Founded 1986
Total employees 750
Annual sales $60 million
Industry Environmental
Growth Openings in past year 50; percentage growth 7%
Contact William Yeo, VP of Human Resources
Tel 303-248-6403
Fax 303-248-6040

Codar Technology, Inc.
2405 Trade Centre Ave.
Longmont, CO 80503

Founded 1980
Total employees 130
Annual sales $25 million
Industries Computer Hardware, Telecommunications
Growth Openings in past year 20; percentage growth 18%
Contact Michael W. Evans, President/CEO
Tel 303-776-0472
Fax 303-776-1806

ConferTech International, Inc.
240 Applewood Tech Center, 2801 Youngfield
Golden, CO 80401

Founded 1976
Total employees 275
Annual sales $25.26 million
Industry Telecommunications

Growth Openings in past year 55; percentage growth 25%
Contact H. Robert Gill, President/CEO
Tel 303-237-5151
Fax 303-233-9051

Cortech, Inc.
6840 North Broadway
Denver, CO 80221

Founded 1982
Total employees 72
Industry Pharmaceuticals
Growth Openings in past year 27; percentage growth 60%
Contact David Crossen, President
Tel 303-650-1200
Fax 303-650-5023

Data Storage Marketing, Inc.
5718 Central Ave.
Boulder, CO 80301

Founded 1987
Total employees 152
Annual sales $71 million
Industry Computer Hardware
Growth Openings in past year 39; percentage growth 34%
Contact Ms. Lynn Cyprian, Personnel Manager
Tel 303-442-4747
Fax 303-442-7985

Denver Instrument Co.
6542 Fig St.
Arvada, CO 80004

Founded 1869
Total employees 160
Annual sales $19 million
Industry Test and Measurement
Growth Openings in past year 12; percentage growth 8%
Contact Scott Schuler, President
Tel 303-431-7255
Fax 303-423-4831

Engineered Data Products, Inc.
2550 West Midway Blvd.
Broomfield, CO 80020

Founded 1969
Total employees 250
Annual sales $20 million
Industries Computer Hardware, Holding Companies
Growth Openings in past year 60; percentage growth 31%
Contact Macy Price, President
Tel 303-465-2800
Fax 303-465-0305

Exabyte Corp.
1685 38th St.
Boulder, CO 80301

Founded 1985
Total employees 950
Annual sales $280 million
Industries Computer Hardware, Factory Automation, Holding Companies
Growth Openings in past year 63; percentage growth 7%
Contact Peter D. Behrendt, President/CEO/COB
Tel 303-442-4333
Fax 303-447-7689

GTG-Fox Environmental Services, Ltd.
4765 Independence St.
Wheat Ridge, CO 80033

Founded 1963
Total employees 50
Annual sales $3.9 million
Industries Advanced Materials, Environmental
Growth Openings in past year 15; percentage growth 42%
Contact Craig Vaughn, President
Tel 303-424-5578
Fax 303-424-5578

Hach Co.
5600 Lindbergh Dr., PO Box 389
Loveland, CO 80537

Founded 1978
Total employees 910
Annual sales $84.74 million
Industries Advanced Materials, Chemicals, Environmental, Factory Automation, Subassemblies and Components, Test and Measurement
Growth Openings in past year 105; percentage growth 13%
Contact Randall A. Petersen, VP of Human Resources
Tel 303-669-3050
Fax 303-669-2932

Hathaway Corp.
8700 Turnpike Dr., Suite 300
Westminster, CO 80030

Founded 1961
Total employees 640
Annual sales $52 million
Industry Holding Companies
Growth Openings in past year 199; percentage growth 45%
Contact Eugene E. Prince, President/COB/CEO
Tel 303-426-1600
Fax 303-426-0932

Hauser Chemical Research, Inc.
5555 Airport Blvd.
Boulder, CO 80301

Founded 1983
Total employees 350
Annual sales $25.6 million
Industry Chemicals
Growth Openings in past year 147; percentage growth 72%
Contact Thomas A. Scales, President
Tel 303-443-4662
Fax 303-441-5800

**Healthwatch, Inc.,
Cambridge Medical
Division**
3400 Industrial Ln., Suite
A
Broomfield, CO 80020

Founded 1983
Total employees 92
Annual sales $8 million
Industry Medical
Growth Openings in past
year 42; percentage
growth 84%
Contact Sanford
Schwartz,
COB/CEO
Tel 303-465-2000
Fax 303-465-2242

Hotsy Corp.
21 Iverness Way East
Englewood, CO 80112

Founded 1970
Total employees 300
Annual sales $40 million
Industries Environmental,
Factory Automation,
Subassemblies and
Components
Growth Openings in past
year 50; percentage
growth 20%
Contact Larry Cohen,
President
Tel 303-792-5200
Fax 303-792-0547

**Information Handling
Services, Inc.**
15 Inverness Way East
Englewood, CO 80150

Founded 1959
Total employees 950
Annual sales $140 million
Industries Computer
Hardware, Computer
Software
Growth Openings In past
year 46; percentage
growth 5%
Contact Ms. Alice
DiFraia,
Director of Human
Resources
Tel 303-790-0600
Fax 303-397-2747

**Johnson Engineering
Corp.**
3055 Center Green Dr.
Boulder, CO 80301

Founded 1973
Total employees 250
Industries Computer
Software, Defense,
Factory Automation,
Manufacturing
Equipment,
Subassemblies and
Components,
Transportation
Growth Openings in past
year 50; percentage
growth 25%
Contact Dale R. Johnson,
President
Tel 303-449-8152
Fax 303-444-8254

Meadowlark Optics, Inc.
7460 Weld County Rd. 1
Longmont, CO 80504

Founded 1982
Total employees 32
Annual sales $1.1 million
Industry Photonics
Growth Openings in past
year 12; percentage
growth 60%
Contact Tom Baur,
President
Tel 303-776-4068
Fax 303-776-5856

**National Renewable
Energy Laboratories**
1617 Cole Blvd.
Golden, CO 80401

Founded 1977
Total employees 800
Industry Energy
Growth Openings in past
year 199; percentage
growth 33%
Contact Duane
Sunderman, Ph.D.,
Director
Tel 303-231-1000
Fax 303-231-1997

OEA, Inc.
34501 East Quincy Ave.,
PO Box 10048
Denver, CO 80250

Founded 1957
Total employees 800
Annual sales $83.7 million
Industry Holding
Companies
Growth Openings in past
year 46; percentage
growth 6%
Contact Ahmed D.
Kafadar,
COB/CEO
Tel 303-693-1248
Fax 303-699-6991

**Otsuka Electronics USA,
Inc.**
2555 Midpoint Dr.
Fort Collins, CO 80525

Founded 1978
Total employees 182
Industry Test and
Measurement
Growth Openings in past
year 26; percentage
growth 16%
Contact Kenji Nakayama,
COB/President
Tel 303-484-0428
Fax 303-484-0487

Pacer, CATS
355 Inverness Dr. South
Englewood, CO 80112

Founded 1976
Total employees 100
Industry Computer
Hardware
Growth Openings in past
year 22; percentage
growth 28%
Contact Israel Greidinger,
President/CEO
Tel 303-649-9818
Fax 303-643-3814

Public Systems Associates, Inc.
303 East 17th Ave., Suite 440
Denver, CO 80203

Founded 1977
Total employees 50
Annual sales $4 million
Industry Computer Software
Growth Openings in past year 15; percentage growth 42%
Contact Kelsey Kennedy, President
Tel 303-831-1260
Fax 303-894-0158

Resource Consultants & Engineers, Inc.
3665 JFK Pkwy., Bldg. 2, Suite 300
Fort Collins, CO 80525

Founded 1979
Total employees 36
Annual sales $3.8 million
Industry Environmental
Growth Openings in past year 19; percentage growth 111%
Contact Peter Legasse, President
Tel 303-223-5556
Fax 303-223-5578

Spectrum Human Resources Systems Corp.
1625 Broadway, Suite 2700
Denver, CO 80202

Founded 1984
Total employees 100
Annual sales $7 million
Industry Computer Software
Growth Openings in past year 30; percentage growth 42%
Contact James Spoor, President
Tel 303-534-8813
Fax 303-595-9970

Synergen, Inc.
1885 33rd St.
Boulder, CO 80301

Founded 1981
Total employees 600
Annual sales $51.4 million
Industry Pharmaceuticals
Growth Openings in past year 208; percentage growth 53%
Contact Ms. Karen Hildebrand, Director of Human Resources
Tel 303-938-6200
Fax 303-938-6268

Syntex Chemicals, Inc.
2075 North 55th St.
Boulder, CO 80301

Founded 1980
Total employees 325
Annual sales $44 million
Industries Biotechnology, Pharmaceuticals
Growth Openings in past year 25; percentage growth 8%
Contact Ms. Pat Bassallo, Director of Human Resources
Tel 303-442-1926
Fax 303-938-6413

Tetrad Corp.
12741 East Caley, Suite 126
Englewood, CO 80111

Founded 1985
Total employees 24
Industry Medical
Growth Openings in past year 15; percentage growth 166%
Contact Dennis Dietz, President
Tel 303-790-7237

Translogic Corp.
10825 East 47th Ave.
Denver, CO 80239

Founded 1915
Total employees 400
Annual sales $47 million
Industry Factory Automation

Growth Openings in past year 100; percentage growth 33%
Contact Dave Lawson, Human Resources Manager
Tel 303-371-7770
Fax 303-373-7932

Vari-L Co., Inc.
11101 East 51st Ave.
Denver, CO 80239

Founded 1953
Total employees 100
Industries Subassemblies and Components, Telecommunications
Growth Openings in past year 15; percentage growth 17%
Contact David Sherman, President/CFO
Tel 303-371-1560
Fax 303-371-0845

XVT Software, Inc.
4900 Pearl East Circle, PO Box 18750
Boulder, CO 80308

Founded 1988
Total employees 65
Industry Computer Software
Growth Openings in past year 20; percentage growth 44%
Contact Marc Rochlind, President
Tel 303-443-4223
Fax 303-443-0969

■ 719 Area Code

Laser Magnetic Storage International Co.
4425 Arrowswest Dr.
Colorado Springs, CO 80907

Founded 1984
Total employees 365
Annual sales $60 million
Industry Computer Hardware

Growth Openings in past
year 15; percentage
growth 4%
Contact Charles D.
Johnston,
President
Tel 719-593-7900
Fax 719-599-8713

**National Systems &
Research Co.**
5475 Mark Dabling Blvd.,
Suite 200
Colorado Springs, CO
80918

Founded 1980
Total employees 580
Annual sales $39 million
Industries Computer
Hardware, Computer
Software, Holding
Companies
Growth Openings in past
year 80; percentage
growth 16%
Contact Michael
Czerkies,
VP of Finance and
Administration
Tel 719-590-8880
Fax 719-590-8983

Omnipoint Corp.
7150 Campus Dr., Suite
155
Colorado Springs, CO
80920

Founded 1987
Total employees 35
Annual sales $4.8 million
Industry
Telecommunications
Growth Openings in past
year 15; percentage
growth 75%
Contact Doug Smith,
President
Tel 719-548-1200
Fax 719-548-1393

**Ramtron International
Corporation**
1850 Ramtron Dr.
Colorado Springs, CO
80921

Founded 1984
Total employees 140
Annual sales $4.5 million
Industry Computer
Hardware
Growth Openings in past
year 40; percentage
growth 40%
Contact David Sikes,
President
Tel 719-481-7000

Connecticut

■ **203 Area Code**

**Accurate Electronics,
Inc.**
215 North Ave.
Bridgeport, CT 06606

Founded 1976
Total employees 110
Annual sales $14 million
Industry Subassemblies
and Components
Growth Openings in past
year 20; percentage
growth 22%
Contact S.P. Judson,
COB/President
Tel 203-366-0214
Fax 203-336-1973

Accutron, Inc.
6 Northwood Dr.
Bloomfield, CT 06002

Founded 1989
Total employees 30
Annual sales $2.3 million
Industry Subassemblies
and Components
Growth Openings in past
year 15; percentage
growth 100%
Contact Vijay Faldu,
President
Tel 203-243-1200
Fax 203-243-1149

**Advanced Medical
Systems, Inc.**
925 Sherman Ave.
Hamden, CT 06514

Founded 1979
Total employees 67
Annual sales $6.5 million
Industries Computer
Software, Medical
Growth Openings in past
year 22; percentage
growth 48%
Contact George
Hojaiban,
President
Tel 203-248-0500
Fax 203-288-9032

**American Consulting
Group, Inc.**
36 State St.
North Haven, CT 06473

Founded 1984
Total employees 60
Annual sales $9.8 million
Industries Computer
Hardware, Computer
Software
Growth Openings in past
year 20; percentage
growth 50%
Contact Carl Mueller,
President
Tel 203-234-2224

**Amphenol Corp.,
Spectra Strip**
720 Sherman Ave.
Hamden, CT 06514

Founded 1972
Total employees 120
Industry Subassemblies
and Components
Growth Openings in past
year 20; percentage
growth 20%
Contact Tim Conlon,
General Manager
Tel 203-281-3200
Fax 203-745-1000

Amring, Inc.
145 North Plains Industrial
Park Rd.
Wallingford, CT 06492

Founded 1971
Total employees 23
Annual sales $2.3 million
Industries Manufacturing
Equipment, Test and
Measurement
Growth Openings in past
year 12; percentage
growth 109%
Contact Richard Fleming,
President
Tel 203-265-6761
Fax 203-949-1933

Bio-Plexus, Inc.
PO Box 826
Tolland, CT 06084

Founded 1987
Total employees 50
Industry Medical
Growth Openings in past
year 24; percentage
growth 92%
Contact Carl Sahi,
President
Tel 203-871-8601
Fax 203-872-9108

Biosystems, Inc.
PO Box 158
Rockfall, CT 06481

Founded 1982
Total employees 65
Annual sales $6 million
Industries Environmental,
Test and Measurement
Growth Openings in past
year 13; percentage
growth 25%
Contact John F. Burt, Jr.,
President
Tel 203-344-1079
Fax 203-344-1068

Computer Management Resources, Inc.
2 Corporate Dr., Suite 249
Shelton, CT 06484

Founded 1981
Total employees 50
Annual sales $5 million

Industry Computer
Hardware
Growth Openings in past
year 31; percentage
growth 163%
Contact Stephen
Michaelson,
President
Tel 203-925-1800
Fax 203-925-1801

Continental Computer Systems, Inc.
835 North Mountain Rd.
Newington, CT 06111

Founded 1985
Total employees 35
Annual sales $10 million
Industry Computer
Hardware
Contact Christopher
Lukas,
President
Tel 203-953-8649
Fax 800-829-3297

Coopers & Lybrand, Solution Thru Technology
41 North Main St.
West Hartford, CT 06107

Founded 1967
Total employees 975
Industry Computer
Software
Growth Openings in past
year 350; percentage
growth 56%
Contact Carl Sellberg,
Managing Partner
Tel 203-521-3284
Fax 203-561-5075

Current, Inc.
PO Box 120183
East Haven, CT 06512

Founded 1966
Total employees 60
Industry Advanced
Materials

Growth Openings in past
year 20; percentage
growth 50%
Contact Albert Prinz,
President
Tel 203-469-1337
Fax 203-467-8435

DataEase International, Inc.
7 Cambridge Dr.
Trumbull, CT 06611

Founded 1982
Total employees 250
Annual sales $28 million
Industries Computer
Software, Holding
Companies
Growth Openings in past
year 130; percentage
growth 108%
Contact Ed Spruck,
Manager of Human
Resources
Tel 203-374-8000
Fax 203-365-2317

DCG Precision Manufacturing Corp.
9 Trowbridge Dr.
Bethel, CT 06801

Founded 1943
Total employees 120
Annual sales $8 million
Industry Manufacturing
Equipment
Growth Openings in past
year 55; percentage
growth 84%
Contact Ms. Joan
Valluzzo,
Personnel Administrator
Tel 203-743-5525
Fax 203-791-1737

Dianon Systems, Inc.
200 Watson Blvd.
Stratford, CT 06497

Founded 1983
Total employees 250
Annual sales $32 million

Industries Computer
Hardware, Medical
Contact Richard A.
Sandberg,
COB/CEO
Tel 203-381-4000
Fax 203-381-4079

Dual-Lite, Inc.
Simm Ln.
Newtown, CT 06470

Founded 1940
Total employees 485
Annual sales $56 million
Industries Energy,
Subassemblies and
Components
Growth Openings in past
year 10; percentage
growth 2%
Contact Ms. Mary Jane
Healy,
Director of Personnel
Tel 203-426-8011
Fax 203-426-7485

Eicon, Inc.
142 Temple St.
New Haven, CT 06510

Founded 1991
Total employees 80
Annual sales $8 million
Industries Environmental,
Holding Companies,
Manufacturing
Equipment
Growth Openings in past
year 30; percentage
growth 60%
Contact Sam Giavara,
President
Tel 203-789-1260
Fax 203-789-8261

**Electronic Film
Capacitors, Inc.**
41 Interstate Ln.
Waterbury, CT 06705

Founded 1981
Total employees 60
Annual sales $14 million
Industry Subassemblies
and Components

Growth Openings in past
year 20; percentage
growth 50%
Contact Guy Bedrossian,
President
Tel 203-755-5629
Fax 203-755-0659

**Electronic Information
Systems, Inc.**
1351 Washington Blvd.
Stamford, CT 06902

Founded 1980
Total employees 120
Annual sales $20 million
Industries Computer
Software,
Telecommunications
Growth Openings in past
year 20; percentage
growth 20%
Contact Joseph Porfeli,
President/CEO
Tel 203-351-4800
Fax 203-961-8632

**Fiberoptic Technology,
Inc.**
28 Quasset Rd.
Pomfret, CT 06258

Founded 1977
Total employees 120
Industry Photonics
Growth Openings in past
year 20; percentage
growth 20%
Contact August W. Loos,
Chief Executive Officer
Tel 203-928-0443
Fax 203-928-7664

Forster Enterprises, Inc.
57 Bristol St.
Waterbury, CT 06708

Founded 1981
Total employees 64
Annual sales $10 million
Industries Energy,
Subassemblies and
Components, Test and
Measurement

Growth Openings in past
year 34; percentage
growth 113%
Contact M.A. Forster,
President
Tel 203-574-3832
Fax 203-755-2973

**General Systems
Solutions, Inc.**
1353 Gold Star Hwy.
Groton, CT 06340

Founded 1989
Total employees 40
Industries Computer
Hardware, Computer
Software
Growth Openings in past
year 12; percentage
growth 42%
Contact Gary M. Gilbert,
President
Tel 203-448-3177
Fax 203-448-3187

Harbor Electronics, Inc.
650 Danbury Rd.
Ridgefield, CT 06877

Founded 1976
Total employees 200
Annual sales $19 million
Industry Subassemblies
and Components
Growth Openings in past
year 50; percentage
growth 33%
Contact Ms. Ann Orrico,
Personnel Manager
Tel 203-438-9625
Fax 203-431-3001

IMRS Inc.
777 Long Ridge Rd.
Stamford, CT 06902

Founded 1981
Total employees 335
Annual sales $45.9 million
Industry Computer
Software
Growth Openings in past
year 74; percentage
growth 28%
Contact James A.
Perakis,
COB/CEO/President
Tel 203-321-3500
Fax 203-322-3904

Information Management Associates, Inc.
6527 Main St.
Trumbull, CT 06611

Founded 1984
Total employees 96
Annual sales $7.5 million
Industry Computer Software
Growth Openings in past year 41; percentage growth 74%
Contact Albert Subbloy, President/CEO
Tel 203-261-4777
Fax 203-261-2516

Inset Systems, Inc.
71 Commerce Dr.
Brookfield, CT 06804

Founded 1982
Total employees 55
Annual sales $6.3 million
Industry Computer Software
Growth Openings in past year 20; percentage growth 57%
Contact Donald J. Skiba, COB/CEO
Tel 203-740-2400
Fax 203-775-5634

Jeneric/Pentron, Inc.
53 North Plains Industrial Rd.
Wallingford, CT 06492

Founded 1967
Total employees 120
Annual sales $16 million
Industries Advanced Materials, Medical
Growth Openings in past year 20; percentage growth 20%
Contact Gordon S. Cohen, MD, President
Tel 203-265-7397
Fax 203-284-0240

Mark Eyelet, Inc.
63 Wakelee Rd.
Wolcott, CT 06716

Founded 1956
Total employees 100
Annual sales $9.9 million
Industries Manufacturing Equipment, Subassemblies and Components
Growth Openings in past year 20; percentage growth 25%
Contact Ms. Sandy Booth, Personnel Manager
Tel 203-756-8847
Fax 203-755-9410

Merocel Corp.
950 Flanders Rd.
Mystic, CT 06355

Founded 1973
Total employees 101
Annual sales $8 million
Industries Advanced Materials, Medical
Growth Openings in past year 26; percentage growth 34%
Contact Ron Cercone, VP of Operations
Tel 203-572-9586
Fax 203-572-7485

MGM Industries, Inc.
925 Sherman Ave.
Hamden, CT 06514

Founded 1963
Total employees 50
Industry Holding Companies
Growth Openings in past year 25; percentage growth 100%
Contact Ed O'Lear, President
Tel 203-288-3523
Fax 203-288-2621

MUST Software International
101 Merritt 7
Norwalk, CT 06856

Founded 1987
Total employees 278
Annual sales $32.3 million
Industry Computer Software
Growth Openings in past year 11; percentage growth 4%
Contact Ms. Karen Flaugh, Director of Human Resources
Tel 203-845-5000
Fax 203-845-5252

Mystech Associates, Inc.
PO Box 220
Mystic, CT 06355

Founded 1971
Total employees 140
Annual sales $12.06 million
Industries Computer Software, Holding Companies, Manufacturing Equipment
Growth Openings in past year 15; percentage growth 12%
Contact Ms. Judith Johns, Manager of Personnel and Administration
Tel 203-536-2663
Fax 203-572-9614

National Medical Research Corp.
25 Main St.
Hartford, CT 06106

Founded 1983
Total employees 70
Annual sales $10 million
Industries Medical, Pharmaceuticals

Growth Openings in past year 25; percentage growth 55%
Contact Ms. Jeanette Staye, Human Resources Manager
Tel 203-724-0091
Fax 203-278-4717

Growth Openings in past year 20; percentage growth 40%
Contact Ms. Vera Lucido, Personnel Director
Tel 203-929-8407
Fax 203-929-0535

Growth Openings in past year 25; percentage growth 9%
Contact Joseph Matrange, Vice President/General Manager
Tel 203-327-6010
Fax 800-631-4005

National Patent Medical
349 Lake Rd.
Dayville, CT 06241

Founded 1920
Total employees 400
Annual sales $50 million
Industries Medical, Pharmaceuticals
Growth Openings in past year 50; percentage growth 14%
Contact Howard Koenig, President/CEO
Tel 203-774-8541
Fax 203-774-1507

Notifier
12 Clintonville Rd.
Northford, CT 06472

Founded 1950
Total employees 200
Annual sales $25 million
Industries Test and Measurement, Telecommunications
Growth Openings in past year 50; percentage growth 33%
Contact Mark Levy, President
Tel 203-484-7161
Fax 203-484-7118

Producto Machine Co.
990 Housatonic Ave., PO Box 780
Bridgeport, CT 06601

Founded 1928
Total employees 272
Annual sales $25 million
Industry Factory Automation
Growth Openings in past year 72; percentage growth 36%
Contact Newman M. Marsilius, III, President
Tel 203-367-8675
Fax 203-335-8776

Neurogen Corp.
35 Northeast Industrial Rd.
Branford, CT 06405

Founded 1987
Total employees 51
Annual sales $5.3 million
Industry Pharmaceuticals
Growth Openings in past year 14; percentage growth 37%
Contact Philip J. Whitcome, President/CEO
Tel 203-488-8201
Fax 203-481-8683

Peak Electronics, Inc.
51 Carlson Rd.
Orange, CT 06477

Founded 1989
Total employees 127
Industry Subassemblies and Components
Growth Openings in past year 27; percentage growth 27%
Contact Paul Carozza, Personnel Administrator
Tel 203-795-0241
Fax 203-795-5804

Programming Resources Co.
875 Asylum Ave.
Hartford, CT 06105

Founded 1971
Total employees 75
Annual sales $8.7 million
Industries Computer Hardware, Computer Software
Growth Openings in past year 18; percentage growth 31%
Contact Steven Weber, President/Owner
Tel 203-728-1428
Fax 203-522-9960

Nitsuko America Corp.
4 Forest Pkwy.
Shelton, CT 06484

Founded 1976
Total employees 70
Annual sales $7 million
Industries Computer Hardware, Telecommunications

Polycast Technology Corp.
70 Carlisle Pl.
Stamford, CT 06902

Founded 1981
Total employees 300
Annual sales $44 million
Industry Advanced Materials

Quamco, Inc., Eldorado Division
336 Boston Post Rd.
Milford, CT 06460

Founded 1984
Total employees 130
Annual sales $15 million
Industry Factory Automation

Growth Openings in past year 14; percentage growth 12%
Contact Ms. Judy Johnson, Human Resources Manager
Tel 203-878-1711
Fax 203-878-6156

Real Decisions Corp.
22 Thorndal Cir.
Darien, CT 06820

Founded 1975
Total employees 80
Annual sales $8 million
Industries Computer Hardware, Computer Software
Growth Openings in past year 13; percentage growth 19%
Contact Len Bergstrom, President
Tel 203-656-1500
Fax 203-656-1659

Reflexite Corp.
315 South St.
New Britain, CT 06050

Founded 1970
Total employees 275
Annual sales $30 million
Industries Advanced Materials, Holding Companies, Photonics, Transportation
Growth Openings in past year 100; percentage growth 57%
Contact David Edgar, VP of Human Resources
Tel 203-223-9297
Fax 203-223-0753

Seitz Corp.
212 Torrington Industrial Park, PO Box 1398
Torrington, CT 06790

Founded 1949
Total employees 230
Industries Computer Hardware, Manufacturing Equipment

Growth Openings in past year 30; percentage growth 15%
Contact Charles Carlson, Director of Human Resources
Tel 203-489-0476
Fax 203-496-1949

Sonalysts, Inc.
215 Pkwy. North, PO Box 280
Waterford, CT 06385

Founded 1973
Total employees 450
Annual sales $31.5 million
Industries Computer Hardware, Computer Software, Factory Automation, Holding Companies, Manufacturing Equipment, Subassemblies and Components
Growth Openings in past year 49; percentage growth 12%
Contact Michael Wunder, Personnel Manager
Tel 203-442-4355
Fax 203-447-8883

Southington Tool & Manufacturing Corp.
300 Atwater St.
Plantsville, CT 06479

Founded 1970
Total employees 59
Annual sales $3 million
Industries Factory Automation, Holding Companies, Manufacturing Equipment, Medical, Subassemblies and Components
Growth Openings in past year 16; percentage growth 37%
Contact Ms. Andrea Kalat, Human Resources Manager
Tel 203-276-0021
Fax 203-621-6100

Spectrum Plastics Molding Resources, Inc.
3 Chestnut St., PO Box 657
Ansonia, CT 06401

Founded 1967
Total employees 62
Annual sales $6 million
Industry Manufacturing Equipment
Growth Openings in past year 14; percentage growth 29%
Contact Pierre Dziubina, President
Tel 203-736-2631
Fax 203-736-6790

Structured Technology Corp.
15 Liberty Way
Niantic, CT 06357

Founded 1982
Total employees 115
Annual sales $10 million
Industries Computer Hardware, Computer Software, Defense, Factory Automation, Test and Measurement, Telecommunications, Transportation
Growth Openings in past year 16; percentage growth 16%
Contact Ms. Dana L. Macy, Purchasing Manager
Tel 203-691-0633
Fax 203-691-1015

Thermatool Corp.
31 Commerce St., PO Box 120769
East Haven, CT 06512

Founded 1952
Total employees 99
Industries Computer Software, Factory Automation, Test and Measurement
Growth Openings in past year 19; percentage growth 23%
Contact Theodore J. Morin, President
Tel 203-468-4100

Thermodynetics, Inc.
651 Day Hill Rd.
Windsor, CT 06095

Founded 1981
Total employees 80
Annual sales $7 million
Industry Holding
Companies
Growth Openings in past
year 15; percentage
growth 23%
Contact Robert
Lieberman,
Controller
Tel 203-683-2005
Fax 203-683-2133

TSI International, Ltd.
45 Danbury Rd.
Wilton, CT 06897

Founded 1979
Total employees 120
Annual sales $13 million
Industry Computer
Software
Growth Openings in past
year 20; percentage
growth 20%
Contact Ms. Connie
Galley,
President
Tel 203-761-8600
Fax 203-762-9677

Virginia Industries, Inc.
1022 Elm St.
Rocky Hill, CT 06067

Founded 1935
Total employees 445
Annual sales $43 million
Industry Holding
Companies
Growth Openings in past
year 26; percentage
growth 6%
Contact John Stupkavich,
Director of Industrial
Relations
Tel 203-563-0111
Fax 203-529-9299

TRC Companies, Inc.
5 Waterside Crossing
Windsor, CT 06095

Founded 1969
Total employees 600
Annual sales $42 million
Industry Holding
Companies
Growth Openings in past
year 149; percentage
growth 33%
Contact Vincent Rocco,
COB/CEO
Tel 203-289-8631
Fax 203-298-6399

University Patents, Inc.
1465 Post Rd. East
Westport, CT 06880

Founded 1966
Total employees 70
Annual sales $1.6 million
Industry Holding
Companies
Growth Openings in past
year 61; percentage
growth 677%
Contact A. Sidney Alpert,
COB/President/CEO
Tel 203-255-6044
Fax 203-254-1102

**Voltarc Technologies,
Inc.**
186 Linwood Ave.
Fairfield, CT 06430

Founded 1927
Total employees 354
Annual sales $31 million
Industries Energy,
Photonics
Growth Openings in past
year 103; percentage
growth 41%
Contact Vinnie Mehta,
President
Tel 203-255-2633
Fax 203-259-1194

TRUMPF, Inc.
Hyde Rd., Farmington
Industrial Park
Farmington, CT 06032

Founded 1967
Total employees 220
Annual sales $50 million
Industries Factory
Automation, Photonics
Growth Openings in past
year 20; percentage
growth 10%
Contact James Bento,
Director of Finance and
Administration
Tel 203-677-9741
Fax 203-678-1704

**Vantage Computer
Systems, Inc.**
100 Great Meadow Rd.
Wethersfield, CT 06109

Founded 1970
Total employees 450
Annual sales $30 million
Industries Computer
Software, Holding
Companies
Growth Openings in past
year 99; percentage
growth 28%
Contact Robert
Maltempo,
Chairman of the Board
Tel 203-721-0694
Fax 203-563-5793

Web Technologies, Inc.
27 Main St.
Oakville, CT 06779

Founded 1980
Total employees 100
Annual sales $20 million
Industry Manufacturing
Equipment
Growth Openings in past
year 15; percentage
growth 17%
Contact Dan Weinick,
Personnel Manager
Tel 203-274-9657
Fax 203-274-1268

Westbrook Technologies

22 Pequot Park Rd., PO Box 910
Westbrook, CT 06498

Founded 1985
Total employees 70
Annual sales $8.1 million
Industry Computer Software
Growth Openings in past year 30; percentage growth 75%
Contact Dennis Graham, President
Tel 203-399-7111
Fax 203-399-7137

Delaware

■ **302 Area Code**

AstroPower, Inc.

Solar Park
Newark, DE 19711

Founded 1983
Total employees 90
Annual sales $5 million
Industries Energy, Manufacturing Equipment
Growth Openings in past year 16; percentage growth 21%
Contact Allen Barnett, President
Tel 302-366-0400
Fax 302-368-6474

ILC Dover, Inc.

PO Box 266
Frederica, DE 19946

Founded 1969
Total employees 625
Annual sales $54 million
Industries Defense, Factory Automation, Test and Measurement, Transportation
Growth Openings in past year 182; percentage growth 41%
Contact Frank Mossman, Director of Human Resources
Tel 302-335-3911
Fax 302-335-0762

District of Columbia

■ **202 Area Code**

Aristotle Industries, Inc.

205 Pennsylvania Ave. Southeast
Washington, DC 20003

Founded 1977
Total employees 45
Industries Computer Hardware, Computer Software
Growth Openings in past year 16; percentage growth 55%
Contact John A. Phillips, President
Tel 202-543-8345
Fax 202-543-6407

Naval Research Laboratory, Space Systems Development Department

4555 Overlook Ave. Southwest
Washington, DC 20375

Founded 1923
Total employees 275
Industries Defense, Transportation
Growth Openings in past year 100; percentage growth 57%
Contact R.E. Eisenhauer, Superintendent
Tel 202-767-0410
Fax 202-767-1952

Florida

■ **305 Area Code**

Arnet Pharmaceutical Corp.

2280 West 77th St.
Hialeah, FL 33016

Founded 1972
Total employees 25
Annual sales $2.2 million
Industry Pharmaceuticals

Growth Openings in past year 15; percentage growth 150%
Contact J.M. Sotomayor, President
Tel 305-558-2929

BLOC Development Corporation

800 Southwest 37th Ave.
Coral Gables, FL 33134

Founded 1986
Total employees 271
Annual sales $26.3 million
Industries Computer Software, Holding Companies
Growth Openings in past year 86; percentage growth 46%
Contact Frank Millman, COB/CEO
Tel 305-567-9931
Fax 305-445-8370

Computer Products, Inc., Process Automation Division

2900 Gateway Dr.
Pompano Beach, FL 33069

Founded 1968
Total employees 130
Annual sales $22 million
Industry Factory Automation
Growth Openings in past year 15; percentage growth 13%
Contact Bob McKenzie, Director of Human Resources
Tel 305-974-5500
Fax 305-979-7371

Deneba Systems, Inc.

7400 Southwest 87th Ave.
Miami, FL 33122

Founded 1986
Total employees 63
Annual sales $10 million
Industry Computer Software

Growth Openings in past year 19; percentage growth 43%
Contact Manny Menendez, President
Tel 305-596-5644
Fax 305-477-5794

Growth Openings in past year 32; percentage growth 18%
Contact Lew Price, Personnel Manager
Tel 305-858-8200
Fax 305-854-6305

Growth Openings in past year 14; percentage growth 66%
Contact Victor Weliky, President
Tel 305-426-4000
Fax 305-960-1471

Diamedix Corp.
2140 North Miami Ave.
Miami, FL 33127

Founded 1986
Total employees 82
Annual sales $9.0 million
Industry Medical
Growth Openings in past year 26; percentage growth 46%
Contact Joseph Giegel, President
Tel 305-324-2300
Fax 305-324-2395

Hobart Airport Systems
6950 Northwest 77th Ct.
Miami, FL 33166

Founded 1917
Total employees 75
Annual sales $8.9 million
Industries Factory Automation, Transportation
Growth Openings in past year 15; percentage growth 25%
Contact Brooks Price, Quality Control Manager
Tel 305-592-5450
Fax 305-477-4105

North American Biologicals, Inc.
16500 North West 15th Ave.
Miami, FL 33169

Founded 1968
Total employees 965
Annual sales $82.4 million
Industries Biotechnology, Pharmaceuticals
Growth Openings in past year 161; percentage growth 20%
Contact Alfred Fernandez, VP of Finance
Tel 305-625-5303
Fax 305-624-1646

Digital Products Corp.
800 Northwest 33rd St.
Pompano Beach, FL 33064

Founded 1970
Total employees 121
Annual sales $8.69 million
Industries Holding Companies, Test and Measurement, Telecommunications
Growth Openings in past year 81; percentage growth 202%
Contact Theodore M. Sabarese, President/CEO
Tel 305-783-9600
Fax 305-783-9609

Masterclip Graphics, Inc.
5201 Ravenswood Rd., Suite 111
Fort Lauderdale, FL 33312

Founded 1991
Total employees 37
Annual sales $4.2 million
Industry Computer Software
Growth Openings in past year 30; percentage growth 428%
Contact Cliff Welles, Chief Executive Officer
Tel 305-983-7440
Fax 305-967-9452

Unipower Corporation
2981 Gateway Dr.
Pompano Beach, FL 33069

Founded 1988
Total employees 155
Annual sales $15 million
Industry Subassemblies and Components
Growth Openings in past year 55; percentage growth 55%
Contact Joe Merino, President
Tel 305-974-2442
Fax 305-971-1837

■ **407 Area Code**

Financial Data Planning Corp.
2140 South Dixie Hwy.
Miami, FL 33133

Founded 1968
Total employees 208
Annual sales $16.31 million
Industry Computer Software

Masyc Southern Corp.
3037 Northwest 25th Ave.
Pompano Beach, FL 33069

Founded 1979
Total employees 35
Annual sales $3 million
Industry Factory Automation

Archive Corp., Maynard Division
36 Skyline Dr.
Lake Mary, FL 32746

Founded 1982
Total employees 600
Annual sales $98 million
Industry Computer Hardware

Growth Openings in past year 248; percentage growth 70%
Contact James Gribben, Director of Human Resources
Tel 407-263-3500
Fax 407-263-3638

Growth Openings in past year 175; percentage growth 70%
Contact Ms. Vicki Goldenson, Director of Human Resources
Tel 407-352-3700
Fax 407-345-8616

Growth Openings in past year 47; percentage growth 167%
Contact J.R. Kennedy, President
Tel 407-331-5500
Fax 407-260-7136

Boca Research, Inc.
6413 Congress Ave.
Boca Raton, FL 33487

Founded 1985
Total employees 100
Annual sales $55 million
Industries Computer Hardware, Telecommunications
Growth Openings in past year 40; percentage growth 66%
Contact Howard Yenke, President/CEO
Tel 407-997-6227
Fax 407-997-0918

BSE Consultants, Inc.
312 South Harbor City Blvd.
Melbourne, FL 32901

Founded 1986
Total employees 25
Industry Manufacturing Equipment
Growth Openings in past year 13; percentage growth 108%
Contact Chris Stapleton, Marketing Director
Tel 407-725-3674
Fax 407-723-1159

Coleman Research Corp.
5950 Lakehurst Dr.
Orlando, FL 32819

Founded 1980
Total employees 425
Annual sales $37 million
Industries Defense, Environmental, Holding Companies, Manufacturing Equipment, Telecommunications

DATAMAX Corp.
4501 Parkway Commerce Blvd.
Orlando, FL 32808

Founded 1980
Total employees 150
Industries Computer Hardware, Computer Software, Subassemblies and Components
Growth Openings in past year 25; percentage growth 20%
Contact Robert Strandberg, President
Tel 407-578-8007
Fax 407-578-8377

Distributed Processing Technology, Inc.
140 Candace Dr.
Maitland, FL 32751

Founded 1977
Total employees 200
Annual sales $20 million
Industry Computer Hardware
Growth Openings in past year 40; percentage growth 25%
Contact Steve Goldman, President
Tel 407-830-5522
Fax 407-260-5366

ECI Telecom, Inc.
927 Fern St.
Altamonte Springs, FL 32701

Founded 1983
Total employees 75
Annual sales $10 million
Industries Subassemblies and Components, Telecommunications

Fiserv, Inc., CBS Division
2601 Technology Dr.
Orlando, FL 32804

Founded 1983
Total employees 178
Annual sales $20 million
Industry Computer Software
Growth Openings in past year 18; percentage growth 11%
Contact Raju Shivdasani, President
Tel 407-299-5400
Fax 407-578-0900

Graseby Electro-Optics, Inc.
12151 Research Pkwy.
Orlando, FL 32826

Founded 1957
Total employees 90
Industries Photonics, Subassemblies and Components, Test and Measurement
Growth Openings in past year 50; percentage growth 125%
Contact Dave Morell, General Manager
Tel 407-282-7700
Fax 407-273-9046

Logicon Eagle Technology, Inc.
950 North Orlando Ave.
Winter Park, FL 32789

Founded 1900
Total employees 470
Annual sales $47 million
Industry Defense

Growth Openings in past year 189; percentage growth 67%
Contact Dr. James F. Harvey, President
Tel 407-629-6010
Fax 407-629-5636

MC Test Service, Inc.
200 East Dr.
Melbourne, FL 32904

Founded 1984
Total employees 165
Annual sales $10 million
Industry Subassemblies and Components
Growth Openings in past year 40; percentage growth 32%
Contact Thomas Winnekowski, President
Tel 407-768-0041
Fax 407-253-0539

Newtrend L.P.
2600 Technology Dr.
Orlando, FL 32804

Founded 1977
Total employees 600
Annual sales $60 million
Industry Computer Software
Growth Openings in past year 100; percentage growth 20%
Contact Mrs. Susan Iwuc, VP of Human Resources
Tel 407-297-0870
Fax 407-292-2528

Q-bit Corp.
2575 Pacific Ave. Northeast
Palm Bay, FL 32905

Founded 1972
Total employees 155
Annual sales $10 million
Industry Subassemblies and Components

Growth Openings in past year 25; percentage growth 19%
Contact Gary R. Callaway, President/General Manager
Tel 407-727-1838
Fax 407-727-3729

Schwartz Electro-Optics, Inc.
3404 North Orange Blossom Trail
Orlando, FL 32804

Founded 1984
Total employees 125
Annual sales $13 million
Industry Holding Companies
Growth Openings in past year 15; percentage growth 13%
Contact William C. Schwartz, President
Tel 407-298-1802
Fax 407-297-1794

Software Technology, Inc.
1511 Park Ave.
Melbourne, FL 32901

Founded 1978
Total employees 200
Annual sales $16 million
Industry Computer Software
Growth Openings in past year 20; percentage growth 11%
Contact Jeff Clift, President
Tel 407-723-3999
Fax 407-676-4510

■ **813 Area Code**

Abra Cadabra Software, Inc.
5565 Ninth St. North
Saint Petersburg, FL 33703

Founded 1985
Total employees 55
Annual sales $6.3 million

Industry Computer Software
Growth Openings in past year 33; percentage growth 150%
Contact Guy Bohner, President
Tel 813-525-4400
Fax 813-525-3254

AMETEK, Inc., Mansfield and Green Division
8600 Somerset Dr.
Largo, FL 34643

Founded 1930
Total employees 150
Industries Environmental, Subassemblies and Components, Test and Measurement, Transportation
Growth Openings in past year 35; percentage growth 30%
Contact Donald L. Whitehead, Vice President/General Manager
Tel 813-536-7831
Fax 813-539-6882

Bausch & Lomb Pharmaceuticals, Inc.
8500 Hidden River Pkwy.
Tampa, FL 33637

Founded 1985
Total employees 300
Industry Pharmaceuticals
Growth Openings in past year 100; percentage growth 50%
Contact Tom Riedhammer, President
Tel 813-975-7700
Fax 813-572-1064

CMS, Inc.
4904 Eisenhower Blvd., Suite 310
Tampa, FL 33634

Founded 1988
Total employees 604
Annual sales $126 million
Industries Defense, Environmental

Growth Openings in past year 105; percentage growth 21%
Contact F.P. Ragano, Chief Executive Officer
Tel 813-882-4477
Fax 813-884-1876

Compass Technology, Inc.
2201 Cantu Ct., Suite 116
Sarasota, FL 34232

Founded 1989
Total employees 100
Annual sales $16 million
Industry Computer Hardware
Growth Openings in past year 90; percentage growth 900%
Contact Peter X. Yates, COB/CEO
Tel 813-371-8000
Fax 813-377-5600

Custom Cable Industries, Inc.
3221 Cherry Palm Dr.
Tampa, FL 33619

Founded 1980
Total employees 168
Annual sales $8 million
Industries Computer Hardware, Subassemblies and Components, Telecommunications
Growth Openings in past year 26; percentage growth 18%
Contact Richard Watson, President
Tel 813-623-2232
Fax 813-626-9630

Dynacs Engineering Co., Inc.
34650 US Hwy. 19 North, Suite 301
Palm Harbor, FL 34684

Founded 1985
Total employees 44
Annual sales $3.5 million
Industries Computer Hardware, Computer Software, Transportation

Growth Openings in past year 12; percentage growth 37%
Contact Ramen Singh, President
Tel 813-784-4035
Fax 813-785-2355

Fischer International Systems Corp.
4073 Merchantile Ave.
Naples, FL 33942

Founded 1982
Total employees 143
Annual sales $16 million
Industries Computer Software, Telecommunications
Growth Openings in past year 53; percentage growth 58%
Contact Art Webber, Controller
Tel 813-643-1500
Fax 813-643-3772

FMC Corp., Food Processing Systems Division
Fairway Ave., PO Box 1708
Lakeland, FL 33802

Founded 1925
Total employees 225
Annual sales $30 million
Industries Advanced Materials, Factory Automation
Growth Openings in past year 25; percentage growth 12%
Contact Charles Cannon, Division Manager
Tel 813-683-5411
Fax 813-680-3677

Group Technologies Corp.
10901 Malcolm McKinnley Dr., MS-08
Tampa, FL 33612
Founded 1965
Total employees 850
Annual sales $100 million

Industries Computer Hardware, Defense, Manufacturing Equipment, Subassemblies and Components, Telecommunications
Growth Openings in past year 49; percentage growth 6%
Contact Ms. Janis Beal, Manager of Human Resources
Tel 813-972-6000
Fax 813-972-6704

GTE Industry Products and Services, Inc.
PO Box 2924
Tampa, FL 33601

Founded 1935
Total employees 600
Annual sales $82 million
Industry Telecommunications
Growth Openings in past year 319; percentage growth 113%
Contact Ms. Christine Strom, Director of Human Resources
Tel 813-273-3000
Fax 813-273-3311

L.E.A. Dynatech, Inc.
6520 Harney Rd.
Tampa, FL 33610

Founded 1971
Total employees 45
Annual sales $5 million
Industry Subassemblies and Components
Growth Openings in past year 15; percentage growth 50%
Contact Robert J. Stanger, President
Tel 813-621-1324
Fax 813-621-8980

Mathematica, Inc.
402 South Kentucky Ave.
Lakeland, FL 33801

Founded 1986
Total employees 45

Industry Computer
Software
Growth Openings in past
year 22; percentage
growth 95%
Contact Derek Hodges,
CEO/President
Tel 813-682-1128
Fax 813-686-5969

Reflectone, Inc.
4908 Tampa West Blvd.
Tampa, FL 33634

Founded 1985
Total employees 560
Annual sales $51 million
Industries Defense,
Transportation
Growth Openings in past
year 27; percentage
growth 5%
Contact Ms. Kelley Rex
Road,
Senior Director of
Human Resources, Admi
Tel 813-885-7481
Fax 813-885-1177

Siemens Power Corp.
PO Box 180
Bradenton, FL 34206

Founded 1978
Total employees 194
Industry Energy
Growth Openings in past
year 18; percentage
growth 10%
Contact John Elrickson,
VP of Human Resources
Tel 813-723-4100
Fax 813-723-4226

Unilens Corp. USA
10431 72nd St. North
Largo, FL 34647

Founded 1982
Total employees 100
Industry Medical
Growth Openings in past
year 33; percentage
growth 49%
Contact Ms. Francine
Swarts,
Personnel Manager
Tel 813-544-2531
Fax 813-545-1883

**Westinghouse Electric
Corp., Electrical
Components Division**
110 Douglas Rd. East, PO
Box 819
Oldsmar, FL 34677

Founded 1982
Total employees 315
Annual sales $39 million
Industries Factory
Automation,
Subassemblies and
Components, Test and
Measurement
Growth Openings in past
year 65; percentage
growth 26%
Contact Steve Marcum,
Plant Manager
Tel 813-855-4621
Fax 813-855-4626

■ **904 Area Code**

Aero Corp.
5530 East Hwy. 90, PO
Box 1909
Lake City, FL 32056

Founded 1951
Total employees 375
Industry Transportation
Growth Openings in past
year 175; percentage
growth 87%
Contact Ms. Barbara
Kuhn,
Personnel Supervisor
Tel 904-752-7911
Fax 904-752-0807

Barr Systems, Inc.
4131 Northwest 28th Ln.
Gainesville, FL 32606

Founded 1978
Total employees 40
Annual sales $4.6 million
Industries Computer
Hardware, Computer
Software,
Subassemblies and
Components,
Telecommunications

Growth Openings in past
year 15; percentage
growth 60%
Contact Anthony J. Barr,
President
Tel 904-371-3050
Fax 904-371-3018

CMS, Data Corp.
124 Marriott Dr., Suite
200
Tallahassee, FL 32301

Founded 1978
Total employees 180
Annual sales $12.83
million
Industries Computer
Software, Holding
Companies
Growth Openings in past
year 55; percentage
growth 44%
Contact P. Scott Kadlec,
Executive Vice President
Tel 904-878-5155
Fax 904-656-4093

Computer Power, Inc.
661 Riverside Ave., Suite
110E
Jacksonville, FL 32204

Founded 1969
Total employees 700
Industry Computer
Software
Growth Openings in past
year 249; percentage
growth 55%
Contact Joseph Eberly,
VP of Human Resources
Tel 904-359-5000
Fax 904-359-5298

Corbel and Co.
1660 Prudential Dr.
Jacksonville, FL 32207

Founded 1974
Total employees 160
Annual sales $18 million
Industries Computer
Software, Holding
Companies

Growth Openings in past
year 35; percentage
growth 28%
Contact Duncan
McPherson,
President
Tel 904-399-5888
Fax 904-399-5551

Growth Openings in past
year 46; percentage
growth 6%
Contact Tom Alexander,
Personnel Manager
Tel 904-968-2191
Fax 904-968-0563

Growth Openings in past
year 14; percentage
growth 7%
Contact Arthur C. Wotiz,
President
Tel 904-730-7511
Fax 904-730-6164

Crestview Aerospace Corp.
5486 Fairchild Rd.
Crestview, FL 32536

Founded 1991
Total employees 50
Annual sales $5.8 million
Industry Transportation
Growth Openings in past
year 20; percentage
growth 66%
Contact Jack Owen,
President
Tel 904-682-2753
Fax 904-682-0489

National High Magnetic Field Laboratory
Florida State University,
1800 E Paul Dirac Dr.
Tallahassee, FL 32306

Founded 1990
Total employees 60
Annual sales $5.8 million
Industry Subassemblies
and Components
Growth Openings in past
year 30; percentage
growth 100%
Contact Dr. Jack Crow,
Director
Tel 904-644-0311
Fax 904-644-0867

TYBRIN Corp.
1283 North Eglin Pkwy.
Shalimar, FL 32579

Founded 1972
Total employees 150
Annual sales $7 million
Industries Computer
Hardware, Computer
Software
Growth Openings in past
year 25; percentage
growth 20%
Contact Ms. Ellen C.
Taylor,
Personnel Manager
Tel 904-651-1150
Fax 904-651-6335

Cuda Products Corp.
6000 Powers Ave.
Jacksonville, FL 32217

Founded 1978
Total employees 100
Annual sales $8.5 million
Industries Medical,
Photonics,
Subassemblies and
Components, Test and
Measurement
Growth Openings in past
year 15; percentage
growth 17%
Contact Joseph Cuda,
President
Tel 904-737-7611
Fax 904-733-4832

PC DOCS, Inc.
124 Marriott Dr., Suite
203
Tallahassee, FL 32301

Founded 1990
Total employees 46
Industry Computer
Software
Growth Openings in past
year 20; percentage
growth 76%
Contact Scott Kadlec,
President
Tel 904-942-3627
Fax 904-942-1517

Georgia

■ 404 Area Code

Advanced Systems Technologies, Inc.
3490 Piedmont Rd.
Northeast, Suite 1410
Atlanta, GA 30305

Founded 1981
Total employees 155
Annual sales $12 million
Industries Defense,
Energy, Environmental,
Manufacturing
Equipment
Growth Openings in past
year 26; percentage
growth 20%
Contact Wayne Knox,
President
Tel 404-240-2930
Fax 404-240-2931

Instrument Control Service, Inc.
2420 Hwy. 29 South
Pensacola, FL 32534

Founded 1967
Total employees 800
Annual sales $42 million
Industry Manufacturing
Equipment

PCR Group, Inc.
8570 Phillips Hwy., Suite
101
Jacksonville, FL 32256

Founded 1953
Total employees 210
Annual sales $30 million
Industries Advanced
Materials, Chemicals,
Holding Companies,
Pharmaceuticals

Agris Corp.
1000 Holcomb Woods
Pkwy., Suite 116
Roswell, GA 30076

Founded 1978
Total employees 72

Industries Computer Software, Holding Companies
Growth Openings in past year 40; percentage growth 125%
Contact Ms. Susan Rasmussen, VP of Operations
Tel 404-587-3324
Fax 404-640-1663

Allied Data Communications Group, Inc.
5375 Oakbrook Pkwy. Norcross, GA 30093

Founded 1978
Total employees 130
Annual sales $17 million
Industries Computer Hardware, Telecommunications
Growth Openings in past year 30; percentage growth 30%
Contact Thomas Beddoe, President
Tel 404-923-4866
Fax 404-923-4833

American Megatrends, Inc.
6145-F North Belt Pkwy. Norcross, GA 30071

Founded 1985
Total employees 130
Industries Computer Hardware, Computer Software, Telecommunications
Growth Openings in past year 30; percentage growth 30%
Contact S. Shankar, President
Tel 404-263-8181
Fax 404-263-9381

Anvic International
3800 New McEver Rd. Acworth, GA 30101

Founded 1977
Total employees 42
Annual sales $5.25 million

Industries Environmental, Test and Measurement
Growth Openings in past year 14; percentage growth 50%
Contact Don Faulkner, President
Tel 404-974-7182
Fax 404-974-2959

Applied Technical Services, Inc.
1190 Atlanta Industrial Dr. Marietta, GA 30066

Founded 1967
Total employees 75
Annual sales $12 million
Industries Advanced Materials, Chemicals, Environmental, Manufacturing Equipment
Growth Openings in past year 20; percentage growth 36%
Contact Jim F. Hills, President
Tel 404-423-1400
Fax 404-424-6415

Atlanta Group Systems, Inc.
2971 Flowers Rd., South 275 Atlanta, GA 30341

Founded 1980
Total employees 100
Annual sales $11 million
Industries Computer Hardware, Computer Software
Growth Openings in past year 30; percentage growth 42%
Contact Paul Jones, Owner/CEO
Tel 404-455-7783
Fax 404-451-5163

AVL Scientific Corp.
33 Mansell Ct., PO Box 337 Roswell, GA 30077

Founded 1973
Total employees 91
Annual sales $13.5 million
Industry Medical

Growth Openings in past year 20; percentage growth 28%
Contact Alfred Marek, President
Tel 404-587-4040
Fax 404-587-4163

Barco Chromatics, Inc.
2558 Mountain Industrial Blvd. Tucker, GA 30084

Founded 1976
Total employees 105
Annual sales $12 million
Industries Computer Hardware, Computer Software
Growth Openings in past year 16; percentage growth 17%
Contact Steve Ames, Controller
Tel 404-493-7000
Fax 404-493-1314

Brock Control Systems, Inc.
2859 Paces Ferry Rd., Suite 1000 Atlanta, GA 30339

Founded 1984
Total employees 159
Annual sales $17.03 million
Industry Computer Software
Growth Openings in past year 49; percentage growth 44%
Contact Ms. Robin Haight, Personnel Coordinator
Tel 404-431-1200
Fax 404-431-1201

Byers Engineering Co.
6285 Barfield Rd. Atlanta, GA 30328

Founded 1971
Total employees 900
Industries Computer Software, Manufacturing Equipment

Growth Openings in past
year 150; percentage
growth 20%
Contact Kenneth G.
Byers, Jr.,
President
Tel 404-843-1000
Fax 404-843-2000

**Chemical Products
Corp.**
PO Box 2470
Cartersville, GA 30120

Founded 1934
Total employees 275
Annual sales $40 million
Industry Chemicals
Growth Openings in past
year 75; percentage
growth 37%
Contact Charles Adams,
Jr.,
President
Tel 404-382-2144
Fax 404-386-6053

**Construction Systems
Associates, Inc.**
2121 Newmarket Pkwy.,
Suite 124
Marietta, GA 30067

Founded 1976
Total employees 100
Annual sales $7.5 million
Industry Computer
Software
Growth Openings in past
year 15; percentage
growth 17%
Contact William B.
Fillman,
VP of Finance
Tel 404-955-3518
Fax 404-956-8748

CryoLife, Inc.
2211 New Market Pkwy.,
Suite 142
Marietta, GA 30067

Founded 1984
Total employees 104
Annual sales $15 million
Industry Biotechnology

Growth Openings in past
year 14; percentage
growth 15%
Contact Steven G.
Anderson,
President
Tel 404-952-1660
Fax 404-952-9743

CytRx Corp.
150 Technology Pkwy.
Norcross, GA 30092

Founded 1985
Total employees 33
Industries Biotechnology,
Pharmaceuticals
Growth Openings in past
year 16; percentage
growth 94%
Contact William V. Fleck,
VP of Human Resources
Tel 404-368-9500
Fax 404-368-0622

Dataradio Corp.
6160 Peachtree
Dunwoody Rd., Suite C-
200
Atlanta, GA 30328

Founded 1984
Total employees 17
Industry
Telecommunications
Growth Openings in past
year 12; percentage
growth 240%
Contact Robert Rouleaux,
President
Tel 404-392-0002
Fax 404-392-9199

DayStar Digital, Inc.
5556 Atlanta Hwy.
Flowery Branch, GA
30542

Founded 1984
Total employees 65
Industries Computer
Hardware,
Telecommunications
Growth Openings in past
year 20; percentage
growth 44%
Contact Andrew Lewis,
President
Tel 404-967-2077
Fax 404-967-3018

**Digital Transmission
Systems, Inc.**
3000 Northwoods Pkwy.,
Bldg. 330
Norcross, GA 30071

Founded 1984
Total employees 59
Annual sales $10 million
Industry
Telecommunications
Contact Joseph Pisula,
President
Tel 404-798-1300
Fax 404-798-1325

**EcoTek Laboratory
Services, Inc.**
3342 International Park
Dr., Southeast
Atlanta, GA 30316

Founded 1988
Total employees 70
Industry Environmental
Growth Openings in past
year 15; percentage
growth 27%
Contact Steve Shutt,
Vice President
Tel 404-244-0827
Fax 404-243-5355

**Elan Pharmaceutical
Research Corp.**
1300 Gould Dr.
Gainesville, GA 30504

Founded 1981
Total employees 72
Annual sales $11 million
Industry Medical
Growth Openings in past
year 20; percentage
growth 38%
Contact Ms. Merla
Sawyers,
Financial Controller
Tel 404-534-8239
Fax 404-534-8247

Expeditor Systems, Inc.
4090 Nine McFarlan Dr.
Alpharetta, GA 30201

Founded 1983
Total employees 50
Annual sales $6.9 million
Industry
Telecommunications

Growth Openings in past year 20; percentage growth 66%
Contact Giles Barton, President
Tel 404-442-9261
Fax 404-664-5214

Growth Openings in past year 53; percentage growth 18%
Contact Dr. Peter Schultz, President
Tel 404-623-6000
Fax 404-623-5640

Growth Openings in past year 25; percentage growth 14%
Contact Albert H. Wiggins, Jr., President/COB
Tel 404-952-8094
Fax 404-984-1223

FormMaker Software, Inc.
1600 Parkwood Circle Northwest, Suite 530
Atlanta, GA 30339

Founded 1983
Total employees 30
Annual sales $3.4 million
Industry Computer Software
Growth Openings in past year 14; percentage growth 87%
Contact Sam Wilkes, III, President
Tel 404-859-9900
Fax 404-859-0216

IMNET, Inc.
8601 Dun Woody Pl., Suite 420
Atlanta, GA 30350

Founded 1986
Total employees 64
Industries Computer Hardware, Computer Software
Growth Openings in past year 32; percentage growth 100%
Contact Kenneth Rardin, President/CEO
Tel 404-998-2200
Fax 404-992-6357

IQ Software Corporation
3295 River Exchange Dr., Suite 550
Norcross, GA 30092

Founded 1984
Total employees 113
Annual sales $13 million
Industry Computer Software
Growth Openings in past year 15; percentage growth 15%
Contact Rick Chitty, President
Tel 404-446-8880
Fax 404-448-4088

Georgia Marble Co.
1201 Roberts Blvd., Bldg. 100
Kennesaw, GA 30144

Founded 1884
Total employees 712
Annual sales $85.2 million
Industries Advanced Materials, Holding Companies
Growth Openings in past year 310; percentage growth 77%
Contact Glenn Mall, Employee Relations Manager
Tel 404-421-6500
Fax 404-421-6507

Industrial Computer Corp.
5871 Glenridge Dr., Suite 300
Atlanta, GA 30328

Founded 1980
Total employees 65
Annual sales $4.9 million
Industry Computer Software
Growth Openings in past year 20; percentage growth 44%
Contact Frank Wingate, President
Tel 404-255-8336
Fax 404-250-0602

KnowledgeWare, Inc.
3340 Peachtree Rd. Northeast, Suite 1100
Atlanta, GA 30326

Founded 1979
Total employees 790
Annual sales $115.08 million
Industry Computer Software
Growth Openings in past year 168; percentage growth 27%
Contact Francis A. Tarkenton, COB/CEO
Tel 404-231-8575

Loral Information Display Systems
6765 Peachtree Industrial Blvd.
Atlanta, GA 30360

Founded 1978
Total employees 350
Annual sales $37 million
Industries Computer Hardware, Defense,

Heraeus Amersil, Inc.
100 Heraeus Blvd.
Buford, GA 30518

Founded 1916
Total employees 343
Annual sales $65 million
Industries Advanced Materials, Photonics

Input Services, Inc.
1130 North Chase Pkwy., Suite 100
Marietta, GA 30067

Founded 1971
Total employees 200
Industry Computer Hardware

Photonics,
Subassemblies and
Components,
Transportation
Growth Openings in past
year 100; percentage
growth 40%
Contact John Crossland,
President
Tel 404-448-1604
Fax 404-448-9163

MarketWare, Inc.
3100 Medlock Bridge Rd.,
Bldg. 500
Norcross, GA 30071

Founded 1988
Total employees 40
Annual sales $4.6 million
Industry Computer
Software
Growth Openings in past
year 20; percentage
growth 100%
Contact Steven
Kirschner,
President
Tel 404-246-1700
Fax 404-246-1750

Mikart, Inc.
2090 Marietta Blvd.
Atlanta, GA 30318

Founded 1975
Total employees 150
Industry Pharmaceuticals
Growth Openings in past
year 50; percentage
growth 50%
Contact Miguel Arteche,
President
Tel 404-351-4510
Fax 404-350-0432

Murex Corp.
3075 Northwoods Cir.
Norcross, GA 30071

Founded 1984
Total employees 80
Annual sales $8.8 million
Industries Biotechnology,
Medical

Growth Openings in past
year 40; percentage
growth 100%
Contact C. Robert
Cusick,
President/CEO
Tel 404-662-0660
Fax 404-447-4989

**National Diagnostics,
Inc.**
305 Patton Dr. Southwest
Atlanta, GA 30336

Founded 1975
Total employees 75
Annual sales $11 million
Industries Biotechnology,
Chemicals,
Pharmaceuticals, Test
and Measurement
Growth Openings in past
year 25; percentage
growth 50%
Contact Dr. Jeffrey
Mirsky, Ph.D.,
President
Tel 404-699-2121
Fax 404-699-2077

**Norton Construction
Products**
4600 Cantrell Rd., PO
Box 2898
Gainesville, GA 30503

Founded 1978
Total employees 250
Annual sales $26 million
Industries Energy,
Factory Automation
Growth Openings in past
year 50; percentage
growth 25%
Contact Trevor Callender,
Personnel Manager
Tel 404-967-3954
Fax 404-967-4287

Peachtree Software, Inc.
1505 Pavilion Pl.
Norcross, GA 30093

Founded 1985
Total employees 130
Annual sales $19.3 million
Industry Computer
Software

Growth Openings in past
year 20; percentage
growth 18%
Contact Lyle Newkirk,
Controller
Tel 404-564-5700
Fax 404-564-5888

Piedmont Olsen Hensly
3200 Professional Pkwy.,
Suite 200
Atlanta, GA 30339

Founded 1944
Total employees 349
Annual sales $14 million
Industries Environmental,
Manufacturing
Equipment
Growth Openings in past
year 4; percentage
growth 1%
Contact Director of
Personnel,
Tel 404-952-8861
Fax 404-984-1160

**RealCom Office
Communications, Inc.**
2030 Powers Ferry Rd.,
Suite 580
Atlanta, GA 30339

Founded 1989
Total employees 220
Annual sales $39 million
Industries Computer
Software,
Telecommunications
Growth Openings in past
year 43; percentage
growth 24%
Contact Thomas
Thorsen,
Director of Human
Resources
Tel 404-859-1100
Fax 404-859-9277

Sales Technologies, Inc.
3399 Peachtree Rd., Suite
700
Atlanta, GA 30326

Founded 1983
Total employees 600
Annual sales $69 million
Industry Computer
Software

Growth Openings in past year 149; percentage growth 33%
Contact James Bensman, CEO/President
Tel 404-841-4000
Fax 404-841-4115

Select Laboratories, Inc.
1168 Airport Pkwy. Southwest, PO Box 2497
Gainesville, GA 30503

Founded 1971
Total employees 190
Annual sales $16 million
Industry Pharmaceuticals
Growth Openings in past year 15; percentage growth 8%
Contact Dale King, President
Tel 404-536-8787
Fax 404-534-8558

SofNet, Inc.
380 Interstate North Pkwy., Suite 150
Atlanta, GA 30339

Founded 1990
Total employees 45
Industry Computer Software
Growth Openings in past year 27; percentage growth 150%
Contact Patrick Dane, President
Tel 404-984-8088
Fax 404-984-9956

Stockholder Systems, Inc.
4411 East Jones Bridge Rd.
Norcross, GA 30092

Founded 1971
Total employees 310
Annual sales $35 million
Industry Computer Software

Growth Openings in past year 50; percentage growth 19%
Contact Larry A. Dean, President
Tel 404-441-3387
Fax 404-242-9927

System Works, Inc.
1640 Powers Ferry Rd., Bldg. 11
Marietta, GA 30067

Founded 1976
Total employees 125
Annual sales $16 million
Industry Computer Software
Growth Openings in past year 25; percentage growth 25%
Contact David P. Welden, President
Tel 404-952-8444
Fax 404-955-2977

Tensar Corp.
1210 Citizens Pkwy.
Morrow, GA 30260

Founded 1984
Total employees 150
Industry Advanced Materials
Growth Openings in past year 25; percentage growth 20%
Contact Ms. Helen Donnelly, Director of Personnel
Tel 404-968-3255
Fax 404-961-8239

United Energy Services Corp.
1110 Northchase Pkwy.
Marietta, GA 30067

Founded 1981
Total employees 650
Annual sales $70 million
Industry Energy
Growth Openings in past year 135; percentage growth 26%
Contact Ms. Linda Kobel, Human Resources Manager
Tel 404-951-8989
Fax 404-984-9375

W.E. Carson Associates, Inc.
6075 Roswell Rd., Suite 523
Atlanta, GA 30328

Founded 1974
Total employees 90
Annual sales $4.55 million
Industries Computer Hardware, Computer Software
Growth Openings in past year 17; percentage growth 23%
Contact W.E. Carson, President
Tel 404-255-0039
Fax 404-255-0361

Westcorp Software Systems, Inc.
2865 Amwiler Rd., Suite 100
Atlanta, GA 30360

Founded 1981
Total employees 25
Annual sales $3 million
Industry Computer Software
Growth Openings in past year 15; percentage growth 150%
Contact Jim Harsler, CEO/President
Tel 404-448-9709
Fax 404-263-0958

Yokogawa Corp. of America
2 Dart Rd.
Newnan, GA 30265

Founded 1957
Total employees 260
Annual sales $36.5 million
Industries Factory Automation, Subassemblies and Components, Test and Measurement
Growth Openings in past year 34; percentage growth 15%
Contact Tadanori Fukuda, President
Tel 404-253-7000
Fax 404-251-2088

■ **706 Area Code**

Noramco, Inc.
PO Box 800001
Athens, GA 30608

Founded 1981
Total employees 200
Industries Chemicals,
  Medical,
  Pharmaceuticals
Contact Ed Graham,
  President
Tel 706-353-4400
Fax 706-353-3205

Surgimach Corp.
1765 Tobacco Rd., PO
  Box 5669
Augusta, GA 30916

Founded 1979
Total employees 32
Annual sales $3 million
Industries Factory
  Automation,
  Manufacturing
  Equipment, Medical
Growth Openings in past
  year 14; percentage
  growth 77%
Contact Lester Fox,
  President
Tel 706-790-7760
Fax 706-798-2923

■ **912 Area Code**

Intermarine USA
PO Box 3045
Savannah, GA 31402

Founded 1987
Total employees 697
Industry Transportation
Growth Openings in past
  year 245; percentage
  growth 54%
Contact Ted Young,
  Managing Director
Tel 912-234-6579

Hawaii

■ **808 Area Code**

**Pacific Marine and
Supply Co., Ltd.**
PO Box 29816
Honolulu, HI 96820

Founded 1944
Total employees 700
Annual sales $53 million
Industry Holding
  Companies
Growth Openings in past
  year 274; percentage
  growth 64%
Contact Steven Loui,
  President
Tel 808-531-7001
Fax 808-523-7668

Idaho

■ **208 Area Code**

Advanced Input Devices
West 250 Aid Dr.
Coeur D'Alene, ID 83814

Founded 1978
Total employees 240
Annual sales $21 million
Industry Computer
  Hardware
Growth Openings in past
  year 40; percentage
  growth 20%
Contact Les Larsen,
  President
Tel 208-765-8000
Fax 208-772-7613

Electronic Controls Co.
PO Box 7246
Boise, ID 83707

Founded 1973
Total employees 110
Industries Photonics,
  Test and Measurement
Growth Openings in past
  year 25; percentage
  growth 29%
Contact James
  Thompson,
  President
Tel 208-376-0707
Fax 208-376-3410

Scientech, Inc.
1690 International Way
Idaho Falls, ID 83402

Founded 1983
Total employees 275
Industries Energy,
  Environmental,
  Manufacturing
  Equipment
Growth Openings in past
  year 75; percentage
  growth 37%
Contact L.J. Ybarrondo,
  Ph.D.,
  President
Tel 208-523-2077
Fax 208-529-4721

Illinois

■ **217 Area Code**

**Cabot Corp., Cab-O-Sil
Division**
Rte. 36 West, PO Box
  188
Tuscola, IL 61953

Founded 1958
Total employees 298
Annual sales $64 million
Industries Advanced
  Materials, Chemicals
Growth Openings in past
  year 48; percentage
  growth 19%
Contact William Reardon,
  Vice President/General
  Manager
Tel 217-253-3370
Fax 217-253-4334

**Construction
Engineering Research
Laboratories**
2902 Newmark Dr., PO
  Box 9005
Champaign, IL 61826

Founded 1969
Total employees 855
Industries Defense,
  Energy, Environmental

Growth Openings in past
year 71; percentage
growth 9%
Contact Daniel Waldo,
Jr.,
Commander Director
Tel 217-352-6511
Fax 217-373-7222

Growth Openings in past
year 13; percentage
growth 7%
Contact Tom Kobylarek,
President
Tel 217-422-8574
Fax 217-422-1417

Growth Openings in past
year 25; percentage
growth 20%
Contact John Blake,
Human Resources
Manager
Tel 309-853-1002
Fax 309-853-1319

Frasca International, Inc.
906 East Airport Rd.
Urbana, IL 61801

Founded 1958
Total employees 165
Industry Transportation
Growth Openings in past
year 15; percentage
growth 10%
Contact Ms. Karen
Crewell,
Director of Personnel
Tel 217-344-9200
Fax 217-344-9207

Hanson Engineers, Inc.
1525 South 6th St.
Springfield, IL 62703

Founded 1954
Total employees 161
Annual sales $15 million
Industries Advanced
Materials,
Environmental,
Manufacturing
Equipment
Growth Openings in past
year 21; percentage
growth 15%
Contact Leo J.
Dondanville, Jr.,
COB/CEO
Tel 217-788-2450
Fax 217-788-2503

IMI Cash Valve Inc
600 East Wabash St.
Decatur, IL 62525

Founded 1940
Total employees 197
Annual sales $23 million
Industry Subassemblies
and Components

Levi, Ray and Shoup, Inc.
2401 West Monroe St.
Springfield, IL 62704

Founded 1979
Total employees 125
Annual sales $12 million
Industries Computer
Hardware, Computer
Software
Growth Openings in past
year 60; percentage
growth 92%
Contact Roger Ray,
Executive Vice President
Tel 217-793-3800
Fax 217-787-3286

Sierra, Inc.
725 McKinley Ave.
Litchfield, IL 62056

Founded 1924
Total employees 75
Industry Subassemblies
and Components
Growth Openings in past
year 15; percentage
growth 25%
Contact Peter Venter,
General Manager
Tel 217-324-9400
Fax 217-324-2461

■ **309 Area Code**

BOMAG USA
2000 Kentville Rd.
Kewanee, IL 61443

Founded 1880
Total employees 150
Annual sales $250 million
Industry Environmental

Peoria Disposal Co.
4700 North Sterling Ave.
Peoria, IL 61615

Founded 1965
Total employees 300
Annual sales $36 million
Industry Environmental
Growth Openings in past
year 30; percentage
growth 11%
Contact Royal J. Coulter,
President
Tel 309-688-0760
Fax 309-688-0881

■ **312 Area Code**

Alfred Benesch & Co.
205 North Michigan, 24th
Floor
Chicago, IL 60601

Founded 1946
Total employees 165
Annual sales $20 million
Industries Manufacturing
Equipment,
Telecommunications
Growth Openings in past
year 19; percentage
growth 13%
Contact Michael
Goodkind,
President
Tel 312-565-0450
Fax 312-565-2497

Carnow, Conibear and Associates, Ltd.
333 West Wacker Dr.,
Suite 1400
Chicago, IL 60606

Founded 1975
Total employees 85
Annual sales $9.3 million
Industry Medical

Growth Openings in past year 15; percentage growth 21%
Contact Dr. Shirley Conibear, Ph.D., President
Tel 312-782-4486
Fax 312-782-5145

Growth Openings in past year 20; percentage growth 15%
Contact Ms. Susan Dunne, Human Resources Manager
Tel 312-266-4444
Fax 312-266-4473

Growth Openings in past year 12; percentage growth 35%
Contact Fred Wood, President/CEO
Tel 312-726-7587
Fax 312-726-1607

CCC Information Services Inc.
640 North LaSalle St., Suite 640
Chicago, IL 60610

Founded 1980
Total employees 700
Annual sales $98 million
Industries Computer Hardware, Computer Software
Growth Openings in past year 249; percentage growth 55%
Contact Ms. Lori Kodrich, Director of Human Resources
Tel 312-787-2640
Fax 312-787-6581

C.P. Hall Co.
7300 South Central Ave.
Chicago, IL 60638

Founded 1919
Total employees 225
Industry Advanced Materials
Growth Openings in past year 25; percentage growth 12%
Contact George Vincent, President
Tel 312-767-4600
Fax 708-458-0428

Datalogics, Inc.
441 West Huron St.
Chicago, IL 60610

Founded 1967
Total employees 150
Industry Computer Software

Homaco, Inc.
1875 West Fullerton Ave.
Chicago, IL 60614

Founded 1968
Total employees 140
Annual sales $11 million
Industry Subassemblies and Components
Growth Openings in past year 20; percentage growth 16%
Contact Bruce D. Holcomb, President
Tel 312-384-5575
Fax 312-384-6080

Information Resources, Inc.
150 North Clinton St.
Chicago, IL 60661

Founded 1986
Total employees 350
Annual sales $65 million
Industries Computer Software, Holding Companies
Growth Openings in past year 49; percentage growth 16%
Contact Jeffrey P. Stamen, President
Tel 312-726-1221

Information Retrieval Companies, Inc.
312 West Randolph St., Suite 610
Chicago, IL 60606

Founded 1983
Total employees 46
Industry Computer Software

Internet Systems Corp.
180 North Stetson, 42nd Floor
Chicago, IL 60601

Founded 1981
Total employees 350
Annual sales $40 million
Industry Computer Software
Growth Openings in past year 59; percentage growth 20%
Contact W. Ron Mahoney, President/CEO
Tel 312-540-0100
Fax 312-540-0118

Mobius Management Systems, Inc.
600 West Fulton St.
Chicago, IL 60661

Founded 1981
Total employees 85
Annual sales $10 million
Industry Computer Software
Growth Openings in past year 20; percentage growth 30%
Contact Joseph Albracht, Executive Vice President
Tel 312-466-4660
Fax 312-466-4680

PRC Environmental Management, Inc.
233 North Michigan Ave., Suite 1620
Chicago, IL 60601

Founded 1982
Total employees 800
Annual sales $100 million
Industry Environmental

Growth Openings in past year 249; percentage growth 45%
Contact Thomas Brisbin, President
Tel 312-856-8700
Fax 312-938-0118

SPSS, Inc.
444 North Michigan Ave., Suite 3000
Chicago, IL 60611

Founded 1975
Total employees 250
Annual sales $36 million
Industry Computer Software
Growth Openings in past year 40; percentage growth 19%
Contact Jack Noonan, President/CEO
Tel 312-329-2400
Fax 312-329-3668

Superior Graphite Co.
120 South Riverside Plaza
Chicago, IL 60606

Founded 1917
Total employees 275
Annual sales $40 million
Industry Advanced Materials
Growth Openings in past year 44; percentage growth 19%
Contact Peter Carney, President
Tel 312-559-2999
Fax 312-559-9064

Zenith Controls, Inc.
830 West 40th St.
Chicago, IL 60609

Founded 1923
Total employees 220
Industries Energy, Subassemblies and Components
Growth Openings in past year 20; percentage growth 10%
Contact Arthur Coren, President
Tel 312-247-6400
Fax 312-247-7805

■ **618 Area Code**

Burlington Environmental, Inc.
210 West Sand Bank Rd.
Columbia, IL 62236

Founded 1975
Total employees 750
Annual sales $125 million
Industry Environmental
Growth Openings in past year 29; percentage growth 4%
Contact John Craig, President
Tel 618-281-7173
Fax 618-281-5120

Marsh Co., Marsh Cornerstone Systems Division
707 East B St.
Belleville, IL 62221

Founded 1983
Total employees 25
Industries Computer Hardware, Computer Software
Growth Openings in past year 13; percentage growth 108%
Contact David Bequette, Director
Tel 618-234-1122
Fax 618-234-1529

■ **708 Area Code**

ACCO USA
770 South Acco Plaza
Wheeling, IL 60090

Founded 1903
Total employees 600
Annual sales $92 million
Industries Computer Hardware, Subassemblies and Components

Growth Openings in past year 248; percentage growth 70%
Contact Ms. Kathy Wolf, VP of Human Resources
Tel 708-541-9500
Fax 800-962-0576

Alltech Associates, Inc.
2051 Waukegan Rd.
Deerfield, IL 60015

Founded 1971
Total employees 140
Annual sales $16 million
Industries Subassemblies and Components, Test and Measurement
Growth Openings in past year 50; percentage growth 55%
Contact Ms. Joanne Topcik, Personnel Manager
Tel 708-948-8600
Fax 708-948-1078

American Colloid Co.
1500 West Shure Dr.
Arlington Heights, IL 60004

Founded 1924
Total employees 879
Annual sales $149 million
Industry Advanced Materials
Growth Openings in past year 102; percentage growth 13%
Contact John Hughes, President/CEO
Tel 708-392-4600
Fax 708-506-6199

Anatol Manufacturing, Inc.
1060 High St.
Mundelein, IL 60060

Founded 1982
Total employees 75
Annual sales $5 million
Industry Factory Automation

Growth Openings in past year 15; percentage growth 25%
Contact Anatol Topolewski, President
Tel 708-949-0330
Fax 708-949-2901

Apollo Colors, Inc.
3000 Dundee Rd., Suite 415
Northbrook, IL 60062

Founded 1969
Total employees 170
Annual sales $40 million
Industry Chemicals
Growth Openings in past year 20; percentage growth 13%
Contact Donald Zalewa, Manager of Human Resources
Tel 708-564-9190
Fax 708-564-9296

Applied Systems, Inc.
2500 Bond St.
University Park, IL 60466

Founded 1980
Total employees 500
Annual sales $45 million
Industry Computer Software
Growth Openings in past year 100; percentage growth 25%
Contact Bob Eustace, COB/CEO
Tel 708-534-5575
Fax 708-534-1216

ARI Technologies, Inc.
600 North First Bank Dr.
Palatine, IL 60067

Founded 1970
Total employees 150
Annual sales $20 million
Industries Environmental, Manufacturing Equipment

Growth Openings in past year 15; percentage growth 11%
Contact Ms. Robyn Silvey, Accounting and Personnel Manager
Tel 708-359-7810
Fax 708-359-3700

ASIC Designs, Inc.
1230 East Diehl Rd., Suite 401
Naperville, IL 60563

Founded 1987
Total employees 33
Industries Manufacturing Equipment, Subassemblies and Components
Growth Openings in past year 18; percentage growth 120%
Contact Robert Patti, President/CEO
Tel 708-505-0404
Fax 708-505-9292

BACG, Inc.
1301 West 22nd St.
Oak Brook, IL 60521

Founded 1988
Total employees 150
Annual sales $17 million
Industry Computer Software
Growth Openings in past year 20; percentage growth 15%
Contact David Gibson, President
Tel 708-571-1616
Fax 708-571-2193

Boots Pharmaceutical, Inc.
300 Tri State International Ctr., Suite 200
Lincolnshire, IL 60069

Founded 1986
Total employees 700
Annual sales $96 million
Industry Pharmaceuticals

Growth Openings in past year 197; percentage growth 39%
Contact Carter H. Eckert, President
Tel 708-405-7400
Fax 708-405-7505

Bran and Luebbe, Inc.
1025 Busch Pkwy.
Buffalo Grove, IL 60089

Founded 1967
Total employees 100
Annual sales $15 million
Industries Subassemblies and Components, Test and Measurement
Growth Openings in past year 25; percentage growth 33%
Contact John Gray, President
Tel 708-520-0700
Fax 708-520-0855

Brunswick Corp., Intellitec Division
131 Eisenhower Ln.
Lombard, IL 60148

Founded 1976
Total employees 40
Annual sales $3 million
Industries Manufacturing Equipment, Subassemblies and Components, Transportation
Growth Openings in past year 15; percentage growth 60%
Contact William H. Slavik, General Manager
Tel 708-268-0010
Fax 708-916-7890

Capsonic Group, Inc.
Fleetwood and Second Sts.
Elgin, IL 60123

Founded 1968
Total employees 185
Annual sales $24 million
Industry Subassemblies and Components

Growth Openings in past year 25; percentage growth 15%
Contact Jim Liautaud, CEO/COB
Tel 708-888-7300
Fax 708-888-7514

Cincinnati Bell Information Systems, Inc., Mobile Division
2 Pierce Pl., Suite 200
Itasca, IL 60143

Founded 1983
Total employees 375
Annual sales $43 million
Industries Computer Hardware, Computer Software
Growth Openings in past year 75; percentage growth 25%
Contact Sheldon Horing, President
Tel 708-775-1700
Fax 708-775-8687

Clean Air Engineering
500 West Wood St.
Palatine, IL 60067

Founded 1973
Total employees 220
Annual sales $23 million
Industry Environmental
Growth Openings in past year 44; percentage growth 25%
Contact William Walker, President
Tel 708-991-3300
Fax 708-991-3385

Continental X-Ray Corp.
2000 South 25th Ave.
Broadview, IL 60153

Founded 1934
Total employees 175
Annual sales $20 million
Industry Medical
Growth Openings in past year 25; percentage growth 16%
Contact Patrick T. Fitzgerald, President/CEO
Tel 708-345-3050
Fax 708-345-1227

Conversational Voice Technologies Corp.
4205 Grove Ave.
Gurnee, IL 60031

Founded 1968
Total employees 50
Industry Telecommunications
Growth Openings in past year 20; percentage growth 66%
Contact Ms. Laura Hinze, President
Tel 708-249-5560

DAI Technologies, Inc.
5100 Academy Dr.
Lisle, IL 60532

Founded 1984
Total employees 65
Industry Test and Measurement
Growth Openings in past year 13; percentage growth 25%
Contact Alan R. Dohner, President
Tel 708-971-2442
Fax 708-971-2642

Danly-Komatsu L.P.
2115 South 54th Ave.
Cicero, IL 60650

Founded 1922
Total employees 631
Annual sales $50 million
Industry Factory Automation
Growth Openings in past year 97; percentage growth 18%
Contact Ronald Cantrell, President
Tel 708-863-2800
Fax 708-863-3049

Dauphin Technology, Inc.
1125 East Saint Charles Rd.
Lombard, IL 60148

Founded 1988
Total employees 45
Annual sales $2 million
Industry Computer Hardware

Growth Openings in past year 25; percentage growth 125%
Contact Alan Yong, President
Tel 708-627-4004
Fax 708-627-7618

Desktop Sales, Inc.
3210 Doolittle
Northbrook, IL 60062

Founded 1988
Total employees 100
Annual sales $16 million
Industry Computer Hardware
Growth Openings in past year 30; percentage growth 42%
Contact Allen Sutker, President
Tel 708-272-9695
Fax 708-272-8244

Dexter Corp., Dexter Packaging Products Division
East Water St.
Waukegan, IL 60085

Founded 1767
Total employees 478
Annual sales $132 million
Industry Advanced Materials
Growth Openings in past year 122; percentage growth 34%
Contact John N. Nuebel, Manager of Personnel
Tel 708-623-4200
Fax 708-623-4295

Enterprise Systems, Inc.
1400 South Wolf Rd., Suite 500
Wheeling, IL 60090

Founded 1981
Total employees 192
Annual sales $16 million
Industry Computer Software

Growth Openings in past year 32; percentage growth 20%
Contact Thomas Pirelli, Chief Executive Officer
Tel 708-537-4800
Fax 708-537-4866

Growth Openings in past year 20; percentage growth 30%
Contact Martin Katz, VP of Operations
Tel 708-948-7180
Fax 708-948-9425

Growth Openings in past year 25; percentage growth 12%
Contact Ms. Virginia Cangelosi, Director of Human Resources
Tel 708-450-2600
Fax 708-450-0943

Gemma International, Inc.
540 Quail Ridge Dr.
Westmont, IL 60559

Founded 1988
Total employees 30
Industry Computer Software
Growth Openings in past year 12; percentage growth 66%
Contact Don Nelson, President/Managing Director
Tel 708-850-4100
Fax 708-850-6814

ICOM Simulations, Inc.
648 South Wheeling Rd.
Wheeling, IL 60090

Founded 1985
Total employees 52
Industry Computer Software
Growth Openings in past year 12; percentage growth 30%
Contact Dennis Defensor, President/CEO
Tel 708-520-4440
Fax 708-459-7456

Lakeview Technology, Inc.
2301 West 22nd St., Suite 206
Oak Brook, IL 60521

Founded 1990
Total employees 53
Industry Computer Software
Growth Openings in past year 15; percentage growth 39%
Contact William Merchantz, President
Tel 708-573-0440
Fax 708-573-0015

Greenbrier & Russel, Inc.
1450 East American Ln.
Schaumburg, IL 60173

Founded 1984
Total employees 200
Industry Computer Software
Growth Openings in past year 60; percentage growth 42%
Contact Nick Blake, VP of Operations
Tel 708-706-4000
Fax 708-706-4020

Kalmus and Associates, Inc.
2424 South 25th Ave.
Broadview, IL 60153

Founded 1937
Total employees 300
Industry Subassemblies and Components
Growth Openings in past year 25; percentage growth 9%
Contact Henry J. Kalmus, Jr., President/CEO
Tel 708-343-7004
Fax 708-343-7016

Lindgren RF Enclosures
400 High Grove Blvd.
Glendale Heights, IL 60139

Founded 1952
Total employees 160
Annual sales $19 million
Industries Factory Automation, Holding Companies, Test and Measurement
Growth Openings in past year 60; percentage growth 60%
Contact Ms. Joyce Curran, Treasurer
Tel 708-307-7200
Fax 708-307-7571

Herbert Friedman & Associates, Inc.
108 Wilmot Rd.
Deerfield, IL 60015

Founded 1971
Total employees 85
Annual sales $10 million
Industry Computer Software

Lab-Line Instruments, Inc.
15th and Bloomingdale Ave., Lab-Line Plaza
Melrose Park, IL 60160

Founded 1952
Total employees 225
Industry Test and Measurement

LoDan Electronics, Inc.
220 West Campus Dr., Suite A
Arlington Heights, IL 60004

Founded 1967
Total employees 190
Industry Subassemblies and Components

Growth Openings in past year 40; percentage growth 26%
Contact Ms. Danielle Rossini, Human Resources Manager
Tel 708-398-5311
Fax 708-398-5340

Growth Openings in past year 15; percentage growth 30%
Contact John B. Kennedy, President
Tel 708-491-3885
Fax 708-491-0682

Growth Openings in past year 45; percentage growth 42%
Contact Ms. Jane Burke, President
Tel 708-866-0150
Fax 708-866-0178

Nunc, Inc.
2000 North Aurora Rd.
Naperville, IL 60563

Founded 1987
Total employees 169
Annual sales $16 million
Industries Biotechnology, Test and Measurement
Growth Openings in past year 29; percentage growth 20%
Contact Verner B. Andersen, President
Tel 708-983-5700
Fax 708-416-2519

Magneco/Metrel, Inc.
223 Interstate Rd.
Addison, IL 60101

Founded 1978
Total employees 220
Annual sales $32 million
Industry Advanced Materials
Growth Openings in past year 20; percentage growth 10%
Contact Charles W. Connors, Chief Executive Officer
Tel 708-543-6660
Fax 708-543-1479

Material Sciences Corp.
2300 East Pratt Blvd.
Elk Grove Village, IL 60007

Founded 1971
Total employees 670
Annual sales $160 million
Industry Holding Companies
Growth Openings in past year 26; percentage growth 4%
Contact Frank Lazowski, VP of Human Resources and Administration
Tel 708-439-8270
Fax 708-439-0737

Otto Engineering, Inc.
2 East Main St.
Carpentersville, IL 60110

Founded 1962
Total employees 200
Annual sales $19 million
Industry Holding Companies
Growth Openings in past year 40; percentage growth 25%
Contact Jack Roeser, President
Tel 708-428-7171
Fax 708-428-1956

Magnetrol International, Inc.
5300 Belmont Rd.
Downers Grove, IL 60515

Founded 1932
Total employees 250
Annual sales $33 million
Industry Test and Measurement
Growth Openings in past year 21; percentage growth 9%
Contact Ms. Mary Saranczak, Personnel Manager
Tel 708-969-4000
Fax 708-969-9489

Monolithic Sensors, Inc.
2800 West Golf Rd.
Rolling Meadows, IL 60008

Founded 1988
Total employees 60
Annual sales $7.1 million
Industry Test and Measurement
Growth Openings in past year 23; percentage growth 62%
Contact Warren Graber, President
Tel 708-437-8090
Fax 708-437-8144

Patrick Engineering, Inc.
346 Taft Ave.
Glen Ellyn, IL 60137

Founded 1979
Total employees 100
Annual sales $7 million
Industry Environmental
Growth Openings in past year 30; percentage growth 42%
Contact Daniel P. Dietzler, President
Tel 708-858-7050
Fax 708-858-6700

Marketing Information Systems, Inc.
1840 Oak Ave.
Evanston, IL 60201

Founded 1981
Total employees 65
Industry Computer Software

NOTIS Systems, Inc.
1007 Church St., 2nd Fl.
Evanston, IL 60201

Founded 1987
Total employees 150
Annual sales $14 million
Industry Computer Software

Polyfoam Packers Corp.
2320 South Foster Ave.
Wheeling, IL 60090

Founded 1946
Total employees 200
Annual sales $21 million
Industry Factory
Automation
Growth Openings in past
year 50; percentage
growth 33%
Contact T. Osterman,
Personnel Manager
Tel 708-398-0110
Fax 708-398-0653

Pre Finish Metals Incorporated
2300 East Pratt Blvd.
Elk Grove Village, IL
60007

Founded 1971
Total employees 660
Annual sales $155 million
Industry Advanced
Materials
Growth Openings in past
year 26; percentage
growth 4%
Contact Frank Lazowski,
VP of Human Resources
Tel 708-439-2210

RainSoft Water Conditioning Co.
2080 Lunt Ave.
Elk Grove Village, IL
60007

Founded 1978
Total employees 120
Industry Environmental
Growth Openings in past
year 20; percentage
growth 20%
Contact John Grayson,
President
Tel 708-437-9400
Fax 708-437-1594

Reichel & Drews, Inc.
1025 West Thorndale
Ave.
Itasca, IL 60143

Founded 1985
Total employees 90
Annual sales $9.1 million

Industry Holding
Companies
Growth Openings in past
year 20; percentage
growth 28%
Contact Curtis Maas,
President
Tel 708-773-2500
Fax 708-773-3414

Richardson Electronics Ltd.
40W267 Keslinger Rd.
LaFox, IL 60147

Founded 1947
Total employees 681
Annual sales $161 million
Industry Subassemblies
and Components
Growth Openings in past
year 33; percentage
growth 5%
Contact Joe Grill,
VP of Human Resources
Tel 708-208-2200
Fax 708-208-2550

Sakata Inx U.S.A. Corp., Computer Products Division
651 Bonnie Ln.
Elk Grove Village, IL
60007

Founded 1970
Total employees 80
Annual sales $40 million
Industry Subassemblies
and Components
Growth Openings in past
year 40; percentage
growth 100%
Contact Ken Morita,
President
Tel 708-593-3211
Fax 708-364-5290

Seaquist Dispensing
1160 North Silver Lake
Rd.
Cary, IL 60013

Founded 1947
Total employees 350
Industry Factory
Automation

Growth Openings in past
year 49; percentage
growth 16%
Contact James Reed,
President
Tel 708-639-2124
Fax 708-639-2142

SoloPak Pharmaceuticals, Inc.
1845 Tonne Rd.
Elk Grove Village, IL
60007

Founded 1970
Total employees 300
Industries Medical,
Pharmaceuticals
Growth Openings in past
year 20; percentage
growth 7%
Contact Dave Dvorak,
Director of Human
Resources
Tel 708-806-0080
Fax 708-806-0087

SunGard Investment Systems, Inc.
11 Salt Creek Ln.
Hinsdale, IL 60521

Founded 1967
Total employees 100
Annual sales $6.9 million
Industry Computer
Software
Growth Openings in past
year 40; percentage
growth 66%
Contact Phillip Dowd,
President
Tel 708-920-3100
Fax 708-920-8038

Surya Electronics, Inc.
600 Windy Point Dr.
Glendale Heights, IL
60139

Founded 1983
Total employees 65
Industries Computer
Software, Manufacturing
Equipment,
Subassemblies and
Components

Growth Openings in past year 15; percentage growth 30%
Contact Pravin Shah, President
Tel 708-858-8000
Fax 708-858-0103

Growth Openings in past year 40; percentage growth 100%
Contact Ms. Lorraine Wilkins, Human Resources Manager
Tel 708-297-0070
Fax 708-699-7864

Growth Openings in past year 33; percentage growth 97%
Contact Dennis Wisnosky, President
Tel 708-357-3000
Fax 708-357-3059

Technologia Systems, Ltd.
8707 Skokie Blvd.
Skokie, IL 60076

Founded 1987
Total employees 44
Annual sales $15 million
Industry Holding Companies
Growth Openings in past year 13; percentage growth 41%
Contact Stanley M. Abramson, Chief Executive Officer
Tel 708-673-8488
Fax 708-673-9244

Timeworks, Inc.
625 Academy Dr.
Northbrook, IL 60062

Founded 1982
Total employees 75
Annual sales $8.7 million
Industry Computer Software
Growth Openings in past year 15; percentage growth 25%
Contact Mark L. Goldberg, President
Tel 708-559-1300
Fax 708-559-1360

Toko America, Inc.
1250 Feehanville Dr.
Mount Prospect, IL 60056

Founded 1965
Total employees 80
Annual sales $7.8 million
Industry Subassemblies and Components

Unitech Systems, Inc.
1240 East Diehl Rd.
Naperville, IL 60563

Founded 1982
Total employees 90
Annual sales $10 million
Industry Computer Software
Growth Openings in past year 22; percentage growth 32%
Contact Madhavan K. Nayer, President
Tel 708-505-1800
Fax 708-505-1812

U.S. Robotics, Inc.
8100 North McCormick Blvd.
Skokie, IL 60076

Founded 1976
Total employees 440
Annual sales $112.43 million
Industries Computer Software, Telecommunications
Growth Openings in past year 37; percentage growth 9%
Contact Ms. Elizabeth Ryan, VP of Human Resources
Tel 708-982-5010
Fax 708-982-5235

Wizdom Systems, Inc.
1300 Iroquois Dr.
Naperville, IL 60563

Founded 1986
Total employees 67
Annual sales $5 million
Industry Holding Companies

Woodhead Industries, Inc.
3411 Woodhead Dr.
Northbrook, IL 60062

Founded 1922
Total employees 816
Annual sales $73.5 million
Industry Holding Companies
Growth Openings in past year 24; percentage growth 3%
Contact Robert Moulton, VP of Human Resources
Tel 708-272-8181

Zebra Technologies Corp.
333 Corporate Woods Pkwy.
Vernon Hills, IL 60061

Founded 1969
Total employees 215
Annual sales $45 million
Industry Computer Hardware
Growth Openings in past year 35; percentage growth 19%
Contact Walter Newborn, Personnel Manager
Tel 708-634-6700
Fax 708-913-8766

■ **815 Area Code**

Barrett Industrial Trucks, Inc.
240 North Prospect St.
Marengo, IL 60152

Founded 1914
Total employees 400
Industries Factory Automation, Holding Companies

Growth Openings in past year 100; percentage growth 33%
Contact Ms. Shirley Kennedy, Personnel Manager
Tel 815-568-6525
Fax 815-568-8340

Climco Coils Co.
400 Oakwood
Morrison, IL 61270

Founded 1950
Total employees 115
Industries Energy, Subassemblies and Components
Growth Openings in past year 20; percentage growth 21%
Contact Jake Beel, Plant Manager
Tel 815-772-2107
Fax 815-772-2195

Coltec Industries Inc, Fairbanks Morse Engine Accessories Operation
6402 Rockton Rd.
Roscoe, IL 61073

Founded 1964
Total employees 85
Industry Subassemblies and Components
Growth Openings in past year 15; percentage growth 21%
Contact Ms. Lorrie Kalke, Personnel Administrator
Tel 815-389-3660
Fax 815-389-1770

Complete Industrial Enterprises, Inc.
1220 Wenzel Rd.
Peru, IL 61354

Founded 1962
Total employees 70
Annual sales $11 million
Industry Holding Companies

Growth Openings in past year 12; percentage growth 20%
Contact Ms. Darlene Krueger, Secretary
Tel 815-224-1510
Fax 815-224-3348

Delavan Process Instrumentation
6402 Rockton Rd.
Roscoe, IL 61073

Founded 1942
Total employees 70
Annual sales $3 million
Industry Test and Measurement
Contact Jim Suchomel, General Manager
Tel 815-389-4915
Fax 815-389-1770

Filtertek, Inc.
11411 Price Rd., PO Box 310
Hebron, IL 60034

Founded 1966
Total employees 800
Annual sales $54 million
Industry Subassemblies and Components
Growth Openings in past year 16; percentage growth 2%
Contact Ms. Jean Wilke, Personnel Manager
Tel 815-648-2416
Fax 815-648-2929

Micro Solutions Computer Products, Inc.
132 West Lincoln Hwy.
De Kalb, IL 60115

Founded 1980
Total employees 50
Industry Computer Hardware
Growth Openings in past year 15; percentage growth 42%
Contact Ms. Debby Armstrong, Marketing Manager
Tel 815-756-3421
Fax 815-756-2928

POWERCORE, Inc.
One Diversatech Dr.
Manteno, IL 60950

Founded 1989
Total employees 50
Industry Computer Software
Growth Openings in past year 25; percentage growth 100%
Contact Richard Juricic, President/CEO
Tel 815-468-3737
Fax 815-468-3867

Indiana

■ **219 Area Code**

Auburn Foundry, Inc.
635 West 11th St.
Auburn, IN 46706

Founded 1911
Total employees 450
Industry Advanced Materials
Growth Openings in past year 69; percentage growth 18%
Contact Walt Bienz, VP of Benefits
Tel 219-925-0900
Fax 219-925-5137

Automatic Technologies Plastics, Inc.
3603 Progress Dr., PO Box 3677
South Bend, IN 46628

Founded 1968
Total employees 496
Annual sales $53 million
Industries Factory Automation, Manufacturing Equipment
Growth Openings in past year 46; percentage growth 10%
Contact Ms. Nancy McKee, Director of Human Resources
Tel 219-289-2404
Fax 219-289-3247

BRC Rubber Group, Inc.
PO Box 227
Churubusco, IN 46723

Founded 1971
Total employees 840
Annual sales $91 million
Industry Manufacturing
Equipment
Growth Openings in past
year 40; percentage
growth 5%
Contact Charles V.
Chaffee,
President
Tel 219-693-2171
Fax 219-693-6511

Crowe Chizek and Co.
330 East Jefferson Blvd.,
PO Box 7
South Bend, IN 46624

Founded 1942
Total employees 600
Annual sales $69 million
Industry Computer
Software
Growth Openings in past
year 100; percentage
growth 20%
Contact Ron Cohen,
Managing Partner
Tel 219-232-3992
Fax 219-236-8692

Crown International, Inc.
1718 West Mishawaka
Rd.
Elkhart, IN 46517

Founded 1955
Total employees 580
Annual sales $76 million
Industry Holding
Companies
Growth Openings in past
year 53; percentage
growth 10%
Contact Clyde Moore,
President
Tel 219-294-8000
Fax 219-294-8329

Crown International, Inc., Fabcom Division
1718 West Mishawaka
Rd.
Elkhart, IN 46517

Founded 1991
Total employees 180
Annual sales $9.5 million
Industries Advanced
Materials, Manufacturing
Equipment
Growth Openings in past
year 30; percentage
growth 20%
Contact Steve Peer,
Division Manager
Tel 219-294-8000
Fax 219-294-8329

Crown International, Inc., Techron Division
1718 West Mishawaka
Rd.
Elkhart, IN 46517

Founded 1982
Total employees 100
Annual sales $13 million
Industry
Telecommunications
Growth Openings in past
year 30; percentage
growth 42%
Contact Don Eger,
Division Manager
Tel 219-294-8300
Fax 219-294-8329

Dwyer Instruments, Inc.
PO Box 373
Michigan City, IN 46360

Founded 1932
Total employees 800
Annual sales $60 million
Industries Holding
Companies,
Subassemblies and
Components, Test and
Measurement
Growth Openings in past
year 199; percentage
growth 33%
Contact Gregg Miller,
Director of Industrial
Relations
Tel 219-879-8000
Fax 219-872-9057

Eaglebrook, Inc.
1150 Junction Ave.
Schererville, IN 46375

Founded 1968
Total employees 200
Industries Advanced
Materials, Chemicals,
Holding Companies
Growth Openings in past
year 50; percentage
growth 33%
Contact Ron Tenny,
President
Tel 219-322-2560
Fax 219-322-8533

Huntington Laboratories, Inc.
970 East Tipton St.
Huntington, IN 46750

Founded 1919
Total employees 450
Annual sales $97 million
Industry Chemicals
Growth Openings in past
year 30; percentage
growth 7%
Contact Bob Smith,
Director of Human
Resources
Tel 219-356-8100
Fax 219-356-6485

PHD, Inc.
PO Box 9070
Fort Wayne, IN 46899

Founded 1957
Total employees 215
Annual sales $27 million
Industries Factory
Automation,
Subassemblies and
Components, Test and
Measurement
Growth Openings in past
year 15; percentage
growth 7%
Contact Ms. Donna
Erenberg,
Personnel Manager
Tel 219-747-6151
Fax 219-747-6754

Indiana

■ 317 Area Code

Bacompt Systems, Inc.
12742 Hamilton Crossing Blvd.
Carmel, IN 46032

Founded 1979
Total employees 40
Annual sales $4 million
Industry Computer Hardware
Growth Openings in past year 15; percentage growth 60%
Contact Paul Ashworth, Executive Vice President
Tel 317-574-7474
Fax 317-574-7475

Boehringer Mannheim Corp., Biochemical Products Division
9115 Hague Rd., PO Box 50414
Indianapolis, IN 46250

Founded 1973
Total employees 250
Annual sales $24 million
Industry Biotechnology
Growth Openings in past year 120; percentage growth 92%
Contact Philip L. DeLong, President
Tel 317-849-9350
Fax 317-576-7317

Dome Software Corp.
655 West Carmel Dr., Suite 151
Carmel, IN 46032

Founded 1981
Total employees 40
Industries Computer Hardware, Computer Software
Growth Openings in past year 22; percentage growth 122%
Contact Dr. Robert D. Hogan, Jr., President
Tel 317-573-8100
Fax 317-573-8109

Endress & Hauser, Inc.
PO Box 246-1
Greenwood, IN 46142

Founded 1970
Total employees 200
Annual sales $23 million
Industries Holding Companies, Test and Measurement
Growth Openings in past year 40; percentage growth 25%
Contact Ms. Patty Harmon, Personnel Manager
Tel 317-535-7138
Fax 317-535-8498

General Devices Co., Inc.
1410 South Post Rd., PO Box 39100
Indianapolis, IN 46239

Founded 1953
Total employees 276
Industries Computer Hardware, Manufacturing Equipment
Growth Openings in past year 26; percentage growth 10%
Contact Maxwell S. Fall, President
Tel 317-897-7000
Fax 317-898-2917

Industrial Dielectrics, Inc.
PO Box 357
Noblesville, IN 46060

Founded 1966
Total employees 200
Annual sales $25 million
Industries Advanced Materials, Manufacturing Equipment
Growth Openings in past year 30; percentage growth 17%
Contact Jon Coleman, Personnel Manager
Tel 317-773-1766
Fax 317-773-3877

Master Software Corp.
8604 Allisonville Rd., Suite 309
Indianapolis, IN 46250

Founded 1983
Total employees 90
Annual sales $5 million
Industry Computer Software
Growth Openings in past year 20; percentage growth 28%
Contact Eugene Schulstad, President
Tel 317-842-7020
Fax 317-576-6110

Muncie Power Products, Inc.
PO Box 548
Muncie, IN 47308

Founded 1934
Total employees 170
Annual sales $16 million
Industries Energy, Subassemblies and Components
Growth Openings in past year 97; percentage growth 132%
Contact Joseph Wilson, President
Tel 317-284-7721
Fax 317-284-6991

Radio Materials Corp.
East Park Ave., PO Box 399
Attica, IN 47918

Founded 1948
Total employees 64
Industry Subassemblies and Components
Growth Openings in past year 20; percentage growth 45%
Contact Joseph Riley, Jr., President
Tel 317-762-2491
Fax 317-762-6814

Rexnord Corp., Roller Chain Operation
220 South Belmont Ave.,
  PO Box 346
Indianapolis, IN 46206

Founded 1871
Total employees 350
Annual sales $34 million
Industries Factory
  Automation,
  Subassemblies and
  Components
Growth Openings in past
  year 120; percentage
  growth 52%
Contact Mark Sabatino,
  Personnel Manager
  Tel 317-267-2200
  Fax 317-267-2248

■ **812 Area Code**

Cook, Inc.
PO Box 489
Bloomington, IN 47402

Founded 1963
Total employees 820
Annual sales $90 million
Industry Holding
  Companies
Growth Openings in past
  year 68; percentage
  growth 9%
Contact Ms. Phyllis
  McCullough,
  President
  Tel 812-339-2235
  Fax 812-339-7316

National Laboratories, Inc.
3210 Claremont Ave.
Evansville, IN 47712

Founded 1969
Total employees 32
Industries Biotechnology,
  Chemicals,
  Environmental
Growth Openings in past
  year 12; percentage
  growth 60%
Contact Ms. Betty Shultz,
  President
  Tel 812-464-9000
  Fax 812-465-5746

Sherry Laboratories
PO Box 2847
Muncie, IN 47307

Founded 1947
Total employees 55
Annual sales $4.3 million
Industries Advanced
  Materials, Environmental
Growth Openings in past
  year 14; percentage
  growth 34%
Contact Mel Barnell,
  President
  Tel 317-747-9000
  Fax 317-747-0228

Digital Audio Disc Corp.
1800 North Fruitridge Ave.
Terre Haute, IN 47804

Founded 1983
Total employees 800
Annual sales $75 million
Industries Computer
  Hardware,
  Telecommunications
Growth Openings in past
  year 175; percentage
  growth 28%
Contact Warren
  Macaroni,
  VP of Human Resources
  Tel 812-462-8100
  Fax 812-466-9125

Samtec, Inc.
PO Box 1147
New Albany, IN 47151

Founded 1975
Total employees 250
Annual sales $45 million
Industry Subassemblies
  and Components
Growth Openings in past
  year 50; percentage
  growth 25%
Contact Sam Shine,
  President
  Tel 812-944-6733
  Fax 812-948-5047

Software Artistry, Inc.
3500 Depauw Blvd., Suite
  1100
Indianapolis, IN 46268

Founded 1988
Total employees 50
Annual sales $5 million
Industry Computer
  Software
Growth Openings in past
  year 30; percentage
  growth 150%
Contact Don Brown,
  Chief Executive Officer
  Tel 317-876-3042
  Fax 317-876-3258

Grote Industries, Inc.
PO Box 1550
Madison, IN 47250

Founded 1901
Total employees 800
Industry Transportation
Growth Openings in past
  year 99; percentage
  growth 14%
Contact Bruce
  Gruemmer,
  VP of Human Resources
  Tel 812-273-2121
  Fax 812-265-8440

Thermwood Corp.
Old Buffaloville Rd.
Dale, IN 47523

Founded 1975
Total employees 150
Annual sales $12.0 million
Industry Holding
  Companies
Growth Openings in past
  year 45; percentage
  growth 42%
Contact Ken Susnajara,
  President
  Tel 812-937-4476
  Fax 812-937-2956

Iowa

■ **319 Area Code**

Howard R. Green Co.
4250 Glass Rd.
Northeast, PO Box 9009
Cedar Rapids, IA 52409

Founded 1913
Total employees 140
Annual sales $6 million
Industries Advanced
  Materials,
  Environmental, Factory
  Automation, Holding
  Companies,
  Manufacturing
  Equipment,
  Subassemblies and
  Components
Growth Openings in past
  year 14; percentage
  growth 11%
Contact Dennis M.
  Schrag,
  Director of Marketing/
  Manager of Human R
Tel 319-395-7805
Fax 319-395-9410

Norand Corp.
550 Second St. Southeast
Cedar Rapids, IA 52401

Founded 1968
Total employees 750
Annual sales $101 million
Industries Computer
  Hardware, Computer
  Software
Growth Openings in past
  year 36; percentage
  growth 5%
Contact Mike Wakefield,
  Personnel Director
Tel 319-369-3100
Fax 319-369-3453

**Oster Communications,
Inc.**
219 Parkade, PO Box 6
Cedar Falls, IA 50613

Founded 1976
Total employees 335
Annual sales $40 million
Industry Holding
  Companies

Growth Openings in past
  year 25; percentage
  growth 8%
Contact Merrill J. Oster,
  President
Tel 319-277-1271
Fax 319-277-7982

Parsons Technology
One Parsons Dr., PO Box
  100
Hiawatha, IA 52233

Founded 1984
Total employees 250
Annual sales $29.8 million
Industry Computer
  Software
Growth Openings in past
  year 122; percentage
  growth 95%
Contact Bob Parsons,
  President
Tel 319-395-9626
Fax 319-395-0217

**Source Data Systems,
Inc.**
950 Ridgemont Dr.
  Northeast
Cedar Rapids, IA 52402

Founded 1978
Total employees 120
Annual sales $12 million
Industries Computer
  Hardware, Computer
  Software
Growth Openings in past
  year 20; percentage
  growth 20%
Contact Gary Ford,
  President
Tel 319-393-3343
Fax 319-393-5173

**University Hygienic
Laboratory**
University of Iowa
Iowa City, IA 52242

Founded 1904
Total employees 150
Annual sales $16 million
Industries Biotechnology,
  Chemicals,
  Environmental, Medical

Growth Openings in past
  year 20; percentage
  growth 15%
Contact William J.
  Hausler, Ph.D.,
  Laboratory Director
Tel 319-335-4500
Fax 319-335-4555

■ **515 Area Code**

Alexander Batteries
PO Box 1508
Mason City, IA 50401

Founded 1967
Total employees 310
Annual sales $30 million
Industries Energy,
  Manufacturing
  Equipment
Growth Openings in past
  year 39; percentage
  growth 14%
Contact Steve
  Alexandres,
  Executive Vice
  President/CEO
Tel 515-423-8955
Fax 515-423-1644

**CE Software Holdings,
Inc.**
1801 Industrial Cir.
West Des Moines, IA
  50265

Founded 1981
Total employees 105
Annual sales $8.64 million
Industry Computer
  Software
Growth Openings in past
  year 40; percentage
  growth 61%
Contact Ms. Janice
  Delperdang,
  Human Resources
  Manager
Tel 515-224-1995
Fax 515-224-4534

Chantland Co.
Hwy. 3 East, PO Box 69
Humboldt, IA 50548

Founded 1961
Total employees 275
Annual sales $32 million

Industries Factory
Automation,
Subassemblies and
Components
Growth Openings in past
year 25; percentage
growth 10%
Contact George Flurey,
Division Manager/
General Manager
Tel 515-332-4040
Fax 515-432-4923

**Compressor Controls
Corp.**
11359 Aurora Ave.
Des Moines, IA 50322

Founded 1975
Total employees 182
Industries Subassemblies
and Components, Test
and Measurement
Growth Openings in past
year 52; percentage
growth 40%
Contact Naum
Staroselsky,
President/CEO
Tel 515-270-0857
Fax 515-270-1331

**Microware Systems
Corp.**
1900 Northwest 114th St.
Des Moines, IA 50325

Founded 1977
Total employees 162
Annual sales $10 million
Industry Computer
Software
Growth Openings in past
year 22; percentage
growth 15%
Contact Ken Kaplan,
President
Tel 515-224-1929
Fax 515-224-1352

■ **712 Area Code**

NOBL Laboratories, Inc.
1568 North Main Ave.
Sioux Center, IA 51250

Founded 1980
Total employees 85
Annual sales $11 million

Industry Pharmaceuticals
Growth Openings in past
year 15; percentage
growth 21%
Contact G. Michael
Daniel, DVM,
President
Tel 712-722-4696
Fax 712-722-0882

Kansas

■ **316 Area Code**

**Cerebral Palsy Research
Foundation of Kansas,
Inc.**
2021 North Old Manor
Wichita, KS 67208

Founded 1970
Total employees 300
Annual sales $11 million
Industries Holding
Companies, Medical
Growth Openings in past
year 50; percentage
growth 20%
Contact Ms. Janet
Thompson,
VP of Human Services
Tel 316-688-1888
Fax 316-688-5678

Lodgistix
Two Brittany Pl., 1938
North Woodlawn, Suite
1
Wichita, KS 67208

Founded 1982
Total employees 280
Annual sales $40 million
Industry Computer
Software
Growth Openings in past
year 49; percentage
growth 21%
Contact Paul Hammar,
President
Tel 316-685-2216
Fax 316-685-1000

■ **913 Area Code**

**Continental Analytical
Services, Inc.**
1804 Glendale Rd.
Salina, KS 67401

Founded 1983
Total employees 75
Annual sales $4.5 million
Industries Advanced
Materials, Environmental
Growth Openings in past
year 36; percentage
growth 92%
Contact Ms. Cindy Unruh,
Director of Human
Resources
Tel 913-827-1273
Fax 913-823-7830

**Custom Metals
Fabricators, Vacu-Blast
Corp.**
PO Box 286
Herington, KS 67449

Founded 1944
Total employees 75
Annual sales $3 million
Industry Factory
Automation
Growth Openings in past
year 15; percentage
growth 25%
Contact Frank Meyer,
President
Tel 913-258-3744
Fax 913-258-2584

**Midwest Grain Products,
Inc.**
1300 Main St.
Atchison, KS 66002

Founded 1941
Total employees 560
Annual sales $227 million
Industries Biotechnology,
Holding Companies
Growth Openings in past
year 208; percentage
growth 59%
Contact Ladd Seaburg,
President/CEO
Tel 913-367-1480
Fax 913-367-0192

Oread Laboratories, Inc.
1501 Wakarusa Dr.
Lawrence, KS 66047

Founded 1983
Total employees 100
Annual sales $5.7 million
Industries Biotechnology,
Chemicals,
Pharmaceuticals
Growth Openings in past
year 25; percentage
growth 33%
Contact Ms. Denise
Snodgrass,
Human Resources
Supervisor
Tel 913-749-0034
Fax 913-841-1991

Smoot Co.
1250 Seminary St., PO
Box 3337
Kansas City, KS 66103

Founded 1965
Total employees 83
Annual sales $10 million
Industries Factory
Automation,
Manufacturing
Equipment
Growth Openings in past
year 28; percentage
growth 50%
Contact David K. Smoot,
President
Tel 913-362-1710
Fax 913-362-7863

Terracon Companies, Inc.
1600 College Blvd.
Lenexa, KS 66219

Founded 1962
Total employees 370
Annual sales $24 million
Industry Holding
Companies
Growth Openings in past
year 70; percentage
growth 23%
Contact Jerry Henson,
Director of Human
Resources
Tel 913-599-6886
Fax 913-599-0574

Kentucky

■ **502 Area Code**

Advanced Production Systems, Inc.
8008 Vinecrest Ave.
Louisville, KY 40222

Founded 1986
Total employees 72
Annual sales $3 million
Industries Computer
Hardware,
Manufacturing
Equipment
Growth Openings in past
year 42; percentage
growth 140%
Contact Don Korfhage,
Chief Executive Officer
Tel 502-423-0882
Fax 502-423-0888

Arch Environmental Equipment, Inc.
5929 Benton Rd.
Paducah, KY 42003

Founded 1976
Total employees 24
Annual sales $4 million
Industries Factory
Automation,
Subassemblies and
Components
Growth Openings in past
year 12; percentage
growth 100%
Contact Neil Archer,
President
Tel 502-898-6821
Fax 502-898-8061

EAS Technologies, Inc.
4124 Taylorsville Rd.
Louisville, KY 40220

Founded 1985
Total employees 23
Annual sales $2.6 million
Industries Computer
Hardware, Computer
Software

Growth Openings in past
year 16; percentage
growth 228%
Contact David L.
Daugherty,
President/CEO
Tel 502-473-1000
Fax 502-473-0990

Electronic Systems USA, Inc.
9410 Bunsen Pkwy.
Louisville, KY 40220

Founded 1979
Total employees 175
Annual sales $20 million
Industries Computer
Hardware, Computer
Software
Growth Openings in past
year 45; percentage
growth 34%
Contact Ken Palmgreen,
Executive Vice
President/COO
Tel 502-495-6700
Fax 502-495-2546

GCA Group, Inc.
PO Box 476
Georgetown, KY 40324

Founded 1963
Total employees 300
Annual sales $23 million
Industry Subassemblies
and Components
Growth Openings in past
year 100; percentage
growth 50%
Contact Greg Martin,
President
Tel 502-863-0936
Fax 502-863-5393

Jideco of Bardstown, Inc.
901 Withrow Ct., PO Box
816
Bardstown, KY 40004

Founded 1986
Total employees 150
Annual sales $14 million
Industry Subassemblies
and Components

Growth Openings in past year 55; percentage growth 57%
Contact Shozo Uchio, President
Tel 502-348-3100
Fax 502-348-3204

Jordan Plating, Inc.
793 Lemmons Mill Rd.,
PO Box 906
Georgetown, KY 40324

Founded 1988
Total employees 70
Annual sales $7.6 million
Industry Manufacturing Equipment
Growth Openings in past year 15; percentage growth 27%
Contact Donald Perry, President
Tel 502-863-9384
Fax 502-863-1255

J-Ron Machine & Tool
635 Bob Posey St.
Henderson, KY 42420

Founded 1980
Total employees 40
Annual sales $4.3 million
Industries Factory Automation, Manufacturing Equipment
Growth Openings in past year 14; percentage growth 53%
Contact Ron Bugg, Owner
Tel 502-827-4953
Fax 502-827-4972

Magnum Mold & Tool Corp.
Hwy. 245
Clermont, KY 40110

Founded 1982
Total employees 56
Annual sales $7.0 million
Industry Factory Automation

Growth Openings in past year 26; percentage growth 86%
Contact Pat Mattingly, President
Tel 502-543-9503
Fax 502-543-2757

NSA Co.
PO Box 500
Hawesville, KY 42348

Founded 1969
Total employees 719
Annual sales $100 million
Industry Advanced Materials
Growth Openings in past year 8; percentage growth 1%
Contact Matt Crooks, Plant Manager
Tel 502-927-6921
Fax 502-927-6543

Service Tool & Die, Inc.
2323 Green St.
Henderson, KY 42420

Founded 1969
Total employees 125
Annual sales $7.8 million
Industries Factory Automation, Holding Companies
Growth Openings in past year 15; percentage growth 13%
Contact Richard E. Fruit, President
Tel 502-827-9582
Fax 502-826-4067

Tri-State Plating, Inc.
1125 South 12th St.
Louisville, KY 40210

Founded 1982
Total employees 40
Annual sales $4.3 million
Industry Manufacturing Equipment
Growth Openings in past year 15; percentage growth 60%
Contact John Keaney, President
Tel 502-587-7397
Fax 502-587-7398

UMI/Data Courier
620 South 3rd St.
Louisville, KY 40202

Founded 1973
Total employees 250
Annual sales $41 million
Industry Computer Hardware
Growth Openings in past year 50; percentage growth 25%
Contact Joe Fitzsimmons, President
Tel 502-583-4111
Fax 502-589-5572

University Medical Associates, P.S.C.
530 South Jackson St.
Louisville, KY 40202

Founded 1975
Total employees 125
Annual sales $7.3 million
Industry Medical
Growth Openings in past year 21; percentage growth 20%
Contact Dr. Richard Redinger, President
Tel 502-588-5233

Zeon Chemicals Kentucky, Inc.
PO Box 34320
Louisville, KY 40232

Founded 1989
Total employees 350
Annual sales $45 million
Industry Advanced Materials
Growth Openings in past year 150; percentage growth 75%
Contact Masamichi Yomura, Chief Executive Officer
Tel 502-775-7600
Fax 502-775-7614

Kentucky

■ 606 Area Code

Alltech, Inc.
3031 Catnip Hill Pike
Nicholasville, KY 40356

Founded 1980
Total employees 140
Annual sales $30 million
Industry Biotechnology
Growth Openings in past
year 21; percentage
growth 17%
Contact Dana Cheeks,
General Manager
Tel 606-885-9613
Fax 606-885-6736

Central Kentucky Processing, Inc.
2580 Palumbo Dr.
Lexington, KY 40509

Founded 1983
Total employees 68
Industry Manufacturing
Equipment
Growth Openings in past
year 13; percentage
growth 23%
Contact James Bishop,
President
Tel 606-266-2247
Fax 606-269-8461

Commonwealth Technology, Inc.
2520 Regency Rd.
Lexington, KY 40503

Founded 1977
Total employees 140
Annual sales $14 million
Industry Environmental
Growth Openings in past
year 15; percentage
growth 12%
Contact Dr. Edward G.
Foree, Ph.D.,
President
Tel 606-276-3506
Fax 606-278-5665

Auto-graph Computer Designing Systems, Inc.
651 Perimeter Dr., Suite 100
Lexington, KY 40517

Founded 1984
Total employees 30
Industry Computer
Software
Growth Openings in past
year 12; percentage
growth 66%
Contact Chuck Cleaton,
General Manager
Tel 606-269-8585
Fax 606-269-9821

Ceramic Coating Co.
PO Box 370
Newport, KY 41072

Founded 1966
Total employees 130
Annual sales $12 million
Industries Advanced
Materials, Holding
Companies,
Subassemblies and
Components
Growth Openings in past
year 20; percentage
growth 18%
Contact Paul Swinford,
Personnel Manager/
Purchasing Agent
Tel 606-781-1915
Fax 606-781-1380

Confederate Plastics, Inc.
1086 Brentwood Ct.
Lexington, KY 40578

Founded 1980
Total employees 50
Annual sales $5 million
Industry Manufacturing
Equipment
Growth Openings in past
year 20; percentage
growth 66%
Contact Stanley
Isenstein,
President
Tel 606-252-8996
Fax 606-255-5929

Balluff, Inc.
8125 Holton Dr., PO Box 937
Florence, KY 41042

Founded 1981
Total employees 43
Annual sales $5.3 million
Industries Factory
Automation,
Subassemblies and
Components, Test and
Measurement
Growth Openings in past
year 13; percentage
growth 43%
Contact John Goyer,
Vice President/General
Manager
Tel 606-727-2200
Fax 606-727-4823

ClinTrials, Inc.
2365 Harrodsburg Rd.,
Suite A290
Lexington, KY 40504

Founded 1980
Total employees 85
Annual sales $11 million
Industries Computer
Software,
Pharmaceuticals
Growth Openings in past
year 50; percentage
growth 142%
Contact William O'Neil,
President
Tel 606-224-2400
Fax 606-224-2430

DataBeam Corp.
3191 Nicholasville Rd.,
Suite 600
Lexington, KY 40503

Founded 1981
Total employees 76
Industries Computer
Software,
Telecommunications
Growth Openings in past
year 37; percentage
growth 94%
Contact John King,
Chief Financial Officer
Tel 606-245-3500
Fax 606-245-3515

Donotech Manufacturing, Inc.
Kendall Spring Rd., PO Box 920
Owingsville, KY 40360

Founded 1982
Total employees 175
Annual sales $17 million
Industry Subassemblies and Components
Growth Openings in past year 25; percentage growth 16%
Contact Verl Ingram, Production Control Manager/Purchasing Ag
Tel 606-674-6319
Fax 606-674-2732

Hughes Display Products Corp.
1501 Newtown Pike
Lexington, KY 40511

Founded 1973
Total employees 150
Annual sales $14 million
Industry Subassemblies and Components
Growth Openings in past year 30; percentage growth 25%
Contact James A. Bottomley, Vice President/General Manager
Tel 606-243-5500
Fax 606-243-5555

Mazak Corp.
8025 Production Dr.
Florence, KY 41042

Founded 1968
Total employees 825
Industry Factory Automation
Growth Openings in past year 25; percentage growth 3%
Contact Fenton Koehler, VP of Personnel
Tel 606-727-5700
Fax 606-727-5865

Post Glover Resistors, Inc.
PO Box 18666
Erlanger, KY 41018

Founded 1892
Total employees 90
Annual sales $7 million
Industry Subassemblies and Components
Growth Openings in past year 15; percentage growth 20%
Contact Neil Gambow, President
Tel 606-283-0778
Fax 606-283-2978

Proctor Davis Ray Engineers
800 Corporate Dr.
Lexington, KY 40503

Founded 1946
Total employees 120
Annual sales $26 million
Industries Computer Software, Energy, Environmental, Manufacturing Equipment, Transportation
Growth Openings in past year 14; percentage growth 13%
Contact Ms. Stephanie Clark, Personnel Manager
Tel 606-223-8000
Fax 606-224-1025

SCT
962 Delaware Ave.
Lexington, KY 40505

Founded 1980
Total employees 155
Annual sales $15 million
Industry Computer Software
Growth Openings in past year 50; percentage growth 47%
Contact Thomas E. Gibbs, President
Tel 606-231-0519
Fax 606-231-0519

SWECO, Inc.
7120 New Buffington Rd.
Florence, KY 41042

Founded 1942
Total employees 200
Annual sales $25 million
Industry Factory Automation
Growth Openings in past year 45; percentage growth 29%
Contact Daniel Kripe, VP of Human Resources
Tel 606-727-5147
Fax 606-727-5122

Your Source, Inc.
3060 Harrodsburg Rd., Suite 203
Lexington, KY 40503

Founded 1989
Total employees 16
Annual sales $1.5 million
Industry Subassemblies and Components
Growth Openings in past year 14; percentage growth 700%
Contact Lannie Stegall, Division Manager
Tel 606-223-7525
Fax 606-223-7525

3-D Enterprises Contracting Corp.
3257 Lochness Dr., PO Box 12588
Lexington, KY 40583

Founded 1956
Total employees 150
Annual sales $20 million
Industry Environmental
Growth Openings in past year 15; percentage growth 11%
Contact Donny Breeding, President
Tel 606-272-6618
Fax 606-273-7206

Louisiana

■ **504 Area Code**

Digicourse, Inc.
5200 Toler St.
Harahan, LA 70123

Founded 1970
Total employees 80
Annual sales $6.9 million
Industry Transportation
Growth Openings in past
year 20; percentage
growth 33%
Contact Roy Kelm,
General Manager
Tel 504-733-6061
Fax 504-734-8627

Discovery Chemicals, Inc.
3502 South Riverview Dr.
Port Allen, LA 70767

Founded 1978
Total employees 75
Annual sales $11 million
Industry Advanced
Materials
Growth Openings in past
year 18; percentage
growth 31%
Contact Jorge Alvarez,
CEO/Executive Vice
President
Tel 504-389-9945
Fax 504-389-9957

Fifth Generation Systems, Inc.
10049 North Reiger Rd.
Baton Rouge, LA 70809

Founded 1984
Total employees 200
Annual sales $50 million
Industries Computer
Software, Holding
Companies
Growth Openings in past
year 30; percentage
growth 17%
Contact Barry L. Bellue,
Sr.,
CEO/President
Tel 504-291-7221
Fax 504-295-3268

G&E Engineering, Inc.
PO Box 77510
Baton Rouge, LA 70879

Founded 1981
Total employees 81
Annual sales $8.6 million
Industry Environmental
Growth Openings in past
year 21; percentage
growth 35%
Contact Richard B.
Adams,
President
Tel 504-292-9007
Fax 504-292-3614

Laser File, Inc.
2001 21st St.
Kenner, LA 70062

Founded 1986
Total employees 40
Annual sales $4.4 million
Industry Medical
Growth Openings in past
year 20; percentage
growth 100%
Contact Steven
Greenstein,
President
Tel 504-469-9977
Fax 504-469-4598

OHM Corporation, Dewatering Division
1090 Cinclare Dr.
Port Allen, LA 70767

Founded 1983
Total employees 140
Annual sales $14 million
Industry Environmental
Growth Openings in past
year 37; percentage
growth 35%
Contact A.B. Carroll,
Manager of Dewatering
Services
Tel 504-389-9596
Fax 504-389-9646

Sunland Fabricators, Inc.
30103 Sunland Dr.
Walker, LA 70785

Founded 1943
Total employees 350
Annual sales $34 million

Industry Subassemblies
and Components
Growth Openings in past
year 79; percentage
growth 29%
Contact Andrew
Kershaw,
Vice President/General
Manager
Tel 504-667-1000
Fax 504-667-1019

TANO Automation, Inc.
3501 Jordan Rd., PO Box
26575
New Orleans, LA 70186

Founded 1961
Total employees 200
Annual sales $16 million
Industries Factory
Automation, Test and
Measurement,
Transportation
Growth Openings in past
year 50; percentage
growth 33%
Contact James S.
Williams,
President
Tel 504-243-2400
Fax 504-246-0808

Thompson Environmental Management, Inc.
PO Box 52141
New Orleans, LA 70152

Founded 1984
Total employees 25
Annual sales $2.6 million
Industry Environmental
Growth Openings in past
year 15; percentage
growth 150%
Contact Shaw Thompson,
President
Tel 504-393-7661
Fax 504-393-7934

Walk, Haydel & Associates, Inc.
600 Carondelet St.
New Orleans, LA 70130

Founded 1959
Total employees 601
Annual sales $30 million

Industries Environmental, Manufacturing Equipment
Growth Openings in past year 101; percentage growth 20%
Contact Pete Quirk, Chief Executive Officer
Tel 504-586-8111
Fax 504-522-0554

Maine

■ **207 Area Code**

Auburn Manufacturing, Inc.
PO Box 220
Mechanic Falls, ME 04256

Founded 1980
Total employees 42
Annual sales $6.2 million
Industry Advanced Materials
Growth Openings in past year 12; percentage growth 40%
Contact Ms. Kathie Leonard, President
Tel 207-345-8271
Fax 207-345-3380

Baker Co.
Sanford Airport, Drawer E
Sanford, ME 04073

Founded 1951
Total employees 220
Annual sales $24 million
Industry Test and Measurement
Growth Openings in past year 40; percentage growth 22%
Contact Dennis Eagelson, President
Tel 207-324-8773

Binax, Inc.
95 Darling Ave.
South Portland, ME 04106

Founded 1986
Total employees 53
Annual sales $4.5 million

Industries Environmental, Medical, Test and Measurement
Growth Openings in past year 27; percentage growth 103%
Contact Roger Piasio, President/CEO
Tel 207-772-3544
Fax 207-761-2074

Emery Waterhouse Co.
Rand Rd.
Portland, ME 04104

Founded 1841
Total employees 323
Annual sales $37 million
Industry Holding Companies
Growth Openings in past year 22; percentage growth 7%
Contact Ernie Lebel, VP of Human Resources
Tel 207-775-2371
Fax 207-775-5206

Hague International
3 Adams St.
South Portland, ME 04106

Founded 1971
Total employees 50
Annual sales $3.9 million
Industries Energy, Environmental, Test and Measurement
Growth Openings in past year 15; percentage growth 42%
Contact Ms. Jackie LaHaye, Director of Personnel
Tel 207-799-7346
Fax 207-799-7643

IDEXX Laboratories, Inc.
One IDEXX Dr.
Westbrook, ME 04092

Founded 1983
Total employees 300
Annual sales $57.65 million
Industries Biotechnology, Computer Software

Growth Openings in past year 100; percentage growth 50%
Contact David E. Shaw, President
Tel 207-856-0300
Fax 207-856-0346

Jackson Laboratory
600 Main St.
Bar Harbor, ME 04609

Founded 1929
Total employees 560
Annual sales $11.8 million
Industry Biotechnology
Growth Openings in past year 27; percentage growth 5%
Contact Ms. Joanne Harris, Personnel Manager
Tel 207-288-3371
Fax 207-288-4152

Maine Poly, Inc.
Rte. 202, PO Box 8
Greene, ME 04236

Founded 1971
Total employees 163
Industry Advanced Materials
Growth Openings in past year 33; percentage growth 25%
Contact Robert Ray, President
Tel 207-946-7440
Fax 207-946-5492

Nutrite Corp.
825 Main St.
Presque Isle, ME 04769

Founded 1980
Total employees 50
Annual sales $40 million
Industry Chemicals
Growth Openings in past year 25; percentage growth 100%
Contact Paul LeBlanc, General Manager
Tel 207-768-5791
Fax 207-764-7550

Olamon Industries
25 River Rd., Indian
Island
Old Town, ME 04468

Founded 1984
Total employees 100
Annual sales $13 million
Industry
Telecommunications
Growth Openings in past
year 15; percentage
growth 17%
Contact Al Marquis,
Plant Manager
Tel 207-827-8051
Fax 207-827-8495

Parker Hannifin Corp., Nichols Portland Division
2400 Congress St.
Portland, ME 04102

Founded 1968
Total employees 460
Annual sales $44 million
Industry Subassemblies
and Components
Growth Openings in past
year 92; percentage
growth 25%
Contact Jurgen Kok,
Vice President/General
Manager
Tel 207-774-6121
Fax 207-774-3601

Maryland

■ **301 Area Code**

American Type Culture Collection
12301 Parklawn Dr.
Rockville, MD 20852

Founded 1925
Total employees 225
Annual sales $12 million
Industries Biotechnology,
Chemicals, Computer
Hardware

Growth Openings in past
year 25; percentage
growth 12%
Contact Ms. Patricia
Holland,
Personnel Administrator
Tel 301-881-2600
Fax 301-231-5826

Andrulis Research Corp.
4600 East-West Hwy.,
Suite 900
Bethesda, MD 20814

Founded 1971
Total employees 235
Industries Computer
Software, Defense, Test
and Measurement
Growth Openings in past
year 35; percentage
growth 17%
Contact Dr. Marilyn W.
Andrulis,
President/CEO
Tel 301-657-1700
Fax 301-657-3555

Angstrohm Precision, Inc.
PO Box 1827
Hagerstown, MD 21740

Founded 1961
Total employees 100
Annual sales $9.7 million
Industry Subassemblies
and Components
Growth Openings in past
year 40; percentage
growth 66%
Contact Donald E.
Hutzell,
General Manager/VP of
Manufacturing
Tel 301-739-8722
Fax 301-797-6852

ATLIS Imaging Systems, Inc.
6011
Rockville, MD 20852

Founded 1990
Total employees 20
Annual sales $5 million
Industry Computer
Software

Growth Openings in past
year 15; percentage
growth 300%
Contact Keith A.
Cunningham, II,
President
Tel 301-770-3000
Fax 301-468-6759

Automated Information Management, Inc.
4403 Forbes Blvd.
Lanham, MD 20706

Founded 1983
Total employees 350
Industries Computer
Hardware,
Manufacturing
Equipment
Growth Openings in past
year 75; percentage
growth 27%
Contact Ms. Cynthia
Hardy,
President
Tel 301-794-8200
Fax 301-794-7268

AVEMCO Corp.
411 Aviation Way
Frederick, MD 21701

Founded 1959
Total employees 400
Annual sales $84.54
million
Industry Holding
Companies
Growth Openings in past
year 23; percentage
growth 6%
Contact William P.
Condon,
President
Tel 301-694-5700
Fax 301-694-4242

AWD Technologies, Inc.
15204 Omega Dr.
Rockville, MD 20850

Founded 1987
Total employees 250
Industry Environmental

Growth Openings in past year 123; percentage growth 96%
Contact Dr. Barry N. Naff, Ph.D., President
Tel 301-948-0040
Fax 301-948-6094

Bioqual, Inc.
9600 Medical Center Dr. Suite 200
Rockville, MD 20850

Founded 1983
Total employees 110
Annual sales $5 million
Industries Biotechnology, Medical
Growth Openings in past year 15; percentage growth 15%
Contact Dr. John C. Landon, Ph.D., President
Tel 301-251-2801
Fax 301-251-1260

BioWhittaker, Inc.
8830 Biggs Ford Rd.
Walkersville, MD 21793

Founded 1947
Total employees 450
Annual sales $51.6 million
Industry Holding Companies
Growth Openings in past year 49; percentage growth 12%
Contact William White, Director of Human Resources
Tel 301-898-7025

Boehringer Mannheim Pharmaceuticals
15204 Omega Dr.
Rockville, MD 20850

Founded 1985
Total employees 150
Industry Pharmaceuticals
Growth Openings in past year 70; percentage growth 87%
Contact Ted Wood, President
Tel 301-216-3900
Fax 301-330-7260

Bohdan Associates, Inc.
220 Girard St.
Gaithersburg, MD 20877

Founded 1983
Total employees 200
Annual sales $91 million
Industry Computer Hardware
Growth Openings in past year 40; percentage growth 25%
Contact Peter B. Zacharkiw, Chief Executive Officer
Tel 301-258-2965
Fax 301-258-9122

Cellco, Inc.
12321 Middlebrook Rd.
Germantown, MD 20874

Founded 1987
Total employees 26
Industries Biotechnology, Medical
Growth Openings in past year 17; percentage growth 188%
Contact R. William Lynn, President/CEO
Tel 301-916-1000
Fax 301-916-1010

Center for Advanced Research in Biotechnology
9600 Gudelsky Dr.
Rockville, MD 20850

Founded 1985
Total employees 54
Industries Biotechnology, Medical
Growth Openings in past year 24; percentage growth 80%
Contact Dr. Walt Stevens, Acting Director
Tel 301-251-2272
Fax 301-251-2255

Computer Technology Services, Inc.
1700 Rockville Pike, Suite 315
Rockville, MD 20852

Founded 1983
Total employees 45
Industries Computer Hardware, Manufacturing Equipment
Growth Openings in past year 15; percentage growth 50%
Contact Dr. Daisy Wallace, President/CEO
Tel 301-468-1160

COMSYS Technical Services, Inc.
4 Research Pl.
Rockville, MD 20850

Founded 1979
Total employees 550
Industries Computer Hardware, Computer Software
Growth Openings in past year 169; percentage growth 44%
Contact Fred Shulman, COB/President
Tel 301-921-3600
Fax 301-921-3670

Cryomedical Sciences, Inc.
1300 Piccard Dr., Suite 102
Rockville, MD 20850

Founded 1989
Total employees 40
Industry Medical
Growth Openings in past year 30; percentage growth 300%
Contact J.J. Finkelstein, COB/CEO/President
Tel 301-417-7070
Fax 301-417-7077

CSC Intelicom, Inc.
6707 Democracy Blvd.
Bethesda, MD 20817

Founded 1977
Total employees 250
Industry Computer
Software
Growth Openings in past
year 50; percentage
growth 25%
Contact Ms. Lynn
Aminzadeh,
Director of Human
Resources
Tel 301-564-6600
Fax 301-571-8399

Data-Prompt, Inc.
11911 Tech Rd.
Silver Spring, MD 20904

Founded 1982
Total employees 145
Annual sales $16 million
Industry Computer
Software
Growth Openings in past
year 20; percentage
growth 16%
Contact Sheldon Katz,
President
Tel 301-622-0900
Fax 301-622-1664

Diagnostic Assay Services, Inc.
9290 Gaither Rd.
Gaithersburg, MD 20877

Founded 1975
Total employees 40
Annual sales $3.5 million
Industry Medical
Growth Openings in past
year 18; percentage
growth 81%
Contact Dr. John Eaton,
President
Tel 301-840-9220

Dynamac Corporation
2275 Research Blvd.
Rockville, MD 20850

Founded 1970
Total employees 420

Industries Computer
Software, Environmental
Contact Elroy Hill,
VP of Human Resources
Tel 301-417-9800
Fax 301-417-9801

Falcon Microsystems, Inc.
1100 Mercantile Ln.
Landover, MD 20785

Founded 1982
Total employees 300
Industry Computer
Software
Growth Openings in past
year 25; percentage
growth 9%
Contact M. Dendy Young,
President
Tel 301-341-0100
Fax 301-386-6424

Fil-Tec, Inc.
PO Box B
Hagerstown, MD 21741

Founded 1978
Total employees 80
Industry Advanced
Materials
Growth Openings in past
year 20; percentage
growth 33%
Contact Vincent
Schoeck,
President
Tel 301-824-6166
Fax 301-824-6938

General Physics Corp.
6700 Alexander Bell Dr.
Columbia, MD 21046

Founded 1966
Total employees 800
Annual sales $73.3 million
Industries Environmental,
Manufacturing
Equipment
Growth Openings in past
year 99; percentage
growth 14%
Contact R. Eugene
Klose,
President
Tel 301-290-2300
Fax 301-290-2600

Genetic Therapy, Inc.
19 Firstfield Rd.
Gaithersburg, MD 20878

Founded 1986
Total employees 87
Annual sales $2.04 million
Industry Biotechnology
Growth Openings in past
year 47; percentage
growth 117%
Contact M. James
Barrett, Ph.D.,
President/CEO
Tel 301-590-2626
Fax 301-948-3774

Geomet Technologies, Inc.
20251 Century Blvd.
Germantown, MD 20874

Founded 1967
Total employees 75
Annual sales $8.0 million
Industry Environmental
Growth Openings in past
year 20; percentage
growth 36%
Contact Bob Durfee,
President
Tel 301-428-9898
Fax 301-428-9482

Global Technology Corp.
11141 Georgia Ave., Suite
115
Silver Spring, MD 20902

Founded 1982
Total employees 60
Annual sales $1 million
Industries Computer
Hardware, Computer
Software
Growth Openings in past
year 12; percentage
growth 25%
Contact Gerald Charles,
President
Tel 301-949-5723

IGEN, Inc.
1530 East Jefferson St.
Rockville, MD 20852

Founded 1982
Total employees 65

Industries Chemicals,
Medical
Growth Openings in past
year 12; percentage
growth 22%
Contact Sam
Wohlstadter,
CEO/COB
Tel 301-984-8000
Fax 301-230-0158

**J.G. Van Dyke &
Associates, Inc.**
6701 Rockledge Dr.
Bethesda, MD 20817

Founded 1978
Total employees 160
Annual sales $17 million
Industries Computer
Hardware, Computer
Software,
Telecommunications
Growth Openings in past
year 25; percentage
growth 18%
Contact J. Gary O. Van
Dyke,
President
Tel 301-897-8970
Fax 301-897-5389

**KCM Computer
Consulting, Inc.**
7833 Walker Dr., Suite
650
Greenbelt, MD 20770

Founded 1986
Total employees 84
Annual sales $9.7 million
Industry Computer
Software
Growth Openings in past
year 34; percentage
growth 68%
Contact Ms. Carmen
Mayfield,
President
Tel 301-345-0707
Fax 301-220-3505

Macro International Inc.
8630 Fenton St.
Silver Spring, MD 20910

Founded 1966
Total employees 375
Annual sales $39 million

Industry Holding
Companies
Growth Openings in past
year 25; percentage
growth 7%
Contact Ms. Millie
Ambrosia,
VP of Human Resources
Tel 301-588-5484
Fax 301-585-3180

Manugistics
2115 East Jefferson St.
Rockville, MD 20852

Founded 1969
Total employees 300
Annual sales $34 million
Industry Computer
Software
Growth Openings in past
year 75; percentage
growth 33%
Contact Gary McKinney,
Director of Human
Resources
Tel 301-984-5000
Fax 301-984-5094

MedImmune, Inc.
35 West Watkins Mill Rd.
Gaithersburg, MD 20878

Founded 1988
Total employees 100
Annual sales $13.1 million
Industries Biotechnology,
Pharmaceuticals
Growth Openings in past
year 25; percentage
growth 33%
Contact Wayne T.
Hockmeyer, Ph.D.,
President
Tel 301-417-0770
Fax 301-417-6289

**Micronetics Design
Corp.**
1375 Piccard Dr., Suite
300
Rockville, MD 20850

Founded 1980
Total employees 52
Industry Computer
Software

Growth Openings in past
year 17; percentage
growth 48%
Contact David Marcus,
Vice President
Tel 301-258-2605
Fax 301-840-8943

MICROS Systems, Inc.
12000 Baltimore Ave.
Beltsville, MD 20705

Founded 1977
Total employees 320
Annual sales $44.3 million
Industries Computer
Hardware, Computer
Software
Growth Openings in past
year 19; percentage
growth 6%
Contact Ronald J.
Kolson,
VP of Finance and
Administration/CFO
Tel 301-490-2000
Fax 301-490-6699

**Molecular Oncology,
Inc.**
19 Firstfield Rd.
Gaithersburg, MD 20878

Founded 1988
Total employees 87
Annual sales $9.5 million
Industry Medical
Growth Openings in past
year 15; percentage
growth 20%
Contact Charles N.
Blitzer,
CEO/COB
Tel 301-590-2600
Fax 301-258-3434

Neutron Products, Inc.
22301 Mount Ephraim
Rd., PO Box 68
Dickerson, MD 20842

Founded 1958
Total employees 90
Annual sales $10 million
Industries Biotechnology,
Chemicals, Medical

Growth Openings in past year 15; percentage growth 20%
Contact Jackson A. Ransohoff, President
Tel 301-349-5001
Fax 301-349-5007

Growth Openings in past year 30; percentage growth 25%
Contact Carlton Josephs, President
Tel 301-459-9100
Fax 301-731-6285

Growth Openings in past year 22; percentage growth 13%
Contact Lawrence Schadegg, President
Tel 301-373-2360
Fax 301-373-3421

Oncor, Inc.
209 Perry Pkwy., Suite 7, PO Box 870
Gaithersburg, MD 20877

Founded 1983
Total employees 150
Annual sales $6.58 million
Industries Biotechnology, Chemicals, Holding Companies, Medical
Growth Openings in past year 70; percentage growth 87%
Contact Steven Turner, President
Tel 301-963-3500
Fax 301-926-6129

Orkand Corp.
8484 Georgia Ave., Suite 1000
Silver Spring, MD 20910

Founded 1970
Total employees 600
Annual sales $20 million
Industries Computer Hardware, Computer Software
Growth Openings in past year 70; percentage growth 13%
Contact Dr. Donald S. Orkand, President
Tel 301-585-8480
Fax 301-565-0828

Pulse Electronics, Inc.
5706 Frederick Ave.
Rockville, MD 20852

Founded 1978
Total employees 140
Annual sales $16 million
Industries Holding Companies, Test and Measurement, Transportation
Growth Openings in past year 15; percentage growth 12%
Contact Emilio Fernandez, President
Tel 301-230-0600
Fax 301-230-0606

One Call Concepts, Inc.
14504 Greenview Dr., Suite 300
Laurel, MD 20708

Founded 1982
Total employees 300
Industry Computer Software
Growth Openings in past year 50; percentage growth 20%
Contact Ms. Susan Volkman, Vice President
Tel 301-776-0202
Fax 410-792-7032

Otsuka Pharmaceutical Co., Ltd., Maryland Research Laboratories
9900 Medical Center Dr.
Rockville, MD 20850

Founded 1985
Total employees 100
Annual sales $11 million
Industries Biotechnology, Pharmaceuticals
Growth Openings in past year 20; percentage growth 25%
Contact Yasuo Iriye, Director
Tel 301-424-9055
Fax 301-424-9054

Racal Communications, Inc.
5 Research Pl.
Rockville, MD 20850

Founded 1955
Total employees 220
Industry Telecommunications
Growth Openings in past year 70; percentage growth 46%
Contact Joe Guilfoyle, Personnel Director
Tel 301-948-4420
Fax 301-948-6015

Optimum Services and Systems, Inc.
4351 Nicole Dr.
Lanham, MD 20706

Founded 1978
Total employees 150
Annual sales $19 million
Industries Computer Hardware, Computer Software

PRB Associates, Inc.
47 Airport View Dr.
Hollywood, MD 20636

Founded 1977
Total employees 188
Industries Computer Software, Defense

Raxco, Inc.
2440 Research Blvd., Suite 200
Rockville, MD 20805

Founded 1977
Total employees 160
Annual sales $20 million
Industry Computer Software

Growth Openings in past year 35; percentage growth 28%
Contact Ms. Lisa Gaslewicz, Director of Personnel and Administration
Tel 301-258-2620
Fax 301-670-3585

R.O.W. Sciences, Inc.
5515 Security Ln., Suite 500
Rockville, MD 20852

Founded 1983
Total employees 325
Annual sales $25 million
Industries Biotechnology, Computer Hardware, Computer Software, Defense
Growth Openings in past year 45; percentage growth 16%
Contact Colin Blough, Human Resources Manager
Tel 301-770-6070
Fax 301-770-6069

Statistica, Inc.
30 West Gude Dr., Suite 300
Rockville, MD 20850

Founded 1977
Total employees 390
Annual sales $36 million
Industries Computer Hardware, Computer Software
Growth Openings in past year 90; percentage growth 30%
Contact John Hakola, Vice President/CAO
Tel 301-424-1911
Fax 301-424-2972

Stephens Engineering Co., Inc.
4601 Forbes Blvd., Suite 300
Lanham, MD 20706

Founded 1976
Total employees 150
Annual sales $20 million

Industries Computer Hardware, Computer Software, Environmental
Growth Openings in past year 20; percentage growth 15%
Contact Ms. Edith Brandt, Director of Human Services
Tel 301-306-9355
Fax 301-306-7116

Synthecell Corp.
7101 Riverwood Dr.
Columbia, MD 21046

Founded 1986
Total employees 50
Annual sales $4.8 million
Industry Holding Companies
Growth Openings in past year 30; percentage growth 150%
Contact Ms. Jean Hugg, Director of Human Resources and Administ
Tel 301-309-1910
Fax 301-309-1916

Texcom, Inc.
4550 Forbes Blvd., Suite 200
Lanham, MD 20706

Founded 1982
Total employees 198
Annual sales $14 million
Industries Computer Hardware, Computer Software, Defense, Telecommunications
Growth Openings in past year 104; percentage growth 110%
Contact Mrs. Ruta Doster, Personnel Manager
Tel 301-794-4400
Fax 301-794-8871

Trusted Information Systems, Inc.
3060 Washington Rd.
Glenwood, MD 21738

Founded 1983
Total employees 80
Industry Computer Hardware

Growth Openings in past year 15; percentage growth 23%
Contact Ms. Linda Aulrich, Personnel Coordinator
Tel 301-854-6889
Fax 301-854-5363

Univax Biologics, Inc.
12280 Wilkins Ave.
Rockville, MD 20852

Founded 1988
Total employees 88
Industry Pharmaceuticals
Growth Openings in past year 64; percentage growth 266%
Contact Ms. Jane Barrett, Human Resources Manager
Tel 301-770-3099
Fax 301-770-3097

Wallac, Inc.
9238 Gaither Rd.
Gaithersburg, MD 20877

Founded 1963
Total employees 68
Annual sales $8.1 million
Industry Test and Measurement
Growth Openings in past year 16; percentage growth 30%
Contact Ms. Ingeborg Graf, Director of Human Resources
Tel 301-963-3200
Fax 301-963-7780

Westat, Inc.
1650 Research Blvd.
Rockville, MD 20850

Founded 1963
Total employees 550
Annual sales $90 million
Industry Computer Hardware

Growth Openings in past year 163; percentage growth 42%
Contact Ms. Patricia Smith, Personnel Director
Tel 301-251-1500
Fax 301-294-2040

Growth Openings in past year 15; percentage growth 33%
Contact Jerry Phillips, Owner/President
Tel 410-329-6801
Fax 410-357-5916

Growth Openings in past year 113; percentage growth 14%
Contact Lou Childress, Director of Human Resources
Tel 410-771-0100
Fax 410-584-7121

A.J. Sackett & Sons Co.
1701 South Highland Ave.
Baltimore, MD 21224

Founded 1897
Total employees 75
Annual sales $6 million
Industry Factory Automation
Growth Openings in past year 25; percentage growth 50%
Contact Larry Taylor, President
Tel 410-276-4466
Fax 410-276-0241

Wilcoxon Research, Inc.
21 Firstfield Rd.
Gaithersburg, MD 20878

Founded 1960
Total employees 105
Annual sales $6 million
Industry Test and Measurement
Growth Openings in past year 20; percentage growth 23%
Contact Ms. Linda Crews, Human Resources Manager
Tel 301-330-8811
Fax 301-330-8873

Better Engineering Manufacturing, Inc.
8361 Town Center Ct.
Baltimore, MD 21236

Founded 1965
Total employees 52
Industry Factory Automation
Growth Openings in past year 12; percentage growth 30%
Contact William K. Hiss, President
Tel 410-931-0000
Fax 410-931-0053

Armco, Inc., Eastern Stainless Division
PO Box 1975
Baltimore, MD 21203

Founded 1900
Total employees 670
Annual sales $100 million
Industry Advanced Materials
Growth Openings in past year 20; percentage growth 3%
Contact Robert Rubino, President
Tel 410-522-6200

XDB Systems, Inc.
14700 Sweitzer Ln.
Laurel, MD 20707

Founded 1982
Total employees 80
Industries Computer Software, Telecommunications
Growth Openings in past year 20; percentage growth 33%
Contact Dr. S. Bing Yao, President
Tel 301-317-6800
Fax 301-317-7701

Computer Sciences Corp., Systems Engineering Division
7471 Candlewood Rd.
Hanover, MD 21076

Founded 1987
Total employees 650
Industry Defense
Growth Openings in past year 249; percentage growth 62%
Contact Robert Rankin, President
Tel 410-684-3500
Fax 410-684-3593

■ **410 Area Code**

AIM, Inc.
19200 Middletown Rd.
Parkton, MD 21120

Founded 1971
Total employees 60
Industry Manufacturing Equipment

Becton Dickinson Microbiology Systems
250 Schilling Cir., PO Box 243
Cockeysville, MD 21030

Founded 1935
Total employees 913
Annual sales $100 million
Industries Biotechnology, Medical, Test and Measurement

Courtland Group, Inc.
10480 Little Patuxent Pkwy., Suite 850
Columbia, MD 21044

Founded 1986
Total employees 20
Annual sales $2.3 million
Industry Computer Software

Growth Openings in past year 12; percentage growth 150%
Contact George J. Trigilio, Jr., President/CEO
Tel 410-730-7668
Fax 410-730-8271

Danfoss Automatic Controls
4971 Mercantile Rd.
Baltimore, MD 21236

Founded 1974
Total employees 135
Annual sales $16 million
Industries Energy, Subassemblies and Components
Growth Openings in past year 20; percentage growth 17%
Contact Robert W. Wilkins, President
Tel 410-931-8250
Fax 410-931-8256

DISC, Inc.
25 Crossroads Dr.
Owings Mills, MD 21117

Founded 1969
Total employees 200
Annual sales $23 million
Industries Computer Software, Holding Companies
Growth Openings in past year 25; percentage growth 14%
Contact Gary F. Taylor, Executive Vice President/CFO
Tel 410-581-2900
Fax 410-581-4600

EVI, Inc.
7138 Columbia Gateway Dr.
Columbia, MD 21046

Founded 1983
Total employees 35
Industry Telecommunications

Growth Openings in past year 13; percentage growth 59%
Contact Peter Horowitz, President
Tel 410-290-1919
Fax 410-290-1925

Fawn Industries, Inc.
311 International Cir., Suite 140
Hunt Valley, MD 21030

Founded 1953
Total employees 400
Annual sales $41 million
Industries Manufacturing Equipment, Subassemblies and Components
Growth Openings in past year 23; percentage growth 6%
Contact John B. Franzone, President/CEO/COB
Tel 410-584-1300
Fax 410-584-1327

Fiber Optic Systems, Inc.
6797 Dorsey Rd.
Baltimore, MD 21227

Founded 1988
Total employees 72
Annual sales $2.5 million
Industry Telecommunications
Growth Openings in past year 42; percentage growth 140%
Contact Ronald M. Hamrah, COB/CEO/President
Tel 410-796-2324
Fax 410-796-2325

Gar-Ron Plastic Corp.
5424 Pulaski Hwy.
Baltimore, MD 21205

Founded 1967
Total employees 50
Annual sales $7 million
Industries Advanced Materials, Manufacturing Equipment

Growth Openings in past year 15; percentage growth 42%
Contact Richard Ruane, President
Tel 410-483-1122
Fax 410-483-1493

Martek Biosciences Corp.
6480 Dobbin Rd.
Columbia, MD 21045

Founded 1985
Total employees 56
Annual sales $3.2 million
Industries Advanced Materials, Biotechnology, Chemicals, Pharmaceuticals
Growth Openings in past year 16; percentage growth 40%
Contact Henry Linsert, COB/CEO
Tel 410-740-0081
Fax 410-740-2985

Maryland Wire Belts, Inc.
Rte. 16, PO Box 67
Church Creek, MD 21622

Founded 1972
Total employees 130
Annual sales $16 million
Industry Factory Automation
Growth Openings in past year 35; percentage growth 36%
Contact Richard A. Loeffler, President
Tel 410-228-7900
Fax 410-228-1647

PharmaKinetics Laboratories, Inc.
302 West Fayette St.
Baltimore, MD 21201

Founded 1975
Total employees 140
Annual sales $13 million
Industry Pharmaceuticals

Growth Openings in past
year 40; percentage
growth 40%
Contact V. Brewster
Jones,
President/CEO
Tel 410-385-4500
Fax 410-385-1957

**Research Support
Instruments, Inc.**
10610 Beaver Dam Rd.
Cockeysville, MD 21030

Founded 1977
Total employees 53
Industries Photonics,
Subassemblies and
Components, Test and
Measurement
Growth Openings in past
year 26; percentage
growth 96%
Contact Robert F.
Crabbs,
President
Tel 410-785-6250
Fax 410-785-1228

**United Container
Machinery Group**
5200 Glen Arm Rd.
Glen Arm, MD 21057

Founded 1986
Total employees 280
Annual sales $42 million
Industry Factory
Automation
Growth Openings in past
year 19; percentage
growth 7%
Contact Richard G.
Osborne,
President/CEO
Tel 410-592-5400
Fax 410-592-5460

US Design Corp.
9075 Guilford
Columbia, MD 21046

Founded 1978
Total employees 42
Annual sales $8 million
Industry Computer
Hardware

Growth Openings in past
year 12; percentage
growth 40%
Contact Bernard F.
McCrory,
President
Tel 410-381-3000
Fax 410-381-3235

Massachusetts

■ **413 Area Code**

**Meadex Technologies,
Inc.**
PO Box 2528
Springfield, MA 01101

Founded 1984
Total employees 37
Annual sales $4.0 million
Industry Photonics
Growth Openings in past
year 12; percentage
growth 48%
Contact Edward F.
Watson,
President
Tel 413-567-3680
Fax 413-567-9068

Millitech Corp.
South Deerfield Research
Park, PO Box 109
South Deerfield, MA
01373

Founded 1982
Total employees 129
Industries
Telecommunications,
Transportation
Growth Openings in past
year 24; percentage
growth 22%
Contact Ms. Gail Carroll,
Director of Human
Resources
Tel 413-665-8551
Fax 413-665-4831

V.I. Corporation
47 Pleasant St.
Northampton, MA 01060

Founded 1986
Total employees 87
Annual sales $10 million

Industry Computer
Software
Growth Openings in past
year 17; percentage
growth 24%
Contact Irwin Jacobs,
President
Tel 413-586-4144
Fax 413-568-3805

■ **508 Area Code**

ADRA Systems, Inc.
59 Technology Dr.
Lowell, MA 01851

Founded 1983
Total employees 150
Industry Computer
Software
Growth Openings in past
year 50; percentage
growth 50%
Contact William L.
Fiedler,
Chief Financial Officer
Tel 508-937-3700
Fax 508-453-2462

**Advanced Cable
Technologies, Inc.**
1 Robert Bonazzoli Ave.
Hudson, MA 01749

Founded 1983
Total employees 300
Annual sales $35 million
Industry Subassemblies
and Components
Growth Openings in past
year 100; percentage
growth 50%
Contact John A. Pino,
President/CEO
Tel 508-562-1200
Fax 508-562-4502

**Advanced NMR
Systems, Inc.**
46 Jonspin Rd.
Wilmington, MA 01887

Founded 1983
Total employees 68
Industry Medical

Growth Openings in past year 21; percentage growth 44%
Contact Ms. Marion Waddington, Human Resource Manager
Tel 508-657-8876
Fax 508-658-3581

Aegis, Inc.
50 Welby Rd.
New Bedford, MA 02745

Founded 1984
Total employees 225
Industry Subassemblies and Components
Growth Openings in past year 25; percentage growth 12%
Contact John Manetti, President
Tel 508-998-3141
Fax 508-995-7315

Aero Plastics, Inc.
720 Mechanic St.
Leominster, MA 01453

Founded 1965
Total employees 100
Annual sales $10 million
Industry Manufacturing Equipment
Growth Openings in past year 25; percentage growth 33%
Contact Jeff Goldberg, President
Tel 508-537-4363
Fax 508-537-9927

Alden Electronics, Inc.
40 Washington St.
Westborough, MA 01581

Founded 1946
Total employees 160
Annual sales $18.1 million
Industries Energy, Holding Companies, Photonics, Test and Measurement, Telecommunications

Growth Openings in past year 25; percentage growth 18%
Contact Lawrence A. Farrington, President
Tel 508-366-8851
Fax 508-898-2427

Alpha-Beta Technology, Inc.
One Innovation Dr.
Worcester, MA 01605

Founded 1988
Total employees 97
Industries Biotechnology, Pharmaceuticals
Growth Openings in past year 57; percentage growth 142%
Contact Spiros Jamas, President/CEO
Tel 508-798-6900
Fax 508-754-2579

Amdex Corp.
76 Treble Cove Rd.
North Billerica, MA 01862

Founded 1985
Total employees 20
Industries Computer Hardware, Factory Automation
Growth Openings in past year 13; percentage growth 185%
Contact Dr. G. Stewart, COB/CEO
Tel 508-663-2070
Fax 508-663-5094

American Flexible Conduit Co.
55 Samuel Barnet Blvd.
New Bedford, MA 02745

Founded 1920
Total employees 280
Industry Subassemblies and Components
Growth Openings in past year 30; percentage growth 12%
Contact Robert Pereira, VP of Operations
Tel 508-998-1131
Fax 508-998-1447

American Medical Instruments, Inc.
97 Cove St., Bldg. 28
New Bedford, MA 02744

Founded 1975
Total employees 140
Annual sales $15 million
Industry Medical
Growth Openings in past year 30; percentage growth 27%
Contact Anthony C. Arrigo, President/COO
Tel 508-993-9169
Fax 508-990-0256

Aries Technology, Inc.
600 Suffolk St.
Lowell, MA 01854

Founded 1984
Total employees 110
Annual sales $12 million
Industry Computer Software
Growth Openings in past year 13; percentage growth 13%
Contact Larry McArthur, COB/President/CEO
Tel 508-453-5310
Fax 508-458-2541

ASA International Ltd.
10 Speen St.
Framingham, MA 01701

Founded 1969
Total employees 200
Annual sales $31.4 million
Industries Computer Software, Holding Companies
Growth Openings in past year 20; percentage growth 11%
Contact Alfred Angelone, Chief Executive Officer
Tel 508-626-2727
Fax 508-626-0645

Aseco Corp.
261 Cedar Hill St.
Marlborough, MA 01752

Founded 1984
Total employees 85

Industry Factory Automation
Growth Openings in past year 20; percentage growth 30%
Contact Michael Vinci, Controller
Tel 508-481-8896
Fax 508-481-0369

Aspen Systems, Inc.
184 Cedar Hill St.
Marlborough, MA 01752

Founded 1984
Total employees 25
Annual sales $2.5 million
Industries Advanced Materials, Energy, Environmental, Manufacturing Equipment, Photonics
Growth Openings in past year 15; percentage growth 150%
Contact Kang P. Lee, President
Tel 508-481-5058
Fax 508-480-0328

Associated X-Ray Imaging Corp.
49 Newark St.
Haverhill, MA 01832

Founded 1984
Total employees 30
Annual sales $3.3 million
Industry Medical
Growth Openings in past year 12; percentage growth 66%
Contact John D. Olenio, President
Tel 508-374-6371
Fax 508-521-2214

Astra Pharmaceutical Products, Inc.
50 Otis St.
Westborough, MA 01581

Founded 1948
Total employees 850
Annual sales $75 million
Industry Pharmaceuticals

Growth Openings in past year 197; percentage growth 30%
Contact Stefan Solzell, Senior Vice President
Tel 508-366-1100
Fax 508-366-7406

Bostik, Inc.
Boston St.
Middleton, MA 01949

Founded 1890
Total employees 450
Annual sales $66 million
Industry Advanced Materials
Growth Openings in past year 99; percentage growth 28%
Contact Ms. Jane Holland, Human Resource Specialist
Tel 508-777-0100
Fax 508-750-7212

Brooks Automation, Inc.
41 Wellman St
Lowell, MA 01851

Founded 1978
Total employees 90
Annual sales $10 million
Industry Manufacturing Equipment
Growth Openings in past year 35; percentage growth 63%
Contact Richard Sullivan, Controller
Tel 508-453-1112
Fax 508-453-3455

Cambridge Automatic
15 Erie Dr.
Natick, MA 01760

Founded 1861
Total employees 28
Annual sales $4 million
Industries Factory Automation, Manufacturing Equipment

Growth Openings in past year 13; percentage growth 86%
Contact Karen Bradley, Treasurer
Tel 508-653-9002
Fax 508-651-3687

Cascade Communications Corp.
239 Littleton Rd.
Westford, MA 01886

Founded 1990
Total employees 28
Annual sales $3.8 million
Industries Computer Software, Telecommunications
Growth Openings in past year 14; percentage growth 100%
Contact Daniel E. Smith, President/CEO
Tel 508-692-2600
Fax 508-692-9214

Chipcom Corp.
118 Turnpike Rd.
Southborough, MA 01772

Founded 1983
Total employees 400
Annual sales $87.3 million
Industry Telecommunications
Growth Openings in past year 50; percentage growth 14%
Contact John Meyer, VP of Human Resources
Tel 508-460-8900
Fax 508-460-8950

ColorAge, Inc.
900 Technology Park Dr., Bldg 8
Billerica, MA 01821

Founded 1980
Total employees 50
Annual sales $5.8 million
Industry Computer Software

Growth Openings in past year 15; percentage growth 42%
Contact Frank Finneran, Controller
Tel 508-667-8585
Fax 508-667-8821

Colorgen, Inc.
1 Federal St.
Billerica, MA 01821

Founded 1985
Total employees 100
Annual sales $11 million
Industries Computer Hardware, Computer Software
Growth Openings in past year 55; percentage growth 122%
Contact John K. O'Brien, COB/CEO/President
Tel 508-663-0029
Fax 508-663-2580

Conversion Devices, Inc.
15 Jonathan Dr.
Brockton, MA 02401

Founded 1987
Total employees 80
Annual sales $7.8 million
Industry Subassemblies and Components
Growth Openings in past year 15; percentage growth 23%
Contact James Zaros, President
Tel 508-559-0880
Fax 508-559-9288

Coral Network Corp.
8 Technology Dr.
Westborough, MA 01581

Founded 1989
Total employees 45
Annual sales $6.2 million
Industry Telecommunications
Growth Openings in past year 15; percentage growth 50%
Contact John Thibault, President/CEO
Tel 508-366-3600
Fax 508-870-1777

Corion Corp.
73 Jeffrey Ave.
Holliston, MA 01746

Founded 1967
Total employees 90
Industry Photonics
Contact David Carls, President/General Manager
Tel 508-429-5065
Fax 508-429-8983

C.R. Bard, Inc., Electrophysiology Division
25 Computer Dr.
Haverhill, MA 01832

Founded 1986
Total employees 200
Annual sales $13 million
Industries Computer Software, Medical
Growth Openings in past year 80; percentage growth 66%
Contact Ms. Karen Uzar, Personnel Director
Tel 508-373-3931
Fax 508-373-3931

CrossComm Corp.
450 Donald Lynch Blvd.
Marlborough, MA 01752

Founded 1986
Total employees 150
Annual sales $16.3 million
Industry Telecommunications
Growth Openings in past year 30; percentage growth 25%
Contact Tad Witkowicz, Founder/President
Tel 508-481-4060
Fax 508-490-5535

Cytyc Corp.
237 Cedar Hill St.
Marlborough, MA 01752

Founded 1987
Total employees 55
Industries Biotechnology, Medical

Growth Openings in past year 20; percentage growth 57%
Contact Ms. Lisa Tweed, Manager of Human Resources
Tel 508-481-1341
Fax 508-481-2173

Datasonics, Inc.
1400 Rte. 28A, PO Box 8
Cataumet, MA 02534

Founded 1980
Total employees 40
Annual sales $4.6 million
Industry Transportation
Growth Openings in past year 12; percentage growth 42%
Contact William Dalton, President
Tel 508-563-9311
Fax 508-563-9312

Design Circuits, Inc.
374 Turnpike Rd.
Southborough, MA 01772

Founded 1985
Total employees 60
Annual sales $5.8 million
Industry Subassemblies and Components
Growth Openings in past year 38; percentage growth 172%
Contact Walter P. Burr, Chief Executive Officer
Tel 508-485-0275
Fax 508-485-1810

Digital Consulting, Inc.
204 Andover St.
Andover, MA 01810

Founded 1981
Total employees 100
Annual sales $18.9 million
Industries Computer Hardware, Computer Software
Growth Openings in past year 47; percentage growth 88%
Contact Ronald J. Gomes, President
Tel 508-470-3870
Fax 508-470-0526

EcoScience Corp.
Three Biotech Park, One
   Innovation Dr.
Worcester, MA 01605

Founded 1982
Total employees 80
Industries Biotechnology,
   Chemicals
Growth Openings in past
   year 49; percentage
   growth 158%
Contact James A. Wylie,
   Jr.,
   President/CEO
Tel 508-754-0300
Fax 508-754-1134

Epoch Systems, Inc.
8 Technology Dr.
Westborough, MA 01581

Founded 1986
Total employees 150
Annual sales $25 million
Industry Computer
   Software
Growth Openings in past
   year 19; percentage
   growth 14%
Contact Christopher D.
   Robert,
   CEO/President
Tel 508-836-4300
Fax 508-366-6853

Fibre Optic Communications Specialists
50 D'Angelo Dr.
Marlborough, MA 01752

Founded 1982
Total employees 60
Industry Photonics
Growth Openings in past
   year 25; percentage
   growth 71%
Contact Ms. Kelly
   Iverson,
   Personnel Manager
Tel 508-480-9600
Fax 508-480-9688

EML Research, Inc.
2 Fox Rd.
Hudson, MA 01749

Founded 1982
Total employees 70
Annual sales $6.8 million
Industries Defense,
   Subassemblies and
   Components
Growth Openings in past
   year 22; percentage
   growth 45%
Contact G. Larry
   Roderick,
   President
Tel 508-562-2933
Fax 508-562-6830

Ergo Computing, Inc.
One Intercontinental Way
Peabody, MA 01960

Founded 1985
Total employees 75
Annual sales $12 million
Industries Computer
   Hardware, Computer
   Software
Growth Openings in past
   year 15; percentage
   growth 25%
Contact Ms. Barbara
   Russell,
   Director of Personnel
Tel 508-535-7510
Fax 508-535-7512

General Metal Finishing Co., Inc.
42 Frank Mossberg Dr.
Attleboro, MA 02703

Founded 1974
Total employees 115
Annual sales $10 million
Industry Manufacturing
   Equipment
Growth Openings in past
   year 22; percentage
   growth 23%
Contact Robert A. Palos,
   President
Tel 508-226-5606
Fax 508-226-5626

Entwistle Co.
Bigelow St.
Hudson, MA 01749

Founded 1954
Total employees 561
Industries Defense,
   Manufacturing
   Equipment
Growth Openings in past
   year 149; percentage
   growth 36%
Contact Paul Salek,
   Personnel Manager
Tel 508-481-4000
Fax 508-562-4808

Fiberspar, Inc.
2380 Cranberry Hwy.
West Wareham, MA
   02576

Founded 1986
Total employees 65
Annual sales $6.3 million
Industry Subassemblies
   and Components
Growth Openings in past
   year 30; percentage
   growth 85%
Contact Peter Quigley,
   President
Tel 508-291-2770
Fax 508-291-2772

GENE-TRAK Systems Corp.
31 New York Ave.
Framingham, MA 01701

Founded 1986
Total employees 150
Industry Medical
Growth Openings in past
   year 20; percentage
   growth 15%
Contact Ms. Donna
   LaDuke,
   Director of Human
   Resources
Tel 508-872-3113
Fax 508-879-6462

Harbor Software, Inc.
40 Beach St., Suite 203
Manchester, MA 01944

Founded 1991
Total employees 20
Industry Computer
Software
Growth Openings in past
year 15; percentage
growth 300%
Contact R.J. Ham,
President
Tel 508-526-1376
Fax 508-526-7728

HBM, Inc.
19 Bartlett St.
Marlborough, MA 01752

Founded 1973
Total employees 120
Annual sales $14 million
Industries Subassemblies
and Components, Test
and Measurement
Growth Openings in past
year 15; percentage
growth 14%
Contact Mike Altwein,
President
Tel 508-624-4500
Fax 508-485-7480

Highland Laboratories, Inc.
159 Chestnut St.
Ashland, MA 01721

Founded 1953
Total employees 43
Annual sales $4.8 million
Industries Factory
Automation,
Subassemblies and
Components
Growth Openings in past
year 18; percentage
growth 72%
Contact James Poitras,
President
Tel 508-881-1570
Fax 508-875-3290

HTI Voice Solutions, Inc.
333 Turnpike Rd.
Southborough, MA 01772

Founded 1986
Total employees 45
Annual sales $6.2 million
Industries Computer
Hardware, Computer
Software,
Telecommunications
Growth Openings in past
year 15; percentage
growth 50%
Contact Kenneth Brater,
President/CEO
Tel 508-485-8400
Fax 508-485-9584

HyperDesk Corp.
2000 West Park Dr.
Westborough, MA 01581

Founded 1990
Total employees 60
Industry Computer
Software
Growth Openings in past
year 20; percentage
growth 50%
Contact Jerry Levin,
Chief Executive Officer
Tel 508-366-5050
Fax 508-898-3841

Iconics, Inc.
100 Foxborough Blvd.
Foxboro, MA 02035

Founded 1986
Total employees 50
Annual sales $8 million
Industry Computer
Software
Growth Openings in past
year 15; percentage
growth 42%
Contact Russ Agrusa,
President
Tel 508-543-8600

Inspex, Inc.
47 Manning Park
Billerica, MA 01821

Founded 1973
Total employees 75
Annual sales $9.4 million
Industry Factory
Automation

Growth Openings in past
year 20; percentage
growth 36%
Contact Mario Maldari,
President
Tel 508-667-5500
Fax 508-663-0011

Intelligent Environments, Inc.
2 Highwood Dr.
Tewksbury, MA 01876

Founded 1985
Total employees 65
Annual sales $10 million
Industry Computer
Software
Growth Openings in past
year 30; percentage
growth 85%
Contact Dr. Terry
Golesworthy, Ph.D.,
President/CEO
Tel 508-640-1080
Fax 508-640-1090

Jaco, Inc.
155 Farm St., PO Box
309
Bellingham, MA 02019

Founded 1973
Total employees 80
Annual sales $7.0 million
Industry Manufacturing
Equipment
Growth Openings in past
year 15; percentage
growth 23%
Contact Alfred P. Rossini,
President
Tel 508-966-2141
Fax 508-966-0167

Keithley Instruments, Inc., Data Acquisition Division
440 Miles Standish Blvd.
Taunton, MA 02780

Founded 1983
Total employees 177
Industries Factory
Automation, Test and
Measurement

Growth Openings in past year 27; percentage growth 18%
Contact Ms. Marcella Nelson, Director of Human Resources
Tel 508-880-3000
Fax 508-880-0179

Keytek Instrument Corp.
260 Fordham Rd.
Wilmington, MA 01887

Founded 1975
Total employees 85
Annual sales $8 million
Industries Factory Automation, Test and Measurement
Growth Openings in past year 20; percentage growth 30%
Contact Peter Richman, President
Tel 508-658-0880
Fax 508-657-4803

Koch Membrane Systems, Inc.
850 Main St.
Wilmington, MA 01887

Founded 1966
Total employees 320
Industries Biotechnology, Environmental
Growth Openings in past year 40; percentage growth 14%
Contact Roger Dillon, Personnel Manager
Tel 508-657-4250
Fax 508-657-5208

Krohn-Hite Corp.
255 Bodwell St.
Avon, MA 02322

Founded 1949
Total employees 35
Annual sales $2.5 million
Industry Factory Automation

Growth Openings in past year 23; percentage growth 191%
Contact Ms. Cheryl Brustin, Accounting Manager
Tel 508-580-1660
Fax 508-583-8989

Leading Edge Products, Inc.
117 Flanders Rd.
Westborough, MA 01581

Founded 1980
Total employees 120
Annual sales $200 million
Industry Computer Hardware
Growth Openings in past year 15; percentage growth 14%
Contact Albert J. Agbay, President
Tel 508-836-4800
Fax 508-836-4504

LFE Industrial Systems
55 Green St.
Clinton, MA 01510

Founded 1946
Total employees 78
Annual sales $14 million
Industry Factory Automation
Growth Openings in past year 20; percentage growth 34%
Contact John Sullivan, Division Director
Tel 508-365-3400
Fax 508-365-3455

Micro Smart
200 Homer Ave.
Ashland, MA 01721

Founded 1980
Total employees 35
Industry Computer Hardware
Growth Openings in past year 20; percentage growth 133%
Contact Mal Gulden, President
Tel 508-872-9090
Fax 508-881-1521

MicroTouch Systems, Inc.
55 Jonspin Rd.
Wilmington, MA 01887

Founded 1982
Total employees 200
Annual sales $18 million
Industries Computer Hardware, Computer Software
Growth Openings in past year 100; percentage growth 100%
Contact James Logan, President
Tel 508-694-9900
Fax 508-694-9980

MPM Corp.
10 Forge Park
Franklin, MA 02038

Founded 1968
Total employees 85
Industry Manufacturing Equipment
Growth Openings in past year 20; percentage growth 30%
Contact Thomas Bagley, President
Tel 508-520-6999
Fax 508-520-2288

MRS Technology, Inc.
10 Elizabeth Dr.
Chelmsford, MA 01824

Founded 1986
Total employees 70
Industry Photonics
Growth Openings in past year 20; percentage growth 40%
Contact Ms. Joanne Carpenter, Employment Manager
Tel 508-250-0450
Fax 508-256-3266

New Media Graphics Corp.
780 Boston Rd.
Billerica, MA 01821

Founded 1981
Total employees 68
Annual sales $7.8 million

Industries Computer
Hardware, Computer
Software
Growth Openings in past
year 16; percentage
growth 30%
Contact Martin Duhms,
COB/President
Tel 508-663-0666
Fax 508-663-6678

**OHM Corporation,
Massachusetts Division**
88-C Elm St.
Hopkinton, MA 01748

Founded 1984
Total employees 70
Annual sales $15 million
Industry Environmental
Growth Openings in past
year 20; percentage
growth 40%
Contact Robert Kelly,
Division Manager
Tel 508-435-9561
Fax 508-435-9641

Omnirel Corp.
205 Crawford St.
Leominster, MA 01453

Founded 1985
Total employees 95
Annual sales $10 million
Industry Subassemblies
and Components
Growth Openings in past
year 15; percentage
growth 18%
Contact John
Catrambone,
President
Tel 508-534-5776
Fax 508-537-4246

Orbotech, Inc.
44 Manning Rd.
Billerica, MA 01821

Founded 1983
Total employees 400
Industries Computer
Hardware, Factory
Automation
Contact David Eisner,
President
Tel 508-667-6037
Fax 508-667-9969

PAGG Corp.
13 Airport Industrial Park
Hopedale, MA 01747

Founded 1981
Total employees 125
Annual sales $20 million
Industries Computer
Hardware,
Subassemblies and
Components
Growth Openings in past
year 20; percentage
growth 19%
Contact Edward Price,
President
Tel 508-478-8544
Fax 508-634-2409

Physical Sciences, Inc.
20 New England Business
Ctr.
Andover, MA 01810

Founded 1973
Total employees 160
Annual sales $12 million
Industries Energy,
Holding Companies,
Transportation
Growth Openings in past
year 35; percentage
growth 28%
Contact George
Caledonia,
President
Tel 508-689-0003
Fax 508-689-3232

PictureTel Corp.
Northwood Towers, 222
Rosewood Dr.
Danvers, MA 01923

Founded 1984
Total employees 741
Annual sales $141 million
Industry
Telecommunications
Growth Openings in past
year 212; percentage
growth 40%
Contact Dr. Norman E.
Gaut,
COB/CEO/President
Tel 508-762-5000
Fax 508-762-5245

**Piggott Wire & Cable
Specialist, Inc.**
PO Box 356
Seekonk, MA 02771

Founded 1977
Total employees 33
Annual sales $4 million
Industry Subassemblies
and Components
Growth Openings in past
year 13; percentage
growth 65%
Contact Burton Piggott,
President/Owner
Tel 508-336-6240
Fax 508-336-3032

**Polymetallurgical, Inc.,
Cooper Wire Division**
262 Broad St.
North Attleboro, MA
02761

Founded 1971
Total employees 70
Industry Advanced
Materials
Contact Armen
Iskenderian,
President
Tel 508-699-0611
Fax 508-695-7512

Precision Robots, Inc.
749 Middlesex Tpke.
Billerica, MA 01821

Founded 1982
Total employees 190
Annual sales $25 million
Industry Factory
Automation
Growth Openings in past
year 60; percentage
growth 46%
Contact Mord Weisler,
President
Tel 508-663-8555
Fax 508-663-9755

**Proconics International,
Inc.**
65 Johnstin Rd.
Wilmington, MA 01801

Founded 1981
Total employees 100
Annual sales $12 million

Industries Factory
Automation,
Manufacturing
Equipment
Growth Openings in past
year 25; percentage
growth 33%
Contact Peter Chiasson,
President
Tel 508-658-7300
Fax 508-658-7685

Proteon, Inc.
9 Technology Dr.
Westborough, MA 01581

Founded 1972
Total employees 450
Annual sales $94.7 million
Industries Computer
Software,
Subassemblies and
Components,
Telecommunications
Growth Openings in past
year 30; percentage
growth 7%
Contact Patrick Courtin,
President/CEO
Tel 508-898-2800
Fax 508-366-8901

Rational Systems, Inc.
220 North Main St.
Natick, MA 01760

Founded 1984
Total employees 48
Annual sales $5.5 million
Industry Computer
Software
Growth Openings in past
year 18; percentage
growth 60%
Contact Terence
Colligan,
President
Tel 508-653-6006
Fax 508-655-2753

RISO, Inc.
300 Rosewood Dr., Suite
210
Danvers, MA 01923

Founded 1987
Total employees 130
Industry Computer
Hardware

Growth Openings in past
year 40; percentage
growth 44%
Contact John Carillon,
President
Tel 508-777-7377
Fax 508-777-2517

Sequoia Systems, Inc.
400 Nickerson Rd.
Marlborough, MA 01752

Founded 1981
Total employees 384
Annual sales $81 million
Industries Computer
Hardware, Computer
Software
Growth Openings in past
year 39; percentage
growth 11%
Contact Carl Lopes,
Director of Human
Resources
Tel 508-480-0800
Fax 508-480-0184

**Siemens Medical
Electronics, Inc.**
16 Electronics Ave.
Danvers, MA 01923

Founded 1988
Total employees 388
Annual sales $42 million
Industry Medical
Growth Openings in past
year 48; percentage
growth 14%
Contact Ms. Dottie
Nestle,
Director of Personnel
Tel 508-750-7500
Fax 508-777-3398

**Smith & Nephew
Dyonics**
160 Dascomb Rd.
Andover, MA 01810

Founded 1986
Total employees 575
Industries Medical,
Photonics

Growth Openings in past
year 48; percentage
growth 9%
Contact Charles
Frederico,
President
Tel 508-470-2800
Fax 508-470-2227

SMT East Corp.
200 Foxborough Blvd.
Foxboro, MA 02035

Founded 1988
Total employees 70
Annual sales $5 million
Industries Manufacturing
Equipment,
Subassemblies and
Components
Growth Openings in past
year 20; percentage
growth 40%
Contact John Baider,
President
Tel 508-543-2600
Fax 508-543-3515

Synernetics Inc.
85 Rangeway Rd.
North Billerica, MA 01862

Founded 1988
Total employees 80
Annual sales $10 million
Industries Computer
Software,
Telecommunications
Growth Openings in past
year 20; percentage
growth 33%
Contact Allan L. Wallack,
President/CEO
Tel 508-670-9009
Fax 508-670-9015

Sytron Corp.
134 Flanders Rd., PO Box
5025
Westborough, MA 01581

Founded 1983
Total employees 100
Annual sales $10 million
Industry Computer
Software

Growth Openings in past year 50; percentage growth 100%
Contact Bob Werbicki, Acting President
Tel 508-898-0100
Fax 508-898-2677

Tech Etch, Inc.
45 Aldrin Rd.
Plymouth, MA 02360

Founded 1961
Total employees 260
Annual sales $15 million
Industries Manufacturing Equipment, Subassemblies and Components
Growth Openings in past year 20; percentage growth 8%
Contact George Keeler, President
Tel 508-747-0300
Fax 508-746-9639

Thermo Environmental Instruments, Inc.
8 West Forge Pkwy.
Franklin, MA 02038

Founded 1970
Total employees 175
Industry Environmental
Growth Openings in past year 35; percentage growth 25%
Contact Denis Holm, President
Tel 508-520-0430
Fax 508-520-1460

Unifi Communications Corp.
4 Federal St.
Billerica, MA 01821

Founded 1989
Total employees 55
Annual sales $1 million
Industry Computer Software
Growth Openings in past year 15; percentage growth 37%
Contact Bob Pokress, President/CEO
Tel 508-663-7570
Fax 508-663-7543

Vicor Corp.
23 Frontage Rd.
Andover, MA 01810

Founded 1981
Total employees 525
Annual sales $55.59 million
Industry Subassemblies and Components
Growth Openings in past year 16; percentage growth 3%
Contact Patrizio Vinciarelli, Ph.D., COB/President
Tel 508-470-2900
Fax 508-475-6715

Viewlogic Systems, Inc.
293 Boston Post Rd. West
Marlborough, MA 01752

Founded 1984
Total employees 358
Annual sales $65.78 million
Industries Computer Software, Holding Companies
Growth Openings in past year 72; percentage growth 25%
Contact Eugene Connolly, VP of Human Resources
Tel 508-480-0881
Fax 508-480-0882

Vision-Sciences, Inc.
6 Strathmore Rd.
Natick, MA 01760

Founded 1990
Total employees 100
Annual sales $5.5 million
Industries Holding Companies, Medical, Photonics
Growth Openings in past year 50; percentage growth 100%
Contact David W. Prigmore, COB/President/CEO
Tel 508-650-9971
Fax 508-650-9976

VMARK Software, Inc.
30 Speen St.
Framingham, MA 01701

Founded 1984
Total employees 105
Annual sales $12.4 million
Industry Computer Software
Growth Openings in past year 55; percentage growth 110%
Contact James Walsh, VP of Finance and Administration
Tel 508-879-3311
Fax 508-879-3332

Walker Magnetics Group, Inc.
17 Rockdale St.
Worcester, MA 01606

Founded 1974
Total employees 500
Industry Holding Companies
Growth Openings in past year 100; percentage growth 25%
Contact Ms. Allyson Picard, Personnel Manager
Tel 508-853-3232
Fax 508-853-3344

XRE Corporation
300 Foster St., PO Box 1154
Littleton, MA 01460

Founded 1971
Total employees 230
Annual sales $40 million
Industry Medical
Growth Openings in past year 80; percentage growth 53%
Contact Ms. Maura Touhy, Personnel Manager
Tel 508-486-9681
Fax 508-486-3426

Zymark Corp.
Zymark Center
Hopkinton, MA 01748

Founded 1981
Total employees 234
Annual sales $27.1 million
Industries Computer
  Software, Factory
  Automation, Test and
  Measurement
Growth Openings in past
  year 14; percentage
  growth 6%
Contact Ms. Pamela
  Duggan,
  Director of Human
  Resources
Tel 508-435-9500
Fax 508-435-3439

American Superconductor Corp.
149 Grove St.
Watertown, MA 02172

Founded 1987
Total employees 67
Annual sales $2.88 million
Industries Advanced
  Materials,
  Subassemblies and
  Components
Growth Openings in past
  year 30; percentage
  growth 81%
Contact Dr. Gregory
  Yurek, Ph.D.,
  COB/President/CEO
Tel 617-923-1122
Fax 617-923-0020

Ascent Technology, Inc.
64 Sidney St., Suite 380
Cambridge, MA 02139

Founded 1986
Total employees 30
Annual sales $3.4 million
Industry Computer
  Software
Growth Openings in past
  year 12; percentage
  growth 66%
Contact Ms. Karen
  Prendergast,
  President
Tel 617-225-0850
Fax 617-225-0822

■ **617 Area Code**

Agency Management Services, Inc.
700 Longwater Dr.
Norwell, MA 02061

Founded 1963
Total employees 700
Annual sales $72 million
Industry Computer
  Software
Growth Openings in past
  year 46; percentage
  growth 7%
Contact Bruce Norton,
  Director of Human
  Resources
Tel 617-982-9400
Fax 617-982-9892

Alkermes, Inc.
64 Sidney St.
Cambridge, MA 02139

Founded 1987
Total employees 70
Industry Medical
Growth Openings in past
  year 40; percentage
  growth 133%
Contact Richard Pops,
  President/CEO
Tel 617-494-0171
Fax 617-494-9263

Application Systems Group
92 Montvale Ave.
Stoneham, MA 02180

Founded 1989
Total employees 95
Industries Computer
  Hardware, Holding
  Companies
Growth Openings in past
  year 65; percentage
  growth 216%
Contact Gary Whear,
  President
Tel 617-279-2790
Fax 617-279-1009

Applied Science and Technology, Inc.
35 Cabot Rd.
Woburn, MA 01801

Founded 1987
Total employees 53
Annual sales $6 million
Industries Holding
  Companies,
  Manufacturing
  Equipment,
  Subassemblies and
  Components
Growth Openings in past
  year 13; percentage
  growth 32%
Contact Dr. Richard S.
  Post, Ph.D.,
  President
Tel 617-933-5560
Fax 617-923-0750

Bachman Information Systems, Inc.
8 New England Executive
Park
Burlington, MA 01803

Founded 1983
Total employees 350
Annual sales $31.5 million
Industry Computer
  Software
Growth Openings in past
  year 120; percentage
  growth 52%
Contact Arnold A. Kraft,
  CEO/President
Tel 617-273-9003
Fax 617-229-9904

Biogen, Inc.
14 Cambridge Ctr.
Cambridge, MA 02142

Founded 1978
Total employees 354
Annual sales $135.11
  million
Industries Biotechnology,
  Pharmaceuticals
Growth Openings in past
  year 24; percentage
  growth 7%
Contact Frank A. Burke,
  VP of Human Resources
Tel 617-252-9200
Fax 617-252-9617

Biopure Corp.
68 Harrison Ave.
Boston, MA 02111

Founded 1963
Total employees 85
Annual sales $4.0 million
Industries Biotechnology,
Pharmaceuticals
Growth Openings in past
year 15; percentage
growth 21%
Contact James O'Shea,
President
Tel 617-350-7800
Fax 617-350-6614

Bird Environmental Systems and Services, Inc.
89 Access Rd., Suite 24
Norwood, MA 02062

Founded 1986
Total employees 80
Annual sales $7 million
Industry Environmental
Growth Openings in past
year 55; percentage
growth 220%
Contact Philip Giantris,
President
Tel 617-255-0108
Fax 617-255-0114

BSC Group
425 Summer St.
Boston, MA 02210

Founded 1965
Total employees 110
Annual sales $7.5 million
Industries Computer
Hardware,
Manufacturing
Equipment
Growth Openings in past
year 20; percentage
growth 22%
Contact David Hays,
Vice President
Tel 617-330-5300
Fax 617-345-8008

Cambridge NeuroScience, Inc.
1 Kendall Sq., Building
700
Cambridge, MA 02139

Founded 1986
Total employees 85
Industries Biotechnology,
Medical,
Pharmaceuticals
Growth Openings in past
year 35; percentage
growth 70%
Contact Elkan R. Gamzu,
President
Tel 617-225-0600
Fax 617-225-2741

Cayman Systems, Inc.
26 Landsdowne St.
Cambridge, MA 02139

Founded 1987
Total employees 90
Annual sales $20 million
Industries Computer
Software,
Telecommunications
Growth Openings in past
year 15; percentage
growth 20%
Contact Ms. Jane
Sanabria,
Personnel Officer
Tel 617-494-1999
Fax 617-494-9270

Center for Blood Research
800 Huntington Ave.
Boston, MA 02115

Founded 1982
Total employees 200
Annual sales $19 million
Industries Holding
Companies, Medical,
Pharmaceuticals
Growth Openings in past
year 100; percentage
growth 100%
Contact Mrs. Robin
Rosenthal,
Personnel Director
Tel 617-731-6470
Fax 617-278-3493

CenterLine Software, Inc.
10 Fawcett St.
Cambridge, MA 02138

Founded 1987
Total employees 135
Annual sales $15 million
Industry Computer
Software
Growth Openings in past
year 45; percentage
growth 50%
Contact Sesha Pratap,
President/CEO
Tel 617-498-3000
Fax 617-868-5004

CeraMem Corp.
12 Clematis Ave.
Waltham, MA 02154

Founded 1986
Total employees 30
Industries Biotechnology,
Test and Measurement
Growth Openings in past
year 15; percentage
growth 100%
Contact Ms. Harriet
Moldau,
Personnel and
Purchasing Manager
Tel 617-899-0467
Fax 617-899-1227

Chase Corp.
50 Braintree Hill Park,
Suite 220
Braintree, MA 02184

Founded 1951
Total employees 140
Annual sales $22.7 million
Industry Holding
Companies
Growth Openings in past
year 20; percentage
growth 16%
Contact Peter Chase,
President/COO
Tel 617-848-2810
Fax 617-843-9639

CLAM Associates, Inc.
101 Main St.
Cambridge, MA 02142

Founded 1987
Total employees 61

Industries Computer Hardware, Computer Software
Growth Openings in past year 41; percentage growth 205%
Contact George Linscott, President
Tel 617-374-7900
Fax 617-252-0820

Growth Openings in past year 12; percentage growth 30%
Contact Tibor Vais, General Manager
Tel 617-661-9440
Fax 617-499-0963

Growth Openings in past year 181; percentage growth 43%
Contact Stephen D.R. Moore, President
Tel 617-821-4500
Fax 617-821-5688

Cognex Corp.
15 Crawford St.
Needham, MA 02194

Founded 1981
Total employees 150
Annual sales $32 million
Industry Factory Automation
Growth Openings in past year 30; percentage growth 25%
Contact Ms. Bina Thompson, Manager of Investor Relations/Treasurer
Tel 617-449-6030
Fax 617-449-4013

Computer Merchant Ltd.
80 Washington St., Bldg. E
Norwell, MA 02061

Founded 1978
Total employees 160
Industry Computer Hardware
Growth Openings in past year 20; percentage growth 14%
Contact John R. Danieli, President
Tel 617-878-1070
Fax 617-878-4712

Cortex Corp.
100 5th Ave., PO Box 9097
Waltham, MA 02254

Founded 1977
Total employees 102
Annual sales $11 million
Industry Computer Software
Growth Openings in past year 17; percentage growth 20%
Contact Ms. Betty Richardson, Director of Human Resources and Administ
Tel 617-622-1900
Fax 617-622-1934

Copley Systems
165 University Ave.
Westwood, MA 02090

Founded 1979
Total employees 120
Annual sales $81 million
Industry Computer Hardware
Growth Openings in past year 20; percentage growth 20%
Contact Michael Moskowitz, President
Tel 617-320-8300
Fax 617-320-8327

Colgate-Hoyt, Gel-Kam
One Colgate Way
Canton, MA 02021

Founded 1959
Total employees 180
Annual sales $50 million
Industries Medical, Pharmaceuticals
Growth Openings in past year 60; percentage growth 50%
Contact Cyrill Siewert, President
Tel 617-821-2880

Costar Corp.
1 Alewife Ctr.
Cambridge, MA 02140

Founded 1946
Total employees 620
Annual sales $74.9 million
Industries Biotechnology, Test and Measurement
Growth Openings in past year 67; percentage growth 12%
Contact Alfred LaGreca, VP of Human Resources
Tel 617-868-6200
Fax 617-868-2076

CompuServe Data Technologies
1000 Massachusetts Ave.
Cambridge, MA 02138

Founded 1972
Total employees 52
Industry Computer Software

Corporate Software, Inc.
275 Dan Rd.
Canton, MA 02021

Founded 1983
Total employees 600
Annual sales $301 million
Industries Computer Hardware, Computer Software

Course Technology, Inc.
One Main St.
Cambridge, MA 02142

Founded 1989
Total employees 45
Industry Computer Software

Growth Openings in past year 15; percentage growth 50%
Contact John M. Connolly, President
Tel 617-225-2595
Fax 617-225-7976

Growth Openings in past year 20; percentage growth 28%
Contact Mel Bosch, President
Tel 617-890-2345
Fax 617-890-4229

Growth Openings in past year 15; percentage growth 13%
Contact Ms. Helen Dolan, Personnel Administrator
Tel 617-935-7444
Fax 617-938-7219

CP Clare Corp., Solid State Products Division
107 Audubon Rd.
Wakefield, MA 01880

Founded 1976
Total employees 75
Annual sales $7.3 million
Industry Subassemblies and Components
Growth Openings in past year 32; percentage growth 74%
Contact Ms. Barbara McGrail, Personnel Administrator
Tel 617-246-4000
Fax 617-246-1356

Delphi McCracken, Inc.
10 Mall Rd.
Burlington, MA 01803

Founded 1971
Total employees 360
Industry Computer Software
Growth Openings in past year 100; percentage growth 38%
Contact Ms. Tricia Schuster, Vice President/General Manager
Tel 617-273-0010
Fax 617-273-1209

Dragon Systems, Inc.
320 Nevada St.
Newton, MA 02160

Founded 1982
Total employees 75
Annual sales $8.7 million
Industries Computer Hardware, Computer Software
Growth Openings in past year 25; percentage growth 50%
Contact Ms. AliceAin Rich, Human Resources Manager
Tel 617-965-5200
Fax 617-527-0372

Dataware Technologies, Inc.
222 Third St.
Cambridge, MA 02142

Founded 1987
Total employees 85
Annual sales $10 million
Industry Computer Software
Growth Openings in past year 35; percentage growth 70%
Contact Kurt Mueller, President
Tel 617-621-0820
Fax 617-621-0307

Desktop Data, Inc.
1601 Trapelo Rd.
Waltham, MA 02154

Founded 1988
Total employees 55
Industries Computer Software, Telecommunications
Growth Openings in past year 15; percentage growth 37%
Contact Don McLagan, President
Tel 617-890-0042
Fax 617-890-1565

D.R.W. Computer Services, Inc.
636 Washington St.
Canton, MA 02021

Founded 1982
Total employees 45
Industries Computer Hardware, Manufacturing Equipment
Growth Openings in past year 15; percentage growth 50%
Contact Dom Rodriguez, President
Tel 617-821-2290
Fax 617-821-2291

Daymarc Corp.
301 Second Ave.
Waltham, MA 02154

Founded 1959
Total employees 90
Industry Factory Automation

Dolan-Jenner Industries, Inc.
Blueberry Hill Industrial Pk., PO Box 1020
Woburn, MA 01801

Founded 1962
Total employees 125
Annual sales $15 million
Industries Factory Automation, Photonics, Test and Measurement

Easel Corp.
25 Corporate Dr.
Burlington, MA 01803

Founded 1981
Total employees 265
Annual sales $28.4 million
Industry Computer Software

Growth Openings in past year 115; percentage growth 76%
Contact R. Douglas Kahn, President
Tel 617-221-2100
Fax 617-221-3099

EDS Personal Communications Corp.
1601 Trapelo Rd.
Waltham, MA 02154

Founded 1986
Total employees 450
Industry Telecommunications
Growth Openings in past year 150; percentage growth 50%
Contact Robert Lentz, Senior Vice President
Tel 617-890-1000
Fax 617-890-0367

EKTRON Applied Imaging, Inc.
23 Crosby Dr.
Bedford, MA 01730

Founded 1986
Total employees 125
Annual sales $20 million
Industries Computer Hardware, Photonics
Growth Openings in past year 45; percentage growth 56%
Contact Philip Considine, President
Tel 617-275-0475
Fax 617-271-1977

Energy Investment, Inc.
286 Congress St
Boston, MA 02210

Founded 1973
Total employees 90
Annual sales $3.7 million
Industries Energy, Manufacturing Equipment

Growth Openings in past year 40; percentage growth 80%
Contact Ms. Mary Myers Kauppila, President
Tel 617-482-8228
Fax 617-482-3784

Epsilon
50 Cambridge St.
Burlington, MA 01803

Founded 1970
Total employees 800
Annual sales $130 million
Industries Computer Hardware, Holding Companies
Growth Openings in past year 199; percentage growth 33%
Contact Robert J. Drummond, President
Tel 617-273-0250
Fax 617-270-6760

Exos, Inc.
2A Gill St.
Woburn, MA 01801

Founded 1988
Total employees 25
Annual sales $3 million
Industry Medical
Growth Openings in past year 15; percentage growth 150%
Contact Carl Muscari, President
Tel 617-933-0022
Fax 617-933-0303

FAX International, Inc.
60 Mall Rd.
Burlington, MA 01803

Founded 1991
Total employees 77
Industry Telecommunications
Growth Openings in past year 49; percentage growth 175%
Contact Douglas J. Ranalli, President
Tel 617-221-0444
Fax 617-221-7210

Focus Enhancements
800 West Cummings Park, Suite 4500
Woburn, MA 01801

Founded 1991
Total employees 35
Annual sales $5.7 million
Industries Computer Hardware, Computer Software, Factory Automation, Subassemblies and Components, Telecommunications
Growth Openings in past year 33; percentage growth 1650%
Contact Thomas Massie, President/CEO
Tel 617-938-8088
Fax 617-938-7741

GCC Technologies, Inc.
209 Burlington Rd.
Bedford, MA 01730

Founded 1980
Total employees 185
Annual sales $50 million
Industries Computer Hardware, Computer Software
Growth Openings in past year 35; percentage growth 23%
Contact Kevin Curran, President/CEO
Tel 617-275-5800
Fax 617-275-1115

Genetics Institute, Inc.
87 Cambridge Park Dr.
Cambridge, MA 02140

Founded 1981
Total employees 700
Annual sales $60.44 million
Industry Biotechnology
Growth Openings in past year 97; percentage growth 16%
Contact Gabriel Schmergel, President/CEO
Tel 617-876-1170
Fax 617-868-1024

GIS/Trans, Ltd.
675 Massachusetts Ave.
Cambridge, MA 02139

Founded 1990
Total employees 25
Industry Computer
Software
Growth Openings in past
year 15; percentage
growth 150%
Contact Simon Lewis,
President
Tel 617-354-2771
Fax 617-354-8964

GZA GeoEnvironmental, Inc.
320 Needham St.
Newton Upper Falls, MA 02164

Founded 1965
Total employees 423
Annual sales $45 million
Industries Environmental,
Test and Measurement
Growth Openings in past
year 21; percentage
growth 5%
Contact Donald T.
Goldberg,
President
Tel 617-969-0050
Fax 617-965-7769

GZA GeoEnvironmental Technologies, Inc.
320 Needham St.
Newton Upper Falls, MA 02164

Founded 1965
Total employees 542
Annual sales $35 million
Industry Holding
Companies
Growth Openings in past
year 16; percentage
growth 3%
Contact James C.
Webber,
Director of Human
Resources
Tel 617-969-0700
Fax 617-969-0715

Hologic, Inc.
590 Lincoln St.
Waltham, MA 02154

Founded 1985
Total employees 150
Annual sales $27 million
Industry Medical
Growth Openings in past
year 20; percentage
growth 15%
Contact Ms. Nancy
Bubeck,
Manager of Human
Resources
Tel 617-893-5100
Fax 617-890-8031

Homisco, Inc.
99 Washington St.
Melrose, MA 02176

Founded 1981
Total employees 43
Annual sales $2.9 million
Industry Computer
Software
Growth Openings in past
year 16; percentage
growth 59%
Contact Ron Contrado,
President
Tel 617-665-1997
Fax 617-665-3013

ImmunoGen, Inc.
60 Hamilton St.
Cambridge, MA 02139

Founded 1981
Total employees 190
Annual sales $3 million
Industry Biotechnology
Growth Openings in past
year 45; percentage
growth 31%
Contact Mitchel Sayare,
Chief Executive Officer
Tel 617-661-9312
Fax 617-661-9334

Infotec Development, Inc., Eastern Division
201 Edgewater Park
Wakefield, MA 01880

Founded 1984
Total employees 125
Annual sales $90.4 million

Industries Computer
Hardware, Computer
Software
Growth Openings in past
year 35; percentage
growth 38%
Contact Paul Saint Jean,
Director of Personnel
and Administration
Tel 617-245-7300
Fax 617-245-7301

Intra Sonix, Inc.
42 Third Ave.
Burlington, MA 01803

Founded 1988
Total employees 70
Annual sales $7.7 million
Industry Medical
Growth Openings in past
year 20; percentage
growth 40%
Contact Donald C.
Freeman, Jr.,
CEO/President
Tel 617-270-9510
Fax 617-270-9585

IPL Systems, Inc.
60 Hickory Dr.
Waltham, MA 02154

Founded 1973
Total employees 133
Annual sales $53 million
Industry Computer
Hardware
Growth Openings in past
year 19; percentage
growth 16%
Contact Greg R.
Grodhaus,
President/CEO
Tel 617-890-6620
Fax 617-890-8128

IRIS Graphics, Inc.
6 Crosby Dr.
Bedford, MA 01730

Founded 1984
Total employees 210
Annual sales $57 million
Industry Computer
Hardware

Growth Openings in past
year 70; percentage
growth 50%
Contact Alphonse M.
Lucchese,
President/CEO
Tel 617-275-8777
Fax 617-275-8590

**John Snow, Inc.,
Fundraising Systems
Division**
210 Lincoln St.
Boston, MA 02111

Founded 1979
Total employees 27
Industry Computer
Software
Growth Openings in past
year 12; percentage
growth 80%
Contact James
Williamson,
Chief Executive Officer
Tel 617-482-9485
Fax 617-482-0617

Kenan Systems Corp.
1 Main St.
Cambridge, MA 02142

Founded 1982
Total employees 105
Annual sales $12 million
Industry Computer
Software
Growth Openings in past
year 20; percentage
growth 23%
Contact Kenan Fahin,
President
Tel 617-225-2200
Fax 617-225-2220

Kronos, Inc.
62 Fourth Ave.
Waltham, MA 02154

Founded 1977
Total employees 550
Annual sales $47.8 million
Industry Computer
Hardware

Growth Openings in past
year 50; percentage
growth 10%
Contact Ms. Mary
Staples,
Director of Human
Resources
Tel 617-890-3232
Fax 617-890-8768

LC Services Corp.
165 New Boston St.
Woburn, MA 01801

Founded 1980
Total employees 22
Industry Chemicals
Growth Openings in past
year 16; percentage
growth 266%
Contact Paul E. Driedger,
President
Tel 617-938-1700
Fax 617-938-5420

Loral Hycor, Inc.
10 Gill St.
Woburn, MA 01801

Founded 1973
Total employees 175
Industry Defense
Growth Openings in past
year 75; percentage
growth 75%
Contact L. James Larson,
President
Tel 617-935-5950
Fax 617-932-3764

**MANAGER SOFTWARE
PRODUCTS INC**
131 Hartwell Ave.
Lexington, MA 02173

Founded 1966
Total employees 300
Annual sales $34 million
Industry Computer
Software
Growth Openings in past
year 50; percentage
growth 20%
Contact Michael Dexter
Smith,
Chief Operating Officer
Tel 617-863-5800
Fax 617-861-6130

Marcam Corporation
95 Wells Ave.
Newton, MA 02159

Founded 1980
Total employees 620
Annual sales $80.35
million
Industry Computer
Software
Growth Openings in past
year 67; percentage
growth 12%
Contact Paul Margolis,
COB/President
Tel 617-965-0220
Fax 617-965-7273

MedChem Products, Inc.
232 West Cummings Park
Woburn, MA 01801

Founded 1972
Total employees 80
Annual sales $22.6 million
Industries Chemicals,
Holding Companies,
Medical
Growth Openings in past
year 32; percentage
growth 66%
Contact Jonathan
Donaldson,
President/CEO
Tel 617-938-9328
Fax 617-938-0657

Medical Parameters, Inc.
30 G Commerce Way
Woburn, MA 01801

Founded 1973
Total employees 70
Industry Medical
Growth Openings in past
year 15; percentage
growth 27%
Contact Ms. Mary Paiva,
Personnel Director
Tel 617-933-5558
Fax 617-935-5931

**Mediq Mobile X-Ray
Services, Inc.**
1417 Hyde Park Ave.
Hyde Park, MA 02136

Founded 1977
Total employees 160
Annual sales $17 million

Industry Medical
Growth Openings in past year 20; percentage growth 14%
Contact Lawrence Smith, President
Tel 617-364-2110
Fax 617-364-4232

Megapulse, Inc.
8 Preston Ct.
Bedford, MA 01730

Founded 1973
Total employees 80
Annual sales $20 million
Industries
Telecommunications, Transportation
Growth Openings in past year 45; percentage growth 128%
Contact Ms. Phyllis Hull, Human Resources Director
Tel 617-275-2010
Fax 617-275-4149

Microcom, Inc.
500 River Ridge Dr.
Norwood, MA 02062

Founded 1980
Total employees 350
Annual sales $73.9 million
Industries Computer Software, Telecommunications
Growth Openings in past year 49; percentage growth 16%
Contact James Dow, President/CEO
Tel 617-551-1000
Fax 617-551-1006

MicroTrac Systems, Inc.
20 Wells Ave..
Newton, MA 02159

Founded 1981
Total employees 55
Industry Computer Software

Growth Openings in past year 20; percentage growth 57%
Contact Lars Perkins, President/CEO
Tel 617-965-4660
Fax 617-965-9654

Mitek Surgical Products, Inc.
27 Providence Hwy.
Norwood, MA 02062

Founded 1985
Total employees 60
Annual sales $13.8 million
Industry Medical
Growth Openings in past year 20; percentage growth 50%
Contact Kenneth Anstey, CEO/President
Tel 617-551-8500
Fax 617-551-8501

Molecular Simulations, Inc.
16 New England Executive Park
Burlington, MA 01803

Founded 1984
Total employees 150
Industry Computer Software
Growth Openings in past year 50; percentage growth 50%
Contact Michael Savage, President/CEO
Tel 617-229-9800
Fax 617-229-9899

Nidec-Power General
152 Will Dr.
Canton, MA 02021

Founded 1979
Total employees 253
Industry Subassemblies and Components
Growth Openings in past year 93; percentage growth 58%
Contact Charles Aubee, General Manager
Tel 617-828-6216
Fax 617-828-3215

Object Design, Inc.
1 New England Executive Park
Burlington, MA 01803

Founded 1988
Total employees 75
Annual sales $8.7 million
Industry Computer Software
Growth Openings in past year 25; percentage growth 50%
Contact Ms. Angela Watz, Administration Manager
Tel 617-270-9797
Fax 617-279-3509

Panametrics, Inc.
221 Crescent St.
Waltham, MA 02154

Founded 1960
Total employees 600
Annual sales $80 million
Industry Holding Companies
Growth Openings in past year 100; percentage growth 20%
Contact David Chleck, Chairman of the Board
Tel 617-899-2719
Fax 617-899-1552

Parametric Technology Corp.
128 Technology Dr.
Waltham, MA 02154

Founded 1985
Total employees 750
Annual sales $86.74 million
Industry Computer Software
Growth Openings in past year 400; percentage growth 114%
Contact Ms. Patricia White, Director of Human Resources
Tel 617-894-7111
Fax 617-891-1069

PB Diagnostic Systems, Inc.
151 University Ave.
Westwood, MA 02090

Founded 1984
Total employees 310
Annual sales $24 million
Industries Biotechnology,
Pharmaceuticals
Growth Openings in past
year 29; percentage
growth 10%
Contact Fareedd Kureshi,
General Manager/Senior
Vice President
Tel 617-320-3000
Fax 617-320-3199

Perception Technology Corp.
40 Shawmut Rd.
Canton, MA 02021

Founded 1968
Total employees 124
Annual sales $16.7 million
Industry Computer
Hardware
Growth Openings in past
year 36; percentage
growth 40%
Contact Ms. Debora
Aubin,
Personnel Director
Tel 617-821-0320
Fax 617-828-7886

PerSeptive Biosystems, Inc.
38 Sidney St.
Cambridge, MA 02139

Founded 1987
Total employees 55
Annual sales $5.01 million
Industry Test and
Measurement
Growth Openings in past
year 17; percentage
growth 44%
Contact Dr. Noubar
Afeyan,
President/CEO
Tel 617-621-1787
Fax 617-621-2575

Pilot Software, Inc.
40 Broad St.
Boston, MA 02109

Founded 1983
Total employees 255
Annual sales $29 million
Industry Computer
Software
Growth Openings in past
year 95; percentage
growth 59%
Contact Ms. Andrea
Johnson,
Human Resources
Manager
Tel 617-350-7035
Fax 617-350-7118

Platelet Research Products, Inc.
313 Pleasant St.
Watertown, MA 02172

Founded 1984
Total employees 25
Industry Medical
Growth Openings in past
year 13; percentage
growth 108%
Contact Dr. Francis
Chao, MD, Ph.D.,
Chief Executive Officer
Tel 617-924-5550
Fax 617-924-5861

Powersoft Corp.
70 Blanchard Rd.
Burlington, MA 01803

Founded 1974
Total employees 106
Annual sales $21.2 million
Industry Computer
Software
Growth Openings in past
year 21; percentage
growth 24%
Contact Mitchell E.
Kertzman,
COB/CEO
Tel 617-229-2200
Fax 617-272-2540

Practice Management Systems, Inc.
140 Gould St.
Needham, MA 02194

Founded 1983
Total employees 200
Industry Computer
Software
Growth Openings in past
year 30; percentage
growth 17%
Contact John Mineck,
President
Tel 617-455-8416

Printed Circuit Corp.
10 Micro Dr.
Woburn, MA 01801

Founded 1963
Total employees 250
Annual sales $24 million
Industries Computer
Hardware,
Subassemblies and
Components
Growth Openings in past
year 29; percentage
growth 13%
Contact Peter Sarmanian,
Chief Executive Officer
Tel 617-935-9570
Fax 617-933-5124

Programart Corp.
124 Mt. Auburn St.
Cambridge, MA 02138

Founded 1969
Total employees 120
Annual sales $13 million
Industry Computer
Software
Growth Openings in past
year 20; percentage
growth 20%
Contact John E. Thron,
President
Tel 617-661-3020
Fax 617-864-6558

Progress Software Corp.
14 Oak Park
Bedford, MA 01730

Founded 1981
Total employees 650
Annual sales $85.1 million

Industry Computer
Software
Growth Openings in past
year 199; percentage
growth 44%
Contact Joseph Alsop,
President
Tel 617-280-4000
Fax 617-280-4095

Repligen Corp.
1 Kendall Sq., Bldg. 700
Cambridge, MA 02139

Founded 1981
Total employees 260
Annual sales $27.3 million
Industries Biotechnology,
Holding Companies,
Medical,
Pharmaceuticals
Growth Openings in past
year 133; percentage
growth 104%
Contact Timothy J.
Morrison,
Director of Human
Resources
Tel 617-225-6000
Fax 617-494-1786

**R.G. Vanderweil
Engineers, Inc.**
266 Summer St.
Boston, MA 02210

Founded 1947
Total employees 250
Annual sales $16 million
Industry Manufacturing
Equipment
Growth Openings in past
year 74; percentage
growth 42%
Contact Gary Vanderweil,
President
Tel 617-423-7423
Fax 617-423-7401

RWA, Inc.
37 Washington St.
Melrose, MA 02176

Founded 1984
Total employees 48

Industries Factory
Automation,
Manufacturing
Equipment,
Subassemblies and
Components
Growth Openings in past
year 18; percentage
growth 60%
Contact Richard Aho,
President
Tel 617-662-9322
Fax 617-662-6032

**Sager Electrical Supply
Co., Inc.**
60 Research Rd.
Hingham, MA 02043

Founded 1887
Total employees 240
Annual sales $80 million
Industry Holding
Companies
Growth Openings in past
year 40; percentage
growth 20%
Contact Raymond
Norton,
President
Tel 617-749-6700
Fax 617-749-3842

Scitex America Corp.
8 Oak Park Dr.
Bedford, MA 01730

Founded 1972
Total employees 508
Annual sales $430 million
Industry Computer
Hardware
Growth Openings in past
year 99; percentage
growth 24%
Contact John J. Whelan,
VP of Human Resources
Tel 617-275-5150
Fax 617-275-3430

**Signal Technology
Corporation**
60 Winter St.
Weymouth, MA 02188

Founded 1981
Total employees 758
Annual sales $75 million
Industry Holding
Companies

Growth Openings in past
year 157; percentage
growth 26%
Contact Dale Peterson,
President/CEO
Tel 617-337-8823
Fax 617-337-8826

**Software Quality
Automation**
10 State St.
Woburn, MA 01801

Founded 1990
Total employees 25
Annual sales $2.9 million
Industry Computer
Software
Growth Openings in past
year 15; percentage
growth 150%
Contact Ron Nordin,
President/CEO
Tel 617-932-0110
Fax 617-932-3280

**Spinnaker Software
Corp.**
201 Broadway
Cambridge, MA 02139

Founded 1982
Total employees 230
Annual sales $30 million
Industries Computer
Software, Holding
Companies
Growth Openings in past
year 100; percentage
growth 76%
Contact Doreen
Donovan,
Human Resources
Manager
Tel 617-494-1200
Fax 617-494-1219

Steinbrecher Corp.
185 New Boston St.
Woburn, MA 01801

Founded 1974
Total employees 90
Annual sales $10 million
Industries Subassemblies
and Components,
Telecommunications

Growth Openings in past year 30; percentage growth 50%
Contact Ms. Patti Boyd, Manager of Human Resources
Tel 617-935-8460
Fax 617-935-8848

Growth Openings in past year 20; percentage growth 11%
Contact John W. Wood, Jr., President/CEO
Tel 617-938-3786
Fax 617-933-4476

Growth Openings in past year 15; percentage growth 11%
Contact Ms. Helen Gardner, Chief Executive Officer
Tel 617-861-6262
Fax 617-861-1852

Synetics Corp.
540 Edgewater Dr.
Wakefield, MA 01880

Founded 1985
Total employees 325
Annual sales $31 million
Industries Computer Hardware, Computer Software, Telecommunications
Growth Openings in past year 40; percentage growth 14%
Contact Bahar Uttam, President
Tel 617-245-9090
Fax 617-245-6311

Technology Integration, Inc.
54 Middlesex Tpke., 2nd Fl.
Bedford, MA 01730

Founded 1984
Total employees 50
Industry Computer Hardware
Growth Openings in past year 15; percentage growth 42%
Contact Richard Hayden, President
Tel 617-275-4545
Fax 617-275-5035

Thermedics, Inc.
470 Wildwood St., PO Box 2999
Woburn, MA 01888

Founded 1983
Total employees 200
Annual sales $46 million
Industries Advanced Materials, Biotechnology, Manufacturing Equipment, Medical, Test and Measurement

Thinking Machines Corp.
245 First St.
Cambridge, MA 02142

Founded 1983
Total employees 500
Annual sales $95 million
Industries Computer Hardware, Computer Software
Growth Openings in past year 50; percentage growth 11%
Contact Ms. Kathy Santoro, Director of Human Resources
Tel 617-876-1111
Fax 617-876-1823

Transkaryotic Therapies, Inc.
195 Albany St.
Cambridge, MA 02139

Founded 1988
Total employees 65
Industry Biotechnology
Growth Openings in past year 35; percentage growth 116%
Contact Ms. Joan Ventola, Purchasing Manager
Tel 617-349-0200
Fax 617-491-7903

UIS, Inc.
420 Bedford St.
Lexington, MA 02173

Founded 1978
Total employees 150
Annual sales $17 million
Industry Computer Software

Vanasse Hangen Bustlin, Inc.
101 Walnut St., PO Box 9151
Watertown, MA 02272

Founded 1979
Total employees 296
Industries Environmental, Manufacturing Equipment
Growth Openings in past year 88; percentage growth 42%
Contact Richard E. Hangen, President
Tel 617-924-1770
Fax 617-924-2286

Venture Tape Corp.
PO Box 384
Rockland, MA 02370

Founded 1980
Total employees 135
Annual sales $22 million
Industry Advanced Materials
Growth Openings in past year 27; percentage growth 25%
Contact Ms. Bonnie Tupper, Personnel Manager
Tel 617-871-5964
Fax 617-871-0065

Vicam
313 Pleasant St.
Watertown, MA 02172

Founded 1986
Total employees 30
Industry Medical

Growth Openings in past
year 13; percentage
growth 76%
Contact Jack Radlow,
President/CEO
Tel 617-926-7045
Fax 617-923-8055

VideoServer, Inc.
50 Forbes Rd.
Lexington, MA 02173

Founded 1990
Total employees 50
Industry
Telecommunications
Growth Openings in past
year 15; percentage
growth 42%
Contact Robert Castle,
President
Tel 617-863-2300
Fax 617-862-2833

**Wellfleet
Communications, Inc.**
15 Crosby Dr.
Bedford, MA 01730

Founded 1986
Total employees 375
Annual sales $36 million
Industries Computer
Software,
Telecommunications
Growth Openings in past
year 194; percentage
growth 107%
Contact Steven Cheheyl,
Senior VP of Finance
and Administration
Tel 617-275-2400
Fax 617-275-5001

**Workgroup Technology
Corp.**
81 Hartwell Ave.
Lexington, MA 02173

Founded 1986
Total employees 35
Industry Computer
Software
Growth Openings in past
year 25; percentage
growth 250%
Contact James Carney,
President
Tel 617-674-2000
Fax 617-674-0034

XLI Corp.
800 West Cummins Park,
Suite 6650
Woburn, MA 01801

Founded 1979
Total employees 35
Annual sales $1.7 million
Industry Computer
Hardware
Growth Openings in past
year 17; percentage
growth 94%
Contact Vincent J. Spoto,
President
Tel 617-932-9199
Fax 617-932-3449

Xylogics, Inc.
53 3rd Ave.
Burlington, MA 01803

Founded 1975
Total employees 170
Annual sales $25.1 million
Industries Computer
Hardware,
Telecommunications
Growth Openings in past
year 20; percentage
growth 13%
Contact Paul Bennett,
Director of Human
Resources
Tel 617-272-8140
Fax 617-273-5392

Michigan

■ **313 Area Code**

Acheson Industries, Inc.
511 Fort St., Suite 315
Port Huron, MI 48060

Founded 1908
Total employees 250
Industry Holding
Companies
Growth Openings in past
year 50; percentage
growth 25%
Contact Herbert A.
Hoover,
President
Tel 313-984-5583
Fax 313-984-5980

Autoflex, Inc.
445 Enterprise Ct.
Bloomfield Hills, MI 48302

Founded 1970
Total employees 80
Annual sales $2.7 million
Industries Computer
Software, Factory
Automation,
Manufacturing
Equipment,
Subassemblies and
Components,
Transportation
Growth Openings in past
year 53; percentage
growth 196%
Contact M. Bahn,
Chief Executive Officer
Tel 313-253-9500
Fax 313-253-9506

**Automated Analysis
Corp.**
2805 South Industrial
Hwy., Suite 100
Ann Arbor, MI 48104

Founded 1983
Total employees 120
Annual sales $5.6 million
Industries Computer
Software, Manufacturing
Equipment
Growth Openings in past
year 35; percentage
growth 41%
Contact S.C. Wang,
Executive Officer
Tel 313-973-1000
Fax 313-973-1190

**Babcock Industries, Inc.,
Acco Systems Division**
12755 East 9 Mile Rd.
Warren, MI 48089

Founded 1919
Total employees 250
Annual sales $31 million
Industry Factory
Automation
Growth Openings in past
year 50; percentage
growth 25%
Contact Donald August,
Industrial Relations
Manager
Tel 313-755-7500
Fax 313-755-7859

Bond Robotics, Inc.
6750 19 Mile Rd.
Sterling Heights, MI
48314

Founded 1978
Total employees 89
Annual sales $11 million
Industry Factory
Automation
Growth Openings in past
year 19; percentage
growth 27%
Contact Irvin D. Bond,
President
Tel 313-254-7600
Fax 313-254-1860

Campbell Services, Inc.
21700 Northwestern Hwy.,
Suite 1070
Southfield, MI 48075

Founded 1971
Total employees 75
Annual sales $8.7 million
Industry Computer
Software
Growth Openings in past
year 15; percentage
growth 25%
Contact Donald
Campbell,
President
Tel 313-559-5955
Fax 313-559-1034

Computer Methods Corp.
13740 Merriman Rd.
Livonia, MI 48150

Founded 1977
Total employees 358
Annual sales $22 million
Industries Computer
Software, Holding
Companies
Growth Openings in past
year 87; percentage
growth 32%
Contact Andrew K.
Stewart,
President
Tel 313-522-5187
Fax 313-522-2705

Conveyor Components Co.
130 Seltzer Rd.
Croswell, MI 48422

Founded 1967
Total employees 119
Annual sales $11 million
Industries Factory
Automation,
Subassemblies and
Components, Test and
Measurement
Growth Openings in past
year 19; percentage
growth 19%
Contact Clint F.
Stimpson,
President
Tel 313-679-4211
Fax 313-679-4510

Eaton Corp., Lebow Products Division
1728 Maplelawn Rd.
Troy, MI 48084

Founded 1956
Total employees 126
Annual sales $14 million
Industries Subassemblies
and Components, Test
and Measurement
Growth Openings in past
year 16; percentage
growth 14%
Contact Chris Fejes,
President
Tel 313-643-0220
Fax 313-643-0259

Ferndale Laboratories, Inc.
780 West Eight Mile Rd.
Ferndale, MI 48220

Founded 1897
Total employees 112
Annual sales $12 million
Industries Medical,
Pharmaceuticals
Growth Openings in past
year 16; percentage
growth 16%
Contact David Bens,
President
Tel 313-548-0900
Fax 313-548-0279

Filtra-Systems Co.
30000 Beck Rd.
Wixom, MI 48393

Founded 1979
Total employees 175
Annual sales $20 million
Industry Holding
Companies
Growth Openings in past
year 15; percentage
growth 9%
Contact Jack Bratten,
President
Tel 313-669-0300
Fax 313-669-0308

HCIA
24 Frank Lloyd Wright Dr.,
PO Box 303
Ann Arbor, MI 48106

Founded 1954
Total employees 285
Annual sales $46 million
Industries Computer
Hardware, Computer
Software
Growth Openings in past
year 145; percentage
growth 103%
Contact George Pillari,
President/CEO
Tel 313-930-7830
Fax 313-930-7611

KMS Advanced Products
700 KMS Pl.
Ann Arbor, MI 48106

Founded 1987
Total employees 50
Annual sales $8.2 million
Industry Computer
Hardware
Growth Openings in past
year 28; percentage
growth 127%
Contact Terry Liddy,
Senior VP of Marketing
Tel 313-769-1780
Fax 313-769-8660

Mallinckrodt Sensor Systems, Inc.
1230 Eisenhower Pl.
Ann Arbor, MI 48108

Founded 1982
Total employees 150
Annual sales $16 million
Industry Medical
Growth Openings in past year 60; percentage growth 66%
Contact Ms. Margaret Spurr,
Manager of Human Resources
Tel 313-973-7000
Fax 313-973-3268

McNamee, Porter and Seeley, Inc.
3131 South State St.
Ann Arbor, MI 48108

Founded 1914
Total employees 190
Annual sales $20 million
Industries Environmental, Manufacturing Equipment
Growth Openings in past year 19; percentage growth 11%
Contact Philip C. Young, President/CEO
Tel 313-665-6000
Fax 313-665-2570

Midwest Rubber
3525 Range Line Rd.
Deckerville, MI 48427

Founded 1946
Total employees 225
Annual sales $12 million
Industry Manufacturing Equipment
Growth Openings in past year 75; percentage growth 50%
Contact Dennis H. Reckinger,
President
Tel 313-376-2085
Fax 313-376-8283

Perceptron, Inc.
23855 Research Dr.
Farmington Hills, MI 48335

Founded 1981
Total employees 77
Annual sales $13 million
Industries Factory Automation, Telecommunications
Growth Openings in past year 17; percentage growth 28%
Contact Ms. Alice Grisham,
Director of Human Resources
Tel 313-478-7710
Fax 313-478-7059

Petro-Chem Processing, Inc.
421 Lycaste St.
Detroit, MI 48214

Founded 1980
Total employees 200
Annual sales $21 million
Industry Environmental
Growth Openings in past year 50; percentage growth 33%
Contact Norm Foster, President
Tel 313-824-5841
Fax 313-824-5842

PVS Chemicals, Inc.
10900 Harper Ave.
Detroit, MI 48213

Founded 1946
Total employees 350
Industries Chemicals, Environmental, Holding Companies
Growth Openings in past year 49; percentage growth 16%
Contact James B. Nicholson,
President
Tel 313-921-1200
Fax 313-921-1378

Sensor Developments, Inc.
PO Box 290
Lake Orion, MI 48361

Founded 1976
Total employees 68
Annual sales $4.0 million
Industries Manufacturing Equipment, Test and Measurement
Growth Openings in past year 18; percentage growth 36%
Contact Albert Brendel, President
Tel 313-391-3000
Fax 313-391-0107

Somanetics Corp.
1653 East Maple Rd.
Troy, MI 48083

Founded 1982
Total employees 39
Industries Medical, Test and Measurement
Growth Openings in past year 28; percentage growth 254%
Contact Gary D. Lewis, COB/CEO/President
Tel 313-689-3050
Fax 313-689-4272

Star Cutter Co.
PO Box 376
Farmington, MI 48332

Founded 1927
Total employees 450
Industries Factory Automation, Manufacturing Equipment
Growth Openings in past year 49; percentage growth 12%
Contact Howard Didier, VP of Personnel
Tel 313-474-8200
Fax 313-474-9518

Traverse Group, Inc.
3772 Plaza Dr.
Ann Arbor, MI 48108

Founded 1975
Total employees 78
Annual sales $8.3 million

Industry Environmental
Growth Openings in past year 18; percentage growth 30%
Contact Dr. John Armstrong,
Chief Executive Officer
Tel 313-747-9300
Fax 313-747-9229

Unitech Engineering, Inc.
32661 Edward Ave.
Madison Heights, MI 48071

Founded 1986
Total employees 75
Annual sales $5.9 million
Industry Manufacturing Equipment
Growth Openings in past year 20; percentage growth 36%
Contact Robert May, President
Tel 313-585-9790
Fax 313-585-0412

X-Ray Industries, Inc., X-R-I Testing Division
1961 Thunderbird Rd.
Troy, MI 48084

Founded 1941
Total employees 100
Annual sales $6 million
Industry Manufacturing Equipment
Growth Openings in past year 20; percentage growth 25%
Contact Scott Thams, President
Tel 313-362-5050
Fax 313-362-4422

■ **517 Area Code**

Hartley Courseware
133 Bridge St., PO Box 419
Dimondale, MI 48821

Founded 1981
Total employees 100
Annual sales $5 million
Industry Computer Software

Growth Openings in past year 35; percentage growth 53%
Contact David Owens, Vice President
Tel 517-646-6458
Fax 517-646-8451

John Brown, Inc., Brown Machine Division
330 North Ross St., PO Box 434
Beaverton, MI 48612

Founded 1982
Total employees 175
Annual sales $25 million
Industries Energy, Factory Automation, Test and Measurement
Growth Openings in past year 19; percentage growth 12%
Contact James Warheit, Director of Human Resources
Tel 517-435-7741
Fax 517-435-2821

MACSTEEL
One Jackson Sq., Suite 500
Jackson, MI 49201

Founded 1974
Total employees 600
Annual sales $69 million
Industry Advanced Materials
Growth Openings in past year 135; percentage growth 29%
Contact Robert V. Kelley, Jr., President
Tel 517-782-0415
Fax 517-782-8736

Morbark Industries, Inc.
PO Box 1000
Winn, MI 48896

Founded 1957
Total employees 550
Annual sales $58 million
Industry Environmental

Growth Openings in past year 50; percentage growth 10%
Contact Norval Morey, President/CEO
Tel 517-866-2800
Fax 517-866-2280

■ **616 Area Code**

Dell Engineering, Inc.
3352 128th Ave.
Holland, MI 49424

Founded 1978
Total employees 75
Annual sales $8.0 million
Industry Environmental
Growth Openings in past year 30; percentage growth 66%
Contact Lee Dell, President
Tel 616-399-3500
Fax 616-399-3777

Eaton Corp., Truck Components Operations Division
13100 East Michigan Ave., PO Box 4013
Kalamazoo, MI 49003

Founded 1914
Total employees 700
Industries Subassemblies and Components, Transportation
Contact Thomas W. O'Boyle, Vice President
Tel 616-342-3000
Fax 616-342-3019

Gast Manufacturing Corp.
PO Box 97
Benton Harbor, MI 49023

Founded 1929
Total employees 580
Annual sales $56 million
Industry Subassemblies and Components

Growth Openings in past
year 80; percentage
growth 16%
Contact Warren Gast,
President
Tel 616-926-6171
Fax 616-927-0808

Gentex Corp.
600 North Centennial St.
Zeeland, MI 49464

Founded 1974
Total employees 450
Annual sales $27 million
Industries Photonics,
Test and Measurement
Growth Openings in past
year 174; percentage
growth 63%
Contact John Van
Haitsma,
Director of Human
Resources
Tel 616-772-1800
Fax 616-772-7348

**Grand Haven Stamped
Products Co.**
1250 Beechtree St.
Grand Haven, MI 49417

Founded 1924
Total employees 263
Annual sales $28 million
Industries Subassemblies
and Components,
Transportation
Growth Openings in past
year 20; percentage
growth 8%
Contact Joe Martella,
General Manager of
Personnel
Tel 616-842-5500
Fax 616-842-7230

**Integrated Metal
Technology, Inc.**
17155 Van Wagoner Rd.
Spring Lake, MI 49456

Founded 1976
Total employees 475
Annual sales $50 million
Industry Manufacturing
Equipment

Growth Openings in past
year 73; percentage
growth 18%
Contact Ms. Sarah Zysk,
Director of Human
Resources
Tel 616-842-2600
Fax 616-847-4300

Manatron, Inc.
2970 South 9th St.
Kalamazoo, MI 49009

Founded 1968
Total employees 140
Annual sales $8 million
Industry Computer
Software
Growth Openings in past
year 40; percentage
growth 40%
Contact Ms. Marge
White,
Personnel Director
Tel 616-375-5300
Fax 616-375-9826

Printek, Inc.
1517 Townline Rd.
Benton Harbor, MI 49022

Founded 1980
Total employees 70
Industry Computer
Hardware
Growth Openings in past
year 20; percentage
growth 40%
Contact Ms. Shirley
Sommers,
Personnel Manager
Tel 616-925-3200
Fax 616-925-8539

Rapistan Demag Corp.
507 Plymouth Ave.
Northeast
Grand Rapids, MI 49505

Founded 1914
Total employees 900
Annual sales $175 million
Industry Factory
Automation

Growth Openings in past
year 398; percentage
growth 79%
Contact B. Bechtel,
VP of Human Resources
Tel 616-451-6525
Fax 616-451-6425

TCH Industries
3040 Charlevoix Dr.
Southeast
Grand Rapids, MI 49546

Founded 1982
Total employees 450
Annual sales $45 million
Industry Manufacturing
Equipment
Growth Openings in past
year 22; percentage
growth 5%
Contact Tom McInerney,
Director of Human
Resources
Tel 616-956-0966
Fax 616-956-9149

**Teledyne Continental
Motors, General
Products**
76 Getty St.
Muskegon, MI 49442

Founded 1972
Total employees 500
Industries Defense,
Manufacturing
Equipment
Growth Openings in past
year 100; percentage
growth 25%
Contact James L.
Johnson,
VP of Personnel and
Industrial Relations
Tel 616-724-2151
Fax 616-724-2796

**WW Engineering &
Science, Inc.**
5555 Glenwood Hills
Pkwy. Southeast, PO
Box 874
Grand Rapids, MI 49588

Founded 1924
Total employees 625
Annual sales $44 million
Industry Environmental

Growth Openings in past year 137; percentage growth 28%
Contact S.S. Saless, President
Tel 616-942-9600
Fax 616-942-6499

X-Rite, Inc.
3100 44th St., Southwest
Grandville, MI 49418

Founded 1958
Total employees 270
Annual sales $29.5 million
Industries Factory Automation, Medical, Photonics, Test and Measurement
Growth Openings in past year 60; percentage growth 28%
Contact Ted Thompson, CEO/President
Tel 616-534-7663
Fax 616-534-9212

Minnesota

■ **218 Area Code**

Chromaline Corp.
4832 Grand Ave.
Duluth, MN 55807

Founded 1953
Total employees 57
Annual sales $4.6 million
Industries Chemicals, Holding Companies, Photonics
Growth Openings in past year 13; percentage growth 29%
Contact Tom Erickson, President
Tel 218-628-2217
Fax 218-628-3245

Zercom Corp.
PO Box 84
Merrifield, MN 56465

Founded 1978
Total employees 170
Industry Subassemblies and Components

Growth Openings in past year 20; percentage growth 13%
Contact Jeff Zernov, President
Tel 218-765-3151
Fax 218-765-3900

■ **507 Area Code**

Waters Instruments, Inc.
2411 Seventh St. Northwest
Rochester, MN 55903

Founded 1960
Total employees 174
Annual sales $11.12 million
Industries Computer Hardware, Medical, Subassemblies and Components, Test and Measurement
Growth Openings in past year 44; percentage growth 33%
Contact Robert Pitel, President/CEO
Tel 507-288-7777
Fax 507-252-3700

■ **612 Area Code**

Advanced Flex, Inc.
15115 Minnetonka Industrial Rd.
Minnetonka, MN 55345

Founded 1972
Total employees 330
Annual sales $32 million
Industries Holding Companies, Subassemblies and Components
Growth Openings in past year 30; percentage growth 10%
Contact Larry G. Bergman, President
Tel 612-930-4800
Fax 612-935-0760

American Guidance Service
4201 Woodland Rd.
Circle Pines, MN 55014

Founded 1957
Total employees 130
Annual sales $15 million
Industry Computer Software
Growth Openings in past year 30; percentage growth 30%
Contact Dr. Gary Robertson, Ph.D., VP of Test Development
Tel 612-786-4343
Fax 612-786-5603

AmeriData, Inc.
10200 51st Ave. North
Minneapolis, MN 55442

Founded 1969
Total employees 300
Annual sales $45 million
Industry Computer Hardware
Growth Openings in past year 25; percentage growth 9%
Contact Ms. Sharon Berglund, Personnel Manager
Tel 612-557-2500
Fax 612-557-6946

Audiotone, Inc.
4120 Olson Memorial Hwy.
Golden Valley, MN 55422

Founded 1949
Total employees 100
Annual sales $29 million
Industry Medical
Growth Openings in past year 20; percentage growth 25%
Contact Paul D'Amico, President
Tel 612-520-9723
Fax 612-520-9529

Barr Engineering Co.
8300 Norman Center Dr.
Minneapolis, MN 55437

Founded 1962
Total employees 212
Annual sales $22 million
Industry Environmental
Growth Openings in past
year 28; percentage
growth 15%
Contact Allan M.
Gebhard,
President
Tel 612-832-2600
Fax 612-835-0186

Blueline Software, Inc.
5775 Wayzata Blvd., Suite
690
Minneapolis, MN 55416

Founded 1985
Total employees 95
Annual sales $15 million
Industry Computer
Software
Growth Openings in past
year 60; percentage
growth 171%
Contact Willard J. Cecchi,
President
Tel 612-542-1072
Fax 612-542-9566

Camax Systems, Inc.
7851 Metro Pkwy.
Minneapolis, MN 55425

Founded 1981
Total employees 90
Annual sales $10 million
Industry Computer
Software
Growth Openings in past
year 20; percentage
growth 28%
Contact Greg Furness,
Chief Financial Officer
Tel 612-854-5300
Fax 612-854-6644

Bergquist Co.
5300 Edina Industrial
Blvd.
Minneapolis, MN 55439

Founded 1964
Total employees 275
Annual sales $26 million
Industries Computer
Hardware,
Subassemblies and
Components
Growth Openings in past
year 87; percentage
growth 46%
Contact Ms. Bonnie
Lyles,
Director of Human
Resources
Tel 612-835-2322
Fax 612-835-4156

Bureau of Engraving, Inc.
3311 Broadway Northeast
Minneapolis, MN 55413

Founded 1898
Total employees 515
Annual sales $48 million
Industry Subassemblies
and Components
Growth Openings in past
year 30; percentage
growth 6%
Contact Ms. Nancy
Erickson,
Director of Human
Resources
Tel 612-623-0900
Fax 612-623-1928

Check Technology Corp.
1284 Corporate Center
Dr., PO Box 105
Saint Paul, MN 55121

Founded 1981
Total employees 170
Annual sales $21.6 million
Industry Computer
Hardware
Growth Openings in past
year 23; percentage
growth 15%
Contact Ms. Barbara
Gandy,
Human Resources
Manager
Tel 612-454-9300
Fax 612-454-0367

Bio-Metric Systems, Inc.
9924 West 74th St.
Eden Prairie, MN 55344

Founded 1979
Total employees 65
Industries Advanced
Materials,
Biotechnology,
Environmental, Medical
Growth Openings in past
year 20; percentage
growth 44%
Contact Dale Olseth,
President
Tel 612-829-2700
Fax 612-829-2743

Burgess Industries, Inc.
2700 Campus Dr.
Plymouth, MN 55441

Founded 1982
Total employees 60
Annual sales $6.5 million
Industries Factory
Automation, Photonics,
Subassemblies and
Components
Growth Openings in past
year 15; percentage
growth 33%
Contact Dennis Burgess,
Sr.,
President
Tel 612-553-0247
Fax 612-553-9289

Coda Music Software
1401 East 79th St.
Bloomington, MN 55425

Founded 1987
Total employees 30
Industry Computer
Software
Growth Openings in past
year 19; percentage
growth 172%
Contact John Paulsen,
General Manager
Tel 612-854-1288
Fax 612-854-4631

Connect Computer Co.
9855 West 78th St.
Eden Prairie, MN 55344

Founded 1985
Total employees 75
Annual sales $8.2 million
Industry Computer
Hardware
Growth Openings in past
year 25; percentage
growth 50%
Contact Ms. Martha
Kieffer,
Vice President
Tel 612-944-0181
Fax 612-944-9298

CyberOptics Corp.
2505 Kennedy St.
Northeast
Minneapolis, MN 55413

Founded 1984
Total employees 70
Annual sales $7.8 million
Industries Factory
Automation, Photonics
Growth Openings in past
year 15; percentage
growth 27%
Contact Dr. Steven K.
Case, Ph.D.,
President
Tel 612-331-5702
Fax 612-331-3826

David Mitchell & Associates, Inc.
2345 Rice St., Suite 205
Saint Paul, MN 55113

Founded 1986
Total employees 130
Annual sales $10 million
Industry Computer
Software
Growth Openings in past
year 15; percentage
growth 13%
Contact David Mitchell,
President
Tel 612-482-0071
Fax 612-482-0976

Digital Solutions, Inc.
6100 Green Valley Dr.,
Suite 170
Minneapolis, MN 55438

Founded 1985
Total employees 33
Annual sales $7 million
Industry Computer
Software
Growth Openings in past
year 16; percentage
growth 94%
Contact Richard Kohout,
Chief Financial Officer
Tel 612-897-3754
Fax 612-897-3739

Doradus Corp.
6095 East River Rd.
Fridley, MN 55432

Founded 1972
Total employees 42
Industry Computer
Software
Growth Openings in past
year 13; percentage
growth 44%
Contact Larry J. Perlick,
Owner
Tel 612-572-1000
Fax 612-572-3927

FSI International, Inc.
322 Lake Hazeltine Dr.
Chaska, MN 55318

Founded 1973
Total employees 425
Annual sales $46.88
million
Industry Manufacturing
Equipment
Growth Openings in past
year 108; percentage
growth 34%
Contact Timothy D. Krieg,
VP of Human Resources
Tel 612-448-5440
Fax 612-448-2825

HEI, Inc.
1495 Steiger Lake Ln.
Victoria, MN 55386

Founded 1968
Total employees 175
Annual sales $10 million
Industry Photonics

Growth Openings in past
year 35; percentage
growth 25%
Contact Gene Courtney,
President
Tel 612-443-2500
Fax 612-443-2668

INCSTAR Corp.
1990 Industrial Blvd., PO
285
Stillwater, MN 55082

Founded 1975
Total employees 400
Annual sales $38.1 million
Industry Medical
Growth Openings in past
year 40; percentage
growth 11%
Contact Orwin Carter,
President/CEO
Tel 612-439-9710
Fax 612-779-7847

Lake Region Manufacturing Co., Inc.
340 Lake Hazeltine Dr.
Chaska, MN 55318

Founded 1947
Total employees 610
Annual sales $67 million
Industry Medical
Growth Openings in past
year 89; percentage
growth 17%
Contact John Van Etta,
Director of Personnel
Tel 612-448-5111
Fax 612-448-3441

Lawson Associates Inc.
1300 Godward St.
Minneapolis, MN 55413

Founded 1975
Total employees 400
Annual sales $31 million
Industry Computer
Software
Growth Openings in past
year 100; percentage
growth 33%
Contact Ms. Kathi Potter,
Director of Human
Resources
Tel 612-379-2633
Fax 612-379-7141

LifeCore Biomedical, Inc.
3515 Lyman Blvd.
Chaska, MN 55318

Founded 1968
Total employees 100
Annual sales $5.88 million
Industries Biotechnology, Holding Companies
Growth Openings in past year 30; percentage growth 42%
Contact Ms. Colleen M. Olson,
VP of Human Resources and Administration
Tel 612-368-4300
Fax 612-368-3411

Lind Electronics Design Co., Inc.
6416 Cambridge St.
Saint Louis Park, MN 55426

Founded 1977
Total employees 25
Annual sales $2.5 million
Industries Subassemblies and Components, Test and Measurement
Growth Openings in past year 13; percentage growth 108%
Contact Leroy Lind, President
Tel 612-927-6303
Fax 612-927-7740

Lumonics Corporation, Laserdyne Division
6690 Shady Oak Rd.
Eden Prairie, MN 55344

Founded 1978
Total employees 70
Industries Manufacturing Equipment, Photonics
Growth Openings in past year 12; percentage growth 20%
Contact R.H. Schmidt, President
Tel 612-941-9530
Fax 612-941-7611

Magnetic Data, Inc.
6754 Shady Oak Rd.
Eden Prairie, MN 55344

Founded 1982
Total employees 500
Annual sales $82 million
Industry Computer Hardware
Growth Openings in past year 77; percentage growth 18%
Contact Ms. Trisha York, Director of Human Resources
Tel 612-941-0453
Fax 612-941-0951

Medtronic, Inc., Promeon Division
6700 Shinglecreek Pkwy.
Brooklyn Center, MN 55430

Founded 1957
Total employees 350
Annual sales $38 million
Industries Energy, Medical
Growth Openings in past year 100; percentage growth 40%
Contact Ms. Colleen Stephans,
Personnel Director
Tel 612-569-1000
Fax 612-561-1002

Micro Control Co.
7956 Main St. Northeast
Minneapolis, MN 55432

Founded 1972
Total employees 100
Annual sales $15 million
Industries Computer Hardware, Computer Software, Factory Automation, Manufacturing Equipment, Test and Measurement
Growth Openings in past year 20; percentage growth 25%
Contact Harold Hamilton, President
Tel 612-786-8750
Fax 612-786-6543

Minco Products, Inc.
7300 Commerce Ln.
Minneapolis, MN 55432

Founded 1956
Total employees 570
Annual sales $30 million
Industries Energy, Subassemblies and Components, Test and Measurement
Growth Openings in past year 17; percentage growth 3%
Contact Karl Schurr, President
Tel 612-571-3121
Fax 612-571-0927

Minntech Corp.
14605 28th Ave. North
Minneapolis, MN 55447

Founded 1974
Total employees 280
Annual sales $29 million
Industries Biotechnology, Medical
Growth Openings in past year 55; percentage growth 24%
Contact Gene Johnson, Director of Human Resources
Tel 612-553-3300
Fax 612-553-3387

Multi-Tech Systems, Inc.
2205 Woodale Dr.
Mounds View, MN 55112

Founded 1970
Total employees 230
Annual sales $67.2 million
Industries Computer Hardware, Telecommunications
Growth Openings in past year 14; percentage growth 6%
Contact Dr. Raghu Sharma, President
Tel 612-785-3500
Fax 612-785-9874

Pace Laboratories, Inc.
1710 Douglas Dr.
Minneapolis, MN 55422

Founded 1978
Total employees 600
Annual sales $34 million
Industries Biotechnology,
Chemicals,
Environmental
Growth Openings in past
year 70; percentage
growth 13%
Contact Ms. Susan V.
Olsen,
Director of Personnel
Tel 612-544-5543
Fax 612-525-3366

Pako Corp.
6550 Wedgewood Rd.
Maple Grove, MN 55369

Founded 1910
Total employees 85
Annual sales $9.2 million
Industry Photonics
Growth Openings in past
year 20; percentage
growth 30%
Contact Richard Reedy,
President
Tel 612-559-7600
Fax 612-559-8787

Possis Medical, Inc.
2905 Northwest Blvd.
Minneapolis, MN 55441

Founded 1956
Total employees 120
Industry Medical
Growth Openings in past
year 35; percentage
growth 41%
Contact Bob Dutcher,
President
Tel 612-550-1010

Reliance Motion Control, Inc.
6950 Washington Ave.
South
Eden Prairie, MN 55344

Founded 1960
Total employees 575

Industries Factory
Automation,
Subassemblies and
Components, Test and
Measurement
Growth Openings in past
year 399; percentage
growth 226%
Contact Jeff Echko,
General Manager
Tel 612-942-3600
Fax 612-942-3636

Remmele Engineering, Inc.
1211 Pierce Butler Rte.
Saint Paul, MN 55104

Founded 1949
Total employees 446
Annual sales $66 million
Industry Factory
Automation
Growth Openings in past
year 13; percentage
growth 3%
Contact Michael Bates,
Director of Personnel
Tel 612-642-5640
Fax 612-642-5668

Serving Software, Inc.
65 Main St., Suite 215
Minneapolis, MN 55414

Founded 1984
Total employees 125
Annual sales $7.05 million
Industry Computer
Software
Growth Openings in past
year 40; percentage
growth 47%
Contact John E. Haugo,
President/CEO
Tel 612-623-4038
Fax 612-623-4506

Shared Resource Management, Inc.
3550 Lexington Ave.
North, Suite 300
Shoreview, MN 55126

Founded 1988
Total employees 85
Annual sales $9.8 million
Industries Computer
Hardware, Computer
Software

Growth Openings in past
year 40; percentage
growth 88%
Contact Leon E. Kline,
President
Tel 612-486-0417
Fax 612-486-0418

Simons Conkey, Inc.
330 Second Ave., Suite
545
Minneapolis, MN 55401

Founded 1956
Total employees 100
Industry Manufacturing
Equipment
Growth Openings in past
year 40; percentage
growth 66%
Contact Rick Sivula,
Vice President/General
Manager
Tel 612-332-8326
Fax 612-332-2423

SL Montevideo Technology, Inc.
2002 Black Oak Ave.
Montevideo, MN 56265

Founded 1974
Total employees 220
Annual sales $21 million
Industries Subassemblies
and Components,
Transportation
Growth Openings in past
year 20; percentage
growth 10%
Contact Robert T.
Reddall,
President
Tel 612-269-6562
Fax 612-269-7662

Suttle Apparatus Corp.
PO Box 548
Hector, MN 55342

Founded 1910
Total employees 500
Annual sales $48 million
Industries Subassemblies
and Components,
Telecommunications

Growth Openings in past year 148; percentage growth 42%
Contact Jeffrey Berg, President/General Manager
Tel 612-848-6711
Fax 612-848-6218

TL Systems Corp.
8700 Wyoming Ave.
Brooklyn Park, MN 55445

Founded 1970
Total employees 140
Industry Factory Automation
Growth Openings in past year 18; percentage growth 14%
Contact Don Demorett, President
Tel 612-424-4700
Fax 612-493-6711

Turck Inc.
3000 Campus Dr.
Minneapolis, MN 55441

Founded 1976
Total employees 100
Annual sales $12 million
Industries Factory Automation, Subassemblies and Components, Test and Measurement
Growth Openings in past year 15; percentage growth 17%
Contact Lawrence G. Worth, Director of Personnel/Manager of Marketi
Tel 612-553-9224
Fax 612-553-0708

UFE, Inc.
1850 South Greeley St., PO Box 7
Stillwater, MN 55082

Founded 1953
Total employees 800
Annual sales $42 million
Industry Manufacturing Equipment

Growth Openings in past year 185; percentage growth 30%
Contact John Podeswa, Personnel Director
Tel 612-439-1561
Fax 612-439-0511

V, G Systems, Inc.
PO Box 840
Lakeville, MN 55044

Founded 1990
Total employees 42
Annual sales $4.8 million
Industry Transportation
Growth Openings in past year 25; percentage growth 147%
Contact Allan L. Peterson, President
Tel 612-469-2002
Fax 612-469-5970

Varitronic Systems, Inc.
300 Interchange North, 300 Hwy. 169 South
Minneapolis, MN 55426

Founded 1983
Total employees 215
Annual sales $39.4 million
Industry Computer Hardware
Growth Openings in past year 22; percentage growth 11%
Contact Scott Drill, COB/President/CEO
Tel 612-542-1580
Fax 612-541-1503

Venturian Corp.
1600 Second St. South
Hopkins, MN 55343

Founded 1987
Total employees 160
Annual sales $40 million
Industry Holding Companies
Growth Openings in past year 50; percentage growth 45%
Contact Gary B. Rappaport, COB/President/CEO
Tel 612-931-2500
Fax 612-931-2402

VTC Inc.
2800 East Old Shakopee Rd.
Bloomington, MN 55425

Founded 1984
Total employees 270
Annual sales $26 million
Industry Subassemblies and Components
Growth Openings in past year 49; percentage growth 22%
Contact Robert Rousseau, Director of Human Resources
Tel 612-853-5100
Fax 612-853-3355

Wenck Associates, Inc.
1800 Pioneer Creek Ctr.
Maple Plain, MN 55359

Founded 1985
Total employees 50
Industry Environmental
Growth Openings in past year 20; percentage growth 66%
Contact Paul Josephson, Vice President
Tel 612-479-4200
Fax 612-479-4242

XATA Corp.
500 East Travelers Trail
Burnsville, MN 55337

Founded 1985
Total employees 24
Annual sales $3 million
Industries Computer Hardware, Computer Software
Growth Openings in past year 16; percentage growth 200%
Contact William Flies, President
Tel 612-894-3680

Zeos International, Ltd.
530 5th Ave. Northwest
Saint Paul, MN 55112

Founded 1981
Total employees 800
Annual sales $230.91 million

Industries Computer
Hardware,
Subassemblies and
Components
Growth Openings in past
year 319; percentage
growth 66%
Contact Greg Herrick,
President
Tel 612-633-4591
Fax 612-633-1325

3M, Identification and Converter Systems Division

3M Ctr., Bldg. 220-7W-03
Saint Paul, MN 55144

Founded 1984
Total employees 150
Annual sales $85 million
Industries Advanced
Materials, Computer
Hardware,
Subassemblies and
Components
Growth Openings in past
year 25; percentage
growth 20%
Contact Robert B. Palma,
Division Vice President/
General Manager
Tel 612-736-4360
Fax 612-737-5568

Mississippi

■ **601 Area Code**

American Laboratories & Research Services

PO Box 15609
Hattiesburg, MS 39402

Founded 1984
Total employees 33
Annual sales $2 million
Industry Environmental
Growth Openings in past
year 13; percentage
growth 65%
Contact Dr. James
Pinson,
President
Tel 601-264-9320
Fax 601-268-7805

Calvert Co., Inc.

2737 Old Brandon Rd.,
PO Box 180288
Pearl, MS 39208

Founded 1957
Total employees 100
Annual sales $12 million
Industry Energy
Growth Openings in past
year 20; percentage
growth 25%
Contact Richard
Campanalie,
President
Tel 601-939-9666
Fax 601-939-9676

US Rubber Reclaiming, Inc.

PO Box 820165
Vicksburg, MS 39182

Founded 1893
Total employees 55
Annual sales $2.9 million
Industries Advanced
Materials, Environmental
Growth Openings in past
year 15; percentage
growth 37%
Contact Bobby LaGrone,
President
Tel 601-636-7071
Fax 601-638-0151

Missouri

■ **314 Area Code**

Accu-Therm, Inc.

821 Lyon St.
Hannibal, MO 63401

Founded 1979
Total employees 125
Annual sales $5 million
Industries Energy,
Manufacturing
Equipment
Growth Openings in past
year 20; percentage
growth 19%
Contact Charles
Bindeman,
President
Tel 314-221-8077
Fax 314-221-7936

Atlas, Soundolier

1859 Intertech Dr.
Fenton, MO 63026

Founded 1935
Total employees 750
Industries Factory
Automation,
Subassemblies and
Components,
Telecommunications
Growth Openings in past
year 50; percentage
growth 7%
Contact Ken Cation,
President
Tel 314-349-3110
Fax 314-349-1251

BioKyowa, Inc.

930 Roosevelt Pkwy.
Chesterfield, MO 63017

Founded 1936
Total employees 100
Annual sales $9.6 million
Industry Biotechnology
Growth Openings in past
year 20; percentage
growth 25%
Contact M. Inoue,
General Manager
Tel 314-532-4070
Fax 314-532-1710

Bock Pharmacal Co.

PO Box 8519
Saint Louis, MO 63126

Founded 1945
Total employees 230
Annual sales $20 million
Industry Pharmaceuticals
Growth Openings in past
year 55; percentage
growth 31%
Contact Lawrence B.
Moskoff,
President
Tel 314-343-0994
Fax 314-343-8167

Brewer Science, Inc.

PO Box GG
Rolla, MO 65401

Founded 1981
Total employees 62
Annual sales $9.2 million

Industries Advanced
Materials, Chemicals,
Photonics, Test and
Measurement
Growth Openings in past
year 17; percentage
growth 37%
Contact Dr. Terry Brewer,
President
Tel 314-364-0300
Fax 314-368-3318

Central Electric Co.
Hwy. 54 South at Rte. BB
Fulton, MO 65251

Founded 1948
Total employees 115
Annual sales $15 million
Industries Energy,
Subassemblies and
Components
Growth Openings in past
year 15; percentage
growth 15%
Contact Charles W.
James,
President
Tel 314-642-6811
Fax 314-642-6844

**Citation Computer
Systems, Inc.**
2312 Millpark Dr.
Maryland Heights, MO
63043

Founded 1979
Total employees 115
Annual sales $12.33
million
Industries Computer
Software, Holding
Companies
Growth Openings in past
year 25; percentage
growth 27%
Contact Ken Brown,
COB/CEO
Tel 314-428-2900
Fax 314-428-7277

Dennis Chemical Co.
2700 Papin St.
Saint Louis, MO 63103

Founded 1936
Total employees 83
Annual sales $23 million

Industries Advanced
Materials, Chemicals,
Holding Companies
Growth Openings in past
year 13; percentage
growth 18%
Contact Aaron Dennis,
President
Tel 314-771-1800
Fax 314-771-8399

**D.W. Ryckman &
Associates, Inc.**
2208 Welsch Industrial Ct.
Saint Louis, MO 63146

Founded 1975
Total employees 80
Annual sales $8.5 million
Industry Holding
Companies
Growth Openings in past
year 20; percentage
growth 33%
Contact Stewart E.
Ryckman,
President/CEO
Tel 314-569-0991
Fax 314-432-2845

Electro-Core, Inc.
Highway A
Washington, MO 63090

Founded 1971
Total employees 50
Annual sales $4.8 million
Industry Subassemblies
and Components
Growth Openings in past
year 15; percentage
growth 42%
Contact Ms. Barbara
Roethlisberger,
President
Tel 314-239-2703
Fax 314-239-0652

Genelco, Inc.
1600 South Brentwood
Blvd.
Saint Louis, MO 63144

Founded 1973
Total employees 200
Annual sales $17 million
Industry Computer
Software

Growth Openings in past
year 20; percentage
growth 11%
Contact Gary Fallert,
Personnel Manager
Tel 314-962-2040
Fax 314-968-9589

K-V Pharmaceutical Co.
2503 South Hanley Rd.
Saint Louis, MO 63144

Founded 1942
Total employees 357
Annual sales $42 million
Industries Holding
Companies,
Pharmaceuticals
Growth Openings in past
year 57; percentage
growth 19%
Contact Marc S.
Hermelin,
Vice Chairman/CEO
Tel 314-645-6600
Fax 314-645-6732

**Nooter/Eriksen
Cogeneration Systems,
Inc.**
3630 South Geyer Rd.,
Suite 310
Saint Louis, MO 63127

Founded 1978
Total employees 115
Industries Energy,
Subassemblies and
Components
Growth Openings in past
year 15; percentage
growth 15%
Contact Dr. Vern Eriksen,
President
Tel 314-957-7800
Fax 314-966-6989

P.D. George & Co.
PO Box 66756
Saint Louis, MO 63166

Founded 1919
Total employees 185
Annual sales $45 million
Industry Advanced
Materials

Growth Openings in past year 25; percentage growth 15%
Contact J.E. George, Jr., President
Tel 314-621-5700
Fax 314-436-1030

Growth Openings in past year 15; percentage growth 100%
Contact Robert Schreiber, President
Tel 314-349-8399
Fax 314-349-8384

Growth Openings in past year 12; percentage growth 36%
Contact H.G. Schwartz, Jr., President
Tel 314-436-7600
Fax 314-421-1935

Plastic Engineered Components, Inc., Moark Mold Division
Rte. 2, Box 1
Poplar Bluff, MO 63901
Founded 1973
Total employees 200
Annual sales $21 million
Industry Manufacturing Equipment
Growth Openings in past year 15; percentage growth 8%
Contact Ms. Jerry Ford, Personnel Manager
Tel 314-785-0871
Fax 314-785-0898

SCS/Compute
12444 Powerscourt Dr., Suite 400
Saint Louis, MO 63131
Founded 1976
Total employees 275
Annual sales $36.6 million
Industry Computer Software
Growth Openings in past year 50; percentage growth 22%
Contact Art Kimbrough, Human Resources Manager
Tel 314-966-1040
Fax 314-966-0545

Talx Corp.
1850 Borman Ct.
Saint Louis, MO 63146
Founded 1973
Total employees 85
Annual sales $9.8 million
Industries Computer Software, Telecommunications
Growth Openings in past year 20; percentage growth 30%
Contact William W. Canfield, President
Tel 314-434-0046
Fax 314-434-9205

Preferred Pipe Products, Inc.
8000 Maryland Ave., Suite 1160
Saint Louis, MO 63105
Founded 1989
Total employees 100
Annual sales $10 million
Industries Holding Companies, Subassemblies and Components
Growth Openings in past year 25; percentage growth 33%
Contact Kevin Eggleton, President
Tel 314-726-2676
Fax 314-726-0013

Storz Instrument Co.
3365 Tree Court Industrial Blvd.
Saint Louis, MO 63122
Founded 1986
Total employees 885
Industry Medical
Growth Openings in past year 26; percentage growth 3%
Contact J. Donald Gaines, President
Tel 314-225-5051
Fax 314-225-7365

Tripos Associates, Inc.
1699 South Hanley Rd., Suite 303
Saint Louis, MO 63144
Founded 1979
Total employees 90
Annual sales $10 million
Industry Computer Software
Growth Openings in past year 24; percentage growth 36%
Contact John McAllister, President
Tel 314-647-1099
Fax 314-647-9241

■ **417 Area Code**

Anderson Engineering, Inc.
730 North Benton Ave.
Springfield, MO 65802
Founded 1958
Total employees 35
Annual sales $1.5 million
Industries Advanced Materials, Environmental

Schreiber, Grana, Yonley, Inc.
271 Wolfner Dr.
Saint Louis, MO 63026
Founded 1992
Total employees 30
Annual sales $4 million
Industry Environmental

Sverdrup Environmental, Inc.
801 North 11th St.
Saint Louis, MO 63101
Founded 1988
Total employees 45
Annual sales $10 million
Industry Environmental

Growth Openings in past year 13; percentage growth 59%
Contact Steve Brady, President
Tel 417-866-2741
Fax 417-866-2778

Growth Openings in past year 50; percentage growth 25%
Contact Mrs. Edith Smith, Personnel Manager
Tel 816-229-3405
Fax 816-229-4615

Growth Openings in past year 15; percentage growth 125%
Contact Ms. Nell Nunn, Chief Executive Officer
Tel 816-468-4622
Fax 816-468-7268

Positronic Industries, Inc.
423 North Campbell Ave., PO Box 8247
Springfield, MO 65801

Founded 1966
Total employees 436
Annual sales $22 million
Industry Subassemblies and Components
Growth Openings in past year 36; percentage growth 9%
Contact Wayne Gilbert, VP of Administration
Tel 417-866-2322
Fax 417-866-4115

Harmon Industries, Inc.
1300 Jefferson Ct.
Blue Springs, MO 64015

Founded 1946
Total employees 800
Annual sales $83 million
Industry Holding Companies
Growth Openings in past year 80; percentage growth 11%
Contact Ronald G. Breshears, VP of Human Resources
Tel 816-229-3345
Fax 816-229-0556

Research Seeds, Inc.
PO Box 1393
Saint Joseph, MO 64502

Founded 1970
Total employees 100
Annual sales $21 million
Industry Holding Companies
Growth Openings in past year 50; percentage growth 100%
Contact Robert Thedinger, President
Tel 816-238-7333
Fax 816-238-7849

■ **816 Area Code**

Cerner Corp.
2800 Rockcreek Pkwy.
Kansas City, MO 64117

Founded 1986
Total employees 450
Annual sales $77.24 million
Industry Computer Software
Growth Openings in past year 22; percentage growth 5%
Contact Neal L. Patterson, COB/CEO
Tel 816-221-1024
Fax 816-474-1742

Info-Data Services, Inc.
510 Walnut St., Suite 100
Kansas City, MO 64106

Founded 1976
Total employees 45
Annual sales $2 million
Industries Computer Hardware, Computer Software
Growth Openings in past year 25; percentage growth 125%
Contact Ronald G. Osborn, President
Tel 816-842-2611
Fax 816-842-9989

Saztec International, Inc.
6700 Corporate Dr., Suite 100
Kansas City, MO 64120

Founded 1976
Total employees 550
Annual sales $25 million
Industries Computer Hardware, Computer Software, Holding Companies
Growth Openings in past year 100; percentage growth 22%
Contact Robert Dunne, CEO/COB
Tel 816-483-6900
Fax 816-241-4966

Fike Corp.
704 South 10th St., PO Box 610
Blue Springs, MO 64015

Founded 1945
Total employees 250
Annual sales $30 million
Industry Holding Companies

Nunn, Yoest, Principals & Associates, Inc.
PO Box 25438
Kansas City, MO 64119

Founded 1986
Total employees 27
Annual sales $8 million
Industries Environmental, Holding Companies

Terracon Environmental Corp.
7810 Northwest 100th St., PO Box 901541
Kansas City, MO 64190

Founded 1985
Total employees 400
Annual sales $42 million
Industry Environmental

Growth Openings in past year 100; percentage growth 33%
Contact James Cunningham, President
Tel 816-891-7717

Wilcox Electric, Inc.
2001 Northeast 46th St.
Kansas City, MO 64116

Founded 1939
Total employees 830
Annual sales $100 million
Industry Transportation
Growth Openings in past year 25; percentage growth 3%
Contact Robert Warren, VP of Human Resources
Tel 816-453-2600
Fax 816-459-4364

Montana

■ **406 Area Code**

Montana Energy Research and Development Institute
PO Box 3809
Butte, MT 59702

Founded 1974
Total employees 300
Annual sales $11 million
Industry Holding Companies
Growth Openings in past year 25; percentage growth 9%
Contact Don Peoples, Chief Executive Officer
Tel 406-782-0463
Fax 406-723-8328

Special Resource Management, Inc.
PO Box 4168
Butte, MT 59702

Founded 1986
Total employees 90
Annual sales $9.6 million
Industry Environmental

Growth Openings in past year 15; percentage growth 20%
Contact Jim Murphy, President
Tel 406-782-4201
Fax 406-782-9968

Nebraska

■ **308 Area Code**

George Risk Industries, Inc.
GRI Plaza, 802 South Elm St.
Kimball, NE 69145

Founded 1965
Total employees 145
Annual sales $6 million
Industry Computer Hardware
Growth Openings in past year 15; percentage growth 11%
Contact Ms. Penney Stull, Personnel Director
Tel 308-235-4645
Fax 308-235-2609

■ **402 Area Code**

HWS Engineering, Inc.
PO Box 80358
Lincoln, NE 68501

Founded 1986
Total employees 60
Annual sales $6 million
Industries Environmental, Manufacturing Equipment
Growth Openings in past year 17; percentage growth 39%
Contact Ron Sorensen, Human Resources Manager
Tel 402-479-2200
Fax 402-479-2276

Terrano Corp.
245 South 84th St.
Lincoln, NE 68510

Founded 1977
Total employees 95
Annual sales $9 million
Industry Computer Software
Growth Openings in past year 20; percentage growth 26%
Contact James A. Terrano, President
Tel 402-483-7831
Fax 402-483-7846

Nevada

■ **702 Area Code**

American Pacific Corp.
3770 Howard Hughes Pkwy., Suite 500
Las Vegas, NV 89109

Founded 1955
Total employees 230
Annual sales $63.08 million
Industry Holding Companies
Growth Openings in past year 105; percentage growth 84%
Contact Fred D. Gibson, Jr., COB/CEO/President
Tel 702-735-2200
Fax 702-735-4876

Carsonite International, Inc.
1301 Hot Springs Rd.
Carson City, NV 89706

Founded 1984
Total employees 140
Industries Advanced Materials, Test and Measurement
Growth Openings in past year 13; percentage growth 10%
Contact D.W. Schmanski, President
Tel 702-883-1076
Fax 702-883-0525

Omnishore Electronics Manufacturing
1700 Forest Way
Carson City, NV 89706

Founded 1990
Total employees 20
Annual sales $1 million
Industries Computer
Hardware,
Subassemblies and
Components
Growth Openings in past
year 14; percentage
growth 233%
Contact Canh Doan,
President
Tel 702-883-8885
Fax 702-687-2836

New Hampshire

■ **603 Area Code**

Assembly Solutions, Inc.
7 Perimeter Rd.
Manchester, NH 03103

Founded 1990
Total employees 55
Annual sales $4 million
Industry Subassemblies
and Components
Growth Openings in past
year 15; percentage
growth 37%
Contact James Pitts,
COB/President/
Treasurer
Tel 603-623-5775
Fax 603-623-2874

Bailey Corp.
700 Lafayette Rd.
Seabrook, NH 03874

Founded 1982
Total employees 510
Annual sales $55 million
Industry Manufacturing
Equipment
Growth Openings in past
year 209; percentage
growth 69%
Contact Martin Waters,
Senior VP of Human
Resources
Tel 603-474-3011
Fax 603-474-8949

Beede Electrical Instrument Co., Inc.
175 South Main St.
Penacook, NH 03303

Founded 1917
Total employees 375
Annual sales $44 million
Industry Test and
Measurement
Growth Openings in past
year 25; percentage
growth 7%
Contact William Kuslaka,
Director of Personnel
Tel 603-753-6362
Fax 603-753-6201

Benchmark Industries, Inc.
215 St. Anselms Dr.
Goffstown, NH 03045

Founded 1982
Total employees 50
Annual sales $5.4 million
Industries Computer
Hardware, Factory
Automation,
Manufacturing
Equipment, Photonics
Growth Openings in past
year 18; percentage
growth 56%
Contact B. Vaine,
Controller
Tel 603-627-8484
Fax 603-627-6788

Browning Thermal Systems, Inc.
PO Box 477
Enfield, NH 03748

Founded 1961
Total employees 28
Annual sales $1 million
Industry Manufacturing
Equipment
Growth Openings in past
year 19; percentage
growth 211%
Contact Joseph Willey,
President
Tel 603-632-7905
Fax 603-632-4031

Coda, Inc.
1155 Elm St.
Manchester, NH 03101

Founded 1979
Total employees 200
Annual sales $29 million
Industry Computer
Software
Growth Openings in past
year 60; percentage
growth 42%
Contact James C. Wood,
President
Tel 603-647-9600
Fax 603-647-4682

Crompton Modutec, Inc.
920 Candia Rd.
Manchester, NH 03109

Founded 1968
Total employees 363
Annual sales $17 million
Industry Test and
Measurement
Growth Openings in past
year 63; percentage
growth 21%
Contact Dana Skaddan,
General Manager
Tel 603-669-5121
Fax 603-622-2690

DEKA Research and Development Corp.
340 Commercial St., 4th
Fl.
Manchester, NH 03101

Founded 1990
Total employees 60
Annual sales $6.6 million
Industry Medical
Growth Openings in past
year 15; percentage
growth 33%
Contact Dean Kamen,
President
Tel 603-669-5139

Dynaco Corporation
PO Box 3209
Derry, NH 03038

Founded 1987
Total employees 250
Annual sales $22 million

Industries Holding
Companies,
Subassemblies and
Components
Growth Openings in past
year 25; percentage
growth 11%
Contact Lyle Jensen,
President/COO
Tel 603-432-1200
Fax 603-432-0361

Ferrofluidics Corp.
40 Simon St.
Nashua, NH 03061

Founded 1969
Total employees 220
Annual sales $27 million
Industries Manufacturing
Equipment,
Subassemblies and
Components
Growth Openings in past
year 55; percentage
growth 33%
Contact Ms. Joan
Deichler,
Director of Personnel
Tel 603-883-9800
Fax 603-883-2308

**Freudenberg-NOK,
Plastic Products
Division**
Grenier Industrial Airpark
Manchester, NH 03103

Founded 1981
Total employees 300
Industries Manufacturing
Equipment,
Subassemblies and
Components
Growth Openings in past
year 118; percentage
growth 64%
Contact Robert Hange,
Vice President/General
Manager
Tel 603-669-4050
Fax 603-627-3718

**Granite
Communications, Inc.**
9 Columbia Dr.
Amherst, NH 03031

Founded 1984
Total employees 35
Annual sales $1 million
Industry Computer
Hardware
Growth Openings in past
year 15; percentage
growth 75%
Contact Pierre Dogan,
President
Tel 603-881-8666
Fax 603-881-4042

**Johnson and Johnston
Associates, Inc.**
130 Rte. 111
Hampstead, NH 03841

Founded 1974
Total employees 40
Annual sales $5 million
Industry Advanced
Materials
Growth Openings in past
year 15; percentage
growth 60%
Contact Charles Donato,
Treasurer
Tel 603-329-5691
Fax 603-329-8307

**Lockheed Sanders, Inc.,
Avionics Division**
95 Canal St., MS NCA1
6244
Nashua, NH 03061

Founded 1932
Total employees 259
Annual sales $100 million
Industries Computer
Hardware, Test and
Measurement,
Transportation
Growth Openings in past
year 129; percentage
growth 99%
Contact Dr. Hugo Poza,
Vice President/General
Manager
Tel 603-885-5182
Fax 603-885-7264

**Nickerson Assembly
Co., Inc.**
PO Box 276
Tilton, NH 03276

Founded 1976
Total employees 55
Annual sales $3.5 million
Industries Holding
Companies,
Subassemblies and
Components
Growth Openings in past
year 30; percentage
growth 120%
Contact Frank Szerlog,
Jr.,
Operations Manager
Tel 603-286-4366
Fax 603-286-7857

Nobis Engineering, Inc.
6 Garvins Falls Rd.
Concord, NH 03301

Founded 1988
Total employees 23
Industry Environmental
Growth Openings in past
year 14; percentage
growth 155%
Contact Nannu Nobis,
President
Tel 603-224-4182
Fax 603-224-2507

**North East
Environmental Products,
Inc.**
17 Technology Dr.
West Lebanon, NH 03784

Founded 1983
Total employees 22
Annual sales $1 million
Industry Environmental
Growth Openings in past
year 13; percentage
growth 144%
Contact Jack Nelson,
Chief Executive Officer
Tel 603-298-7061
Fax 603-298-7063

Palette Systems Corp.
6 Trafalgar Square
Nashua, NH 03063

Founded 1983
Total employees 57

Industry Computer
Software
Growth Openings in past
year 20; percentage
growth 54%
Contact Ms. Carolyn
Bernier,
Office Manager
Tel 603-886-1230
Fax 603-886-4799

Primary Rate, Inc.
24 Flagstone Dr.
Hudson, NH 03051

Founded 1989
Total employees 30
Annual sales $5 million
Industry Computer
Software
Growth Openings in past
year 15; percentage
growth 100%
Contact Mark Galvin,
President
Tel 603-889-3600
Fax 603-889-5544

**Renaissance Design,
Inc.**
PO Box 733
Hampton, NH 03862

Founded 1988
Total employees 28
Annual sales $1.6 million
Industries Computer
Hardware, Computer
Software, Factory
Automation
Growth Openings in past
year 13; percentage
growth 86%
Contact David Whally,
President
Tel 603-964-6736
Fax 603-964-1525

Softdesk, Inc.
7 Liberty Hill Rd.
Henniker, NH 03242

Founded 1985
Total employees 100
Industry Computer
Software

Growth Openings in past
year 25; percentage
growth 33%
Contact Jessie Devitte,
President
Tel 603-428-3199

Tally Systems Corp.
PO Box 70
Hanover, NH 03755

Founded 1990
Total employees 55
Annual sales $6.3 million
Industry Computer
Software
Growth Openings in past
year 30; percentage
growth 120%
Contact Ted
Jastrzembski,
President
Tel 603-643-1300
Fax 603-643-9366

**Thermal Technology,
Inc., Brew Division**
90 Airport Rd.
Concord, NH 03301

Founded 1955
Total employees 50
Industry Factory
Automation
Growth Openings in past
year 20; percentage
growth 66%
Contact George
Johnston,
President
Tel 603-225-6605
Fax 603-224-3798

Wilcom Products, Inc.
PO Box 508
Laconia, NH 03247

Founded 1967
Total employees 120
Annual sales $15 million
Industry Factory
Automation
Growth Openings in past
year 35; percentage
growth 41%
Contact Ms. Debora Vien,
Personnel Manager
Tel 603-524-2622
Fax 603-528-3804

New Jersey

■ **201 Area Code**

**Allied-Signal Inc.,
Metglas Products
Division**
6 Eastmans Rd.
Parsippany, NJ 07054

Founded 1977
Total employees 300
Industry Advanced
Materials
Growth Openings in past
year 100; percentage
growth 50%
Contact George A.
Kerekes,
Manager of Employee
Relations
Tel 201-581-7500
Fax 201-581-7581

Biomatrix, Inc.
65 Railroad Ave.
Ridgefield, NJ 07657

Founded 1981
Total employees 70
Annual sales $2.7 million
Industry Biotechnology
Growth Openings in past
year 17; percentage
growth 32%
Contact Dr. Endre
Balazs,
CEO/Chief Scientific
Officer
Tel 201-945-9550
Fax 201-945-0363

BISYS Group, Inc.
150 Clove Rd.
Little Falls, NJ 07424

Founded 1969
Total employees 700
Annual sales $74.53
million
Industries Computer
Hardware, Computer
Software

Growth Openings in past
year 46; percentage
growth 7%
Contact Mark J.
Rybarczyk,
VP of Human Resources
Tel 201-812-8600
Fax 201-812-1217

Bogen Communications, Inc.
50 Spring St.
Ramsey, NJ 07446

Founded 1932
Total employees 87
Annual sales $18 million
Industry
Telecommunications
Growth Openings in past
year 27; percentage
growth 45%
Contact John H. Ochtera,
President
Tel 201-934-8500
Fax 201-934-9832

Cambrex Corp.
1 Meadowlands Plaza
East Rutherford, NJ
07073

Founded 1981
Total employees 780
Annual sales $133.6
million
Industry Holding
Companies
Growth Openings in past
year 271; percentage
growth 53%
Contact Paul A.
Zdrodowski,
VP of Administration
Tel 201-804-3000
Fax 201-804-9852

**Cincinnati Milacron, Inc.,
Sano Division**
150 Dayton Ave.
Passaic, NJ 07055

Founded 1971
Total employees 170
Annual sales $17 million
Industry Factory
Automation

Growth Openings in past
year 20; percentage
growth 13%
Contact Al England,
President
Tel 201-779-2800
Fax 201-779-3408

**Computron
Technologies Corp.**
301 Rte. 17 North
Rutherford, NJ 07070

Founded 1973
Total employees 250
Annual sales $20 million
Industry Computer
Software
Growth Openings in past
year 55; percentage
growth 28%
Contact Andreas
Typaldos,
President
Tel 201-935-3400
Fax 201-935-7678

**Deltronic Crystal
Industries, Inc.**
60 Harding Ave.
Dover, NJ 07801

Founded 1972
Total employees 48
Annual sales $5.2 million
Industries Holding
Companies, Photonics,
Subassemblies and
Components
Growth Openings in past
year 18; percentage
growth 60%
Contact Robert Howe,
Operations Manager
Tel 201-361-2222
Fax 201-361-0722

**Fairchild Corporation,
Camloc Products
Division**
601 Rte. 46 West
Hasbrouck Heights, NJ
07604

Founded 1942
Total employees 220
Annual sales $25 million

Industries Subassemblies
and Components, Test
and Measurement
Growth Openings in past
year 15; percentage
growth 7%
Contact Jim Portalatin,
Director of Human
Resources
Tel 201-288-8300
Fax 201-288-8065

Fidelity Medical, Inc.
6 Vreeland Rd.
Florham Park, NJ 07932

Founded 1978
Total employees 80
Annual sales $5.3 million
Industries Computer
Software, Medical
Growth Openings in past
year 20; percentage
growth 33%
Contact Dr. Werner
Haas,
President
Tel 201-377-0400
Fax 201-377-0734

Fujinon, Inc.
10 High Point Dr.
Wayne, NJ 07470

Founded 1970
Total employees 200
Annual sales $25 million
Industries Medical,
Photonics
Growth Openings in past
year 80; percentage
growth 66%
Contact S. Takada,
President
Tel 201-633-5600
Fax 201-633-5216

GeoTek Industries, Inc.
50 Spring St.
Ramsey, NJ 07446

Founded 1989
Total employees 425
Annual sales $36.78
million
Industry Holding
Companies

Growth Openings in past year 25; percentage growth 6%
Contact Yaron Eitan, President/CEO
Tel 201-825-7080
Fax 201-818-9526

Growth Openings in past year 14; percentage growth 8%
Contact David Kennedy, Human Resources Manager
Tel 201-361-2310
Fax 201-989-5405

Growth Openings in past year 93; percentage growth 86%
Contact Nicholas Menonna, Jr., President
Tel 201-854-7777
Fax 201-854-1771

Global Turnkey Systems, Inc.
4 North St.
Waldwick, NJ 07463

Founded 1969
Total employees 90
Annual sales $10 million
Industries Computer Software, Holding Companies
Growth Openings in past year 19; percentage growth 26%
Contact Robert Farina, President
Tel 201-445-5050
Fax 201-445-1648

Industrial Devices, Inc.
260 Railroad Ave.
Hackensack, NJ 07601

Founded 1946
Total employees 290
Annual sales $17 million
Industries Photonics, Subassemblies and Components
Growth Openings in past year 14; percentage growth 5%
Contact Bernard P. Schnoll, President/CEO
Tel 201-489-8989
Fax 201-489-6911

Materials Processing Technology, Inc.
95 Prince St.
Paterson, NJ 07501

Founded 1978
Total employees 65
Annual sales $4.5 million
Industries Chemicals, Pharmaceuticals
Growth Openings in past year 15; percentage growth 30%
Contact Norman D. Alworth, COB/CEO/President
Tel 201-279-4133
Fax 201-279-4435

Graphnet, Inc.
329 Alfred Ave.
Teaneck, NJ 07666

Founded 1974
Total employees 250
Annual sales $34 million
Industry Telecommunications
Growth Openings in past year 50; percentage growth 25%
Contact Ms. Marina Case, Human Resources
Tel 201-837-5100
Fax 201-833-3888

Isomedix Inc.
11 Apollo Dr.
Whippany, NJ 07981

Founded 1973
Total employees 300
Annual sales $25 million
Industries Holding Companies, Medical
Growth Openings in past year 80; percentage growth 36%
Contact John Masefield, COB/CEO/President
Tel 201-887-4700
Fax 201-887-1476

Olflex Wire and Cable, Inc.
30 Plymouth St.
Fairfield, NJ 07004

Founded 1976
Total employees 50
Industry Subassemblies and Components
Growth Openings in past year 20; percentage growth 66%
Contact John Ciccone, Senior Vice President
Tel 201-575-1101
Fax 201-575-7178

Howmet Corp., Dover Alloy Division
9 Roy St., PO Box 371
Dover, NJ 07801

Founded 1967
Total employees 185
Annual sales $27 million
Industry Advanced Materials

KTI Holdings, Inc.
7000 Blvd. East
Guttenberg, NJ 07093

Founded 1982
Total employees 200
Annual sales $70 million
Industry Holding Companies

Personal Diagnostics, Inc.
8 Morris Ave.
Mountain Lakes, NJ 07046

Founded 1980
Total employees 130
Annual sales $11 million
Industries Holding Companies, Medical

New Jersey

Growth Openings in past year 20; percentage growth 18%
Contact John H. Micheal, COB/President
Tel 201-335-4486
Fax 201-335-8365

PharmaControl Corp.
661 Palisade Ave.
Englewood Cliffs, NJ 07632

Founded 1981
Total employees 213
Annual sales $30 million
Industries Holding Companies, Medical, Pharmaceuticals
Growth Openings in past year 18; percentage growth 9%
Contact Max A. Tester, M.D., COB/CEO/President
Tel 201-567-9004

Racal-Redac, Inc.
1000 Wyckoff Ave.
Mahwah, NJ 07430

Founded 1973
Total employees 200
Annual sales $23 million
Industry Computer Software
Growth Openings in past year 50; percentage growth 33%
Contact Geoff Mann, Director of Human Resources
Tel 201-848-8000
Fax 201-848-8189

Stauff Corp.
21-25 Industrial Park
Waldwick, NJ 07463

Founded 1974
Total employees 70
Annual sales $10 million
Industries Factory Automation, Subassemblies and Components, Test and Measurement

Growth Openings in past year 20; percentage growth 40%
Contact Manfred Riegg, President
Tel 201-444-7800
Fax 201-444-7852

Synaptic Pharmaceutical Corp.
215 College Rd.
Paramus, NJ 07652

Founded 1987
Total employees 70
Industry Pharmaceuticals
Growth Openings in past year 15; percentage growth 27%
Contact Ms. Kathleen P. Mullinix, Ph, President/CEO
Tel 201-261-1331
Fax 201-261-0623

Troy Corp.
72 Eagle Rock Ave.
East Hanover, NJ 07936

Founded 1952
Total employees 175
Annual sales $50 million
Industry Chemicals
Growth Openings in past year 25; percentage growth 16%
Contact Darel Smith, President
Tel 201-884-4300
Fax 201-884-4317

United Water Resources Inc.
200 Old Hook Rd.
Harrington Park, NJ 07640

Founded 1886
Total employees 720
Annual sales $162 million
Industry Holding Companies
Growth Openings in past year 15; percentage growth 2%
Contact Donald L. Correll, President/CEO
Tel 201-784-9434
Fax 201-767-2892

Vital Signs, Inc.
20 Campus Rd.
Totowa, NJ 07512

Founded 1972
Total employees 600
Annual sales $56 million
Industries Holding Companies, Medical
Growth Openings in past year 100; percentage growth 20%
Contact Terence Wall, President/CEO
Tel 201-790-1330
Fax 201-790-3307

Warner Insurance Services, Inc.
17-01 Pollitt Dr.
Fair Lawn, NJ 07410

Founded 1971
Total employees 511
Annual sales $90.5 million
Industry Holding Companies
Growth Openings in past year 43; percentage growth 9%
Contact Harvey Krieger, COB/President
Tel 201-794-4800
Fax 201-791-9113

Warner-Lambert Co., Warner Chilcott Laboratories Division
201 Tabor Rd.
Morris Plains, NJ 07950

Founded 1987
Total employees 154
Annual sales $80 million
Industry Pharmaceuticals
Growth Openings in past year 46; percentage growth 42%
Contact Nick Holihan, General Manager
Tel 201-540-2000
Fax 201-540-3283

■ **609 Area Code**

ARMS, Inc.
4 Kings Hwy. East
Haddonfield, NJ 08033

Founded 1968
Total employees 311
Annual sales $36 million
Industries Computer
Hardware, Computer
Software
Growth Openings in past
year 61; percentage
growth 24%
Contact Nathan Konecky,
President/CEO
Tel 609-795-5000
Fax 609-795-9850

AW Computer Systems, Inc.
9000-A Commerce Pkwy.
Mount Laurel, NJ 08054

Founded 1973
Total employees 52
Annual sales $9 million
Industries Computer
Hardware, Computer
Software
Growth Openings in past
year 19; percentage
growth 57%
Contact Nicholas
Ambrus,
COB/CEO
Tel 609-234-3939
Fax 609-234-9377

Bluestone Consulting, Inc.
1200 Church St., Suite 7
Mount Laurel, NJ 08054

Founded 1989
Total employees 45
Industries Computer
Hardware, Computer
Software
Growth Openings in past
year 25; percentage
growth 125%
Contact Mel Baiada,
President
Tel 609-727-4600
Fax 609-778-8125

Bohlin Instruments, Inc.
2540 Rte. 130
Cranbury, NJ 08512

Founded 1987
Total employees 50
Annual sales $8 million
Industry Test and
Measurement
Growth Openings in past
year 30; percentage
growth 150%
Contact Tommy Lindgren,
President
Tel 609-655-4447
Fax 609-655-1475

Crestek, Inc.
Scotch Rd., Mercer
County Airport, PO Box
7266
Trenton, NJ 08628

Founded 1980
Total employees 230
Annual sales $25 million
Industry Holding
Companies
Growth Openings in past
year 80; percentage
growth 53%
Contact J. Michael
Goodson,
COB/CEO
Tel 609-883-4000
Fax 609-883-6452

Curtis Young Corp.
1050 Taylors Ln.
Cinnaminson, NJ 08077

Founded 1954
Total employees 200
Industry Computer
Hardware
Growth Openings in past
year 25; percentage
growth 14%
Contact Ms. Deborah
Lee,
Personnel Manager
Tel 609-665-6650
Fax 609-786-1705

Datapro Information Services Group
600 Delran Pkwy.
Delran, NJ 08075

Founded 1970
Total employees 600
Annual sales $82 million
Industry Computer
Hardware
Growth Openings in past
year 100; percentage
growth 20%
Contact Ms. Renie
Crowder,
Manager of Human
Resources
Tel 609-764-0100
Fax 609-764-2812

Dataram Corp.
PO Box 7528
Princeton, NJ 08543

Founded 1967
Total employees 150
Annual sales $40 million
Industry Computer
Hardware
Growth Openings in past
year 25; percentage
growth 20%
Contact Ms. Linda
Colmenares,
Director of Human
Resources
Tel 609-799-0071
Fax 609-799-6734

Formation, Inc.
121 Whittendale Dr.
Moorestown, NJ 08057

Founded 1970
Total employees 250
Annual sales $30 million
Industries Computer
Hardware,
Manufacturing
Equipment,
Subassemblies and
Components
Growth Openings in past
year 69; percentage
growth 38%
Contact Ms. Carol
Johnson,
VP of Personnel
Tel 609-234-5020
Fax 609-234-5242

Garry Electronics
23 Front St.
Salem, NJ 08079

Founded 1978
Total employees 250
Annual sales $3 million
Industry Subassemblies
and Components
Growth Openings in past
year 50; percentage
growth 25%
Contact Gerald Eddis,
President
Tel 609-935-7603
Fax 609-935-0102

JBA International, Inc.
161 Gaither Dr. Suite 200
Mount Laurel, NJ 08054

Founded 1981
Total employees 200
Industries Computer
Hardware, Computer
Software
Growth Openings in past
year 50; percentage
growth 33%
Contact Alistair Clague,
President/CEO
Tel 609-231-9400
Fax 609-231-9874

**Novo Nordisk
Pharmaceuticals, Inc.**
100 Overlook Ctr.
Princeton, NJ 08540

Founded 1982
Total employees 300
Annual sales $28 million
Industry Biotechnology
Growth Openings in past
year 50; percentage
growth 20%
Contact Ms. Sara Jane
MacKenzie,
VP of Human Resources
and Administration
Tel 609-987-5800
Fax 609-921-8082

**Hydrocarbon Research,
Inc.**
100 Overlook Center,
Suite 400
Princeton, NJ 08540

Founded 1946
Total employees 99
Annual sales $6.8 million
Industries Advanced
Materials, Energy
Growth Openings in past
year 14; percentage
growth 16%
Contact Peter Quinn,
President
Tel 609-987-3017
Fax 609-987-0204

Liposome Co., Inc.
One Research Way,
Princeton Forrestal
Center
Princeton, NJ 08540

Founded 1981
Total employees 100
Annual sales $8.83 million
Industry Biotechnology
Growth Openings in past
year 30; percentage
growth 42%
Contact Leon M.
Rosenson, Ph.D.,
VP of Administration
Tel 609-452-7060
Fax 609-452-1890

Rees Scientific Corp.
1007 Whitehead Rd. EXT
Trenton, NJ 08638

Founded 1983
Total employees 30
Industry Test and
Measurement
Growth Openings in past
year 18; percentage
growth 150%
Contact Dr. Rees
Thomas, Ph.D.,
President
Tel 609-530-1055
Fax 609-530-1094

IGI, Inc.
2285 East Landis Ave.
Vineland, NJ 08360

Founded 1977
Total employees 185
Annual sales $22 million
Industry Holding
Companies
Growth Openings in past
year 14; percentage
growth 8%
Contact Edward B.
Hagar,
COB/CEO
Tel 609-691-2411
Fax 609-691-1177

**Materials Electronic
Products Corp.**
1040 Spruce St.
Trenton, NJ 08648

Founded 1959
Total employees 275
Industries Energy,
Subassemblies and
Components
Growth Openings in past
year 50; percentage
growth 22%
Contact Robert V.
Jensen,
President
Tel 609-393-4178
Fax 609-393-9461

■ **908 Area Code**

Alacrity Systems, Inc.
43 Newburg Rd.
Hackettstown, NJ 07840

Founded 1987
Total employees 35
Annual sales $4.8 million
Industry
Telecommunications
Growth Openings in past
year 15; percentage
growth 75%
Contact James R. Folts,
CEO/President
Tel 908-813-2400
Fax 908-813-2490

Anadigics, Inc.
35 Technology Dr.
Warren, NJ 07059

Founded 1985
Total employees 220
Annual sales $14 million
Industry Subassemblies
and Components
Growth Openings in past
year 109; percentage
growth 98%
Contact Ronald
Rosenzweig,
President/CEO
Tel 908-668-5000
Fax 908-668-5068

Anadigics, Inc.
35 Technology Dr.
Warren, NJ 07059

Founded 1985
Total employees 200
Industry Subassemblies
and Components
Growth Openings in past
year 110; percentage
growth 122%
Contact Ronald
Rosenzweig,
CEO/President
Tel 908-668-5000
Fax 908-668-5068

Anaquest, Inc.
110 Allen Rd., PO Box
804
Liberty Corner, NJ 07938

Founded 1910
Total employees 679
Annual sales $88 million
Industries Biotechnology,
Pharmaceuticals
Growth Openings in past
year 227; percentage
growth 50%
Contact Charles
Niederer,
VP of Human Resources
Tel 908-647-9200
Fax 908-604-7652

Aromat Corp.
629 Central Ave.
New Providence, NJ
07974

Founded 1974
Total employees 400
Industry Subassemblies
and Components
Growth Openings in past
year 50; percentage
growth 14%
Contact Ms. June
Bowden,
Senior Manager of
Human Resource
Tel 908-464-3550
Fax 908-464-8513

Avionic Instruments, Inc.
1414 Randolph Ave., PO
Box 498
Avenel, NJ 07001

Founded 1976
Total employees 165
Industry Subassemblies
and Components
Contact A.H. Reinfeld,
Chief Executive Officer
Tel 908-388-3500
Fax 908-382-4996

Celgene Corporation
7 Powder Horn Dr., PO
Box 4914
Warren, NJ 07060

Founded 1986
Total employees 70
Annual sales $3 million
Industries Chemicals,
Environmental
Growth Openings in past
year 24; percentage
growth 52%
Contact John L. Ufheil,
President/CEO/COB
Tel 908-271-1001

Coburn Corp.
1650 Corporate Rd. West
Lakewood, NJ 08701

Founded 1973
Total employees 115
Annual sales $12 million
Industry Photonics

Growth Openings in past
year 16; percentage
growth 16%
Contact Joseph W.
Coburn, II,
President/CEO
Tel 908-367-5511
Fax 908-367-2908

Computer Systems Development, Inc.
242 Old New Brunswick
Rd.
Piscataway, NJ 08854

Founded 1970
Total employees 200
Industries Computer
Hardware, Computer
Software
Growth Openings in past
year 125; percentage
growth 166%
Contact Ms. Rosemary
Sarafian,
President
Tel 908-562-0100
Fax 908-562-0102

Electronic Associates, Inc.
185 Monmouth Pkwy.
West Long Branch, NJ
07764

Founded 1945
Total employees 400
Annual sales $42.21
million
Industries Computer
Hardware,
Subassemblies and
Components, Test and
Measurement
Growth Openings in past
year 30; percentage
growth 8%
Contact Ms. Paula
Cohen,
Director of Human
Resources
Tel 908-229-1100
Fax 908-229-1329

Globe Manufacturing Sales, Inc.
1159 Rte. 22
Mountainside, NJ 07092

Founded 1945
Total employees 125
Industries Computer
Hardware,
Subassemblies and
Components
Growth Openings in past
year 35; percentage
growth 38%
Contact Arthur Kurz,
President
Tel 908-232-7301
Fax 908-232-4729

GynoPharma, Inc.
50 Division St.
Somerville, NJ 08876

Founded 1984
Total employees 170
Annual sales $18 million
Industry Medical
Growth Openings in past
year 20; percentage
growth 13%
Contact Louis Frisina,
President
Tel 908-725-3100
Fax 908-725-5838

Hillmann Environmental Co.
1089 Cedar Ave.
Union, NJ 07083

Founded 1985
Total employees 100
Annual sales $12 million
Industry Environmental
Growth Openings in past
year 20; percentage
growth 25%
Contact Chris Hillmann,
President
Tel 908-686-3335
Fax 908-686-2636

Keptel, Inc.
56 Park Rd.
Tinton Falls, NJ 07724

Founded 1983
Total employees 500
Annual sales $48.5 million

Industries Factory
Automation,
Telecommunications
Growth Openings in past
year 100; percentage
growth 25%
Contact Richard K. Laird,
CEO/President
Tel 908-389-8800
Fax 908-389-4595

Numerax, Inc.
555 Rte. One South
Iselin, NJ 08830

Founded 1969
Total employees 185
Annual sales $9 million
Industries Computer
Hardware, Computer
Software, Transportation
Growth Openings in past
year 37; percentage
growth 25%
Contact Marc Cooper,
President
Tel 908-602-7231
Fax 908-855-4986

Ortho Pharmaceutical Corp., Advanced Care Products Division
1001 US Hwy. 202, PO
Box 610
Raritan, NJ 08869

Founded 1887
Total employees 195
Industries Medical,
Pharmaceuticals
Growth Openings in past
year 85; percentage
growth 77%
Contact R.B. Miller,
President
Tel 908-218-6000
Fax 908-218-8649

Osteotech, Inc.
1151 Shrewsbury Ave.
Shrewsbury, NJ 07702

Founded 1986
Total employees 100
Annual sales $8.0 million
Industries Biotechnology,
Medical,
Pharmaceuticals

Growth Openings in past
year 20; percentage
growth 25%
Contact John Callan,
VP of Operations
Tel 908-542-2800
Fax 908-542-2906

Private Formulations, Inc.
460 Plainfield Ave.
Edison, NJ 08818

Founded 1979
Total employees 200
Annual sales $25 million
Industry Pharmaceuticals
Growth Openings in past
year 32; percentage
growth 19%
Contact Ms. Irma
Gonzalez,
Director of Human
Resources
Tel 908-985-7100
Fax 908-819-3332

Science Management Corp.
PO Box 0600
Basking Ridge, NJ 07920

Founded 1946
Total employees 378
Annual sales $45.6 million
Industry Holding
Companies
Growth Openings in past
year 71; percentage
growth 23%
Contact Ms. Virginia
Brandt,
Director of Human
Resources
Tel 908-647-7000
Fax 908-647-1446

Verbex Voice Systems, Inc.
1090 King Georges Post
Rd., Bldg. 107
Edison, NJ 08837

Founded 1986
Total employees 40
Annual sales $6.5 million
Industries Computer
Hardware, Computer
Software

Growth Openings in past year 13; percentage growth 48%
Contact Alan G. Stromberg, President/CEO
Tel 908-225-5225
Fax 908-225-7764

Voyager Software Corp
1163 Shrewsbury Ave.
Shrewsbury, NJ 07702

Founded 1988
Total employees 75
Annual sales $30 million
Industry Holding Companies
Growth Openings in past year 15; percentage growth 25%
Contact Roger Paradis, President
Tel 908-389-1700
Fax 908-389-9227

New Mexico

■ **505 Area Code**

Bohannan-Huston, Inc.
7500 Jefferson Northeast
Albuquerque, NM 87109

Founded 1959
Total employees 110
Industry Computer Software
Growth Openings in past year 15; percentage growth 15%
Contact Larry Huston, Chief Executive Officer
Tel 505-823-1000
Fax 505-821-0892

Cell Robotics, Inc.
2715 Broadbent Pkwy. Northeast
Albuquerque, NM 87107

Founded 1988
Total employees 20
Industry Test and Measurement

Growth Openings in past year 14; percentage growth 233%
Contact Ronald Lohrding, President
Tel 505-343-1131
Fax 505-344-8112

Los Alamos Technical Associates, Inc.
1650 Trinity Dr., PO Box 410
Los Alamos, NM 87544

Founded 1976
Total employees 385
Annual sales $19.5 million
Industries Defense, Environmental
Growth Openings in past year 22; percentage growth 6%
Contact D.B. Geran, Manager of Human Resources
Tel 505-662-9080
Fax 505-662-1725

Rio Grande Albuquerque, Inc.
6901 Washington Northeast
Albuquerque, NM 87109

Founded 1944
Total employees 215
Annual sales $27 million
Industry Holding Companies
Growth Openings in past year 33; percentage growth 18%
Contact Hugh Bell, President
Tel 505-345-8511
Fax 505-344-9671

Sparton Technology, Inc.
4901 Rockaway Blvd.
Rio Rancho, NM 87124

Founded 1962
Total employees 321
Annual sales $38 million
Industries Defense, Energy, Subassemblies and Components, Test and Measurement

Growth Openings in past year 32; percentage growth 11%
Contact Kendall Karn, Employee Relations Manager
Tel 505-892-5300
Fax 505-892-5515

Tech Reps, Inc.
5000 Marble Ave. Northeast, Suite 222
Albuquerque, NM 87110

Founded 1974
Total employees 172
Annual sales $15 million
Industries Computer Software, Environmental
Growth Openings in past year 32; percentage growth 22%
Contact Donald Tiano, President
Tel 505-266-5678
Fax 505-260-1163

New York

■ **212 Area Code**

Alpine Group, Inc.
1790 Broadway, 15th Floor
New York, NY 10019

Founded 1957
Total employees 375
Annual sales $6.3 million
Industry Holding Companies
Growth Openings in past year 75; percentage growth 25%
Contact Steven S. Elbaum, COB/CEO
Tel 212-757-3333
Fax 212-757-3423

Applied Business Technology Corp.
361 Broadway
New York, NY 10013

Founded 1981
Total employees 150
Annual sales $17 million

Industry Computer
Software
Growth Openings in past
year 20; percentage
growth 15%
Contact Christopher
Murray,
President
Tel 212-219-8945
Fax 212-219-3925

Comtex Systems, Inc.
40 Broad St.
New York, NY 10004

Founded 1976
Total employees 250
Industry Computer
Software
Growth Openings in past
year 50; percentage
growth 25%
Contact Michael Mullins,
President
Tel 212-480-2600
Fax 212-480-2625

CRC, Inc.
575 Lexington Ave.
New York, NY 10022

Founded 1979
Total employees 50
Annual sales $7.0 million
Industries Computer
Hardware, Computer
Software
Growth Openings in past
year 15; percentage
growth 42%
Contact Joshua
Wurzburger,
President
Tel 212-906-1000
Fax 212-906-9500

FD Consulting, Inc.
22 Cortlandt St., 8th Floor
New York, NY 10007

Founded 1977
Total employees 107
Annual sales $14 million
Industry Computer
Software

Growth Openings in past
year 32; percentage
growth 42%
Contact Frank Dechirico,
President
Tel 212-766-1420
Fax 212-766-1422

**Fusion Systems Group,
Inc.**
225 Broadway, 24th Fl.
New York, NY 10007

Founded 1988
Total employees 95
Annual sales $11 million
Industry Computer
Software
Growth Openings in past
year 25; percentage
growth 35%
Contact Henry
Wyszomierski,
President
Tel 212-285-8001
Fax 212-285-8705

Instinet Corp.
757 3rd Ave.
New York, NY 10017

Founded 1969
Total employees 200
Industry Computer
Hardware
Growth Openings in past
year 40; percentage
growth 25%
Contact Ms. Meredith
Lowe,
VP of Human Resources
Tel 212-310-9500
Fax 212-935-2131

**Investment Dealers'
Digest, Inc.**
2 World Trade Ctr.
New York, NY 10048

Founded 1935
Total employees 300
Annual sales $49 million
Industries Computer
Hardware, Holding
Companies

Growth Openings in past
year 50; percentage
growth 20%
Contact Jim Pierson,
Director of Human
Resources
Tel 212-432-0045
Fax 212-321-9617

JYACC, Inc.
116 John St.
New York, NY 10038

Founded 1978
Total employees 200
Annual sales $12 million
Industry Computer
Software
Growth Openings in past
year 25; percentage
growth 14%
Contact Ms. Annette
Cappola,
VP of Human Resources
Tel 212-267-7722
Fax 212-608-6753

**Microbank Software,
Inc.**
80 Broad St.
New York, NY 10004

Founded 1984
Total employees 63
Annual sales $9 million
Industry Computer
Software
Growth Openings in past
year 13; percentage
growth 26%
Contact Brian Twibell,
President
Tel 212-363-5600
Fax 212-363-5891

**Novo Nordisk of North
America, Inc.**
405 Lexington Ave., Suite
6200
New York, NY 10017

Founded 1981
Total employees 858
Annual sales $263.71
million
Industry Holding
Companies

Growth Openings in past year 137; percentage growth 19%
Contact Harry H. Penner, President
Tel 212-867-0123
Fax 212-867-0298

Public Health Research Institute
455 First Ave.
New York, NY 10016

Founded 1942
Total employees 150
Industries Biotechnology, Medical
Growth Openings in past year 25; percentage growth 20%
Contact Lewis Weinstein, President
Tel 212-578-0800
Fax 212-578-0804

Systems Strategies, Inc.
1 Penn Plaza
New York, NY 10119

Founded 1976
Total employees 135
Annual sales $15 million
Industry Computer Software
Growth Openings in past year 25; percentage growth 22%
Contact Ms. Lisa Ente, Personnel Director
Tel 212-279-8400
Fax 212-967-8368

Vista Concepts, Inc.
5 Hanover Square
New York, NY 10004

Founded 1979
Total employees 150
Annual sales $25 million
Industry Computer Software
Growth Openings in past year 20; percentage growth 15%
Contact Tony Termini, Assistant Director of Employment and Rec
Tel 212-943-9070
Fax 212-943-0904

■ **315 Area Code**

CABLExpress Corp.
500 East Brighton Ave.
Syracuse, NY 13210

Founded 1978
Total employees 46
Industries Computer Software, Factory Automation, Subassemblies and Components, Telecommunications
Growth Openings in past year 21; percentage growth 84%
Contact Bill Pomeroy, President
Tel 315-476-3000
Fax 315-476-3034

Clestra Cleanroom Technology
7000 Performance Dr.
North Syracuse, NY 13212

Founded 1983
Total employees 150
Annual sales $50 million
Industries Energy, Manufacturing Equipment, Test and Measurement
Growth Openings in past year 75; percentage growth 100%
Contact Daniel Ackermann, President
Tel 315-452-5200
Fax 315-452-5252

Feldmeier Equipment, Inc.
6800 Town Line Rd., PO Box 474
Syracuse, NY 13211

Founded 1952
Total employees 84
Annual sales $6 million
Industries Energy, Factory Automation

Growth Openings in past year 19; percentage growth 29%
Contact R.H. Feldmeier, President
Tel 315-454-8608
Fax 315-454-3701

G.W. Lisk Co., Inc.
2 South St.
Clifton Springs, NY 14432

Founded 1949
Total employees 350
Industries Holding Companies, Subassemblies and Components, Test and Measurement, Transportation
Growth Openings in past year 49; percentage growth 16%
Contact I.A. Morris, President
Tel 315-462-2611
Fax 315-462-7661

IEC Electronics Corp.
105 Norton St., PO Box 271
Newark, NY 14513

Founded 1966
Total employees 700
Annual sales $60 million
Industry Subassemblies and Components
Growth Openings in past year 97; percentage growth 16%
Contact Ms. Ellie Faro, Personnel Manager
Tel 315-331-7742
Fax 315-331-3547

M.S. Kennedy Corp.
8170 Thompson Rd.
Cicero, NY 13039

Founded 1971
Total employees 80
Annual sales $4.5 million
Industry Subassemblies and Components

Growth Openings in past year 15; percentage growth 23%
Contact R. Roehm, Operations Manager
Tel 315-699-9201
Fax 315-699-8023

OBG Technical Services, Inc.
5000 Brittonfield Pkwy., PO Box 5240
Syracuse, NY 13221

Founded 1981
Total employees 82
Annual sales $23.7 million
Industry Environmental
Growth Openings in past year 21; percentage growth 34%
Contact Terry L. Brown, PE, President
Tel 315-437-6400
Fax 315-437-9800

O'Brien & Gere Engineers, Inc.
5000 Brittonfield Pkwy., PO Box 4873
Syracuse, NY 13221

Founded 1945
Total employees 580
Annual sales $58 million
Industry Environmental
Growth Openings in past year 28; percentage growth 5%
Contact Peter R. Koval, PE, Vice President
Tel 315-437-6100
Fax 315-463-7554

OP-TECH Environmental Services, Inc.
Old River Rd., PO Box 5182
Massena, NY 13662

Founded 1976
Total employees 50
Annual sales $3 million
Industry Environmental

Growth Openings in past year 30; percentage growth 150%
Contact Richard L. Elander, President
Tel 315-764-1917
Fax 315-764-9453

Philips Broad Band Network, Inc.
100 Fairgrounds Dr.
Manlius, NY 13104

Founded 1988
Total employees 550
Annual sales $59 million
Industries Manufacturing Equipment, Photonics, Telecommunications
Growth Openings in past year 50; percentage growth 10%
Contact Chet Wilk, Manager of Human Resources
Tel 315-682-9105
Fax 315-682-9005

Syracuse Research Corp.
Merril Ln.
Syracuse, NY 13210

Founded 1957
Total employees 185
Annual sales $19 million
Industries Chemicals, Computer Software, Environmental, Transportation
Growth Openings in past year 14; percentage growth 8%
Contact Edward Moore, Manager of Human Resources
Tel 315-426-3200
Fax 315-425-1339

Volpi Manufacturing USA, Inc.
26 Aurelius Ave.
Auburn, NY 13021

Founded 1979
Total employees 43
Annual sales $4 million

Industries Photonics, Test and Measurement, Telecommunications
Growth Openings in past year 21; percentage growth 95%
Contact Ueli Armbruster, Vice President/General Manager
Tel 315-255-1737
Fax 315-255-1202

Williamsville Co.
200 Seward Ave., PO Box 438
Utica, NY 13502

Founded 1960
Total employees 125
Annual sales $2 million
Industry Factory Automation
Growth Openings in past year 25; percentage growth 25%
Contact George Weaver, President
Tel 315-735-9252
Fax 315-797-0058

Young & Franklin Inc.
942 Old Liverpool Rd.
Liverpool, NY 13088

Founded 1918
Total employees 100
Annual sales $8.3 million
Industries Holding Companies, Subassemblies and Components
Growth Openings in past year 20; percentage growth 25%
Contact Ms. Carol Hawkins, Personnel Manager
Tel 315-457-3110
Fax 315-457-9204

■ 516 Area Code

Appgen Business Software, Inc.
4320 Veteran's Memorial Hwy.
Holbrook, NY 11741

Founded 1977
Total employees 55
Annual sales $6.3 million
Industry Computer Software
Growth Openings in past year 30; percentage growth 120%
Contact Marc Andre, President
Tel 516-471-3200
Fax 516-471-3291

Applied Digital Data Systems, Inc.
100 Marcus Blvd., PO Box 18001
Hauppauge, NY 11788

Founded 1969
Total employees 525
Annual sales $86 million
Industry Computer Hardware
Growth Openings in past year 25; percentage growth 5%
Contact Steve Green, Director of Human Resources and Administ
Tel 516-342-7000
Fax 516-342-7378

Center Laboratories
35 Channel Dr.
Port Washington, NY 11050

Founded 1979
Total employees 115
Annual sales $15 million
Industry Pharmaceuticals
Growth Openings in past year 15; percentage growth 15%
Contact Ms. Lee Viesta, Personnel Manager
Tel 516-767-1873
Fax 516-767-4229

Curative Technologies, Inc.
14 Research Way, Box 9052
East Setauket, NY 11733

Founded 1987
Total employees 211
Annual sales $6.26 million
Industries Biotechnology, Medical, Pharmaceuticals
Growth Openings in past year 91; percentage growth 75%
Contact Russell B. Whitman, President
Tel 516-689-7000
Fax 516-689-7067

Medsonic, Inc.
1938 New Hwy.
Farmingdale, NY 11735

Founded 1955
Total employees 70
Annual sales $3.5 million
Industries Environmental, Factory Automation, Test and Measurement
Growth Openings in past year 21; percentage growth 42%
Contact Michael Juliano, President
Tel 516-694-9555
Fax 516-694-9412

Merit Electronic Design Co., Ltd.
190 Rodeo Dr.
Edgewood, NY 11717

Founded 1977
Total employees 85
Annual sales $5 million
Industry Subassemblies and Components
Growth Openings in past year 25; percentage growth 41%
Contact Emmanuel Intoci, President
Tel 516-667-9699
Fax 516-667-9853

Miltope Group, Inc.
1770 Walt Whitman Rd.
Melville, NY 11747

Founded 1975
Total employees 650
Annual sales $103.1 million
Industries Computer Hardware, Holding Companies
Growth Openings in past year 49; percentage growth 8%
Contact Ms. Rita Lowe, Personnel Director
Tel 516-420-0200
Fax 516-756-7606

Miteq, Inc.
100 Davids Dr.
Hauppauge, NY 11788

Founded 1969
Total employees 350
Annual sales $29 million
Industry Telecommunications
Growth Openings in past year 23; percentage growth 7%
Contact Ms. Patricia A. Albano, Director of Human Resources
Tel 516-436-7400
Fax 516-864-1586

North Atlantic Industries, Inc.
60 Plant Ave.
Hauppauge, NY 11788

Founded 1954
Total employees 450
Annual sales $59.4 million
Industries Computer Hardware, Holding Companies, Telecommunications
Growth Openings in past year 99; percentage growth 28%
Contact L. Stanton, Director of Human Resources
Tel 516-582-6500
Fax 516-582-8652

Oncogene Science, Inc.
106 Charles Lindbergh
Blvd.
Uniondale, NY 11553

Founded 1983
Total employees 112
Annual sales $10 million
Industries Biotechnology,
Chemicals, Holding
Companies, Medical
Growth Openings in past
year 34; percentage
growth 43%
Contact Gary Frashier,
President/CEO
Tel 516-222-0023
Fax 516-222-0114

Periphonics Corp.
4000 Veterans Memorial
Hwy.
Bohemia, NY 11716

Founded 1970
Total employees 250
Annual sales $41 million
Industry Computer
Hardware
Growth Openings in past
year 50; percentage
growth 25%
Contact Ms. Janet
Anderson,
Director of Human
Resources
Tel 516-467-0500
Fax 516-737-8520

Precise Optics/PME, Inc.
239 South Fehr Way
Bay Shore, NY 11706

Founded 1953
Total employees 39
Annual sales $7.1 million
Industries Medical,
Photonics,
Telecommunications
Contact Leonard Corso,
Director
Tel 516-242-6600
Fax 516-242-4421

Renco Electronics, Inc.
60 Jeffryn Blvd. East
Deer Park, NY 11729

Founded 1955
Total employees 200

Industry Subassemblies
and Components
Growth Openings in past
year 40; percentage
growth 25%
Contact Bruce A.
Rensing,
President/CEO
Tel 516-586-5566
Fax 516-586-5562

RFI Corp.
100 Pine Aire Dr.
Bay Shore, NY 11706

Founded 1980
Total employees 135
Annual sales $13 million
Industries Manufacturing
Equipment,
Subassemblies and
Components
Growth Openings in past
year 40; percentage
growth 42%
Contact Sy Rubin,
President
Tel 516-231-6400
Fax 516-231-6465

Software Engineering of America, Inc.
2001 Marcus Ave.
Lake Success, NY 11042

Founded 1982
Total employees 250
Annual sales $67 million
Industry Computer
Software
Growth Openings in past
year 50; percentage
growth 25%
Contact Salvatore
Simeone,
President/CEO
Tel 516-328-7000
Fax 516-354-4015

Spellman High Voltage Electronics Corp.
7 Fairchild Ave.
Plainview, NY 11803

Founded 1947
Total employees 190
Annual sales $14 million
Industries Subassemblies
and Components, Test
and Measurement

Growth Openings in past
year 29; percentage
growth 18%
Contact Ms. Carol
Stewart,
Human Resource
Manager
Tel 516-349-8686
Fax 516-349-8699

Struthers Electronics
300 Rte. 109
West Babylon, NY 11704

Founded 1962
Total employees 86
Industry Subassemblies
and Components
Growth Openings in past
year 56; percentage
growth 186%
Contact Ms. Florence
Isaacson,
President
Tel 516-422-3000
Fax 516-422-3192

Telephonics Corp., Electronic Systems Division
815 Broad Hollow Rd.
Farmingdale, NY 11735

Founded 1990
Total employees 50
Annual sales $15 million
Industries Defense,
Factory Automation
Growth Openings in past
year 20; percentage
growth 66%
Contact Z.J.
Papazissimos,
President
Tel 516-755-7000
Fax 516-755-7010

United Capital Corp.
111 Great Neck Rd.,
Suite 401
Great Neck, NY 11021

Founded 1980
Total employees 550
Annual sales $70.88
million
Industry Holding
Companies

Growth Openings in past year 100; percentage growth 22%
Contact A.E. Petrocelli, COB/CEO/President
Tel 516-466-6464

■ **518 Area Code**

MapInfo Corp.
200 Broadway
Troy, NY 12180

Founded 1986
Total employees 125
Annual sales $14 million
Industry Computer Software
Growth Openings in past year 35; percentage growth 38%
Contact Brian D. Owen, President/CEO
Tel 518-274-6000
Fax 518-274-6066

Shaker Computer & Management Services, Inc.
50 Century Hill Dr.
Latham, NY 12110

Founded 1976
Total employees 54
Annual sales $6.2 million
Industry Computer Software
Growth Openings in past year 14; percentage growth 35%
Contact Richard L. Werner, President
Tel 518-786-7200
Fax 518-786-7298

■ **607 Area Code**

ABB Traction, Inc.
East 18th St.
Elmira, NY 14903

Founded 1986
Total employees 700
Annual sales $81 million
Industry Transportation

Growth Openings in past year 197; percentage growth 39%
Contact Lutz Elsner, President
Tel 607-732-5251
Fax 607-732-6614

Array Analysis, Inc.
200 Langmuir/Brown Rd.
Ithaca, NY 14850

Founded 1983
Total employees 50
Annual sales $6.3 million
Industries Factory Automation, Test and Measurement
Growth Openings in past year 20; percentage growth 66%
Contact Spencer Silverstein, President/CEO
Tel 607-257-6800
Fax 607-257-6871

CBORD Group, Inc.
61 Brown Rd.
Ithaca, NY 14850

Founded 1975
Total employees 112
Industry Computer Software
Growth Openings in past year 20; percentage growth 21%
Contact John E. Alexander, President
Tel 607-257-2410
Fax 607-257-1902

Deltown Specialties
1712 Deltown Plaza
Fraser, NY 13753

Founded 1968
Total employees 106
Annual sales $10 million
Industry Biotechnology
Growth Openings in past year 16; percentage growth 17%
Contact Simon Kooyman, President
Tel 607-746-3082
Fax 607-746-2710

Endicott Research Group, Inc.
2601 Wayne St., PO Box 269
Endicott, NY 13760

Founded 1979
Total employees 120
Annual sales $6.5 million
Industry Subassemblies and Components
Growth Openings in past year 20; percentage growth 20%
Contact Ms. Betty Davis, Personnel Administrator
Tel 607-754-9187
Fax 607-754-9255

ENSCO, Inc., Instrumentation Software Systems Division
1195 Taylor Rd.
Owego, NY 13827

Founded 1985
Total employees 150
Annual sales $17 million
Industry Computer Software
Growth Openings in past year 75; percentage growth 100%
Contact Todd Laudman, Division Manager
Tel 607-687-4110
Fax 607-687-4733

ETL Testing Laboratories, Inc.
Industrial Park
Cortland, NY 13045

Founded 1896
Total employees 300
Industries Manufacturing Equipment, Subassemblies and Components, Test and Measurement
Growth Openings in past year 75; percentage growth 33%
Contact Eric Birch, COB/CEO
Tel 607-753-6711
Fax 607-756-9891

Hilliard Corp.
100 West Fourth St.
Elmira, NY 14902

Founded 1905
Total employees 220
Annual sales $18 million
Industry Subassemblies
and Components
Growth Openings in past
year 20; percentage
growth 10%
Contact Ms. Lois Place,
Personnel Director
Tel 607-733-7121
Fax 607-733-3009

■ 716 Area Code

Alliance Automation Systems
400 Trabold Rd.
Rochester, NY 14624

Founded 1961
Total employees 125
Annual sales $13 million
Industries Factory
Automation,
Manufacturing
Equipment
Growth Openings in past
year 12; percentage
growth 10%
Contact Stuart Rodman,
COB/CEO
Tel 716-426-2700
Fax 716-426-3788

American Sigma, Inc.
11601 Maple Ridge Rd.,
PO Box 120
Medina, NY 14103

Founded 1984
Total employees 132
Annual sales $18.5 million
Industries Environmental,
Test and Measurement
Growth Openings in past
year 23; percentage
growth 21%
Contact Gerald Allen,
Supervisor of Materials
Management
Tel 716-798-5580
Fax 716-798-5599

Bergmann Associates Engineers, Architects, Surveyors PC
1 South Washington St.
Rochester, NY 14614

Founded 1980
Total employees 175
Annual sales $18 million
Industries Energy,
Environmental,
Manufacturing
Equipment
Growth Openings in past
year 45; percentage
growth 34%
Contact Donald J.
Bergmann,
President
Tel 716-232-5135
Fax 716-232-4652

Electronic Technology Group, Inc.
315 North Main St.
Jamestown, NY 14701

Founded 1987
Total employees 220
Annual sales $16 million
Industry Holding
Companies
Growth Openings in past
year 20; percentage
growth 10%
Contact Frank Costanzo,
COB/CEO
Tel 716-488-9699
Fax 716-483-5107

Fresnel Optics, Inc.
1300 Mount Read Blvd.
Rochester, NY 14606

Founded 1970
Total employees 110
Annual sales $11 million
Industry Photonics
Growth Openings in past
year 46; percentage
growth 71%
Contact John Egger,
President
Tel 716-647-1140
Fax 716-254-4940

Genencor International, Inc.
4 Cambridge Pl., 1870
South Winton Rd.
Rochester, NY 14618

Founded 1990
Total employees 550
Annual sales $125 million
Industries Biotechnology,
Chemicals
Growth Openings in past
year 72; percentage
growth 15%
Contact Dennis Raup,
Director of Human
Resources
Tel 716-256-5200
Fax 716-244-9988

Graham Manufacturing Co., Inc.
20 Florence Ave.
Batavia, NY 14020

Founded 1936
Total employees 350
Annual sales $43 million
Industry Energy
Growth Openings in past
year 29; percentage
growth 9%
Contact Al Cadena,
President
Tel 716-343-2216
Fax 716-343-1097

Hampshire Instruments, Inc.
10 Carlson Rd.
Rochester, NY 14610

Founded 1984
Total employees 130
Annual sales $12 million
Industry Subassemblies
and Components
Growth Openings in past
year 40; percentage
growth 44%
Contact Ms. Donna
Urella,
Personnel Administrator
Tel 716-482-4070
Fax 716-482-6497

Harsco Corp., Sherwood Division
120 Church St.
Lockport, NY 14094

Founded 1853
Total employees 500
Annual sales $50 million
Industries Medical,
Subassemblies and
Components
Growth Openings in past
year 100; percentage
growth 25%
Contact K.F. Bruch, III,
General Manager
Tel 716-433-3891
Fax 716-433-1275

JML Optical Industries, Inc.
690 Portland Ave.
Rochester, NY 14621

Founded 1972
Total employees 100
Annual sales $10 million
Industries Factory
Automation,
Manufacturing
Equipment, Photonics
Growth Openings in past
year 20; percentage
growth 25%
Contact Joseph M.
Lobozzo, Jr.,
President
Tel 716-342-8900
Fax 716-342-6125

Microwave Data Systems
300 Main St.
East Rochester, NY
14445

Founded 1985
Total employees 110
Annual sales $13 million
Industry
Telecommunications
Growth Openings in past
year 20; percentage
growth 22%
Contact Paul Jacobs,
President
Tel 716-385-7560
Fax 716-385-7923

Moscom Corp.
3750 Monroe Ave.
Pittsford, NY 14534

Founded 1983
Total employees 160
Annual sales $15.8 million
Industries Computer
Software, Holding
Companies,
Telecommunications
Growth Openings in past
year 34; percentage
growth 26%
Contact Albert J.
Montevecchio,
COB/President/CEO
Tel 716-381-6000
Fax 716-383-6800

Hazmat Environmental Group, Inc.
New Village Industrial Pk.,
60 Commerce Dr.
Buffalo, NY 14218

Founded 1984
Total employees 150
Industry Environmental
Growth Openings in past
year 50; percentage
growth 50%
Contact Dennis Dintino,
President
Tel 716-827-7200
Fax 716-827-7217

LaBella Associates, P.C.
300 State St.
Rochester, NY 14614

Founded 1978
Total employees 85
Annual sales $5 million
Industries Environmental,
Manufacturing
Equipment
Growth Openings in past
year 20; percentage
growth 30%
Contact Salvatore
LaBella,
President
Tel 716-454-6110
Fax 716-454-3066

International Imaging Materials, Inc.
310 Commerce Dr.
Amherst, NY 14228

Founded 1983
Total employees 500
Annual sales $82 million
Industry Computer
Hardware
Growth Openings in past
year 199; percentage
growth 66%
Contact Michael
Drennan,
VP of Finance
Tel 716-691-6333
Fax 716-691-3395

Magnetic Technologies Corp.
770 Linden Ave.
Rochester, NY 14625

Founded 1969
Total employees 150
Annual sales $14 million
Industries Computer
Hardware,
Manufacturing
Equipment
Growth Openings in past
year 70; percentage
growth 87%
Contact Gordon McNeil,
President
Tel 716-385-8711
Fax 716-385-5625

Performance Technologies, Inc.
315 Science Pkwy.
Rochester, NY 14620

Founded 1981
Total employees 150
Annual sales $24 million
Industries Computer
Hardware, Computer
Software, Holding
Companies
Growth Openings in past
year 67; percentage
growth 80%
Contact John Slusser,
President/COO
Tel 716-256-0200
Fax 716-256-0791

STS Duotek, Inc.
7500 West Henrietta Rd.,
PO Box 349
Rush, NY 14543

Founded 1978
Total employees 85
Annual sales $8.1 million
Industry Biotechnology
Growth Openings in past
year 31; percentage
growth 57%
Contact Richard
Whitbourne,
Chief Executive Officer
Tel 716-533-1672
Fax 716-533-1796

Taylor Devices, Inc.
90 Taylor Dr.
North Tonawanda, NY
14120

Founded 1955
Total employees 85
Annual sales $4.97 million
Industry Subassemblies
and Components
Growth Openings in past
year 14; percentage
growth 19%
Contact Douglas P.
Taylor,
President/COB
Tel 716-694-0800
Fax 716-695-6015

**University of Rochester
Lab for Laser
Energetics**
250 East River Rd.
Rochester, NY 14623

Founded 1970
Total employees 200
Industries Medical,
Photonics
Growth Openings in past
year 80; percentage
growth 66%
Contact Robert McCrory,
Ph.D.,
Director
Tel 716-275-5101
Fax 716-275-5960

**Wilson Greatbatch, Ltd.,
Medical Division**
10000 Wehrle Dr.
Clarence, NY 14031

Founded 1979
Total employees 510
Annual sales $68 million
Industry Energy
Growth Openings in past
year 59; percentage
growth 13%
Contact Edward Voboro,
President/CEO
Tel 716-759-6901
Fax 716-759-8579

■ **718 Area Code**

**American Healthware
Systems, Inc.**
4522 Fort Hamilton Pkwy.
Brooklyn, NY 11219

Founded 1978
Total employees 70
Industry Computer
Software
Growth Openings in past
year 30; percentage
growth 75%
Contact George
Weinberger,
President
Tel 718-435-6300
Fax 718-435-0275

**Chromex Corp., Ink
Division**
19 Clay St.
Brooklyn, NY 11222

Founded 1964
Total employees 200
Annual sales $43 million
Industry Chemicals
Growth Openings in past
year 50; percentage
growth 33%
Contact Irving M.
Wolbrom,
President
Tel 718-389-2860
Fax 718-389-2474

CIC International, Inc.
38-01 23rd Ave.
Astoria, NY 11105

Founded 1930
Total employees 252
Industries Defense,
Manufacturing
Equipment
Growth Openings in past
year 152; percentage
growth 152%
Contact Michael Kane,
President
Tel 718-204-0900
Fax 718-728-7663

**Eon Labs
Manufacturing, Inc.**
227-15 North Conduit
Ave.
Laurelton, NY 11413

Founded 1970
Total employees 130
Annual sales $73 million
Industry Pharmaceuticals
Growth Openings in past
year 15; percentage
growth 13%
Contact Ms. Maria
Sinnott,
Human Resources
Director
Tel 718-276-8600
Fax 718-949-3120

**Industrial Acoustics Co.,
Inc.**
1160 Commerce Ave.
Bronx, NY 10462

Founded 1949
Total employees 770
Annual sales $80.99
million
Industries Environmental,
Test and Measurement,
Transportation
Growth Openings in past
year 144; percentage
growth 23%
Contact Raymond E.
Svana,
Assistant VP of Human
Resources
Tel 718-931-8000
Fax 718-863-1138

Keystone Electronics Corp.
31-07 20th Rd.
Astoria, NY 11105

Founded 1943
Total employees 102
Industry Subassemblies and Components
Growth Openings in past year 22; percentage growth 27%
Contact Richard David, President/CEO
Tel 718-956-8900
Fax 718-956-9040

Teleport Communications Group
1 Teleport Dr.
Staten Island, NY 10311

Founded 1984
Total employees 250
Annual sales $34 million
Industries Photonics, Telecommunications
Growth Openings in past year 25; percentage growth 11%
Contact William Baldwin, VP of Administration
Tel 718-983-2000
Fax 718-983-2147

Belmay, Inc.
200 Corporate Blvd. South
Yonkers, NY 10701

Founded 1932
Total employees 100
Annual sales $21 million
Industry Chemicals
Growth Openings in past year 20; percentage growth 25%
Contact Alan Kestin, President
Tel 914-376-1515
Fax 914-376-1784

■ **914 Area Code**

Redound Industries
19 Clay St.
Brooklyn, NY 11222

Founded 1964
Total employees 200
Annual sales $22 million
Industry Holding Companies
Growth Openings in past year 50; percentage growth 33%
Contact Irving M. Wolbrom, President
Tel 718-389-2860
Fax 718-389-2474

Alsthom International, Inc.
4 Skyline Dr.
Hawthorne, NY 10532

Founded 1967
Total employees 50
Annual sales $5.9 million
Industries Energy, Factory Automation, Subassemblies and Components, Transportation
Growth Openings in past year 20; percentage growth 66%
Contact Paul Jancek, President
Tel 914-347-5155
Fax 914-347-5432

Carl Zeiss, Inc.
One Zeiss Dr.
Thornwood, NY 10594

Founded 1925
Total employees 600
Annual sales $65 million
Industries Factory Automation, Medical, Photonics, Test and Measurement, Telecommunications
Growth Openings in past year 100; percentage growth 20%
Contact Larry Hart, VP of Human Resources
Tel 914-747-1800
Fax 914-682-8296

Republic Wire and Cable
58-60 Grand Ave.
Maspeth, NY 11378

Founded 1851
Total employees 165
Annual sales $35 million
Industry Subassemblies and Components
Growth Openings in past year 35; percentage growth 26%
Contact John S. Moore, Vice President/General Manager
Tel 718-326-0001
Fax 718-894-6667

American White Cross Labs, Inc.
40 Nardozzi Pl.
New Rochelle, NY 10802

Founded 1913
Total employees 450
Annual sales $35 million
Industry Medical
Growth Openings in past year 150; percentage growth 50%
Contact Richard Orentzel, President
Tel 914-632-3045
Fax 914-632-3071

Danbury Pharmacal, Inc.
12 Stoneleigh Ave., PO Box 990
Carmel, NY 10512

Founded 1931
Total employees 700
Annual sales $96 million
Industry Pharmaceuticals
Growth Openings in past year 197; percentage growth 39%
Contact Paul Kirkwood, VP of Human Resources
Tel 914-225-1700
Fax 914-225-1763

Dataverse Corporation
PO Box 937
New Paltz, NY 12561

Founded 1980
Total employees 19
Annual sales $1 million
Industry Computer
Software
Growth Openings in past
year 13; percentage
growth 216%
Contact Judah
Reichenthal,
President
Tel 914-255-2201

Gotham Ink & Color Co., Inc.
19 Kay Fries Dr.
Stony Point, NY 10980

Founded 1937
Total employees 60
Annual sales $8.2 million
Industry Chemicals
Growth Openings in past
year 13; percentage
growth 27%
Contact Dave Smith,
Corporate Vice
President/General
Manager
Tel 914-947-4000
Fax 914-947-3270

Intergen Company
2 Manhattanville Rd.
Purchase, NY 10577

Founded 1910
Total employees 45
Annual sales $4.3 million
Industries Biotechnology,
Pharmaceuticals
Growth Openings in past
year 20; percentage
growth 80%
Contact Robert J.
Beckman,
President
Tel 914-694-1700
Fax 914-694-1429

Mearl Corporation
217 North Highland Ave.
Ossining, NY 10562

Founded 1933
Total employees 700

Industries Advanced
Materials, Chemicals,
Holding Companies
Growth Openings in past
year 97; percentage
growth 16%
Contact Dominic A.
Pinciaro,
President
Tel 914-941-7450
Fax 914-941-2311

Medical Laboratory Automation, Inc.
270 Marble Ave.
Pleasantville, NY 10570

Founded 1963
Total employees 350
Annual sales $50 million
Industry Medical
Growth Openings in past
year 35; percentage
growth 11%
Contact Richard E.
Scordato,
President
Tel 914-747-3020
Fax 914-747-0498

Microbiz Corp.
500 Airport Executive
Park
Spring Valley, NY 10977

Founded 1987
Total employees 76
Annual sales $8.8 million
Industry Computer
Software
Growth Openings in past
year 31; percentage
growth 68%
Contact Craig Aberle,
President
Tel 914-425-9500
Fax 914-425-4598

Regeneron Pharmaceuticals, Inc.
777 Old Saw Mill River
Rd.
Tarrytown, NY 10591

Founded 1988
Total employees 190
Industry Pharmaceuticals

Growth Openings in past
year 80; percentage
growth 72%
Contact Dr. Leonard
Schleifer, MD, P,
CEO/President
Tel 914-347-7000
Fax 914-347-2113

Schott America Glass & Scientific Products, Inc.
3 Odell Plaza
Yonkers, NY 10701

Founded 1963
Total employees 100
Industries Photonics,
Test and Measurement
Growth Openings in past
year 50; percentage
growth 100%
Contact Hans Moeller,
President
Tel 914-968-8900
Fax 914-968-4422

Vicon Fiberoptics, Inc.
90 Secor Ln.
Pelham Manor, NY 10803

Founded 1968
Total employees 40
Annual sales $1.5 million
Industries Medical,
Photonics
Growth Openings in past
year 15; percentage
growth 60%
Contact Leonard Scrivo,
President
Tel 914-738-5006

Witco Corp., Chemprene Division
570 Fishkill Ave.
Beacon, NY 12508

Founded 1926
Total employees 265
Annual sales $33 million
Industries Advanced
Materials, Factory
Automation,
Manufacturing
Equipment

Growth Openings in past year 65; percentage growth 32%
Contact Edward B. Kerin, Vice President/General Manager
Tel 914-831-2800
Fax 914-831-4639

North Carolina

■ **704 Area Code**

AGIE USA, Ltd.
PO Box 220
Davidson, NC 28036

Founded 1964
Total employees 150
Annual sales $18 million
Industry Factory Automation
Growth Openings in past year 30; percentage growth 25%
Contact Gabriele Carinci, President
Tel 704-892-8011
Fax 704-896-7512

FMC Corp., Lithium Division
449 North Cox Rd., PO Box 3925
Gastonia, NC 28054

Founded 1948
Total employees 650
Annual sales $130 million
Industries Advanced Materials, Chemicals, Pharmaceuticals
Growth Openings in past year 19; percentage growth 3%
Contact T.K. Johnson, Manager of Human Resources
Tel 704-868-5300
Fax 704-868-5370

HydroLogic, Inc.
122 Lyman St.
Asheville, NC 28801

Founded 1986
Total employees 130
Annual sales $10 million

Industries Biotechnology, Chemicals, Environmental, Holding Companies
Growth Openings in past year 70; percentage growth 116%
Contact Thomas R. Barr, President
Tel 704-254-5169
Fax 704-252-9711

Info Systems of North Carolina, Inc.
7500 East Independence Blvd.
Charlotte, NC 28227

Founded 1978
Total employees 230
Industry Computer Software
Growth Openings in past year 70; percentage growth 43%
Contact William J. Gaughan, Vice Chairman/COO
Tel 704-535-7180
Fax 704-567-8958

Network Computing Corp.
5301 77 Center Dr.
Charlotte, NC 28217

Founded 1971
Total employees 115
Annual sales $13 million
Industry Computer Software
Growth Openings in past year 15; percentage growth 15%
Contact George Mackie, President
Tel 704-525-8810

Perfection Gear, Inc.
9 North Bear Creek Rd.
Asheville, NC 28806

Founded 1934
Total employees 84
Industry Factory Automation

Growth Openings in past year 12; percentage growth 16%
Contact Ms. Mary Hager, Personnel Manager
Tel 704-253-0000
Fax 704-251-0971

Rexroth Corp., Star Linear Systems Division
9432 Southern Pine Blvd.
Charlotte, NC 28273

Founded 1966
Total employees 60
Industries Photonics, Subassemblies and Components
Growth Openings in past year 20; percentage growth 50%
Contact G.C. Blankemeyer, Controller/Director of Employee Relation
Tel 704-523-2088
Fax 704-523-4099

Schaefer Systems International, Inc.
10021 Westlake Dr., PO Box 7009
Charlotte, NC 28241

Founded 1985
Total employees 50
Annual sales $10 million
Industries Environmental, Factory Automation
Growth Openings in past year 20; percentage growth 66%
Contact Arnold Heuzen, General Manager
Tel 704-588-2150
Fax 704-588-1862

Textron, Inc., Townsend Division
5250-77 Center Dr., Suite 300
Charlotte, NC 28217

Founded 1920
Total employees 750
Industries Factory Automation, Subassemblies and Components

Growth Openings in past year 50; percentage growth 7%
Contact Robert P. Ross, President
Tel 704-525-8003
Fax 704-525-8565

Growth Openings in past year 90; percentage growth 56%
Contact W. Keith Stoneback, President
Tel 919-362-0842
Fax 919-387-8225

Growth Openings in past year 50; percentage growth 10%
Contact G.C. Verkerk, President/CEO
Tel 919-549-8263
Fax 919-248-6462

W.S. Tyler, Inc.
3200 Bessemer City Rd., PO Box 8900
Gastonia, NC 28053

Founded 1988
Total employees 600
Annual sales $71 million
Industries Environmental, Test and Measurement
Growth Openings in past year 50; percentage growth 9%
Contact Donald Whitehouse, Director of Human Resources
Tel 704-629-2214
Fax 704-865-6533

Captive-Aire Systems, Inc.
112 Wheaton Dr.
Youngsville, NC 27596

Founded 1980
Total employees 160
Annual sales $26 million
Industries Energy, Subassemblies and Components
Growth Openings in past year 60; percentage growth 60%
Contact Robert Luddy, President
Tel 919-554-2414

Electronic Data Systems Corp., Local Governments Division
4800 Six Forks Rd., Six Forks Ctr.
Raleigh, NC 27609

Founded 1976
Total employees 160
Annual sales $18 million
Industry Computer Software
Growth Openings in past year 20; percentage growth 14%
Contact Harvey Braswell, Division Manager
Tel 919-783-8000
Fax 919-783-1000

■ **919 Area Code**

Alphatronix, Inc.
4022 Stirrup Creek Dr., Suite 315
Durham, NC 27713

Founded 1988
Total employees 60
Annual sales $9.8 million
Industry Computer Hardware
Growth Openings in past year 25; percentage growth 71%
Contact Dr. Robert P. Freese, President
Tel 919-544-0001
Fax 919-544-4079

Cardiovascular Diagnostics, Inc.
PO Box 14025
Research Triangle Park, NC 27709

Founded 1986
Total employees 28
Industry Medical
Growth Openings in past year 13; percentage growth 86%
Contact Jonathan M. Lawrie, President
Tel 919-544-2952
Fax 919-544-1454

Embrex, Inc.
PO Box 13989
Research Triangle Park, NC 27709

Founded 1985
Total employees 50
Industries Biotechnology, Pharmaceuticals
Growth Openings in past year 20; percentage growth 66%
Contact Ms. Helen J. Makarezyk, Personnel Supervisor
Tel 919-941-5185
Fax 919-941-5186

AMSCO Scientific
10002 Lufkin Rd., PO Box 747
Apex, NC 27502

Founded 1989
Total employees 250
Annual sales $310 million
Industry Test and Measurement

CompuChem Corp.
3308 Chapel Hill/Nelson Hwy., PO Box 12652
Research Triangle Park, NC 27709

Founded 1982
Total employees 550
Annual sales $58 million
Industries Environmental, Medical

Envirochem Environmental Services, Inc.
1005 Investment Blvd.
Apex, NC 27502

Founded 1981
Total employees 70
Annual sales $7 million
Industry Environmental

Growth Openings in past
year 20; percentage
growth 40%
Contact Jerry Deakle,
President
Tel 919-362-9010
Fax 919-362-9005

Growth Openings in past
year 200; percentage
growth 40%
Contact Bruce Muller,
President
Tel 919-892-8081
Fax 919-892-9600

Growth Openings in past
year 75; percentage
growth 33%
Contact Gene Bedell,
President
Tel 919-380-5000
Fax 919-469-1910

**Environmental
Diagnostic, Inc.**
1238 Anthony Rd., PO
Box 908
Burlington, NC 27215

Founded 1970
Total employees 47
Annual sales $2.7 million
Industries Biotechnology,
Manufacturing
Equipment, Medical,
Photonics, Test and
Measurement
Growth Openings in past
year 13; percentage
growth 38%
Contact James D.
Skinner,
President/CEO
Tel 919-226-6311
Fax 919-229-4471

**Novo Nordisk
Biochemical, Inc.**
1003 State Rd.
Franklinton, NC 27525

Founded 1978
Total employees 97
Annual sales $9.3 million
Industry Biotechnology
Growth Openings in past
year 13; percentage
growth 15%
Contact Ms. Joanne
Steiner,
Human Resources
Manager
Tel 919-494-2014
Fax 919-494-5465

**Wandel & Goltermann
Technologies, Inc.**
1030 Swabia Ct.
Research Triangle Park,
NC 27709

Founded 1966
Total employees 220
Industries Factory
Automation,
Subassemblies and
Components, Test and
Measurement
Growth Openings in past
year 20; percentage
growth 10%
Contact Matt Weitz,
Personnel Manager
Tel 919-941-5730
Fax 919-941-5751

**High Point Chemical
Corp.**
243 Woodbine, PO Box
2316
High Point, NC 27260

Founded 1945
Total employees 175
Annual sales $24 million
Industries Advanced
Materials, Chemicals
Growth Openings in past
year 19; percentage
growth 12%
Contact R. Morton,
Manager of Human
Resources
Tel 919-884-2214
Fax 919-884-5039

Pioneer Software, Inc.
5540 Centerview Dr.
Raleigh, NC 27606

Founded 1986
Total employees 100
Annual sales $11 million
Industry Computer
Software
Growth Openings in past
year 70; percentage
growth 233%
Contact Richard
Halcomb,
President
Tel 919-859-2220
Fax 919-859-9334

North Dakota

■ **701 Area Code**

Great Plains Software
1701 Southwest 38th St.
Fargo, ND 58103

Founded 1980
Total employees 500
Industry Computer
Software
Growth Openings in past
year 180; percentage
growth 56%
Contact Ms. Jodi Uecker-
Rust,
Director of Operations
Tel 701-281-0550
Fax 701-281-3171

Morganite, Inc.
1 Morganite Dr.
Dunn, NC 28334

Founded 1964
Total employees 700
Annual sales $76 million
Industry Advanced
Materials

Seer Technologies, Inc.
8000 Regency Pkwy.
Cary, NC 27511

Founded 1990
Total employees 300
Annual sales $34 million
Industry Computer
Software

Ohio

■ **216 Area Code**

Acromed Corp.
3303 Carnegie Ave.
Cleveland, OH 44115

Founded 1983
Total employees 60
Annual sales $20 million
Industry Medical
Growth Openings in past
  year 12; percentage
  growth 25%
Contact Hans Eekhof,
  President
  Tel 216-431-9900
  Fax 216-431-1075

AMRESCO, Inc.
30175 Solon Industrial
  Pkwy.
Solon, OH 44139

Founded 1976
Total employees 95
Annual sales $9.1 million
Industries Advanced
  Materials,
  Biotechnology,
  Chemicals, Medical
Growth Openings in past
  year 15; percentage
  growth 18%
Contact Ms. Carol Takiff,
  Personnel Director
  Tel 216-349-1199
  Fax 216-349-1182

Antenna Specialists Co.
30500 Bruce Industrial
  Pkwy.
Solon, OH 44139

Founded 1953
Total employees 380
Annual sales $52 million
Industries Subassemblies
  and Components,
  Telecommunications
Growth Openings in past
  year 79; percentage
  growth 26%
Contact Ms. Susan
  VanDale,
  Director of Personnel
  Tel 216-349-8400
  Fax 216-349-8407

Bicron Corp.
12345 Kinsman Rd.
Newbury, OH 44065

Founded 1969
Total employees 250
Annual sales $25 million
Industry Test and
  Measurement
Growth Openings in past
  year 29; percentage
  growth 13%
Contact Ms. Donna
  Lashchuk,
  Director of Personnel
  Tel 216-564-2251
  Fax 216-564-8047

Bliss-Salem, Inc.
530 South Ellsworth Ave.
Salem, OH 44460

Founded 1857
Total employees 240
Industries Computer
  Hardware, Factory
  Automation,
  Manufacturing
  Equipment, Test and
  Measurement
Growth Openings in past
  year 30; percentage
  growth 14%
Contact Michael Zugay,
  President
  Tel 216-337-3444
  Fax 216-337-7067

Conceptual Systems Corp.
730 SOM Center Rd.
Mayfield Village, OH
  44143

Founded 1982
Total employees 70
Industry Computer
  Software
Growth Openings in past
  year 45; percentage
  growth 180%
Contact Nicholas
  Rosenstein, Ph.D.,
  President
  Tel 216-449-0600
  Fax 216-449-0600

Crest Rubber Co.
6408 Newton Falls Rd.,
  PO Box 312
Ravenna, OH 44266

Founded 1960
Total employees 77
Annual sales $2 million
Industry Manufacturing
  Equipment
Growth Openings in past
  year 15; percentage
  growth 24%
Contact Ms. Cindy
  Moore,
  General Manager
  Tel 216-296-4015
  Fax 216-296-4684

Cyberex, Inc.
7171 Industrial Park Blvd.
Mentor, OH 44060

Founded 1968
Total employees 120
Industries Energy,
  Subassemblies and
  Components
Growth Openings in past
  year 20; percentage
  growth 20%
Contact Gus Stevens,
  President/COO
  Tel 216-946-1783
  Fax 216-946-5963

DeCarlo Paternite & Associates, Inc.
6133 Rockside Rd.
Independence, OH 44131

Founded 1976
Total employees 115
Industry Computer
  Software
Growth Openings in past
  year 12; percentage
  growth 11%
Contact Vincent T.
  DeCarlo,
  President
  Tel 216-524-2121
  Fax 216-524-2845

Dover Chemical Corp.
Dept. DV-26, PO Box 40
Dover, OH 44622

Founded 1947
Total employees 105
Annual sales $22 million
Industries Advanced
Materials, Chemicals
Growth Openings in past
year 20; percentage
growth 23%
Contact J. Fette,
President
Tel 216-343-7711
Fax 216-364-1579

Gougler Industries, Inc.
805 Lake St.
Kent, OH 44240

Founded 1924
Total employees 250
Industry Holding
Companies
Growth Openings in past
year 25; percentage
growth 11%
Contact H. Saito,
President
Tel 216-673-5821
Fax 216-673-8838

North East Chemical Corp.
3301 Monroe Ave.
Cleveland, OH 44113

Founded 1983
Total employees 70
Annual sales $7.4 million
Industry Environmental
Growth Openings in past
year 20; percentage
growth 40%
Contact Ernest Q. Petrey,
Jr.,
Chief Executive Officer
Tel 216-961-8618
Fax 216-961-7812

GBS Computer Systems, Inc.
1035 North Meridian Rd.
Youngstown, OH 44509

Founded 1978
Total employees 92
Annual sales $16 million
Industries Computer
Hardware, Computer
Software
Growth Openings in past
year 12; percentage
growth 15%
Contact Ms. Anna
Lanhan,
Personnel Manager
Tel 216-797-2700
Fax 216-797-2724

Harwick Chemical Corp.
60 South Seiberling St.
Akron, OH 44305

Founded 1935
Total employees 350
Annual sales $76 million
Industries Advanced
Materials, Chemicals
Growth Openings in past
year 20; percentage
growth 6%
Contact Roger T. Reed,
President/CEO
Tel 216-798-9300
Fax 216-798-0214

Novar Electronics Corp.
24 Brown St.
Barberton, OH 44203

Founded 1963
Total employees 200
Annual sales $26 million
Industry Energy
Growth Openings in past
year 50; percentage
growth 33%
Contact J.H. Ott,
President of Novar
Electronics
Tel 216-745-0074
Fax 216-745-7401

General Computer Corp.
2045 Midway Dr.
Twinsburg, OH 44087

Founded 1970
Total employees 230
Annual sales $13.5 million
Industries Computer
Software, Holding
Companies
Growth Openings in past
year 55; percentage
growth 31%
Contact Richard
Pilarczyk,
President
Tel 216-425-3241
Fax 216-425-3249

Liquid Control Corp.
7576 Freedom Ave.
Northwest, PO Box
2747
North Canton, OH 44720

Founded 1975
Total employees 90
Annual sales $5 million
Industries Factory
Automation, Test and
Measurement
Growth Openings in past
year 20; percentage
growth 28%
Contact William Schiltz,
President
Tel 216-494-1313
Fax 216-494-5383

Pressco Technology, Inc.
29200 Aurora Rd.
Cleveland, OH 44139

Founded 1966
Total employees 130
Annual sales $15 million
Industry Factory
Automation
Growth Openings in past
year 20; percentage
growth 18%
Contact Don W. Cochran,
President
Tel 216-498-2600
Fax 216-498-2615

Production Machinery Corp.
8500 Station St.
Mentor, OH 44060

Founded 1955
Total employees 100
Annual sales $10 million
Industries Holding Companies, Manufacturing Equipment
Growth Openings in past year 15; percentage growth 17%
Contact J.R. Deering, VP of Finance and Administration
Tel 216-255-3437
Fax 216-255-3430

Radiometer America, Inc.
811 Sharon Dr.
Westlake, OH 44145

Founded 1961
Total employees 280
Annual sales $57 million
Industries Medical, Subassemblies and Components, Test and Measurement
Growth Openings in past year 14; percentage growth 5%
Contact Dennis Cada, Director of Human Resources
Tel 216-871-8900
Fax 216-871-8117

Research Oil Co.
2777 Broadway Ave.
Cleveland, OH 44115

Founded 1932
Total employees 150
Annual sales $15 million
Industries Energy, Environmental
Growth Openings in past year 15; percentage growth 11%
Contact Alan Gressel, President
Tel 216-623-8383
Fax 216-623-8393

Ricerca, Inc.
7528 Auburn Rd.
Painesville, OH 44077

Founded 1990
Total employees 300
Annual sales $65 million
Industries Biotechnology, Chemicals, Environmental, Medical
Growth Openings in past year 20; percentage growth 7%
Contact Dr. James Scozzie, President
Tel 216-357-3300
Fax 216-354-4415

Steris Corp.
9450 Pineneedle Dr.
Mentor, OH 44060

Founded 1985
Total employees 150
Annual sales $16 million
Industries Chemicals, Medical
Growth Openings in past year 60; percentage growth 66%
Contact Bill R. Sanford, President
Tel 216-354-2600
Fax 216-639-4457

Synthetic Products Co.
1000 Wayside Rd.
Cleveland, OH 44110

Founded 1917
Total employees 350
Annual sales $100 million
Industry Advanced Materials
Growth Openings in past year 79; percentage growth 29%
Contact Tom Jennings, President
Tel 216-531-6010
Fax 216-283-5331

Teledyne Hyson
10367 Brecksville Rd.
Brecksville, OH 44141

Founded 1941
Total employees 250
Annual sales $24 million

Industry Subassemblies and Components
Growth Openings in past year 100; percentage growth 66%
Contact John Terrell, President
Tel 216-526-5900
Fax 216-838-7684

Thomas Steel Strip Corp.
Delaware Ave. Northwest
Warren, OH 44485

Founded 1921
Total employees 600
Annual sales $89 million
Industry Advanced Materials
Growth Openings in past year 12; percentage growth 2%
Contact Charlie Van Horn, Director of Human Resources
Tel 216-841-6222
Fax 216-841-6260

Victoreen, Inc.
6000 Cochran Rd.
Cleveland, OH 44139

Founded 1928
Total employees 360
Annual sales $28 million
Industries Holding Companies, Test and Measurement
Growth Openings in past year 18; percentage growth 5%
Contact Ms. Carol Loucka, Director of Human Resources
Tel 216-248-9300
Fax 216-248-9301

■ 419 Area Code

Green Manufacturing, Inc.
1032 South Maple St., PO Box 408
Bowling Green, OH 43402

Founded 1952
Total employees 130
Annual sales $7 million
Industry Subassemblies and Components
Growth Openings in past year 30; percentage growth 30%
Contact Jeff Snook, President
Tel 419-352-9484
Fax 419-354-2087

Systems Alternatives, Inc.
1705 Indian Wood Cir., Suite 100
Maumee, OH 43537

Founded 1981
Total employees 45
Industry Computer Software
Contact John Underwood, President
Tel 419-891-1100
Fax 419-891-1045

Wahl Refractories, Inc.
South State Rte. 19, PO Box 530
Fremont, OH 43420

Founded 1919
Total employees 80
Industry Advanced Materials
Growth Openings in past year 30; percentage growth 60%
Contact Daniel W. Lease, President
Tel 419-334-2658
Fax 419-334-9445

WIL Research Laboratories, Inc.
1407 George Rd.
Ashland, OH 44805

Founded 1933
Total employees 130
Annual sales $8 million
Industry Pharmaceuticals
Growth Openings in past year 25; percentage growth 23%
Contact Dr. Joe Holoon, President
Tel 419-289-8700
Fax 419-289-3650

■ 513 Area Code

Advanced Assembly Automation, Inc.
313 Mound St.
Dayton, OH 45407

Founded 1978
Total employees 160
Annual sales $25 million
Industry Factory Automation
Growth Openings in past year 30; percentage growth 23%
Contact John Logan, President
Tel 513-222-3030
Fax 513-223-3334

Cables To Go, Inc.
1501 Webster St.
Dayton, OH 45404

Founded 1985
Total employees 85
Annual sales $9.6 million
Industries Photonics, Subassemblies and Components, Telecommunications
Growth Openings in past year 35; percentage growth 70%
Contact Jeff Hyman, President
Tel 513-224-8646
Fax 800-331-2841

Campbell Group
100 Production Dr.
Harrison, OH 45030

Founded 1979
Total employees 800
Annual sales $150 million
Industries Factory Automation, Subassemblies and Components
Growth Openings in past year 199; percentage growth 33%
Contact Richard Heiman, President
Tel 513-367-4811
Fax 513-367-3176

Cincinnati Sub-Zero Products, Inc.
12011 Mosteller Rd.
Cincinnati, OH 45241

Founded 1940
Total employees 115
Annual sales $17 million
Industries Holding Companies, Test and Measurement
Growth Openings in past year 15; percentage growth 15%
Contact Leonard Berke, President
Tel 513-772-8810
Fax 513-772-9119

Environmental Enterprises, Inc.
10163 Cincinnati Dayton Rd.
Cincinnati, OH 45241

Founded 1976
Total employees 146
Annual sales $15 million
Industry Environmental
Growth Openings in past year 46; percentage growth 46%
Contact Daniel McCabe, President
Tel 513-772-2818
Fax 513-782-8950

Globe Motors
2275 Stanley Ave.
Dayton, OH 45404

Founded 1987
Total employees 550
Annual sales $44 million
Industry Subassemblies
and Components
Growth Openings in past
year 17; percentage
growth 3%
Contact Steve
Hendrickson,
Director of Human
Resources
Tel 513-228-3171
Fax 513-229-8531

Kohol Systems, Inc.
980 Senate Dr.
Dayton, OH 45459

Founded 1978
Total employees 43
Annual sales $5.1 million
Industries Computer
Software, Factory
Automation,
Transportation
Growth Openings in past
year 13; percentage
growth 43%
Contact Neil Reif,
VP of Operations
Tel 513-439-5200
Fax 513-439-5204

Meridian Diagnostics, Inc.
3471 River Hills Dr.
Cincinnati, OH 45244

Founded 1977
Total employees 120
Annual sales $11 million
Industries Biotechnology,
Chemicals, Medical,
Pharmaceuticals
Growth Openings in past
year 20; percentage
growth 20%
Contact Frank Seurkamp,
Vice President/
Treasurer
Tel 513-271-3700
Fax 513-271-0124

Precision Industrial Automation, Inc.
3520 Ibsen Ave.
Cincinnati, OH 45209

Founded 1945
Total employees 240
Annual sales $25 million
Industry Factory
Automation
Growth Openings in past
year 40; percentage
growth 20%
Contact R.W. Rothfusz,
President
Tel 513-351-3300
Fax 513-351-4666

RJO Enterprises, Inc., Systems Acquisition and Logistics Division
101 Woodman Dr., Suite
100
Dayton, OH 45431

Founded 1984
Total employees 160
Annual sales $15.8 million
Industries Computer
Hardware, Defense
Growth Openings in past
year 50; percentage
growth 45%
Contact Bill Bowser,
Vice President/Director
Tel 513-252-8609
Fax 513-252-8609

Simpson Industries, Inc., Troy Operations
2001 Corporate Dr.
Troy, OH 45373

Founded 1985
Total employees 150
Annual sales $14 million
Industry Subassemblies
and Components
Growth Openings in past
year 32; percentage
growth 27%
Contact Jim Drake,
General Manager
Tel 513-339-2677
Fax 513-339-2680

Spectra-Physics, Inc., Construction & Agricultural Division
5475 Kellenburger Rd.
Dayton, OH 45424

Founded 1983
Total employees 750
Annual sales $81 million
Industry Photonics
Growth Openings in past
year 150; percentage
growth 25%
Contact David
Studebaker,
Personnel Manager
Tel 513-233-8921
Fax 513-233-9004

Systech Environmental Corp.
245 North Valley Rd.
Xenia, OH 45385

Founded 1969
Total employees 240
Annual sales $11 million
Industry Environmental
Growth Openings in past
year 14; percentage
growth 6%
Contact Steven Zimmer,
Senior VP of Finance
and Administration
Tel 513-372-8077
Fax 513-372-8099

Tastemaker
1199 Edison
Cincinnati, OH 45216

Founded 1931
Total employees 400
Annual sales $87 million
Industry Chemicals
Growth Openings in past
year 150; percentage
growth 60%
Contact Ms. Terri Bonar-
Stewart,
VP of Human Resources
Tel 513-948-8000
Fax 513-948-5607

ZestoTherm, Inc.
311 Northland Blvd.
Cincinnati, OH 45246

Founded 1984
Total employees 110

Industries Energy,
Manufacturing
Equipment
Growth Openings in past
year 40; percentage
growth 57%
Contact David Holwadel,
President
Tel 513-772-3066
Fax 513-772-3269

■ **614 Area Code**

BMA Technologies, Inc.
196 South Main St.
Marion, OH 43302

Founded 1930
Total employees 350
Annual sales $37 million
Industry Holding
Companies
Growth Openings in past
year 49; percentage
growth 16%
Contact Charles W.
Wright,
Chief Executive Officer
Tel 614-383-1660
Fax 614-383-6010

**Dodson-Lindblom
Associates, Inc.**
6121 Huntley Rd.
Columbus, OH 43229

Founded 1950
Total employees 100
Industry Manufacturing
Equipment
Growth Openings in past
year 45; percentage
growth 81%
Contact James Siebert,
President
Tel 614-848-4141
Fax 614-848-6712

**R.D. Zande &
Associates, Ltd.**
1237 Dublin Rd.
Columbus, OH 43215

Founded 1968
Total employees 160
Annual sales $12 million
Industry Environmental

Growth Openings in past
year 42; percentage
growth 35%
Contact Richard D.
Zande,
CEO/President
Tel 614-486-4383
Fax 614-486-4387

**Roxane Laboratories,
Inc.**
PO Box 16532
Columbus, OH 43216

Founded 1886
Total employees 450
Annual sales $62 million
Industry Pharmaceuticals
Growth Openings in past
year 99; percentage
growth 28%
Contact Gerald C. Wojta,
President
Tel 614-276-4000
Fax 614-274-0974

Sensotec, Inc.
1200 Chesapeake Ave.
Columbus, OH 43212

Founded 1973
Total employees 210
Annual sales $22 million
Industries Subassemblies
and Components, Test
and Measurement,
Transportation
Growth Openings in past
year 31; percentage
growth 17%
Contact John Easton,
President
Tel 614-488-5926
Fax 614-486-0506

**Symix Computer
Systems Inc.**
2800 Corporate Exchange
Dr.
Columbus, OH 43231

Founded 1979
Total employees 250
Annual sales $24.5 million
Industry Computer
Software

Growth Openings in past
year 50; percentage
growth 25%
Contact Doug Foust,
Human Resources
Manager
Tel 614-523-7000
Fax 614-895-2504

**Telesis Marking
Systems Corp.**
20700 U.S. Rte. 23, PO
Box 5000
Chillicothe, OH 45601

Founded 1971
Total employees 80
Annual sales $9.5 million
Industry Factory
Automation
Growth Openings in past
year 15; percentage
growth 23%
Contact John Robertson,
President/CEO
Tel 614-642-3200
Fax 614-642-2037

Tosoh SMD, Inc.
3515 Grove City Rd.
Grove City, OH 43123

Founded 1978
Total employees 220
Annual sales $23 million
Industry Manufacturing
Equipment
Growth Openings in past
year 40; percentage
growth 22%
Contact William Koch,
VP of Human Resources
Tel 614-875-7912
Fax 614-875-0031

Oklahoma

■ **405 Area Code**

Central Plastics Co.
PO Box 3129
Shawnee, OK 74801

Founded 1955
Total employees 200
Annual sales $25 million

Industries Factory
Automation,
Subassemblies and
Components
Growth Openings in past
year 35; percentage
growth 21%
Contact Phill Pourchot,
President
Tel 405-273-6302
Fax 800-733-5993

Governair
4841 North Sewell
Oklahoma City, OK 73118

Founded 1937
Total employees 180
Industry Energy
Growth Openings in past
year 15; percentage
growth 9%
Contact Ms. Lee Young,
Director of Personnel
Tel 405-525-6546
Fax 405-528-4724

KF Industries, Inc.
1500 Southeast 89th St.,
PO Box 95249
Oklahoma City, OK 73149

Founded 1874
Total employees 283
Annual sales $48 million
Industries Energy,
Subassemblies and
Components
Growth Openings in past
year 48; percentage
growth 20%
Contact Bill D. Neimann,
President
Tel 405-631-1533
Fax 405-631-5034

LB&M Associates, Inc.
211 Southwest A Ave.
Lawton, OK 73501

Founded 1982
Total employees 170
Industries Computer
Hardware, Defense,
Environmental,
Transportation

Growth Openings in past
year 120; percentage
growth 240%
Contact Rudy Alverrado,
Chief Executive Officer
Tel 405-355-1471
Fax 405-357-9360

SSI, Photo I.D.
1027 Waterwood Pkwy.
Edmond, OK 73034

Founded 1969
Total employees 325
Industries Computer
Hardware, Photonics
Growth Openings in past
year 239; percentage
growth 277%
Contact Ron Goade,
President
Tel 405-359-6000
Fax 405-359-6528

■ **918 Area Code**

**Eagle-Picher Industries,
Inc., Eagle-Picher
Research Laboratory**
200 9th Ave. North East,
PO Box 1090
Miami, OK 74354

Founded 1957
Total employees 200
Annual sales $26 million
Industries Chemicals,
Environmental,
Manufacturing
Equipment,
Subassemblies and
Components
Growth Openings in past
year 35; percentage
growth 21%
Contact Carl Holmes,
Personnel Manager
Tel 918-542-1801
Fax 918-542-3223

**Pulsafeeder, Inc.,
Electronics Control
Operation**
2800 South 24th St. West
Muskogee, OK 74401

Founded 1976
Total employees 105
Annual sales $9 million

Industries Subassemblies
and Components, Test
and Measurement
Growth Openings in past
year 15; percentage
growth 16%
Contact Bob Williams,
Vice President/General
Manager
Tel 918-683-0238
Fax 918-683-4858

Oregon

■ **503 Area Code**

**Advance Machine
Technology**
8411 North Denver Ave.
Portland, OR 97217

Founded 1987
Total employees 90
Industry Factory
Automation
Growth Openings in past
year 15; percentage
growth 20%
Contact Victor Nelson,
President
Tel 503-285-6282
Fax 503-283-4403

**Advanced Power
Technology, Inc.**
405 Southwest Columbia
St.
Bend, OR 97702

Founded 1984
Total employees 115
Annual sales $10 million
Industry Subassemblies
and Components
Growth Openings in past
year 15; percentage
growth 15%
Contact Patrick Sireta,
President/CEO
Tel 503-382-8028
Fax 503-388-0364

Agritope, Inc.
8505 Southwest
  Creekside Pl.
Beaverton, OR 97005

Founded 1987
Total employees 40
Industry Biotechnology
Growth Openings in past
  year 20; percentage
  growth 100%
Contact Dr. Adolph Ferro,
  Ph.D.,
  President
Tel 503-641-6115
Fax 503-643-2781

Analogy, Inc.
9205 Southwest Gemini
  Dr., PO Box 1669
Beaverton, OR 97005

Founded 1985
Total employees 90
Annual sales $10 million
Industry Computer
  Software
Growth Openings in past
  year 30; percentage
  growth 50%
Contact Roger Barkus,
  VP of Finance and
  Administration
Tel 503-626-9700
Fax 503-643-3361

Biamp Systems, Ltd.
14270 Northwest Science
  Park Dr.
Portland, OR 97229

Founded 1989
Total employees 70
Annual sales $7 million
Industry
  Telecommunications
Growth Openings in past
  year 15; percentage
  growth 27%
Contact Ralph Lockart,
  President
Tel 503-641-7287
Fax 503-626-0281

Cadre Technologies, Inc.
19545 Northwest Von
  Newmann Dr.
Beaverton, OR 97006

Founded 1982
Total employees 355
Annual sales $41 million
Industry Computer
  Software
Growth Openings in past
  year 11; percentage
  growth 3%
Contact Bill Winslow,
  VP of Human Resources
Tel 503-690-1300
Fax 503-690-1320

Central Point Software, Inc.
15220 Northwest
  Greenbrier Pkwy., Suite
  200
Beaverton, OR 97006

Founded 1981
Total employees 357
Annual sales $83.7 million
Industry Computer
  Software
Growth Openings in past
  year 57; percentage
  growth 19%
Contact Ms. Nancy
  Andrews,
  Human Resources
  Manager
Tel 503-690-8088
Fax 503-690-8083

Dynamix, Inc.
99 West 10th Ave., Suite
  224
Eugene, OR 97401

Founded 1979
Total employees 134
Annual sales $15 million
Industry Computer
  Software
Growth Openings in past
  year 49; percentage
  growth 57%
Contact Jeffrey Tunnell,
  President
Tel 503-343-0772
Fax 503-344-1754

Electronic Controls Design, Inc.
4287 A Southeast
  International Way
Milwaukie, OR 97222

Founded 1964
Total employees 120
Annual sales $14 million
Industry Holding
  Companies
Growth Openings in past
  year 15; percentage
  growth 14%
Contact Ms. Evelyn
  Irvine,
  Controller
Tel 503-659-6100
Fax 503-659-4422

Epitope, Inc.
8505 Southwest
  Creekside Pl.
Beaverton, OR 97005

Founded 1979
Total employees 140
Annual sales $3 million
Industries Biotechnology,
  Holding Companies,
  Medical
Growth Openings in past
  year 20; percentage
  growth 16%
Contact Dr. Adolph J.
  Ferro, Ph.D.,
  President/CEO
Tel 503-641-6115
Fax 503-643-2781

Kentrox Industries, Inc.
14375 Northwest Science
  Park Dr., PO Box 10704
Portland, OR 97210

Founded 1967
Total employees 300
Annual sales $41 million
Industries Computer
  Hardware, Computer
  Software,
  Subassemblies and
  Components,
  Telecommunications

Growth Openings in past year 50; percentage growth 20%
Contact Ms. Karen Callin, Director of Human Resources
Tel 503-643-1681
Fax 503-641-3341

Growth Openings in past year 15; percentage growth 100%
Contact Stephen Saltzman, President
Tel 503-274-2800
Fax 503-274-0670

Growth Openings in past year 34; percentage growth 45%
Contact Gene White, President
Tel 503-644-1960
Fax 503-526-4700

Pikes Peak Mining Co.
500 Multnomah St. Northeast, Suite 1200
Portland, OR 97232

Founded 1978
Total employees 150
Industry Advanced Materials
Growth Openings in past year 100; percentage growth 200%
Contact Thomas Albanese, President
Tel 503-731-2000

OrCAD, Inc.
3175 Northwest Aloclek Dr.
Hillsboro, OR 97124

Founded 1985
Total employees 77
Annual sales $8.9 million
Industry Computer Software
Growth Openings in past year 27; percentage growth 54%
Contact Michael Bosworth, CEO/President
Tel 503-690-9881
Fax 503-690-9891

Microflect Co., Inc.
3575 25th St. Southeast, PO Box 12985
Salem, OR 97309

Founded 1956
Total employees 119
Annual sales $16 million
Industry Telecommunications
Growth Openings in past year 14; percentage growth 13%
Contact Ms. Terrie Smith, Personnel Coordinator
Tel 503-363-9267
Fax 503-363-4613

Planar Systems, Inc.
1400 Northwest Compton Dr.
Beaverton, OR 97006

Founded 1983
Total employees 150
Industry Photonics
Growth Openings in past year 25; percentage growth 20%
Contact James Hurd, President
Tel 503-690-1100
Fax 503-690-1244

PERCON, Inc.
1720 Willow Creek Cir., Suite 530
Eugene, OR 97402

Founded 1983
Total employees 30
Industry Computer Hardware
Growth Openings in past year 12; percentage growth 66%
Contact Michael Coughlin, President
Tel 503-344-1189
Fax 503-344-1399

Molecular Probes, Inc.
4849 Pitchford Ave., PO Box 22010
Eugene, OR 97402

Founded 1975
Total employees 120
Industries Biotechnology, Chemicals
Growth Openings in past year 15; percentage growth 14%
Contact Ms. Tamara TenBrook, Personnel Director
Tel 503-465-8300
Fax 503-344-6504

Praegitzer Industries, Inc.
1270 Monmouth Cutoff
Dallas, OR 97338

Founded 1981
Total employees 600
Industry Subassemblies and Components
Growth Openings in past year 100; percentage growth 20%
Contact Robert L. Praegitzer, President
Tel 503-623-9273
Fax 503-623-5438

Photon Kinetics, Inc.
9405 Southwest Gemini Dr.
Beaverton, OR 97005

Founded 1979
Total employees 109
Annual sales $13 million
Industries Computer Software, Factory Automation, Test and Measurement

Now Software, Inc.
319 Southwest Washington St., 11th Floor
Portland, OR 97204

Founded 1990
Total employees 30
Industry Computer Software

Precision Interconnect Corporation
16640 Southwest 72nd Ave.
Portland, OR 97224

Founded 1972
Total employees 460
Annual sales $25 million
Industries Subassemblies and Components, Telecommunications
Growth Openings in past year 109; percentage growth 31%
Contact Ms. Holly Borden, Personnel Manager
Tel 503-620-9400
Fax 503-620-7131

Protocol Systems, Inc.
8500 Southwest Creekside Pl.
Beaverton, OR 97005

Founded 1986
Total employees 211
Annual sales $29.09 million
Industry Medical
Growth Openings in past year 41; percentage growth 24%
Contact Ms. Trudel Wiedemann, Director of Human Resources
Tel 503-526-8500
Fax 503-526-4200

Summit Information Systems Corp.
850 Southwest 35th St., PO Box 3003
Corvallis, OR 97339

Founded 1980
Total employees 140
Annual sales $16 million
Industry Computer Software
Growth Openings in past year 15; percentage growth 12%
Contact Ms. Susan Dunham, Personnel Manager
Tel 503-758-5888
Fax 503-758-5701

Supra Corp.
7101 Supra Dr. Southwest
Albany, OR 97321

Founded 1985
Total employees 90
Annual sales $14 million
Industries Computer Hardware, Telecommunications
Growth Openings in past year 45; percentage growth 100%
Contact John Wiley, President
Tel 503-967-9075
Fax 503-926-9370

Timberline Software Corp.
PO Box 728
Beaverton, OR 97075

Founded 1971
Total employees 192
Annual sales $14.9 million
Industry Computer Software
Growth Openings in past year 21; percentage growth 12%
Contact John Gorman, President/CEO
Tel 503-626-6775
Fax 503-641-7498

TSSI
8205 South West Creekside Pl.
Beaverton, OR 97005

Founded 1979
Total employees 72
Annual sales $10 million
Industry Computer Software
Growth Openings in past year 20; percentage growth 38%
Contact Ms. Ronnie Kamka, Manager of Human Resources and Administr
Tel 503-643-9281
Fax 503-646-4954

VTECH Computers, Inc.
10430 Southwest Fifth St.
Beaverton, OR 97005

Founded 1985
Total employees 300
Industry Computer Hardware
Growth Openings in past year 40; percentage growth 15%
Contact Abe Gish, President
Tel 503-646-3424
Fax 503-626-7845

Pennsylvania

■ **215 Area Code**

ABEC, Inc.
6390 Hedgewood Dr.
Allentown, PA 18106

Founded 1974
Total employees 60
Industries Biotechnology, Manufacturing Equipment
Growth Openings in past year 20; percentage growth 50%
Contact Dave Trout, President
Tel 215-366-7800
Fax 215-395-8147

Advanced Chemical Technologies, Inc.
450 Allentown Dr., Allentown Business Park
Allentown, PA 18103

Founded 1984
Total employees 50
Annual sales $7 million
Industry Chemicals
Growth Openings in past year 15; percentage growth 42%
Contact Shari Naghshineh, President
Tel 215-433-4066
Fax 215-433-4601

AST Data Group Corp.
100 High Point Dr.
Chalfont, PA 18914

Founded 1979
Total employees 160
Annual sales $18 million
Industry Computer
  Software
Growth Openings in past
  year 87; percentage
  growth 119%
Contact Zach Bergreen,
  President/CEO
Tel 215-822-8888
Fax 215-997-9060

Bentley Systems, Inc.
690 Pennsylvania Dr.
Exton, PA 19341

Founded 1984
Total employees 65
Industry Computer
  Software
Growth Openings in past
  year 23; percentage
  growth 54%
Contact Keith Bentley,
  President
Tel 215-458-5000
Fax 215-458-1060

CFM Technologies, Inc.
1380 Enterprise Dr.
West Chester, PA 19380

Founded 1984
Total employees 60
Annual sales $2 million
Industries Energy,
  Manufacturing
  Equipment
Growth Openings in past
  year 19; percentage
  growth 46%
Contact Roger Carolin,
  President
Tel 215-696-8300
Fax 215-696-8309

Drexelbrook Engineering Co.
205 Keith Valley Rd.
Horsham, PA 19044

Founded 1960
Total employees 350
Annual sales $41 million

Industry Test and
  Measurement
Growth Openings in past
  year 49; percentage
  growth 16%
Contact Steven Fierce,
  President
Tel 215-674-1234
Fax 215-674-2731

Echo Data Services, Inc.
15 East Uwchlan Ave.,
  Marsh Creek Corporate
  Ctr.
Exton, PA 19341

Founded 1983
Total employees 50
Industry
  Telecommunications
Growth Openings in past
  year 20; percentage
  growth 66%
Contact Stephen R.
  Roberts,
  President
Tel 215-363-2400
Fax 215-363-2421

Electronic Connectors, Inc.
125 South Fifth St.
Reading, PA 19602

Founded 1960
Total employees 44
Annual sales $4.3 million
Industry Subassemblies
  and Components
Growth Openings in past
  year 13; percentage
  growth 41%
Contact Dean Fronheiser,
  President
Tel 215-374-3796
Fax 215-374-0630

Enzymatics, Inc.
500 Enterprise Rd.
Horsham, PA 19044

Founded 1985
Total employees 80
Annual sales $8.8 million
Industry Medical

Growth Openings in past
  year 40; percentage
  growth 100%
Contact Donald Kuhla,
  Chief Operating Officer
Tel 215-674-3288
Fax 215-674-3273

Fluid Energy Processing and Equipment Co.
PO Box 200
Hatfield, PA 19440

Founded 1955
Total employees 100
Annual sales $15 million
Industries Chemicals,
  Holding Companies
Growth Openings in past
  year 35; percentage
  growth 53%
Contact Peter Zielinski,
  President
Tel 215-368-2510
Fax 215-368-6235

Gist-Brocades Food Ingredients, Inc.
2200 Renaissance Blvd.
King of Prussia, PA 19406

Founded 1987
Total employees 235
Annual sales $36 million
Industries Biotechnology,
  Chemicals
Growth Openings in past
  year 35; percentage
  growth 17%
Contact Kevin Kraus,
  President/CEO
Tel 215-272-4040
Fax 215-272-5695

GMIS Inc.
5 Country View Rd.
Malvern, PA 19355

Founded 1983
Total employees 120
Annual sales $10.5 million
Industry Computer
  Software

Growth Openings in past year 60; percentage growth 100%
Contact Thomas R. Owens, President/CEO
Tel 215-296-3838
Fax 215-640-9876

Great Valley Products, Inc.
600 Clark Ave.
King of Prussia, PA 19406

Founded 1987
Total employees 70
Annual sales $11 million
Industries Computer Hardware, Computer Software
Growth Openings in past year 35; percentage growth 100%
Contact Gerard Bucas, President
Tel 215-337-8770
Fax 215-337-9922

Heraeus Electro-Nite Co.
9901 Blue Grass Rd.
Philadelphia, PA 19114

Founded 1975
Total employees 350
Annual sales $45 million
Industries Factory Automation, Test and Measurement
Growth Openings in past year 20; percentage growth 6%
Contact Paul W. Sabol, Director of Administration
Tel 215-464-4200
Fax 215-698-7793

InterDigital Communications Corp.
2200 Renaissance Blvd., Suite 105
King of Prussia, PA 19406

Founded 1972
Total employees 180
Annual sales $50 million
Industries Holding Companies, Telecommunications

Growth Openings in past year 20; percentage growth 12%
Contact William W. Erdman, President/CEO
Tel 215-278-7800
Fax 215-278-6801

JWS Delavau Co., Inc.
2140 Germantown Ave.
Philadelphia, PA 19122

Founded 1847
Total employees 160
Annual sales $13 million
Industry Pharmaceuticals
Growth Openings in past year 60; percentage growth 60%
Contact Richard Leff, President
Tel 215-235-1100
Fax 215-235-2202

Lemmon Co.
650 Cathill Rd.
Sellersville, PA 18960

Founded 1945
Total employees 400
Annual sales $105 million
Industry Pharmaceuticals
Growth Openings in past year 23; percentage growth 6%
Contact William Fletcher, President
Tel 215-723-5544
Fax 215-721-9669

MG Industries, Specialty Gas Division
1 Steel Rd. East
Morrisville, PA 19482

Founded 1969
Total employees 122
Annual sales $22 million
Industries Chemicals, Manufacturing Equipment, Test and Measurement
Growth Openings in past year 14; percentage growth 12%
Contact John Summers, Personnel Manager
Tel 215-736-5200
Fax 215-736-5240

Moyco Industries, Inc.
2054 West Clearfield St.
Philadelphia, PA 19132

Founded 1893
Total employees 163
Annual sales $9 million
Industry Holding Companies
Growth Openings in past year 63; percentage growth 63%
Contact Marvin E. Sternberg, President
Tel 215-229-0470
Fax 215-229-3291

Norwood Industries, Inc.
57 Morehall Rd.
Frazer, PA 19355

Founded 1972
Total employees 80
Annual sales $10 million
Industry Advanced Materials
Growth Openings in past year 15; percentage growth 23%
Contact Robert Frye, General Manager
Tel 215-647-3500
Fax 215-296-2575

Ntron, Inc.
820 Springdale Dr.
Exton, PA 19341

Founded 1976
Total employees 125
Annual sales $14 million
Industry Test and Measurement
Growth Openings in past year 50; percentage growth 66%
Contact Terry Halpern, President
Tel 215-524-8800
Fax 215-524-8807

O'Brien Environmental Energy
225 South Eighth St.
Philadelphia, PA 19106

Founded 1981
Total employees 300
Annual sales $110 million

Industry Energy
Growth Openings in past
year 199; percentage
growth 197%
Contact Frank O'Brien,
III,
COB/CEO
Tel 215-627-5500
Fax 215-922-5227

Ohmicron Corp.
375 Pheasant Run
Newtown, PA 18940

Founded 1985
Total employees 48
Annual sales $1 million
Industries Biotechnology,
Chemicals,
Environmental, Medical,
Photonics
Growth Openings in past
year 20; percentage
growth 71%
Contact Ms. Marion
Kohn,
Human Resource
Manager
Tel 215-860-5115
Fax 215-860-5213

**Oppenheimer Precision
Products**
2475 Wyandotte Rd.
Willow Grove, PA 19090

Founded 1971
Total employees 190
Annual sales $19 million
Industry Transportation
Growth Openings in past
year 15; percentage
growth 8%
Contact Ms. Barbara
Carver,
Personnel Manager
Tel 215-674-9100
Fax 215-674-0423

Polybac Corp.
3894 Courtney St.
Bethlehem, PA 18017

Founded 1977
Total employees 40
Annual sales $4.2 million
Industry Environmental

Growth Openings in past
year 15; percentage
growth 60%
Contact Stephen
Salvesen,
Chief Operating Officer
Tel 215-867-7338
Fax 215-861-0991

Primavera Systems, Inc.
Two Bala Plaza
Bala Cynwyd, PA 19004

Founded 1983
Total employees 152
Annual sales $19 million
Industry Computer
Software
Growth Openings in past
year 34; percentage
growth 28%
Contact Ms. Barrie
Novak,
Director of Human
Resources
Tel 215-667-8600
Fax 215-667-7894

Quad Systems Corp.
2 Electronic Dr.
Horsham, PA 19044

Founded 1981
Total employees 185
Annual sales $12 million
Industries Factory
Automation,
Manufacturing
Equipment
Growth Openings in past
year 35; percentage
growth 23%
Contact Tony Drury,
Chief Financial Officer
Tel 215-657-6202
Fax 215-657-5013

RAM Industries
Morgantown Rd., Rte.
#1, Box 39
Reading, PA 19607

Founded 1971
Total employees 205
Annual sales $25 million
Industry Subassemblies
and Components

Growth Openings in past
year 14; percentage
growth 7%
Contact David Walton,
President
Tel 215-376-7102
Fax 215-375-8667

Resco Products, Inc.
PO Box 108
Norristown, PA 19404

Founded 1945
Total employees 570
Annual sales $66 million
Industries Advanced
Materials, Holding
Companies
Growth Openings in past
year 70; percentage
growth 14%
Contact W.T. Tredennick,
President
Tel 215-279-5010
Fax 215-279-6070

STV Group, Inc.
11 Robinson St., PO Box
459
Pottstown, PA 19464

Founded 1968
Total employees 960
Annual sales $75.8 million
Industries Environmental,
Manufacturing
Equipment
Growth Openings in past
year 88; percentage
growth 10%
Contact William Rex,
Vice President
Tel 215-326-4600
Fax 215-326-2718

**SunGard Computer
Services, Inc.**
401 North Broad St.,
Suite 600
Philadelphia, PA 19108

Founded 1972
Total employees 125
Annual sales $1 million
Industries Computer
Hardware, Computer
Software

Growth Openings in past
year 25; percentage
growth 25%
Contact Mike Muratore,
Chief Executive Officer
Tel 215-351-1300
Fax 215-351-1356

U.S. Bioscience, Inc.
100 Front St.
Conshohocken, PA 19428

Founded 1987
Total employees 120
Annual sales $3.35 million
Industries Medical,
Pharmaceuticals
Growth Openings in past
year 50; percentage
growth 71%
Contact Dr. Philip Schein,
President
Tel 215-832-0570
Fax 215-832-4500

Vertex Inc.
1041 Old Cassatt Rd.
Berwyn, PA 19312

Founded 1976
Total employees 92
Annual sales $10 million
Industry Computer
Software
Growth Openings in past
year 12; percentage
growth 15%
Contact Bill Boyer,
Controller
Tel 215-640-4200
Fax 215-640-1207

Vortec Corp.
3770 Ridge Pike
Collegeville, PA 19426

Founded 1984
Total employees 35
Annual sales $3.1 million
Industries Energy,
Environmental,
Manufacturing
Equipment
Growth Openings in past
year 13; percentage
growth 59%
Contact James Hnat,
President
Tel 215-489-2255
Fax 215-489-3185

■ **412 Area Code**

Algor, Inc.
150 Beta Dr.
Pittsburgh, PA 15238

Founded 1976
Total employees 60
Annual sales $7 million
Industry Computer
Software
Growth Openings in past
year 15; percentage
growth 33%
Contact Michael L.
Bussler,
President
Tel 412-967-2700
Fax 412-967-2781

Ansoft Corporation
Four Station Sq., Suite
660
Pittsburgh, PA 15219

Founded 1984
Total employees 50
Industry Computer
Software
Growth Openings in past
year 14; percentage
growth 38%
Contact Nick Csendes,
President/CEO
Tel 412-261-3200
Fax 412-471-9427

Bacharach, Inc.
625 Alpha Dr.
Pittsburgh, PA 15238

Founded 1909
Total employees 323
Industries Factory
Automation, Test and
Measurement
Growth Openings in past
year 16; percentage
growth 5%
Contact Mrs. Linda May,
Human Resources
Coordinator
Tel 412-963-2000
Fax 412-963-2091

**Baker Environmental
Inc.**
420 Rouser Rd.
Coraopolis, PA 15108

Founded 1981
Total employees 265
Annual sales $18 million
Industry Environmental
Growth Openings in past
year 85; percentage
growth 47%
Contact Andrew P. Pajak,
President
Tel 412-269-6000
Fax 412-269-6097

Biodecision, Inc.
5900 Penn Ave.
Pittsburgh, PA 15206

Founded 1971
Total employees 130
Annual sales $6 million
Industry Holding
Companies
Growth Openings in past
year 30; percentage
growth 30%
Contact Edward
McGolugh,
Director of Human
Resources
Tel 412-363-3300
Fax 412-362-5783

**Chester Environmental
Group, Inc.**
PO Box 15851
Pittsburgh, PA 15244

Founded 1910
Total employees 722
Annual sales $50 million
Industry Environmental
Growth Openings in past
year 48; percentage
growth 7%
Contact D. Ward,
Director of Human
Resources
Tel 412-269-5700
Fax 412-269-5749

DXI, Inc.
200 High Tower Blvd.,
Suite 202
Pittsburgh, PA 15205

Founded 1987
Total employees 37
Industry Computer
Software
Growth Openings in past
year 15; percentage
growth 68%
Contact Robert Ryan,
President
Tel 412-788-2466
Fax 412-788-4230

Extrude Hone Corp.
8075 Pennsylvania Ave.,
PO Box 527
Irwin, PA 15642

Founded 1966
Total employees 120
Annual sales $25 million
Industries Factory
Automation, Holding
Companies,
Manufacturing
Equipment
Growth Openings in past
year 14; percentage
growth 13%
Contact C. Gary Dinsel,
VP of Operations
Tel 412-863-5900
Fax 412-863-8759

International Communication Materials, Inc.
Rte. 119 South, PO Box
716
Connellsville, PA 15425

Founded 1978
Total employees 127
Annual sales $20 million
Industry Computer
Hardware
Growth Openings in past
year 25; percentage
growth 24%
Contact Ms. Paula Price,
Controller
Tel 412-628-1014
Fax 412-628-1214

Electronic Technology Systems, Inc.
12th St., Schreiber
Industrial Park
New Kensington, PA
15068

Founded 1984
Total employees 87
Annual sales $8.1 million
Industries Energy,
Subassemblies and
Components
Growth Openings in past
year 17; percentage
growth 24%
Contact Ron Walko,
President
Tel 412-335-1300
Fax 412-335-2450

GAI Consultants, Inc.
570 Beatty Rd.
Monroeville, PA 15146

Founded 1958
Total employees 430
Annual sales $16 million
Industries Energy,
Environmental
Growth Openings in past
year 29; percentage
growth 7%
Contact Anthony M.
DiGioia, Jr.,
President
Tel 412-856-6400
Fax 412-856-4970

Invotech Manufacturing Co.
17 University Dr.
Lemont Furnace, PA
15456

Founded 1988
Total employees 40
Annual sales $4 million
Industry Manufacturing
Equipment
Growth Openings in past
year 25; percentage
growth 166%
Contact Alan Kirk,
President
Tel 412-437-8020
Fax 412-437-8048

Ensys
3424 William Penn Hwy.
Pittsburgh, PA 15235

Founded 1989
Total employees 35
Annual sales $2.3 million
Industry Computer
Software
Growth Openings in past
year 15; percentage
growth 75%
Contact Joe Salvucci,
President
Tel 412-825-3333
Fax 412-825-3339

GSI
1380 Old Freeport Rd.
Pittsburgh, PA 15238

Founded 1972
Total employees 200
Annual sales $22 million
Industry Computer
Software
Growth Openings in past
year 25; percentage
growth 14%
Contact Ms. Pati
Henderson,
Personnel Director
Tel 412-963-6770
Fax 412-963-6779

Keynote Systems, Inc.
500 Standard Life Bldg.,
345 Fourth Ave.
Pittsburgh, PA 15222

Founded 1975
Total employees 875
Industry Computer
Software
Growth Openings in past
year 246; percentage
growth 39%
Contact Thomas
McCarthy,
President
Tel 412-261-0187
Fax 412-261-1073

Kipin Industries, Inc.
513 Green Garden Rd.
Aliquippa, PA 15001

Founded 1979
Total employees 60
Annual sales $2.5 million
Industry Environmental
Growth Openings in past
year 17; percentage
growth 39%
Contact Peter Kipin,
President
Tel 412-495-6200
Fax 412-495-2219

Koppel Steel Corp.
6th Ave. and Mount, PO
Box 750
Beaver Falls, PA 15010

Founded 1988
Total employees 440
Annual sales $65 million
Industries Advanced
Materials,
Subassemblies and
Components
Growth Openings in past
year 239; percentage
growth 118%
Contact James Barger,
Manager of Human
Resources
Tel 412-843-7100
Fax 412-847-4071

Michael Baker Jr., Inc.,
Transportation Division
420 Rouser Rd.
Coraopolis, PA 15108

Founded 1946
Total employees 382
Annual sales $35 million
Industries Energy,
Transportation
Growth Openings in past
year 41; percentage
growth 12%
Contact John Hayward,
Senior Vice President/
General Manager
Tel 412-269-6000

Microbac Labs, Inc.
4721 McKnight Rd.
Pittsburgh, PA 15237

Founded 1890
Total employees 200
Industries Environmental,
Holding Companies,
Medical
Growth Openings in past
year 50; percentage
growth 33%
Contact Trevor Boyce,
President
Tel 412-369-9900
Fax 412-931-0473

Mylan Laboratories, Inc.
1030 Century Bldg., 130
Seventh St.
Pittsburgh, PA 15222

Founded 1961
Total employees 690
Annual sales $131.94
million
Industries Holding
Companies,
Pharmaceuticals
Growth Openings in past
year 248; percentage
growth 56%
Contact Milan Puskar,
President/Vice
Chairman
Tel 412-232-0100
Fax 412-232-0123

Pakco Industrial
Ceramics, Inc.
55 Hillview Ave.
Latrobe, PA 15650

Founded 1980
Total employees 100
Annual sales $15 million
Industry Advanced
Materials
Growth Openings in past
year 25; percentage
growth 33%
Contact Ms. Marylou
Hamachu,
Personnel Manager
Tel 412-539-6000
Fax 412-539-6070

Peak Technical
Services, Inc.
3424 William Penn Hwy.
Pittsburgh, PA 15235

Founded 1967
Total employees 650
Industries Chemicals,
Energy, Holding
Companies
Growth Openings in past
year 49; percentage
growth 8%
Contact Joe Salvucci,
President
Tel 412-825-3900
Fax 412-825-3339

Swindell Dressler
International Company
P.O. Box 15541
Pittsburgh, PA 15244

Founded 1915
Total employees 58
Annual sales $6.3 million
Industries Factory
Automation,
Manufacturing
Equipment
Growth Openings in past
year 13; percentage
growth 28%
Contact Andrew M.
Halapin,
President
Tel 412-788-7100
Fax 412-788-7110

Tuscarora Plastics, Inc.
PO Box 448
New Brighton, PA 15066

Founded 1962
Total employees 900
Annual sales $85 million
Industry Advanced
Materials
Growth Openings in past
year 43; percentage
growth 5%
Contact John P. O'Leary,
Jr.,
President
Tel 412-843-8200

United Sciences, Inc.
5310 North Pioneer Rd.
Gibsonia, PA 15044

Founded 1978
Total employees 45
Annual sales $6.1 million
Industry Environmental
Growth Openings in past
  year 25; percentage
  growth 125%
Contact John Traina,
  President
Tel 412-443-8610
Fax 412-443-4025

U.S. Filter, Inc.
181 Thorn Hill Rd.
Warrendale, PA 15086

Founded 1950
Total employees 85
Annual sales $5.3 million
Industry Environmental
Growth Openings in past
  year 35; percentage
  growth 70%
Contact Gerald Rogers,
  Vice President and
  General Manager
Tel 412-772-0044
Fax 412-772-1360

Westinghouse Electric Corp., Distribution and Control Business Unit
875 Greentree Rd., 5
  Park Way Ctr.
Pittsburgh, PA 15220

Founded 1886
Total employees 400
Annual sales $36 million
Industries Energy,
  Photonics,
  Subassemblies and
  Components, Test and
  Measurement,
  Telecommunications
Growth Openings in past
  year 50; percentage
  growth 14%
Contact J.L. Becherer,
  Vice President/General
  Manager
Tel 412-937-6100
Fax 412-937-6357

■ 717 Area Code

Altec Industries, Inc.
250 Laird St.
Plains, PA 18705

Founded 1927
Total employees 200
Annual sales $19 million
Industry Subassemblies
  and Components
Growth Openings in past
  year 50; percentage
  growth 33%
Contact Ted Meadows,
  Human Resources
  Manager
Tel 717-822-3104

American Hydro Corp.
135 Stonewood Rd., PO
  Box 3039
York, PA 17402

Founded 1986
Total employees 99
Annual sales $15 million
Industries Energy,
  Subassemblies and
  Components
Growth Openings in past
  year 19; percentage
  growth 23%
Contact Selim Chacour,
  President
Tel 717-755-5300
Fax 717-755-5522

C-TEC Corp., Cellular Plus
1400 Spruce St.
Avoca, PA 18641

Founded 1985
Total employees 140
Industry
  Telecommunications
Growth Openings in past
  year 37; percentage
  growth 35%
Contact Marc Elgaway,
  Executive VP of Mobile
  Services
Tel 717-654-7587
Fax 717-883-8888

Flight Systems, Inc.
Hempt Rd., PO Box 25
Mechanicsburg, PA 17055

Founded 1968
Total employees 100
Annual sales $8 million
Industries Subassemblies
  and Components, Test
  and Measurement
Growth Openings in past
  year 20; percentage
  growth 25%
Contact Robert Shaffner,
  President
Tel 717-697-0333
Fax 717-697-5350

InterCon Systems, Inc.
1000 Rosedale Ave.
Middletown, PA 17057

Founded 1985
Total employees 100
Annual sales $9.7 million
Industry Subassemblies
  and Components
Growth Openings in past
  year 40; percentage
  growth 66%
Contact Mrs. Marianne
  Neidich,
  Personnel Coordinator
Tel 717-540-5660
Fax 717-540-5839

ITT Corporation, ITT Engineered Valves
33 Centerville Rd., PO
  Box 6164
Lancaster, PA 17603

Founded 1950
Total employees 400
Annual sales $39 million
Industry Subassemblies
  and Components
Growth Openings in past
  year 100; percentage
  growth 33%
Contact Bob DiGironimo,
  Personnel Manager
Tel 717-291-1901
Fax 717-291-2025

Lancaster Laboratories, Inc.
2425 New Holland Pike
Lancaster, PA 17601

Founded 1961
Total employees 460
Annual sales $26 million
Industries Biotechnology,
Chemicals,
Environmental,
Pharmaceuticals
Growth Openings in past
year 50; percentage
growth 12%
Contact Dr. Earl H. Hess,
Ph.D.,
President/CEO
Tel 717-656-2301
Fax 717-656-2681

Phoenix Contact Inc.
PO Box 4100
Harrisburg, PA 17111

Founded 1981
Total employees 123
Industries Factory
Automation,
Subassemblies and
Components
Growth Openings in past
year 23; percentage
growth 23%
Contact Ms. Melissa
Tsenoff,
Human Resources
Manager
Tel 717-944-1300
Fax 717-944-1625

Skelly and Loy, Inc.
2601 North Front St.
Harrisburg, PA 17110

Founded 1969
Total employees 145
Industry Environmental
Growth Openings in past
year 35; percentage
growth 31%
Contact Ms. Sandy Loy,
VP of Marketing
Tel 717-232-0593
Fax 717-232-1799

Svedala Industries, Inc., Grinding Division
240 Arch St., PO Box 15-
312
York, PA 17405

Founded 1983
Total employees 250
Annual sales $100 million
Industries Advanced
Materials, Energy,
Factory Automation,
Manufacturing
Equipment
Growth Openings in past
year 50; percentage
growth 25%
Contact Andy Benco,
General Manager of the
Grinding Divion
Tel 717-843-8671
Fax 717-845-5154

Tampella Power Corp.
2600 Reach Rd.
Williamsport, PA 17701

Founded 1986
Total employees 400
Industries Environmental,
Subassemblies and
Components
Growth Openings in past
year 80; percentage
growth 25%
Contact Dan Smith,
Director of Human
Resources
Tel 717-326-3361
Fax 717-327-3121

Thoren Caging Systems, Inc.
PO Box 586
Hazelton, PA 18201

Founded 1978
Total employees 55
Industries Biotechnology,
Medical
Growth Openings in past
year 40; percentage
growth 266%
Contact William Thomas,
President
Tel 717-455-5041
Fax 717-454-3500

Topflight Corp.
160 East Ninth Ave., PO
Box 2847
York, PA 17405

Founded 1943
Total employees 215
Industry Computer
Hardware
Growth Openings in past
year 15; percentage
growth 7%
Contact Ms. Susan
Hayes,
Director of Human
Resources
Tel 717-843-9901
Fax 717-845-6087

■ **814 Area Code**

Accu-Weather, Inc.
619 West College Ave.
State College, PA 16801

Founded 1962
Total employees 240
Annual sales $39 million
Industries Computer
Hardware, Computer
Software, Environmental
Growth Openings in past
year 20; percentage
growth 9%
Contact Ms. Bev Grothy,
Personnel Manager
Tel 814-237-0309
Fax 814-238-1339

Autoclave Engineers, Inc.
2930 West 22nd St.
Erie, PA 16512

Founded 1945
Total employees 730
Annual sales $80.2 million
Industries Holding
Companies,
Subassemblies and
Components, Test and
Measurement
Growth Openings in past
year 55; percentage
growth 8%
Contact Ms. Cecily
Gingrich,
Personnel Supervisor
Tel 814-838-5700
Fax 814-833-0145

Pennsylvania

Brockway Pressed Metals, Inc.
921 Clark St.
Brockway, PA 15824

Founded 1953
Total employees 260
Annual sales $20 million
Industry Subassemblies and Components
Growth Openings in past year 30; percentage growth 13%
Contact Randall Newell, Personnel Manager
Tel 814-268-3455
Fax 814-265-1274

Carlisle Companies, Inc., Motion Control Industries, Inc.
Gillis Ave.
Ridgway, PA 15853

Founded 1964
Total employees 250
Annual sales $60 million
Industries Advanced Materials, Subassemblies and Components
Growth Openings in past year 50; percentage growth 25%
Contact William M. Skelley, VP of Personnel
Tel 814-773-3185
Fax 814-776-5479

Comptek Research, Inc., ISS Division
1610 Linden Ave.
Erie, PA 16505

Founded 1985
Total employees 56
Annual sales $5.4 million
Industry Subassemblies and Components
Growth Openings in past year 14; percentage growth 33%
Contact Michael Munnings, Vice President/General Manager
Tel 814-838-8660
Fax 814-833-3219

Creative Pultrusions, Inc.
Pleasantville Industrial Park, PO Box 6
Alum Bank, PA 15521

Founded 1973
Total employees 240
Industries Advanced Materials, Manufacturing Equipment
Growth Openings in past year 40; percentage growth 20%
Contact Bill Harclerode, Manufacturing Supervisor
Tel 814-839-4186
Fax 814-839-4276

Delta Computer Systems, Inc.
PO Box 1824
Altoona, PA 16603

Founded 1968
Total employees 92
Industry Computer Software
Growth Openings in past year 12; percentage growth 15%
Contact James R. Yates, President
Tel 814-944-1651
Fax 814-942-0125

Earl E. Knox Co.
1111 Bacon St.
Erie, PA 16512

Founded 1930
Total employees 100
Annual sales $8 million
Industry Holding Companies
Growth Openings in past year 50; percentage growth 100%
Contact Robert Knox, President
Tel 814-459-2754
Fax 814-455-2770

Erie Ceramic Arts Co.
3120 West 22nd St., PO Box 8324
Erie, PA 16505

Founded 1946
Total employees 187
Annual sales $5 million
Industries Advanced Materials, Computer Hardware
Growth Openings in past year 37; percentage growth 24%
Contact Ms. Nancy Kospick, Director of Personnel
Tel 814-833-7758
Fax 814-838-7584

Knox Western
1111 Bacon St.
Erie, PA 16512

Founded 1979
Total employees 70
Annual sales $10 million
Industry Subassemblies and Components
Growth Openings in past year 13; percentage growth 22%
Contact Robert Knox, President
Tel 814-459-2754
Fax 814-455-8493

KOA Speer Electronics, Inc.
Bolivar Dr., PO Box 547
Bradford, PA 16701

Founded 1939
Total employees 120
Industry Subassemblies and Components
Growth Openings in past year 46; percentage growth 62%
Contact K. Kakinoki, President
Tel 814-362-5536
Fax 814-362-8883

Molded Fiber Glass Companies, Union City Division
55 Fourth Ave.
Union City, PA 16438

Founded 1948
Total employees 200
Annual sales $12 million
Industries Advanced Materials, Environmental, Manufacturing Equipment, Transportation
Growth Openings in past year 12; percentage growth 6%
Contact Gerald Bender, President
Tel 814-438-3841
Fax 814-438-2284

PHB Polymeric
8152 West Ridge Rd.
Fairview, PA 16415

Founded 1984
Total employees 75
Annual sales $4 million
Industry Manufacturing Equipment
Growth Openings in past year 25; percentage growth 50%
Contact William Hilbert, Sr., President/CEO
Tel 814-474-2683
Fax 814-474-5868

Spectrum Control, Inc.
6000 West Ridge Rd.
Erie, PA 16506

Founded 1968
Total employees 610
Annual sales $34.9 million
Industries Subassemblies and Components, Telecommunications
Growth Openings in past year 209; percentage growth 52%
Contact George Van Horn, Director of Human Resources
Tel 814-835-4000
Fax 814-835-9000

Rhode Island

■ **401 Area Code**

American Power Conversion Corp.
132 Fairgrounds Rd., PO Box 278
West Kingston, RI 02892

Founded 1981
Total employees 560
Annual sales $93 million
Industries Computer Software, Energy, Subassemblies and Components
Growth Openings in past year 133; percentage growth 31%
Contact Rodger B. Dowdell, Jr., President/CEO
Tel 401-789-5735
Fax 401-789-3710

CytoTherapeutics, Inc.
2 Richmond St.
Providence, RI 02903

Founded 1989
Total employees 70
Industry Biotechnology
Growth Openings in past year 15; percentage growth 27%
Contact Seth A. Rudnick, MD, Chief Executive Officer
Tel 401-272-3310

Early Cloud and Co.
Aquidneck Industrial Park
Newport, RI 02840

Founded 1981
Total employees 165
Annual sales $18 million
Industries Computer Hardware, Computer Software
Growth Openings in past year 40; percentage growth 32%
Contact Bob Pardini, Director of Human Resources
Tel 401-849-0500
Fax 401-849-1190

Electronic Book Technologies, Inc.
One Richmond Sq.
Providence, RI 02906

Founded 1989
Total employees 33
Annual sales $2.5 million
Industry Computer Software
Growth Openings in past year 20; percentage growth 153%
Contact Lou Reynolds, President
Tel 401-421-9550
Fax 401-421-9551

Environmental Science Services, Inc.
532 Atwells Ave.
Providence, RI 02908

Founded 1981
Total employees 50
Annual sales $5.3 million
Industry Environmental
Growth Openings in past year 20; percentage growth 66%
Contact Ken Dreyer, President
Tel 401-421-0398
Fax 401-421-5731

Hanna Instruments
584 Park East Dr.
Woonsocket, RI 02895

Founded 1978
Total employees 70
Annual sales $7.9 million
Industries Environmental, Test and Measurement
Growth Openings in past year 35; percentage growth 100%
Contact Rich Bouvier, International Marketing Manager
Tel 401-765-7500
Fax 401-765-7575

Laser Fare, Inc.
1 Industrial Dr. South, Lan-Rex Industrial Park
Smithfield, RI 02917

Founded 1980
Total employees 45

Industries Manufacturing Equipment, Photonics
Growth Openings in past year 12; percentage growth 36%
Contact Terry Feeley, President
Tel 401-231-4400
Fax 401-231-4674

NEPTCO, Inc.
PO Box 2323
Pawtucket, RI 02861

Founded 1953
Total employees 420
Industry Advanced Materials
Growth Openings in past year 20; percentage growth 5%
Contact Guy Marini, President
Tel 401-722-5500
Fax 401-722-6378

Network Solutions, Inc.
475 Kilvert St.
Warwick, RI 02886

Founded 1976
Total employees 81
Annual sales $4 million
Industries Computer Hardware, Computer Software
Growth Openings in past year 26; percentage growth 47%
Contact Richard Hawkins, President/CEO
Tel 401-732-9000
Fax 401-732-9009

Science Applications International Corp., Ocean, Science, and Technology Division
221 Third St.
Newport, RI 02840

Founded 1979
Total employees 120
Annual sales $22 million
Industries Defense, Environmental, Transportation

Growth Openings in past year 70; percentage growth 140%
Contact Dave Pearson, Division Manager
Tel 401-847-4210
Fax 401-849-1585

Taco, Inc.
1160 Cranston St.
Cranston, RI 02920

Founded 1936
Total employees 400
Annual sales $46 million
Industries Energy, Subassemblies and Components
Growth Openings in past year 100; percentage growth 33%
Contact John H. White, President
Tel 401-942-8000
Fax 401-942-2360

Thielsch Engineering Associates, Inc.
195 Frances Ave.
Cranston, RI 02910

Founded 1984
Total employees 100
Industries Advanced Materials, Environmental
Growth Openings in past year 25; percentage growth 33%
Contact Helmut Thielsch, President
Tel 401-467-6454
Fax 401-467-2398

Toray Plastics America, Inc.
50 Belver Ave.
North Kingstown, RI 02852

Founded 1972
Total employees 350
Annual sales $52 million
Industry Advanced Materials

Growth Openings in past year 100; percentage growth 40%
Contact Harvey Greenhalgh, Director of Human Resources
Tel 401-294-4511
Fax 401-294-2154

South Carolina

■ **803 Area Code**

Computer Dynamic, Inc.
107 South Main St.
Greer, SC 29650

Founded 1981
Total employees 100
Industry Computer Hardware
Growth Openings in past year 40; percentage growth 66%
Contact Kurt Priester, President
Tel 803-877-8700
Fax 803-879-2030

Computer Dynamics, Inc.
105 South Main St.
Greer, SC 29650

Founded 1981
Total employees 80
Annual sales $6 million
Industry Computer Hardware
Growth Openings in past year 35; percentage growth 77%
Contact Kurt Priester, President
Tel 803-877-7471
Fax 803-879-2030

JM Smith Corp., QS/1 Data Systems Division
PO Box 6052
Spartanburg, SC 29304

Founded 1959
Total employees 400
Industry Computer Software

Growth Openings in past year 100; percentage growth 33%
Contact James Wilson, Human Resources Manager
Tel 803-578-9455
Fax 803-578-6966

Zeus Industrial Products, Inc.
501 Blvd. St., PO Box 2167
Orangeburg, SC 29116

Founded 1966
Total employees 330
Annual sales $32 million
Industries Manufacturing Equipment, Medical, Subassemblies and Components
Growth Openings in past year 30; percentage growth 10%
Contact Bob Cornell, Personnel Manager
Tel 803-531-2174
Fax 803-533-5694

South Dakota

■ **605 Area Code**

Daktronics, Inc.
331 32nd Ave., PO Box 128
Brookings, SD 57006

Founded 1968
Total employees 426
Annual sales $46 million
Industries Computer Hardware, Holding Companies, Photonics, Test and Measurement
Growth Openings in past year 13; percentage growth 3%
Contact Ms. Carla Gatzke, Personnel Manager
Tel 605-697-4000
Fax 605-697-5171

Tennessee

■ **615 Area Code**

Alco Chemical
909 Mueller Dr.
Chattanooga, TN 37406

Founded 1978
Total employees 140
Annual sales $30 million
Industry Chemicals
Growth Openings in past year 15; percentage growth 12%
Contact Ms. Barbara Atchley, Human Resources Manager
Tel 615-629-1405
Fax 615-698-8723

Avecor, Inc.
PO Box 278
Vonore, TN 37885

Founded 1885
Total employees 200
Annual sales $43 million
Industry Chemicals
Growth Openings in past year 50; percentage growth 33%
Contact Len Klarich, President
Tel 615-884-6625
Fax 615-884-6176

Computational Systems, Inc.
835 Innovation Dr.
Knoxville, TN 37932

Founded 1984
Total employees 210
Annual sales $17 million
Industries Computer Software, Test and Measurement
Growth Openings in past year 20; percentage growth 10%
Contact Ron Moore, President
Tel 615-675-2110
Fax 615-675-3100

Control Technology
PO Box 59003
Knoxville, TN 37950

Founded 1980
Total employees 80
Industry Factory Automation
Growth Openings in past year 20; percentage growth 33%
Contact Mark Medley, President
Tel 615-584-0440
Fax 615-584-5720

CTI, Inc.
810 Innovation Dr., PO Box 22999
Knoxville, TN 37933

Founded 1984
Total employees 200
Annual sales $14 million
Industries Holding Companies, Medical
Growth Openings in past year 25; percentage growth 14%
Contact Ms. Kathy Coleman, Human Resources Manager
Tel 615-966-7539
Fax 615-966-8955

Cubic Corp., Precision Systems Division
1308 South Washington St., PO Box 821
Tullahoma, TN 37388

Founded 1912
Total employees 169
Industries Photonics, Transportation
Growth Openings in past year 49; percentage growth 40%
Contact Ms. Carolyn Mitchell, Human Resources Administrator
Tel 615-455-8524
Fax 615-455-0699

Dalcon International, Inc.
1321 Murfreesboro Rd.,
4th Floor
Nashville, TN 37217

Founded 1978
Total employees 85
Annual sales $6 million
Industry Computer
Software
Growth Openings in past
year 25; percentage
growth 41%
Contact Ms. Ann
Koresdoski,
Accounting Manager
Tel 615-366-4300
Fax 615-361-3800

Franklin Industrial Minerals
612 10th Ave. North
Nashville, TN 37203

Founded 1911
Total employees 400
Industry Advanced
Materials
Growth Openings in past
year 50; percentage
growth 14%
Contact Nelson
Severinghaus,
President
Tel 615-259-4222
Fax 615-726-2693

Oak Ridge Research Institute
113 Union Valley Rd.
Oak Ridge, TN 37830

Founded 1981
Total employees 130
Industries Chemicals,
Environmental, Medical
Growth Openings in past
year 60; percentage
growth 85%
Contact Ms. Nancy Peck,
Director of Human
Resources
Tel 615-482-9604
Fax 615-481-5020

EcoTek, Inc.
1219 Banner Hill Rd.
Erwin, TN 37650

Founded 1987
Total employees 150
Annual sales $5 million
Industries Environmental,
Holding Companies
Growth Openings in past
year 42; percentage
growth 38%
Contact Colman B.
Woodhall,
CEO/President
Tel 615-743-6186
Fax 615-743-7837

Micro Craft, Inc.
PO Box 370
Tullahoma, TN 37388

Founded 1958
Total employees 400
Annual sales $47 million
Industries Factory
Automation,
Manufacturing
Equipment
Growth Openings in past
year 40; percentage
growth 11%
Contact Dan J. Marcum,
President
Tel 615-455-2664
Fax 615-455-7060

OSCO, Inc.
618 Grassmere Park,
Suite 7
Nashville, TN 37211

Founded 1966
Total employees 189
Annual sales $20 million
Industry Environmental
Growth Openings in past
year 39; percentage
growth 26%
Contact L.E. Wilson,
President
Tel 615-832-0081
Fax 615-832-0712

First Data Systems, Inc.
1187 Vultee Blvd.
Nashville, TN 37217

Founded 1974
Total employees 68
Annual sales $6 million
Industry Computer
Software
Growth Openings in past
year 16; percentage
growth 30%
Contact Patrick Vaden,
President/CEO
Tel 615-361-8404
Fax 615-361-0798

National Recovery Technologies, Inc.
566 Mainstream Dr.
Nashville, TN 37228

Founded 1982
Total employees 48
Annual sales $12 million
Industry Environmental
Growth Openings in past
year 14; percentage
growth 41%
Contact Charles Crow,
President
Tel 615-734-6400
Fax 615-734-6410

Porcelain Industries, Inc.
20 Ceco Rd.
Dickson, TN 37055

Founded 1959
Total employees 183
Annual sales $19 million
Industry Manufacturing
Equipment
Growth Openings in past
year 30; percentage
growth 19%
Contact John Walsh,
President
Tel 615-446-7400
Fax 615-446-5450

Science Applications International Corp., Environmental Compliance Group
301 Laboratory Rd., PO Box 2501
Oak Ridge, TN 37831

Founded 1972
Total employees 350
Annual sales $37 million
Industry Environmental
Growth Openings in past year 38; percentage growth 12%
Contact Barry Goss, Group Senior Vice President
Tel 615-482-9031
Fax 615-481-8593

Steward, Inc.
PO Box 510
Chattanooga, TN 37401

Founded 1876
Total employees 300
Annual sales $20 million
Industry Advanced Materials
Growth Openings in past year 50; percentage growth 20%
Contact Lee Atchley, Manager of Personnel
Tel 615-867-4100
Fax 615-867-4102

Synercom
100 Westwood Pl., Suite 400
Brentwood, TN 37027

Founded 1982
Total employees 40
Annual sales $5 million
Industry Computer Software
Growth Openings in past year 12; percentage growth 42%
Contact George Owens, President
Tel 615-377-6990
Fax 615-371-0135

■ 901 Area Code

AZO, Inc.
4445 Malone Rd.
Memphis, TN 38118

Founded 1978
Total employees 70
Annual sales $8.8 million
Industry Factory Automation
Growth Openings in past year 15; percentage growth 27%
Contact Robert Moore, President
Tel 901-794-9480
Fax 901-794-9934

Cedar Chemical Corp.
5100 Poplar Ave., Suite 2414
Memphis, TN 38137

Founded 1985
Total employees 600
Annual sales $100 million
Industry Chemicals
Growth Openings in past year 100; percentage growth 20%
Contact Zwi Waldman, President
Tel 901-685-5348
Fax 901-684-5398

Jefferson Pilot Data Services, Inc.
75 Crossover Ln., Suite 141
Memphis, TN 38117

Founded 1969
Total employees 221
Industries Computer Hardware, Computer Software
Growth Openings in past year 21; percentage growth 10%
Contact Ms. Jodie Broussard, Personnel Director
Tel 901-762-8000
Fax 901-762-8038

WIS-CON Total Power Corp.
3409 Democrat Rd.
Memphis, TN 38118

Founded 1983
Total employees 300
Annual sales $29 million
Industry Subassemblies and Components
Growth Openings in past year 100; percentage growth 50%
Contact Ms. Betty Smith, Plant Administrator/ Human Resources Mana
Tel 901-665-7711
Fax 901-665-7710

Texas

■ 210 Area Code

DATA RACE, Inc.
11550 Interstate 10 West
San Antonio, TX 78230

Founded 1983
Total employees 214
Annual sales $21.7 million
Industries Computer Hardware, Telecommunications
Growth Openings in past year 64; percentage growth 42%
Contact Herb Hensley, President
Tel 210-558-1900
Fax 210-558-1929

Docucon, Inc.
9100 IH 10 West
San Antonio, TX 78230

Founded 1988
Total employees 120
Annual sales $19 million
Industry Computer Hardware
Growth Openings in past year 50; percentage growth 71%
Contact Ms. Alice Hopkins, Personnel Manager
Tel 210-593-0183
Fax 210-593-0139

Meyer Machine Co.
3528 Fredricksburg Rd.
San Antonio, TX 78201

Founded 1935
Total employees 120
Annual sales $10 million
Industry Factory
Automation
Growth Openings in past
year 20; percentage
growth 20%
Contact Eugene Teeter,
President
Tel 210-736-1811
Fax 210-736-9452

Operational Technologies Corp.
4100 North West Loop
410, Suite 230
San Antonio, TX 78229

Founded 1986
Total employees 145
Annual sales $8 million
Industries Defense,
Environmental, Holding
Companies,
Subassemblies and
Components
Growth Openings in past
year 55; percentage
growth 61%
Contact Max Navarro,
President
Tel 210-731-0000
Fax 210-731-0008

Remote Operating Systems, Inc.
121 Interpark Blvd., Suite
601
San Antonio, TX 78216

Founded 1984
Total employees 34
Industries Computer
Software,
Environmental, Test and
Measurement
Growth Openings in past
year 14; percentage
growth 70%
Contact William W. Dunn,
Chief Executive Officer
Tel 210-496-0661
Fax 210-496-0135

■ 214 Area Code

Altsys Corp.
269 West Renner Rd.
Richardson, TX 75080

Founded 1984
Total employees 70
Annual sales $8 million
Industry Computer
Software
Growth Openings in past
year 35; percentage
growth 100%
Contact Earl Allen,
Technical Support
Manager
Tel 214-680-2060
Fax 214-680-0537

American Medical Electronics, Inc.
250 East Arapaho Rd.
Richardson, TX 75081

Founded 1982
Total employees 230
Annual sales $27.15
million
Industry Medical
Growth Openings in past
year 90; percentage
growth 64%
Contact Ms. LaVonne
Chimbel,
VP of Human Resources
Tel 214-918-8400
Fax 214-918-8490

AMX Corp.
11995 Forestgate Dr.
Dallas, TX 75243

Founded 1982
Total employees 120
Annual sales $16 million
Industry
Telecommunications
Growth Openings in past
year 20; percentage
growth 20%
Contact Scott Miller,
President
Tel 214-644-3048
Fax 214-907-2053

Argo Data Resource Corp.
12770 Coit Rd., Suite 600
Dallas, TX 75248

Founded 1980
Total employees 50
Annual sales $5.8 million
Industry Computer
Software
Growth Openings in past
year 20; percentage
growth 66%
Contact Max Martin,
President
Tel 214-386-4949
Fax 214-991-1214

Barracuda Technologies, Inc.
315 Seahawk Dr.
De Soto, TX 75115

Founded 1981
Total employees 100
Industries Advanced
Materials, Transportation
Growth Openings in past
year 50; percentage
growth 100%
Contact Delton Kelley,
Human Resources
Manager
Tel 214-224-8441
Fax 214-228-2667

Benchmarq Microelectronics, Inc.
2611 Westgrove, Suite
101
Carrollton, TX 75006

Founded 1989
Total employees 85
Industry Subassemblies
and Components
Growth Openings in past
year 20; percentage
growth 30%
Contact Derrell Coker,
President
Tel 214-407-0011
Fax 214-407-9845

Bird Life Design, Inc.
2735 Beltline Rd.
Carrollton, TX 75006

Founded 1976
Total employees 110
Annual sales $15 million
Industry Medical
Growth Openings in past
  year 43; percentage
  growth 64%
Contact Jeff Roski,
  President
  Tel 214-418-8800
  Fax 214-416-6929

CNet, Inc.
4975 Preston Park Blvd.,
  8th Floor
Plano, TX 75093

Founded 1986
Total employees 40
Annual sales $5 million
Industry Computer
  Software
Growth Openings in past
  year 12; percentage
  growth 42%
Contact David M.
  Zumwalt,
  President
  Tel 214-690-3333
  Fax 214-867-6800

Control Products Corp.
PO Box 531109
Grand Prairie, TX 75053

Founded 1963
Total employees 106
Annual sales $10 million
Industries Defense,
  Holding Companies,
  Transportation
Growth Openings in past
  year 20; percentage
  growth 23%
Contact H. Wayne
  Hanks,
  Chief Executive Officer
  Tel 214-264-0368
  Fax 214-262-1653

C-Power Companies, Inc.
2007-B Industrial Ln.
Rockwall, TX 75087

Founded 1986
Total employees 400
Industries Energy,
  Manufacturing
  Equipment, Test and
  Measurement
Growth Openings in past
  year 150; percentage
  growth 60%
Contact Ms. Dee
  Goleman,
  Director of Human
  Resources
  Tel 214-771-4303
  Fax 214-771-0462

Cuplex, Inc.
1500 East Hwy. 66
Garland, TX 75040

Founded 1973
Total employees 435
Annual sales $34 million
Industry Subassemblies
  and Components
Growth Openings in past
  year 85; percentage
  growth 24%
Contact Ron Ryno,
  President
  Tel 214-276-0333
  Fax 214-276-3401

Cyten Circuit Design, Inc.
11601 North Plano Rd.,
  Suite 118
Dallas, TX 75243

Founded 1985
Total employees 30
Industry Subassemblies
  and Components
Growth Openings in past
  year 15; percentage
  growth 100%
Contact E. Winkelmann,
  President
  Tel 214-341-1069
  Fax 214-341-1173

Datotek, Inc.
3801 Realty Rd.
Dallas, TX 75244

Founded 1969
Total employees 130
Annual sales $25 million
Industries Computer
  Hardware, Computer
  Software,
  Telecommunications
Growth Openings in past
  year 30; percentage
  growth 30%
Contact Ms. E. Calvert,
  Personnel Manager
  Tel 214-241-4491
  Fax 214-241-6735

Dental Plan, Inc.
3633B Broadway
Garland, TX 75043

Founded 1980
Total employees 30
Annual sales $4.5 million
Industry Computer
  Software
Growth Openings in past
  year 18; percentage
  growth 150%
Contact Fred Gharis,
  President
  Tel 214-271-0457
  Fax 214-840-2926

GEAC Computers, Inc.
14140 Midway Rd., Suite
  105
Dallas, TX 75244

Founded 1977
Total employees 250
Industry Computer
  Software
Growth Openings in past
  year 90; percentage
  growth 56%
Contact Michael
  Greenough,
  VP of U.S. Operations
  Tel 214-490-3482
  Fax 214-960-9728

Hogan Systems, Inc.
5080 Spectrum Dr., Suite 400E
Dallas, TX 75248

Founded 1977
Total employees 400
Annual sales $56.11 million
Industry Computer Software
Growth Openings in past year 40; percentage growth 11%
Contact W. Daniel Johnson, Senior VP of Human Resources
Tel 214-386-0020
Fax 214-386-0315

Ideal Learning, Inc.
8505 Freeport Pkwy., Suite 360
Irving, TX 75063

Founded 1982
Total employees 42
Annual sales $4 million
Industry Computer Software
Growth Openings in past year 14; percentage growth 50%
Contact Gary D. Volding, President/COB
Tel 214-929-4201
Fax 214-929-4548

Interphase Corporation
13800 Senlac
Dallas, TX 75234

Founded 1974
Total employees 275
Annual sales $40 million
Industries Computer Software, Telecommunications
Growth Openings in past year 30; percentage growth 12%
Contact Ms. Paula Jandura, VP of Administration
Tel 214-919-9000
Fax 214-919-9200

InterVoice, Inc.
17811 Waterview Pkwy.
Dallas, TX 75252

Founded 1983
Total employees 300
Annual sales $44.5 million
Industries Computer Hardware, Computer Software, Telecommunications
Growth Openings in past year 50; percentage growth 20%
Contact Daniel D. Hammond, COB/CEO
Tel 214-669-3988
Fax 214-907-1079

Lacerte Microcomputer Corporation
4835 LBJ Frwy., 10th Fl.
Dallas, TX 75244

Founded 1978
Total employees 150
Industry Computer Software
Growth Openings in past year 25; percentage growth 20%
Contact Larry Lacerte, President
Tel 214-490-8500
Fax 214-770-8689

Lear Data Info-Services, Inc.
5910 North Central
Dallas, TX 75206

Founded 1965
Total employees 75
Annual sales $6.5 million
Industry Computer Software
Growth Openings in past year 15; percentage growth 25%
Contact Bruce Smith, Chief Executive Officer
Tel 214-360-9008
Fax 214-363-1384

Luminator Aircraft Products
1200 East Plano Pkwy.
Plano, TX 75074

Founded 1969
Total employees 90
Annual sales $10 million
Industry Transportation
Growth Openings in past year 30; percentage growth 50%
Contact John Hartzler, President
Tel 214-424-6511
Fax 214-423-8515

Mactronix, Inc.
13434 Floyd Circle
Dallas, TX 75243

Founded 1982
Total employees 120
Industry Factory Automation
Growth Openings in past year 40; percentage growth 50%
Contact John Lau, President
Tel 214-690-0028
Fax 214-690-0074

Magflux Corp.
1101 East Walnut
Garland, TX 75040

Founded 1976
Total employees 75
Industry Subassemblies and Components
Growth Openings in past year 25; percentage growth 50%
Contact C. Glynn Davis, President
Tel 214-272-8572
Fax 214-272-6897

Micrografx, Inc.
1303 Arapahoe Rd.
Richardson, TX 75081

Founded 1982
Total employees 320
Annual sales $30 million
Industry Computer Software

Growth Openings in past
year 100; percentage
growth 45%
Contact Paul Grayson,
COB/CEO
Tel 214-234-1769
Fax 214-234-2410

Growth Openings in past
year 37; percentage
growth 27%
Contact Gary Hegna,
President/CEO/COB
Tel 214-484-5200
Fax 214-888-0688

Growth Openings in past
year 55; percentage
growth 45%
Contact Gary A.
Andersen,
President/CEO
Tel 214-233-2903
Fax 214-387-8148

Midwest Magnetics, Inc.
600 South Sherman St.,
Suite 102
Richardson, TX 75081

Founded 1981
Total employees 50
Annual sales $6.9 million
Industry
Telecommunications
Growth Openings in past
year 18; percentage
growth 56%
Contact Paul Voss,
President
Tel 214-235-9551
Fax 214-235-9586

Precision Technology, Inc.
10860 Switzer Ave., Suite
108
Dallas, TX 75238

Founded 1978
Total employees 25
Industry Subassemblies
and Components
Growth Openings in past
year 13; percentage
growth 108%
Contact Carl McCleskey,
President/CEO
Tel 214-343-0131
Fax 214-343-8216

Senlsys, Inc.
1600 West Plano Pkwy.
Plano, TX 75075

Founded 1983
Total employees 100
Industry Photonics
Growth Openings in past
year 50; percentage
growth 100%
Contact Wes Pitts,
President
Tel 214-422-1844
Fax 214-423-4661

Software of the Future, Inc.
PO Box 531650
Grand Prairie, TX 75053

Founded 1979
Total employees 40
Annual sales $7 million
Industry Computer
Software
Growth Openings in past
year 15; percentage
growth 60%
Contact David Ricks,
Chief Executive Officer
Tel 214-264-2626
Fax 214-262-7338

NetWorth, Inc.
8404 Esters Blvd.
Irving, TX 75063

Founded 1984
Total employees 141
Annual sales $17 million
Industries Computer
Software,
Telecommunications
Growth Openings in past
year 81; percentage
growth 135%
Contact John McHale,
President/COB/CEO
Tel 214-929-1700
Fax 214-929-1720

Quest Medical, Inc.
4103 Billy Mitchell Dr.
Dallas, TX 75244

Founded 1978
Total employees 200
Annual sales $13 million
Industries Holding
Companies, Medical
Growth Openings in past
year 30; percentage
growth 17%
Contact Ms. Corinne
Olszowka,
Manager of Human
Resources
Tel 214-387-2740
Fax 214-387-0501

Sterling Software, Inc., Directions Division
15301 Dallas Pkwy., Suite
400
Dallas, TX 75248

Founded 1976
Total employees 70
Industry Computer
Software
Growth Openings in past
year 15; percentage
growth 27%
Contact Mark Alexander,
Senior Vice President/
Controller
Tel 214-788-2580
Fax 214-788-1049

OpenConnect Systems, Inc.
2711 LBJ Frwy.
Dallas, TX 75234

Founded 1982
Total employees 172
Annual sales $16 million
Industries Computer
Software,
Telecommunications

RF Monolithics, Inc.
4441 Sigma Rd.
Dallas, TX 75244

Founded 1979
Total employees 175
Annual sales $15 million
Industries Subassemblies
and Components,
Telecommunications

Tigon Voice Messaging Network
17080 Dallas Pkwy.
Dallas, TX 75248

Founded 1983
Total employees 220
Industry
Telecommunications
Contact Bruce Simpson,
President/CEO
Tel 214-733-2700
Fax 214-733-2737

United States Data Corporation
2435 North Central Expwy.
Richardson, TX 75080

Founded 1974
Total employees 230
Annual sales $30 million
Industry Computer Software
Growth Openings in past year 40; percentage growth 21%
Contact John Pellegrini,
Director of Human Resources
Tel 214-680-9700
Fax 214-669-8318

VLSI Packaging Corp.
1161 Executive Dr. West
Richardson, TX 75081

Founded 1984
Total employees 100
Industries Defense, Subassemblies and Components, Test and Measurement
Growth Openings in past year 20; percentage growth 25%
Contact Rolf Haberecht,
Chief Executive Officer
Tel 214-437-5506
Fax 214-644-1286

Vortech Data, Inc.
2929 North Central Express, Suite 101
Richardson, TX 75080

Founded 1985
Total employees 100
Annual sales $11 million

Industries Computer Software, Medical
Growth Openings in past year 50; percentage growth 100%
Contact Allen Griebenow,
CEO/President
Tel 214-994-1200
Fax 214-994-1310

Whitehall Corp.
2659 Nova Dr., PO Box 29709
Dallas, TX 75229

Founded 1963
Total employees 522
Annual sales $20 million
Industry Holding Companies
Growth Openings in past year 130; percentage growth 33%
Contact George F. Baker,
COB/CEO/President
Tel 214-247-8747
Fax 214-247-2024

York Chemical Corp.
3309 East Carpenter Frwy.
Irving, TX 75062

Founded 1979
Total employees 70
Annual sales $3 million
Industry Chemicals
Growth Openings in past year 20; percentage growth 40%
Contact Al Castagnoli,
President
Tel 214-438-6744
Fax 214-721-1460

■ 409 Area Code

Clif Mock Co., Inc.
Johnson Rd., FM 2854,
PO Box 1159
Conroe, TX 77305

Founded 1978
Total employees 100
Industries Factory Automation, Test and Measurement

Growth Openings in past year 20; percentage growth 25%
Contact James H. Miller,
President
Tel 409-588-1171
Fax 409-588-1783

OI Corporation
PO Box 2980
College Station, TX 77841

Founded 1969
Total employees 140
Annual sales $18 million
Industry Environmental
Growth Openings in past year 26; percentage growth 22%
Contact William W. Botts,
COB/President/CEO
Tel 409-690-1711
Fax 409-690-0440

■ 512 Area Code

Acoustic Systems, Inc.
415 East Saint Elmo Rd.
Austin, TX 78745

Founded 1971
Total employees 75
Annual sales $5 million
Industries Environmental, Test and Measurement, Telecommunications
Growth Openings in past year 25; percentage growth 50%
Contact Ms. Cindy Nutt,
Personnel Manager
Tel 512-444-1961
Fax 512-444-2282

American Microelectronics Inc.
1611 Headway Cir., Bldg. 3
Austin, TX 78754

Founded 1987
Total employees 265
Annual sales $10 million
Industries Manufacturing Equipment, Subassemblies and Components

Growth Openings in past year 189; percentage growth 248%
Contact James Draper, President/CEO
Tel 512-339-0001
Fax 512-339-0002

AMP Packaging Systems, Inc.
700-E Jeffrey Way
Round Rock, TX 78664

Founded 1986
Total employees 165
Industry Computer Hardware
Growth Openings in past year 30; percentage growth 22%
Contact Don Pope, Controller
Tel 512-244-5200
Fax 512-244-5112

Columbia Scientific Industries Corp.
11950 Jollyville Rd., PO Box 203190
Austin, TX 78720

Founded 1968
Total employees 75
Annual sales $7 million
Industries Environmental, Test and Measurement, Telecommunications
Growth Openings in past year 25; percentage growth 50%
Contact Gerald Phillips, President
Tel 512-258-5191
Fax 512-258-5004

Consolidated Technologies, Inc.
2170 Woodward St., Suite 100
Austin, TX 78744

Founded 1970
Total employees 57
Annual sales $2.75 million
Industries Chemicals, Pharmaceuticals

Growth Openings in past year 16; percentage growth 39%
Contact William Cone, President
Tel 512-445-5100
Fax 512-445-5515

Crystal Semiconductor Corp.
PO Box 17847
Austin, TX 78760

Founded 1984
Total employees 240
Annual sales $23 million
Industry Subassemblies and Components
Growth Openings in past year 79; percentage growth 49%
Contact John McGovern, VP of Finance
Tel 512-445-7222
Fax 512-445-7581

Intera Technologies, Inc.
6850 Austin Center Blvd., Suite 300
Austin, TX 78759

Founded 1974
Total employees 111
Annual sales $11 million
Industry Environmental
Growth Openings in past year 61; percentage growth 122%
Contact S.B. Pahwa, President
Tel 512-346-2000
Fax 512-346-9436

International Biomedical, Inc.
8508 Cross Park Dr.
Austin, TX 78754

Founded 1957
Total employees 80
Industry Holding Companies
Growth Openings in past year 20; percentage growth 33%
Contact A.J. Segars, President
Tel 512-873-0033
Fax 512-873-9090

Netserv, Inc.
PO Box 9390
Austin, TX 78766

Founded 1983
Total employees 32
Annual sales $3.5 million
Industries Computer Hardware, Telecommunications
Growth Openings in past year 12; percentage growth 60%
Contact D. Dayal, President
Tel 512-453-8844
Fax 512-453-9650

Origin Systems, Inc.
110 Wild Basin Rd., Suite 230
Austin, TX 78746

Founded 1983
Total employees 165
Annual sales $19 million
Industry Computer Software
Growth Openings in past year 65; percentage growth 65%
Contact Robert Garriott, President
Tel 512-328-5490
Fax 512-328-3825

Penoco, Inc.
PO Box 2567
Corpus Christi, TX 78403

Founded 1986
Total employees 30
Industry Chemicals
Growth Openings in past year 16; percentage growth 114%
Contact R.L. Horne, President
Tel 512-881-9205
Fax 512-881-8570

Southwest Network Services, Inc.
9130 Jollyville Rd., Suite 200
Austin, TX 78759

Founded 1987
Total employees 100
Annual sales $9.2 million

Industry
Telecommunications
Growth Openings in past
year 30; percentage
growth 42%
Contact Otis Brinkley,
CEO/President
Tel 512-795-3000
Fax 512-795-3008

Growth Openings in past
year 100; percentage
growth 50%
Contact Walter T. Thirion,
Chief Executive Officer
Tel 512-836-1935
Fax 512-836-2840

Growth Openings in past
year 99; percentage
growth 28%
Contact Darrell Shook,
Human Resources
Manager
Tel 512-834-2266
Fax 512-834-9250

Sterling Information Group, Inc.
PO Box 61148
Austin, TX 78716

Founded 1985
Total employees 42
Industry Computer
Software
Growth Openings in past
year 17; percentage
growth 68%
Contact Chip Wolfe,
President
Tel 512-327-0090
Fax 512-327-0197

Tivoli Systems, Inc.
6034 West Courtyard Dr.,
Suite 210
Austin, TX 78730

Founded 1989
Total employees 90
Annual sales $10 million
Industry Computer
Software
Growth Openings in past
year 48; percentage
growth 114%
Contact Frank Moss,
President/CEO
Tel 512-794-9070
Fax 512-794-0623

■ **713 Area Code**

Aprogenex, Inc.
8000 El Rio
Houston, TX 77054

Founded 1989
Total employees 32
Industries Biotechnology,
Medical
Growth Openings in past
year 16; percentage
growth 100%
Contact Ms. Laura Farr,
Human Resources
Manager
Tel 713-748-5114
Fax 713-748-6012

Tessco Group, Inc.
300 Industrial Ave.
Georgetown, TX 78626

Total employees 270
Annual sales $19 million
Industries Manufacturing
Equipment,
Subassemblies and
Components, Test and
Measurement
Growth Openings in past
year 29; percentage
growth 12%
Contact Rand Mueller,
President/CEO
Tel 512-863-8742
Fax 512-863-0002

VTEL Corp.
1901 West Braker Ln.
Austin, TX 78758

Founded 1984
Total employees 175
Annual sales $26.07
million
Industry
Telecommunications
Growth Openings in past
year 105; percentage
growth 150%
Contact Carson Brown,
Director of Human
Resources
Tel 512-834-2700
Fax 512-834-3792

Astro International Corp.
100 Park Ave.
League City, TX 77573

Founded 1973
Total employees 100
Industries Environmental,
Test and Measurement
Growth Openings in past
year 25; percentage
growth 33%
Contact Ms. Susan Boyd,
Personnel Manager
Tel 713-332-2484
Fax 713-554-6795

Thomas-Conrad Corp.
1908-R Kramer Ln.
Austin, TX 78758

Founded 1988
Total employees 300
Annual sales $34 million
Industries Computer
Software,
Subassemblies and
Components,
Telecommunications

XETEL Corporation
8100 Cameron Rd., Suite
150
Austin, TX 78753

Founded 1984
Total employees 450
Annual sales $50 million
Industry Subassemblies
and Components

Automaker, Inc.
4030 Bluebonnet Dr.
Stafford, TX 77477

Founded 1985
Total employees 150
Annual sales $12 million
Industry Factory
Automation
Contact James B. Morris,
Chief Operating Officer
Tel 713-240-7424
Fax 713-240-6301

Biles and Associates
6161 Savoy Dr.
Houston, TX 77036

Founded 1970
Total employees 50
Annual sales $5.8 million
Industry Computer
Software
Growth Openings in past
year 20; percentage
growth 66%
Contact Ms. Margaret
Landers,
Secretary/Treasurer
Tel 713-789-8880
Fax 713-789-5524

BMC Software, Inc.
PO Box 2002
Sugar Land, TX 77487

Founded 1979
Total employees 700
Annual sales $130.11
million
Industry Computer
Software
Growth Openings in past
year 197; percentage
growth 39%
Contact Max P. Watson,
Jr.,
President
Tel 713-240-8800
Fax 713-242-6523

CDR Environmental, Inc.
20515 State Hwy. 249,
Suite 380
Houston, TX 77070

Founded 1984
Total employees 40
Annual sales $4.2 million
Industry Environmental
Growth Openings in past
year 12; percentage
growth 42%
Contact Don
Couperthwaite,
President
Tel 713-370-6700
Fax 713-370-9292

Cogniseis Development, Inc.
2401 Portsmouth St.
Houston, TX 77098

Founded 1987
Total employees 225
Industry Computer
Software
Growth Openings in past
year 75; percentage
growth 50%
Contact Pat Poe,
COB/President
Tel 713-526-3273
Fax 713-630-3968

Community Health Computing, Inc.
5 Greenway Plaza, Suite
1900
Houston, TX 77046

Founded 1973
Total employees 310
Annual sales $35 million
Industry Computer
Software
Growth Openings in past
year 110; percentage
growth 55%
Contact Errol Robinson,
Director of Human
Resources
Tel 713-960-1907
Fax 713-840-3300

Cyberonics, Inc.
17448 Hwy 3, Suite 100
Webster, TX 77598

Founded 1987
Total employees 40
Industry Medical
Growth Openings in past
year 20; percentage
growth 100%
Contact Allen Hill,
Chief Executive Officer
Tel 713-332-1375
Fax 713-332-3615

Daniel Valve Co.
PO Box 40421
Houston, TX 77240

Founded 1962
Total employees 200
Annual sales $19 million

Industry Subassemblies
and Components
Growth Openings in past
year 25; percentage
growth 14%
Contact Ken Chickering,
III,
President
Tel 713-469-0550
Fax 713-894-1332

Develco, Inc.
7000 Hollister St.
Houston, TX 77210

Founded 1958
Total employees 200
Industries Energy, Test
and Measurement,
Telecommunications
Growth Openings in past
year 100; percentage
growth 100%
Contact Patrick Herbert,
President
Tel 713-744-4200
Fax 713-744-4438

Diagnostic Systems Laboratories, Inc.
445 Medical Center Blvd.
Webster, TX 77598

Founded 1981
Total employees 60
Annual sales $6.6 million
Industries Chemicals,
Medical
Growth Openings in past
year 19; percentage
growth 46%
Contact Gopal Savjani,
President
Tel 713-332-9678
Fax 713-338-1895

Dixie Chemical Co., Inc.
PO Box 130410
Houston, TX 77219

Founded 1946
Total employees 200
Annual sales $37 million
Industries Advanced
Materials, Chemicals

Growth Openings in past
year 30; percentage
growth 17%
Contact Gary Mossman,
President
Tel 713-863-1947
Fax 713-863-8316

Growth Openings in past
year 19; percentage
growth 76%
Contact Joe Wakil,
President
Tel 713-465-1921
Fax 713-465-2418

Growth Openings in past
year 15; percentage
growth 42%
Contact Timothy Farrell,
Chief Executive Officer
Tel 713-496-9400
Fax 713-496-1090

EGC Corp.
11718 McGallion, PO Box
16080
Houston, TX 77222

Founded 1959
Total employees 325
Annual sales $48 million
Industries Advanced
Materials, Factory
Automation,
Manufacturing
Equipment,
Subassemblies and
Components
Growth Openings in past
year 75; percentage
growth 30%
Contact John Ostroot,
President
Tel 713-447-8611
Fax 713-931-2201

FSSL, Inc.
525 Julie Rivers Dr.
Sugar Land, TX 77478

Founded 1985
Total employees 80
Industries Energy,
Manufacturing
Equipment,
Subassemblies and
Components, Test and
Measurement
Growth Openings in past
year 20; percentage
growth 33%
Contact Robert A. Mintz,
General Manager
Tel 713-240-1122
Fax 713-240-0951

Genosys Biotechnology, Inc.
8701-A New Trails Dr.
The Woodlands, TX
77381

Founded 1987
Total employees 34
Industries Biotechnology,
Chemicals
Growth Openings in past
year 13; percentage
growth 61%
Contact Tim McGrath,
President
Tel 713-363-3693
Fax 713-363-2212

Energy BioSystems Corp.
3608 Research Forrest
Dr., B7
The Woodlands, TX
77381

Founded 1989
Total employees 35
Industry Environmental
Growth Openings in past
year 28; percentage
growth 400%
Contact John H. Webb,
President/CEO
Tel 713-364-6100
Fax 713-364-6110

Fugro-McClelland (Environmental), Inc.
PO Box 740010
Houston, TX 77274

Founded 1990
Total employees 90
Annual sales $9.6 million
Industry Environmental
Growth Openings in past
year 30; percentage
growth 50%
Contact Robert Benning,
President
Tel 713-772-3700
Fax 713-778-5560

GHG Corp.
1300 Hercules Ave., Suite
111
Houston, TX 77058

Founded 1979
Total employees 72
Industry Computer
Software
Growth Openings in past
year 12; percentage
growth 20%
Contact I.J. Galvan,
President
Tel 713-488-8806
Fax 713-488-1838

Eyesys Laboratories, Inc.
2776 Bingle Rd.
Houston, TX 77055

Founded 1986
Total employees 44
Annual sales $7.8 million
Industry Medical

FutureSoft Engineering, Inc.
1001 South Dairy Ashford,
Suite 101
Houston, TX 77077

Founded 1982
Total employees 50
Annual sales $5.8 million
Industry Computer
Software

Henley International, Inc.
104 Industrial Blvd.
Sugar Land, TX 77478

Founded 1976
Total employees 600
Annual sales $60 million
Industries Computer
Hardware, Holding
Companies, Medical

Growth Openings in past year 100; percentage growth 20%
Contact Kenneth W. Davidson, COB/President/CEO
Tel 713-240-2442
Fax 713-240-2577

Kaneka Texas Corp.
17 South Briar Hollow Ln., Suite 307
Houston, TX 77027

Founded 1983
Total employees 200
Annual sales $70 million
Industry Advanced Materials
Growth Openings in past year 100; percentage growth 100%
Contact Dr. H. Yasui, President
Tel 713-840-1751
Fax 713-552-0133

KRUG Life Sciences Inc., Houston Division
1290 Hercules Dr., Suite 120
Houston, TX 77058

Founded 1959
Total employees 356
Annual sales $42 million
Industries Defense, Medical, Telecommunications, Transportation
Growth Openings in past year 36; percentage growth 11%
Contact James M. Vanderploeg, MD, General Manager
Tel 713-488-5970
Fax 713-488-8503

LBMS, Inc.
1800 West Loop South, Suite 1800
Houston, TX 77027

Founded 1988
Total employees 80
Annual sales $40 million
Industries Computer Hardware, Computer Software

Growth Openings in past year 15; percentage growth 23%
Contact John Bantleman, COO/CEO
Tel 713-623-0414
Fax 713-623-4955

Litwin Process Automation
1250 West Sam Houston Pkwy. South, PO Box 1281
Houston, TX 77251

Founded 1986
Total employees 185
Annual sales $23 million
Industries Computer Hardware, Factory Automation, Manufacturing Equipment
Growth Openings in past year 55; percentage growth 42%
Contact Boyd Bergen, President
Tel 713-268-8200
Fax 713-268-7469

Molecular Structure Corp.
3200 Research Forest Dr.
The Woodlands, TX 77381

Founded 1973
Total employees 42
Industries Chemicals, Computer Software, Test and Measurement
Growth Openings in past year 12; percentage growth 40%
Contact Dr. Jan M. Troup, President
Tel 713-363-1033
Fax 713-292-2472

NYNEX DPI
12946 Dairy Ashford, Suite 300
Sugar Land, TX 77478

Founded 1979
Total employees 175
Annual sales $20 million

Industry Computer Software
Growth Openings in past year 115; percentage growth 191%
Contact Joe Bonocore, President
Tel 713-491-7200
Fax 713-240-7144

Powell Electrical Manufacturing Co.
PO Box 12818
Houston, TX 77075

Founded 1947
Total employees 550
Annual sales $73 million
Industry Energy
Growth Openings in past year 149; percentage growth 37%
Contact Thomas Powell, Chief Executive Officer
Tel 713-944-6900
Fax 713-947-4453

Roussel Environmental Health, Inc.
3741 Red Bluff Rd., Suite 200
Pasadena, TX 77503

Founded 1973
Total employees 45
Annual sales $9.7 million
Industry Chemicals
Growth Openings in past year 15; percentage growth 50%
Contact Tim Driscoll, President
Tel 713-477-0900
Fax 713-940-2422

Sterling Electronics Corporation
PO Box 1229
Houston, TX 77251

Founded 1940
Total employees 493
Annual sales $101.5 million
Industry Holding Companies

Growth Openings in past year 33; percentage growth 7%
Contact M.S. Spolane, COB/CEO
Tel 713-627-9800
Fax 713-629-3939

Growth Openings in past year 189; percentage growth 78%
Contact Michael L. Jeane, COB/CEO/President
Tel 713-367-1983
Fax 713-364-2240

Growth Openings in past year 49; percentage growth 12%
Contact R.F. Hupp, VP of Administration
Tel 806-665-3701
Fax 806-665-3216

Tanox Biosystems, Inc.
10301 Stella Link Rd., Suite 110
Houston, TX 77025

Founded 1986
Total employees 41
Industry Biotechnology
Growth Openings in past year 13; percentage growth 46%
Contact Dr. Nancy T. Chang, President/CEO
Tel 713-664-2288
Fax 713-664-8914

Triplex Pharmaceutical, Inc.
9391 Grogan's Mill Rd.
The Woodlands, TX 77380

Founded 1989
Total employees 41
Industry Pharmaceuticals
Growth Openings in past year 21; percentage growth 105%
Contact Ms. Laurie Pinkerton, Human Resources Manager
Tel 713-363-8761
Fax 713-363-1168

■ **817 Area Code**

Alan Plummer and Associates, Inc.
841 West Mitchell St.
Arlington, TX 76013

Founded 1978
Total employees 54
Industries Environmental, Manufacturing Equipment
Growth Openings in past year 19; percentage growth 54%
Contact Alan Plummer, President
Tel 817-461-1491
Fax 817-860-3339

Tescorp Seismic Products, Inc.
6209 Windfern Rd.
Houston, TX 77040

Founded 1981
Total employees 150
Annual sales $11 million
Industries Holding Companies, Subassemblies and Components
Growth Openings in past year 30; percentage growth 25%
Contact Don Fussell, President
Tel 713-462-6608
Fax 713-460-1633

■ **806 Area Code**

Goodpasture, Inc.
PO Box 912
Brownfield, TX 79316

Founded 1946
Total employees 125
Annual sales $17 million
Industry Chemicals
Growth Openings in past year 25; percentage growth 25%
Contact Ken Muldrow, President
Tel 806-637-2541
Fax 806-637-2541 X242

Alcon Laboratories, Inc., Ophthalmic Division
6201 South Fwy.
Fort Worth, TX 76134

Founded 1947
Total employees 500
Annual sales $68 million
Industry Pharmaceuticals
Growth Openings in past year 199; percentage growth 66%
Contact Richard Sisson, Executive Vice President
Tel 817-293-0450
Fax 817-551-4352

TETRA Technologies, Inc.
25231 Grogan Mill Rd.
The Woodlands, TX 77380

Founded 1981
Total employees 431
Annual sales $85.26 million
Industries Environmental, Holding Companies

IRI International, Inc.
PO Box 1101
Pampa, TX 79065

Founded 1985
Total employees 450
Annual sales $48 million
Industries Advanced Materials, Energy, Manufacturing Equipment

Altai, Inc.
624 Six Flags Dr., Suite 150
Arlington, TX 76011

Founded 1979
Total employees 100
Annual sales $9.5 million
Industries Computer Hardware, Computer Software

Growth Openings in past year 20; percentage growth 25%
Contact James P. Williams, President/CEO
Tel 817-640-8911
Fax 817-633-4449

Growth Openings in past year 148; percentage growth 42%
Contact Scott Whittenburg, President
Tel 817-868-5000
Fax 817-354-9145

Growth Openings in past year 50; percentage growth 20%
Contact Glenn L. Smith, President
Tel 817-483-4422
Fax 817-483-0931

First Community Services, Inc.
4400 Swanner Loop
Killeen, TX 76543

Founded 1973
Total employees 60
Industries Computer Hardware, Computer Software
Growth Openings in past year 20; percentage growth 50%
Contact Ms. Sandy Thorpe,
Human Resources Manager
Tel 817-690-5185
Fax 817-680-5735

FWT, Inc.
PO Box 8597
Fort Worth, TX 76124

Founded 1959
Total employees 80
Industry Telecommunications
Growth Openings in past year 26; percentage growth 48%
Contact T. Moore, President
Tel 817-457-3060
Fax 817-429-6010

Graham Magnetics, Inc.
4001 Airport Frwy., Suire 400
Bedford, TX 76021

Founded 1964
Total employees 500
Industry Computer Hardware

Larus Industries, Inc.
2220 West Peter Smith St.
Fort Worth, TX 76102

Founded 1976
Total employees 70
Industry Subassemblies and Components
Growth Openings in past year 15; percentage growth 27%
Contact Weldon Johnson, President
Tel 817-332-2994
Fax 817-877-4009

Marvel Communications Corporation
6000D Old Hemphill Rd.
Fort Worth, TX 76134

Founded 1974
Total employees 75
Industry Telecommunications
Growth Openings in past year 35; percentage growth 87%
Contact Ms. Sheila Simmons,
Secretary/Treasurer
Tel 817-568-0177
Fax 817-293-4441

Mouser Electronics
2363 Hwy. 287 North
Mansfield, TX 76063

Founded 1964
Total employees 300
Annual sales $39 million
Industries Energy, Photonics, Subassemblies and Components, Test and Measurement, Telecommunications

PDX, Inc.
101 Jim Wright Frwy. South, Suite 200
Fort Worth, TX 76108

Founded 1983
Total employees 105
Annual sales $12 million
Industry Holding Companies
Growth Openings in past year 40; percentage growth 61%
Contact Ken Hill, President
Tel 817-246-6760
Fax 817-246-0131

Tecnol, Inc.
7201 Industrial Park Blvd.
Fort Worth, TX 76180

Founded 1976
Total employees 850
Annual sales $71 million
Industry Holding Companies
Growth Openings in past year 248; percentage growth 41%
Contact Ms. DeLania Truly,
VP of Corporate Communications and Human
Tel 817-581-6424
Fax 817-581-9354

■ **903 Area Code**

Vertex Communications Corp.
2600 Longview St., PO Box 1277
Kilgore, TX 75662

Founded 1973
Total employees 390
Annual sales $40 million

Industries Holding
Companies,
Telecommunications
Growth Openings in past
year 45; percentage
growth 13%
Contact J. Rex
Vardeman,
President
Tel 903-984-0555
Fax 903-984-1826

Utah

■ **801 Area Code**

Allen Communication, Inc.
5225 Wiley Post Way
Salt Lake City, UT 84116

Founded 1981
Total employees 105
Industry Computer
Software
Growth Openings in past
year 30; percentage
growth 40%
Contact Steven W. Allen,
President
Tel 801-537-7800
Fax 801-537-7805

Ballard Medical Products
12050 Lone Peak Pkwy.
Draper, UT 84020

Founded 1978
Total employees 480
Annual sales $38.1 million
Industry Medical
Growth Openings in past
year 120; percentage
growth 33%
Contact Ms. Geri Stelling,
Director of Personnel
Tel 801-572-6800
Fax 801-572-6999

Burton Group
PO Box 3448
Salt Lake City, UT 84110

Founded 1989
Total employees 25

Industries Computer
Hardware,
Telecommunications
Growth Openings in past
year 14; percentage
growth 127%
Contact Craig Burton,
President
Tel 801-943-1966

CardioPulmonics, Inc.
5060 Amelia Earhart Dr.
Salt Lake City, UT 84116

Founded 1985
Total employees 50
Industry Medical
Growth Openings in past
year 14; percentage
growth 38%
Contact George Sims,
President/CEO
Tel 801-350-3600
Fax 801-350-3610

Datachem Laboratories, Inc.
960 West Levoy Dr.
Salt Lake City, UT 84123

Founded 1971
Total employees 215
Annual sales $21 million
Industry Environmental
Growth Openings in past
year 15; percentage
growth 7%
Contact James Nelson,
President
Tel 801-266-7700
Fax 801-268-9992

Dayna Communications, Inc.
50 South Main, 5th Floor
Salt Lake City, UT 84144

Founded 1977
Total employees 90
Annual sales $15 million
Industries Computer
Hardware, Computer
Software
Growth Openings in past
year 30; percentage
growth 50%
Contact Brad Romney,
President/CEO
Tel 801-531-0600
Fax 801-359-9135

DHI Computing Service, Inc.
1525 West 820 North, PO
Box 51427
Provo, UT 84603

Founded 1954
Total employees 180
Annual sales $20 million
Industries Computer
Hardware, Computer
Software, Holding
Companies
Growth Openings in past
year 20; percentage
growth 12%
Contact Bliss H. Crandall,
President
Tel 801-373-8518

EDO Corp., Acoustics Division
2645 South 300 West
Salt Lake City, UT 84115

Founded 1926
Total employees 400
Annual sales $26 million
Industries Advanced
Materials, Defense,
Subassemblies and
Components, Test and
Measurement,
Transportation
Growth Openings in past
year 50; percentage
growth 14%
Contact Brian Burke,
Manager of Personnel
Tel 801-486-7481
Fax 801-484-3301

Gentner Communications Corp.
1825 Research Way
Salt Lake City, UT 84119

Founded 1981
Total employees 65
Annual sales $8 million
Industries Subassemblies
and Components,
Telecommunications
Growth Openings in past
year 15; percentage
growth 30%
Contact Russell D.
Gentner,
Chief Executive Officer
Tel 801-975-7200
Fax 801-977-0087

Gull Laboratories, Inc.
1011 East 4800 South
Salt Lake City, UT 84117

Founded 1974
Total employees 126
Annual sales $7 million
Industries Medical,
Pharmaceuticals
Growth Openings in past
year 16; percentage
growth 14%
Contact Dr. Myron W.
Wentz, Ph.D.,
COB/President
Tel 801-263-3524
Fax 801-265-9268

HGM Medical Laser Systems, Inc.
3959 West 1820 South
Salt Lake City, UT 84104

Founded 1983
Total employees 200
Annual sales $22 million
Industries Medical,
Photonics
Growth Openings in past
year 50; percentage
growth 33%
Contact William
McMahon,
President
Tel 801-972-0500
Fax 801-972-4884

Hyclone Laboratories, Inc.
1725 South Hyclone Rd.
Logan, UT 84321

Founded 1975
Total employees 200
Annual sales $25 million
Industries Biotechnology,
Medical
Growth Openings in past
year 50; percentage
growth 33%
Contact Greg Cox,
Personnel Manager
Tel 801-753-4584
Fax 801-753-4589

IOMED, Inc.
1290 West 2320 South,
Suite A
Salt Lake City, UT 84119

Founded 1974
Total employees 120
Annual sales $6 million
Industry Medical
Growth Openings in past
year 40; percentage
growth 50%
Contact Ms. Mary
Crowther,
Director of
Administration
Tel 801-975-1191
Fax 801-975-7366

Macrotech Fluid Sealing, Inc., Polyseal Division
1754 West 500 South
Salt Lake City, UT 84104

Founded 1974
Total employees 130
Annual sales $12 million
Industry Subassemblies
and Components
Growth Openings in past
year 20; percentage
growth 18%
Contact Ted Witte,
Personnel Director
Tel 801-973-9171
Fax 801-973-9188

Megahertz Corp.
4505 South Wasatch
Blvd.
Salt Lake City, UT 84124

Founded 1985
Total employees 160
Industry
Telecommunications
Growth Openings in past
year 63; percentage
growth 64%
Contact Spencer Kirk,
President
Tel 801-272-6000
Fax 801-272-6077

Megawest Systems, Inc.
345 Bearcat Dr.
Salt Lake City, UT 84115

Founded 1979
Total employees 45

Industry Computer
Software
Growth Openings in past
year 14; percentage
growth 45%
Contact Michael
Archuleta,
President
Tel 801-487-0788
Fax 801-466-7206

Ohmeda, Salt Lake Division
4745 Wiley Post Way, 650
Plaza 6
Salt Lake City, UT 84116

Founded 1981
Total employees 63
Annual sales $6.0 million
Industries Medical,
Pharmaceuticals
Growth Openings in past
year 13; percentage
growth 26%
Contact Mark Nelson,
Director of Operations
Tel 801-364-2021
Fax 801-364-2070

Research Industries Corp.
6864 South 300 West
Midvale, UT 84047

Founded 1968
Total employees 175
Annual sales $17.5 million
Industry Holding
Companies
Growth Openings in past
year 65; percentage
growth 59%
Contact Michael Kelly,
VP of Operations
Tel 801-562-0200
Fax 801-562-1122

Rogers & Associates Engineering Corp.
515 East, 4500 South
Salt Lake City, UT 84107

Founded 1980
Total employees 43
Annual sales $3 million
Industries Environmental,
Manufacturing
Equipment

Growth Openings in past year 16; percentage growth 59%
Contact Vern C. Rogers, Ph.D., President
Tel 801-263-1600
Fax 801-262-1527

SoftSolutions Technology Corp.
625 South State St.
Orem, UT 84058

Founded 1990
Total employees 100
Industry Computer Software
Growth Openings in past year 15; percentage growth 17%
Contact Kenneth Duncan, President
Tel 801-226-6000
Fax 801-224-0920

Theratech, Inc.
417 Wakara Way, Suite 100
Salt Lake City, UT 84108

Founded 1985
Total employees 90
Annual sales $2.56 million
Industries Medical, Pharmaceuticals
Growth Openings in past year 40; percentage growth 80%
Contact Dr. Dinesh Patel, Ph.D., President/CEO
Tel 801-583-6028
Fax 801-583-6042

3M, Health Information Systems Department
575 West Murray Blvd., PO Box 57900
Murray, UT 84157

Founded 1981
Total employees 500
Industry Computer Software

Growth Openings in past year 100; percentage growth 25%
Contact Brian Hewitt, General Manager
Tel 801-265-4400
Fax 801-263-3658

Vermont

■ **802 Area Code**

Bio-Tek Instruments, Inc.
Highland Industrial Park, PO Box 998
Winooski, VT 05404

Founded 1965
Total employees 190
Annual sales $22 million
Industries Factory Automation, Test and Measurement
Growth Openings in past year 29; percentage growth 18%
Contact Ms. Kathleen Gilpin, Director of M.I.S. and Human Resources
Tel 802-655-4040
Fax 802-655-7941

IDX Systems Corp.
1400 Shelburne Rd., PO Box 1070
Burlington, VT 05402

Founded 1969
Total employees 810
Annual sales $100 million
Industries Computer Software, Holding Companies
Growth Openings in past year 106; percentage growth 15%
Contact Dean Haller, Corporate Human Resources Manager
Tel 802-862-1022
Fax 802-862-6848

IDX Systems Corp., Systems Division
1400 Shelburn Rd., PO Box 1070
Burlington, VT 05402

Founded 1969
Total employees 80
Annual sales $9.2 million
Industry Computer Software
Growth Openings in past year 27; percentage growth 50%
Contact Jim Crook, Vice President
Tel 802-658-2664
Fax 802-862-6848

Janos Technology, Inc.
Rte. 35
Townshend, VT 05353

Founded 1970
Total employees 75
Annual sales $8.1 million
Industries Photonics, Test and Measurement
Growth Openings in past year 25; percentage growth 50%
Contact Gil Bigelow, Personnel Director
Tel 802-365-7714
Fax 802-365-4596

Virginia

■ **703 Area Code**

Adroit Systems, Inc.
209 Madison St.
Alexandria, VA 22314

Founded 1983
Total employees 85
Annual sales $6 million
Industries Computer Software, Telecommunications, Transportation
Growth Openings in past year 30; percentage growth 54%
Contact Ms. Kathryn Edwards, Personnel Administrator
Tel 703-684-2900
Fax 703-836-7411

Advanced Communication Systems, Inc.
1900 North Beauregard St., Suite 300
Alexandria, VA 22311

Founded 1987
Total employees 125
Industries Defense, Telecommunications
Growth Openings in past year 25; percentage growth 25%
Contact George Robinson, President
Tel 703-553-4389
Fax 703-820-8435

Advanced Technology Systems, Inc.
800 Follin Ln., Suite 270
Vienna, VA 22180

Founded 1978
Total employees 350
Annual sales $18.1 million
Industries Computer Hardware, Computer Software
Growth Openings in past year 100; percentage growth 40%
Contact Ms. Elsie Love, Personnel Manager
Tel 703-242-0030
Fax 703-242-5220

American Communications Co.
14200 Park Meadow Dr.
Chantilly, VA 22021

Founded 1975
Total employees 250
Annual sales $41 million
Industries Computer Hardware, Telecommunications
Growth Openings in past year 50; percentage growth 25%
Contact Donald Kirk, Vice President
Tel 703-968-6300
Fax 703-968-5151

American Systems Corp.
14200 Park Meadow Dr.
Chantilly, VA 22021

Founded 1975
Total employees 750
Industry Holding Companies
Growth Openings in past year 125; percentage growth 20%
Contact Thomas H. Curran, President/CEO
Tel 703-968-6300
Fax 703-968-5151

Autometric, Inc.
5301 Shawnee Rd.
Alexandria, VA 22312

Founded 1957
Total employees 175
Annual sales $18 million
Industry Holding Companies
Growth Openings in past year 19; percentage growth 12%
Contact Ms. Wendy Harrison, Director of Human Resources
Tel 703-658-4000
Fax 703-658-4021

Autometric, Inc., Autometric Service Division
5301 Shawnee Rd.
Alexandria, VA 22312

Founded 1957
Total employees 200
Industries Computer Software, Photonics
Growth Openings in past year 50; percentage growth 33%
Contact Don Hardison, Senior Vice President
Tel 703-658-4000
Fax 703-658-4021

BCI, Inc.
5160 Parkstone Dr., Suite 190
Chantilly, VA 22021

Founded 1979
Total employees 300
Annual sales $41 million
Industry Telecommunications
Growth Openings in past year 50; percentage growth 20%
Contact Ron Graves, President
Tel 703-222-8300
Fax 703-222-0205

Best Programs, Inc.
11413 Isaac Newton Southwest
Reston, VA 22090

Founded 1982
Total employees 250
Annual sales $17 million
Industries Computer Software, Holding Companies
Growth Openings in past year 110; percentage growth 78%
Contact James F. Petersen, President
Tel 703-709-5200
Fax 703-709-9359

BTG, Inc.
1945 Old Gallows Rd.
Vienna, VA 22182

Founded 1982
Total employees 300
Annual sales $30 million
Industries Computer Hardware, Computer Software, Holding Companies
Growth Openings in past year 15; percentage growth 5%
Contact Winder Heller, Director of Human Resources
Tel 703-556-6518
Fax 703-556-9290

CEXEC, Inc.
7918 Jones Branch Dr.,
Suite 700
Mc Lean, VA 22102

Founded 1976
Total employees 190
Industries Computer
Hardware,
Manufacturing
Equipment,
Telecommunications
Growth Openings in past
year 90; percentage
growth 90%
Contact James Moss,
Executive Vice President
Tel 703-893-3220
Fax 703-556-0829

DCS Corp.
1330 Braddock Pl.
Alexandria, VA 22314

Founded 1977
Total employees 265
Annual sales $23 million
Industries Defense,
Manufacturing
Equipment,
Subassemblies and
Components
Growth Openings in past
year 25; percentage
growth 10%
Contact James T. Wood,
President
Tel 703-683-8430
Fax 703-684-7229

Dewberry & Davis
8401 Arlington Blvd.
Fairfax, VA 22031

Founded 1959
Total employees 992
Industry Manufacturing
Equipment
Growth Openings in past
year 39; percentage
growth 4%
Contact Richard Renner,
Assistant Director of
Human Resources
Tel 703-849-0100
Fax 703-849-0118

Dual, Inc.
2101 Wilson Blvd., Suite
600
Arlington, VA 22201

Founded 1983
Total employees 240
Annual sales $18 million
Industries Manufacturing
Equipment,
Subassemblies and
Components
Growth Openings in past
year 30; percentage
growth 14%
Contact Ms. Nancy
Streeter,
Director of
Administration
Tel 703-527-3500
Fax 703-527-0829

Coastal Remediation, Inc.
310 First St.
Roanoke, VA 24011

Founded 1989
Total employees 150
Annual sales $21 million
Industry Environmental
Growth Openings in past
year 100; percentage
growth 200%
Contact James L. Van
Lanen,
President
Tel 703-983-0222

Delta Research Corp.
1501 Wilson Blvd., Suite
1200
Arlington, VA 22209

Founded 1972
Total employees 80
Annual sales $7.2 million
Industry Computer
Software
Growth Openings in past
year 13; percentage
growth 19%
Contact Ms. Nancy
Turner,
Treasurer
Tel 703-841-1900
Fax 703-247-8343

Datatel, Inc.
4375 Fair Lakes Ct.
Fairfax, VA 22033

Founded 1968
Total employees 145
Annual sales $20 million
Industry Computer
Software
Growth Openings in past
year 25; percentage
growth 20%
Contact Ms. Ginger
Piercy,
VP of Finance
Tel 703-968-9000
Fax 703-968-4625

Deltek Systems, Inc.
8280 Greensboro Dr.
Mc Lean, VA 22102

Founded 1983
Total employees 125
Annual sales $14 million
Industry Computer
Software
Growth Openings in past
year 25; percentage
growth 25%
Contact Ken de Laski,
President
Tel 703-734-8606
Fax 703-734-0346

Electronic Instrumentation and Technology, Inc.
108 Carpenter Dr.
Sterling, VA 22170

Founded 1977
Total employees 112
Annual sales $8.8 million
Industry Subassemblies
and Components
Growth Openings in past
year 12; percentage
growth 12%
Contact Joe May,
President
Tel 703-478-0700
Fax 703-478-0291

ENSCO, Inc.
5400 Port Royal Rd.
Springfield, VA 22151

Founded 1969
Total employees 380
Annual sales $28 million
Industry Holding
Companies
Growth Openings in past
year 29; percentage
growth 8%
Contact Ms. Joanne
McDonald,
Director of
Administration
Tel 703-321-9000
Fax 703-321-4529

ENVIRON Corp.
4350 North Fairfax Dr.
Arlington, VA 22203

Founded 1982
Total employees 230
Annual sales $24 million
Industry Environmental
Growth Openings in past
year 100; percentage
growth 76%
Contact Ms. Cindi
Hollomon,
Director of
Administration and
Human Res
Tel 703-516-2300
Fax 703-516-2345

**Fastcomm
Communications Corp.**
45472 Holiday Dr.
Sterling, VA 22170

Founded 1985
Total employees 40
Annual sales $5.5 million
Industries Subassemblies
and Components,
Telecommunications
Growth Openings in past
year 17; percentage
growth 73%
Contact Robert Dennis,
President
Tel 703-318-7750
Fax 703-787-4625

Genetics & IVF Institute
3020 Javier Rd.
Fairfax, VA 22031

Founded 1984
Total employees 210
Annual sales $20 million
Industry Biotechnology
Growth Openings in past
year 29; percentage
growth 16%
Contact Joseph D.
Schulman, MD,
COB/CEO
Tel 703-698-7355
Fax 703-698-3963

Global Associates, Ltd.
2300 Clarendon Blvd.,
Suite 205
Arlington, VA 22201

Founded 1986
Total employees 60
Annual sales $4 million
Industries Computer
Hardware, Defense,
Manufacturing
Equipment,
Telecommunications
Growth Openings in past
year 22; percentage
growth 57%
Contact John W. Asher,
President/CEO
Tel 703-351-5660
Fax 703-351-5650

**Healthy Buildings
International, Inc.**
10378 Democracy Ln.
Fairfax, VA 22030

Founded 1981
Total employees 50
Industry Environmental
Growth Openings in past
year 25; percentage
growth 100%
Contact Gray Robertson,
President
Tel 703-352-0102
Fax 703-352-0151

**Information
Management
Consultants, Inc.**
7915 Westpark Dr.
Mc Lean, VA 22102

Founded 1981
Total employees 160
Annual sales $12 million
Industry Computer
Software
Growth Openings in past
year 60; percentage
growth 60%
Contact Sudhakar
Shenoy,
President
Tel 703-893-3100
Fax 703-237-2620

**Information Technology
and Applications Corp.**
1875 Campus Commons
Dr.
Reston, VA 22091

Founded 1986
Total employees 60
Annual sales $6.9 million
Industries Computer
Software, Defense
Growth Openings in past
year 12; percentage
growth 25%
Contact James E.
Scrivener,
President
Tel 703-391-8822
Fax 703-391-8879

InterCon Systems Corp.
950 Herndon Pkwy., Suite
420
Herndon, VA 22070

Founded 1988
Total employees 50
Annual sales $5.8 million
Industry Computer
Software
Growth Openings in past
year 25; percentage
growth 100%
Contact Kurt Baumann,
President
Tel 703-709-5500
Fax 703-709-5555

Logicon, Inc., Operating Systems
2100 Washington Blvd.
Arlington, VA 22204

Founded 1969
Total employees 175
Annual sales $18 million
Industry Defense
Growth Openings in past year 19; percentage growth 12%
Contact Dan B. Wallace, Vice President/General Manager
Tel 703-486-3500
Fax 703-920-7086

Management Engineers, Inc.
1893 Preston White Dr.
Reston, VA 22091

Founded 1975
Total employees 64
Annual sales $5 million
Industry Computer Software
Growth Openings in past year 34; percentage growth 113%
Contact Peter W. Kauffman, President
Tel 703-476-6700
Fax 703-620-4858

Metters Industries, Inc.
8200 Greensboro Dr.
Mc Lean, VA 22102

Founded 1981
Total employees 400
Annual sales $43 million
Industry Defense
Growth Openings in past year 40; percentage growth 11%
Contact Samuel Metters, Chief Executive Officer
Tel 703-821-3300
Fax 703-821-3996

Michael Baker Jr., Inc., Civil and Water Resources Division
3601 Eisenhower Ave.
Alexandria, VA 22304

Founded 1946
Total employees 440
Annual sales $28 million
Industries Computer Software, Environmental, Manufacturing Equipment, Telecommunications
Growth Openings in past year 190; percentage growth 76%
Contact Edward Wiley, Senior Vice President/ General Manager
Tel 703-960-8800
Fax 703-960-9125

NCI Information Systems, Inc.
8260 Greensboro Dr., Suite 400
Mc Lean, VA 22102

Founded 1986
Total employees 110
Annual sales $12 million
Industry Computer Software
Growth Openings in past year 70; percentage growth 175%
Contact Ms. Kathy Kander, Human Resources Manager
Tel 703-903-0325
Fax 703-903-0325

Netrix Corp.
13595 Dulles Technology Dr.
Herndon, VA 22071

Founded 1985
Total employees 154
Annual sales $31.39 million
Industry Telecommunications

Growth Openings in past year 14; percentage growth 10%
Contact Charles W. Stein, President
Tel 703-742-6000
Fax 703-742-4048

NPRI, Inc.
602 Cameron St.
Alexandria, VA 22314

Founded 1981
Total employees 75
Annual sales $8.7 million
Industry Computer Software
Growth Openings in past year 15; percentage growth 25%
Contact Ron Charnock, President
Tel 703-683-9090
Fax 703-684-3439

Person-System Integration, Ltd.
2401 Huntington Ave.
Alexandria, VA 22303

Founded 1977
Total employees 130
Industries Computer Hardware, Defense, Factory Automation
Growth Openings in past year 45; percentage growth 52%
Contact Dr. James McGuinness, Ph.D., President
Tel 703-960-5555
Fax 703-960-5575

Quality Systems, Inc.
4000 Legato Rd., Suite 1100
Fairfax, VA 22033

Founded 1981
Total employees 301
Annual sales $24.2 million
Industries Computer Hardware, Computer Software

Growth Openings in past year 106; percentage growth 54%
Contact Robert C. Dehaven, Chief Executice Officer
Tel 703-352-9200
Fax 703-352-9216

Radiation Systems, Inc.
1501 Moran Rd.
Sterling, VA 22170

Founded 1960
Total employees 890
Annual sales $140 million
Industries Holding Companies, Telecommunications
Growth Openings in past year 388; percentage growth 77%
Contact Leo Flynn, Director of Human Resources
Tel 703-450-5680
Fax 703-450-4706

RBC, Inc.
Two Colonial Pl., 2101 Wilson Blvd., Suite 801
Arlington, VA 22201

Founded 1975
Total employees 150
Annual sales $10.3 million
Industries Computer Hardware, Computer Software, Defense, Holding Companies
Growth Openings in past year 15; percentage growth 11%
Contact Ms. Reine DeHart, VP of Administration and Finance
Tel 703-243-9550
Fax 703-243-7854

Rehau, Inc.
Edwards Ferry Rd., PO Box 1706
Leesburg, VA 22075

Founded 1952
Total employees 150
Annual sales $15 million

Industries Manufacturing Equipment, Medical, Subassemblies and Components
Growth Openings in past year 50; percentage growth 50%
Contact J. Burke, VP of Human Resources
Tel 703-777-5255
Fax 703-777-3053

Resource Applications, Inc.
2980 Fairview Park Dr., Suite 1000
Falls Church, VA 22042

Founded 1979
Total employees 120
Industry Environmental
Growth Openings in past year 70; percentage growth 140%
Contact Dr. Tara Singh, President
Tel 703-698-2000
Fax 703-698-2030

Resource Consultants, Inc.
1960 Gallows Rd.
Vienna, VA 22027

Founded 1979
Total employees 700
Annual sales $75 million
Industry Defense
Growth Openings in past year 197; percentage growth 39%
Contact Ronald S. Newlan, President
Tel 703-893-6120
Fax 703-893-0917

Robbins-Gioia, Inc.
209 Madison St.
Alexandria, VA 22314

Founded 1981
Total employees 310
Annual sales $20 million
Industry Computer Software

Growth Openings in past year 60; percentage growth 24%
Contact John Gioia, President
Tel 703-548-7006
Fax 703-684-5189

SRA Technologies, Inc.
4700 King St., Suite 300
Alexandria, VA 22302

Founded 1975
Total employees 200
Annual sales $19 million
Industry Holding Companies
Growth Openings in past year 30; percentage growth 17%
Contact Ms. Loretta Zachman, Personnel Manager
Tel 703-671-7171
Fax 703-671-7438

SRA Technologies, Inc., Life Sciences Division
4700 King St.
Alexandria, VA 22302

Founded 1986
Total employees 80
Annual sales $9 million
Industry Biotechnology
Growth Openings in past year 35; percentage growth 77%
Contact Dr. Al Hellman, Ph.D., Vice President
Tel 703-671-7171
Fax 703-671-7438

SWL Inc.
1900 Gallows Rd.
Vienna, VA 22182

Founded 1964
Total employees 330
Annual sales $30 million
Industries Computer Hardware, Defense, Manufacturing Equipment, Subassemblies and Components

Growth Openings in past year 30; percentage growth 10%
Contact Ms. Arlene Rimson, Human Resource Director
Tel 703-506-5000
Fax 703-506-0585

Growth Openings in past year 14; percentage growth 233%
Contact Ron Oklewicz, President
Tel 703-834-9000
Fax 703-834-1235

Growth Openings in past year 17; percentage growth 29%
Contact Ms. Sue Guest, Personnel Director
Tel 703-471-7070
Fax 703-471-1165

■ 804 Area Code

Systar, Inc.
205 Van Buren St., Suite 350
Herndon, VA 22070

Founded 1984
Total employees 70
Annual sales $20 million
Industry Computer Software
Growth Openings in past year 40; percentage growth 133%
Contact Ronald K. Hamrick, President/CEO
Tel 703-834-5510
Fax 703-834-9040

VDO-Yazaki Corp.
980 Brooke Rd., PO Box 2897
Winchester, VA 22601

Founded 1977
Total employees 756
Annual sales $89 million
Industries Photonics, Test and Measurement, Transportation
Growth Openings in past year 56; percentage growth 8%
Contact Duffy McDonald, Director of Human Resources
Tel 703-665-0100
Fax 703-662-2515

B&W Fuel Co.
3315 Old Forest Rd., PO box 10935
Lynchburg, VA 24506

Founded 1987
Total employees 421
Annual sales $77 million
Industry Energy
Growth Openings in past year 35; percentage growth 9%
Contact Robert H. Ihde, President
Tel 804-385-2000
Fax 804-385-3663

Systems Research and Applications Corp.
2000 15th St. North
Arlington, VA 22201

Founded 1978
Total employees 830
Annual sales $66 million
Industries Manufacturing Equipment, Telecommunications
Growth Openings in past year 109; percentage growth 15%
Contact Jerry Yates, VP of Administration
Tel 703-558-4700
Fax 703-558-4788

Verdix Corp.
205 Van Buren St., 4th Fl.
Herndon, VA 22070

Founded 1982
Total employees 128
Annual sales $19 million
Industries Computer Software, Telecommunications
Growth Openings in past year 20; percentage growth 18%
Contact Ralph Alexander, President/CEO
Tel 703-318-5800
Fax 703-318-9304

Busch, Inc.
516 Viking Dr.
Virginia Beach, VA 23452

Founded 1975
Total employees 135
Industry Subassemblies and Components
Growth Openings in past year 25; percentage growth 22%
Contact Ms. Lynne Hartley, Personnel Manager
Tel 804-463-7800
Fax 804-463-7407

TelePad Corp.
1861 Wiehle Ave., Suite 350
Reston, VA 22090

Founded 1990
Total employees 20
Industries Computer Hardware, Computer Software

Vidar Systems, Inc.
520 Herndon Pkwy.
Herndon, VA 22070

Founded 1984
Total employees 75
Industry Computer Hardware

Goldschmidt Chemical Corp.
914 East Randolph Rd., PO Box 1299
Hopewell, VA 23860

Founded 1979
Total employees 107
Annual sales $15 million
Industry Advanced Materials

Growth Openings in past year 37; percentage growth 52%
Contact Ms. Linda Gutridge, Personnel Manager
Tel 804-541-8658
Fax 804-541-2783

Hickson DanChem Corp.
1975 Richmond Rd., PO Box 400
Danville, VA 24543

Founded 1942
Total employees 117
Annual sales $25 million
Industries Advanced Materials, Chemicals
Growth Openings in past year 12; percentage growth 11%
Contact Elliot H. Baum, President
Tel 804-797-8100
Fax 804-799-2814

Lee Laboratories, Inc.
2820 North Normandy Dr.
Petersburg, VA 23805

Founded 1976
Total employees 70
Industry Pharmaceuticals
Growth Openings in past year 38; percentage growth 118%
Contact Michael E. Zaleski, President
Tel 804-862-1990
Fax 804-862-3246

Maida Development Co.
20 Libby St., PO Box 3529
Hampton, VA 23663

Founded 1947
Total employees 350
Annual sales $24 million
Industry Subassemblies and Components

Growth Openings in past year 100; percentage growth 40%
Contact Donald H. Merritt, President
Tel 804-723-0785
Fax 804-722-1194

MiniComputer Co., Health Care Management Systems Division
2116 West Laburnum Ave., Suite 108
Richmond, VA 23227

Founded 1976
Total employees 70
Annual sales $3.9 million
Industry Computer Software
Growth Openings in past year 20; percentage growth 40%
Contact Richard B. Usry, President
Tel 804-359-5700
Fax 804-359-1090

nVIEW Corp.
860 Omni Blvd.
Newport News, VA 23606

Founded 1986
Total employees 85
Annual sales $16.8 million
Industries Computer Hardware, Telecommunications
Growth Openings in past year 45; percentage growth 112%
Contact William Donaldson, CEO/President
Tel 804-873-1354
Fax 804-873-2153

Science & Technology Corp.
101 Research Dr.
Hampton, VA 23666

Founded 1979
Total employees 325
Industries Computer Software,

Environmental, Photonics, Transportation
Growth Openings in past year 125; percentage growth 62%
Contact Dr. Ardash Deepak, President
Tel 804-865-1894
Fax 804-865-1294

Simplimatic Engineering Co.
PO Box 11709
Lynchburg, VA 24506

Founded 1962
Total employees 500
Annual sales $63 million
Industry Factory Automation
Growth Openings in past year 119; percentage growth 31%
Contact Harry Tatum, Human Resources Director
Tel 804-582-1200
Fax 804-582-1284

Washington

■ **206 Area Code**

Aldus Corp.
411 First Ave. South, Suite 200
Seattle, WA 98104

Founded 1984
Total employees 886
Annual sales $167.5 million
Industries Computer Software, Holding Companies
Growth Openings in past year 194; percentage growth 28%
Contact Paul Brainerd, President/CEO
Tel 206-622-5500

Applied Geotechnology Inc.
PO Box 3885
Bellevue, WA 98009

Founded 1977
Total employees 115
Annual sales $10 million
Industry Environmental
Growth Openings in past year 15; percentage growth 15%
Contact John Newby, President
Tel 206-453-8383
Fax 206-646-9523

Asymetrix Corp.
110-110th Ave., Suite 700
Bellevue, WA 98004

Founded 1985
Total employees 200
Annual sales $23 million
Industry Computer Software
Growth Openings in past year 100; percentage growth 100%
Contact Paul Allen, President
Tel 206-462-0501
Fax 206-455-3071

Cellpro, Inc.
22322 20th Ave.
Southeast, Suite 100
Bothell, WA 98021

Founded 1989
Total employees 70
Annual sales $1 million
Industry Biotechnology
Growth Openings in past year 30; percentage growth 75%
Contact Dr. Christopher Porter,
Vice Chairman/CEO
Tel 206-485-7644
Fax 206-485-4787

Applied Microsystems Corp.
5020 148th Ave.
Northeast, PO Box 97002
Redmond, WA 98073

Founded 1979
Total employees 240
Industries Computer Hardware, Computer Software, Factory Automation
Growth Openings in past year 22; percentage growth 10%
Contact Eric J. Peterson, VP of Finance and Administration
Tel 206-882-2000
Fax 206-883-3049

Augat Communications Group, Inc.
23315 66th Ave. South
Kent, WA 98032

Founded 1976
Total employees 225
Industries Photonics, Telecommunications
Growth Openings in past year 75; percentage growth 50%
Contact Larry Buffington, President
Tel 206-854-9802
Fax 206-813-1001

Columbia Analytical Services, Inc.
1317 South 13th Ave.
Kelso, WA 98626

Founded 1986
Total employees 200
Industry Chemicals
Growth Openings in past year 127; percentage growth 173%
Contact Ms. Alicia Pulaski,
Human Resources Manager
Tel 206-577-7222
Fax 206-636-1068

ARNAV Systems, Inc.
PO Box 73730
Puyallup, WA 98373

Founded 1970
Total employees 80
Annual sales $10 million
Industries Computer Hardware, Transportation
Growth Openings in past year 30; percentage growth 60%
Contact Frank Williams, President/CEO
Tel 206-847-3550
Fax 206-847-3966

Cascade Design Automation Corp.
3650 131st Ave.
Southeast, Suite 650
Bellevue, WA 98006

Founded 1991
Total employees 65
Annual sales $10 million
Industry Computer Software
Growth Openings in past year 17; percentage growth 35%
Contact Ms. Lee Frazer, Director of Personnel
Tel 206-643-0200
Fax 206-649-7600

Digital Systems International, Inc.
6464 185th Pl. Northeast
Redmond, WA 98052

Founded 1978
Total employees 400
Annual sales $52 million
Industry Telecommunications
Growth Openings in past year 100; percentage growth 33%
Contact Michael L. Darland, President/CEO
Tel 206-881-7544
Fax 206-556-8022

Electronic Specialty Corp.
14511 North East 13th Ave.
Vancouver, WA 98685

Founded 1983
Total employees 120
Industries Subassemblies and Components, Test and Measurement
Growth Openings in past year 20; percentage growth 20%
Contact Frank Preve, President
Tel 206-574-5000
Fax 206-573-4635

Emcon Northwest, Inc.
18912 North Creek Pkwy., Suite 210
Bothell, WA 98011

Founded 1974
Total employees 210
Annual sales $22 million
Industry Environmental
Growth Openings in past year 80; percentage growth 61%
Contact Ms. Cecilia Simonis, Director of Human Resources
Tel 206-485-5000
Fax 206-486-9766

Fleck Co., Inc.
3410 A St. Southeast
Auburn, WA 98002

Founded 1967
Total employees 90
Annual sales $9.8 million
Industry Manufacturing Equipment
Growth Openings in past year 15; percentage growth 20%
Contact Mrs. Darlene Locken, Personnel Manager
Tel 206-833-5900
Fax 206-833-2245

FourGen Software, Inc.
115 Northeast 100th St.
Seattle, WA 98125

Founded 1983
Total employees 90
Industry Computer Software
Growth Openings in past year 15; percentage growth 20%
Contact Gary Gagliardi, President
Tel 206-522-0055
Fax 206-522-0053

IC Designs
12020 113th Ave. Northeast
Kirkland, WA 98034

Founded 1985
Total employees 40
Industry Subassemblies and Components
Growth Openings in past year 20; percentage growth 100%
Contact Dr. John Q. Torode, President
Tel 206-821-9202
Fax 206-820-8959

ICOS Corp.
22021 20th Ave. Southeast
Bothell, WA 98021

Founded 1989
Total employees 102
Industry Pharmaceuticals
Growth Openings in past year 22; percentage growth 27%
Contact Ms. Susan Moore, Personnel Manager
Tel 206-485-1900
Fax 206-485-1911

Immunex Corp.
51 University St.
Seattle, WA 98101

Founded 1981
Total employees 611
Annual sales $62.6 million
Industry Biotechnology
Growth Openings in past year 80; percentage growth 15%
Contact Ms. Anita Williamson, Human Resources Director
Tel 206-587-0430
Fax 206-587-0606

Industrial Systems, Inc.
18720 142nd Ave. Northeast
Woodinville, WA 98072

Founded 1979
Total employees 40
Annual sales $4.6 million
Industry Computer Software
Growth Openings in past year 15; percentage growth 60%
Contact Max J. Morgan, President
Tel 206-481-6325
Fax 206-481-0506

Interlinq Software Corp.
10230 Northeast Points Dr., Suite 200
Kirkland, WA 98033

Founded 1982
Total employees 126
Annual sales $9.33 million
Industry Computer Software
Growth Openings in past year 36; percentage growth 40%
Contact Ms. Sandra Scribner, Human Resources Manager
Tel 206-827-1112
Fax 206-827-0927

Interpoint Corp.
10301 Willows Rd.
Redmond, WA 98052

Founded 1969
Total employees 500
Annual sales $36 million
Industries Holding Companies, Subassemblies and Components

Growth Openings in past year 50; percentage growth 11%
Contact Ms. Shannon Dillingham, Director of Personnel
Tel 206-882-3100
Fax 206-882-1990

Growth Openings in past year 20; percentage growth 33%
Contact Don Sytsma, COB/CEO/President
Tel 206-251-9411
Fax 206-251-0621

Growth Openings in past year 18; percentage growth 5%
Contact Nicholas Dykstra, VP of Finance and Administration
Tel 206-487-8200
Fax 206-487-3787

Luxar Corp.
19204 Northcreek Pkwy., Suite 100
Bothell, WA 98011

Founded 1987
Total employees 60
Industries Medical, Photonics
Growth Openings in past year 15; percentage growth 33%
Contact Ms. Kathy Laakmann, President
Tel 206-483-4142
Fax 206-483-6844

Microscan Systems, Inc.
939 Industry Dr.
Tukwila, WA 98188

Founded 1982
Total employees 65
Annual sales $10 million
Industry Computer Hardware
Growth Openings in past year 15; percentage growth 30%
Contact Ms. Elizabeth Hall, Personnel Manager
Tel 206-575-3060
Fax 206-575-1904

Quinton Instrument Co.
2121 Terry Ave.
Seattle, WA 98121

Founded 1961
Total employees 691
Annual sales $76 million
Industries Medical, Telecommunications
Growth Openings in past year 91; percentage growth 15%
Contact Ed Schnebele, Director of Personnel
Tel 206-223-7373
Fax 206-223-8465

Maple Systems, Inc.
1930 220th St. Southeast
Bothell, WA 98021

Founded 1983
Total employees 35
Industry Computer Hardware
Growth Openings in past year 15; percentage growth 75%
Contact Ms. Gail St. Peter, Secretary
Tel 206-486-4477
Fax 206-486-4589

Model & Instrument Development Corp.
861 Poplar Pl.
Seattle, WA 98144

Founded 1932
Total employees 50
Annual sales $5 million
Industries Computer Hardware, Medical
Growth Openings in past year 20; percentage growth 66%
Contact Jim Cairns, President/CEO
Tel 206-325-0715
Fax 206-322-6463

Raima Corp.
1605 Northwest Sammamish Rd.
Issaquah, WA 98027

Founded 1982
Total employees 90
Annual sales $8.1 million
Industry Computer Software
Growth Openings in past year 20; percentage growth 28%
Contact J. Robert Newton, President
Tel 206-557-0200
Fax 206-557-5200

Meteor Communications Corp.
6020 South 190th Ave.
Kent, WA 98032

Founded 1975
Total employees 80
Annual sales $5.3 million
Industries Energy, Holding Companies

Panlabs, Inc.
11804 North Creek Pkwy. South
Bothell, WA 98011

Founded 1970
Total employees 370
Annual sales $18 million
Industry Holding Companies

SeaMED Corp.
11810 North Creek Pkwy. North
Bothell, WA 98011

Founded 1976
Total employees 90
Annual sales $12 million
Industries Factory Automation, Medical

Growth Openings in past year 30; percentage growth 50%
Contact Robert W. Berg, President/CEO
Tel 206-485-3399
Fax 206-487-1736

Sierra Geophysics, Inc.
11255 Kirkland Way
Kirkland, WA 98033

Founded 1978
Total employees 300
Industry Computer Software
Growth Openings in past year 145; percentage growth 93%
Contact Dr. Robert S. Hart, President/CEO
Tel 206-822-5200
Fax 206-827-3893

Spry, Inc.
316 Occidental Ave. South
Seattle, WA 98104

Founded 1987
Total employees 25
Industry Computer Software
Growth Openings in past year 15; percentage growth 150%
Contact David Pool, President
Tel 206-447-0300

Teltone Corp.
22121 20th Ave. Southeast
Bothell, WA 98021

Founded 1968
Total employees 100
Annual sales $13 million
Industries Subassemblies and Components, Telecommunications
Growth Openings in past year 15; percentage growth 17%
Contact Ms. Marnie Vitt, Human Resource Manager
Tel 206-487-1515
Fax 206-487-2288

Traveling Software, Inc.
18702 North Creek Pkwy.
Bothell, WA 98011

Founded 1982
Total employees 120
Industry Computer Software
Growth Openings in past year 24; percentage growth 25%
Contact Mark Eppley, COB/CEO
Tel 206-483-8088
Fax 206-487-1284

Walker, Richer and Quinn, Inc.
2815 Eastlake Ave. East
Seattle, WA 98102

Founded 1981
Total employees 250
Annual sales $40 million
Industry Computer Software
Growth Openings in past year 50; percentage growth 25%
Contact Ms. Char Harrington, Personnel Director
Tel 206-324-0350
Fax 206-322-8151

Wall Data, Inc.
17769 Northeast 78th Pl.
Redmond, WA 98052

Founded 1982
Total employees 221
Annual sales $31.79 million
Industry Computer Software
Growth Openings in past year 71; percentage growth 47%
Contact Ms. Jane Graham, Director of Administration and Human Res
Tel 206-883-4777
Fax 206-885-9250

■ **509 Area Code**

Hewlett-Packard Co., Spokane Division
East 24001 Mission Ave.
Liberty Lake, WA 99019

Founded 1979
Total employees 850
Industries Factory Automation, Subassemblies and Components, Telecommunications
Growth Openings in past year 148; percentage growth 21%
Contact James Rundle, General Manager
Tel 509-921-4001

Johnson Matthey Electronics, Inc.
East 15128 Euclid Ave.
Spokane, WA 99216

Founded 1961
Total employees 260
Annual sales $33 million
Industries Advanced Materials, Manufacturing Equipment, Subassemblies and Components
Growth Openings in past year 60; percentage growth 30%
Contact Geoff Wild, General Manager
Tel 509-924-2200
Fax 509-922-8617

Wisconsin

■ **414 Area Code**

A&A Manufacturing Co., Inc.
2300 South Calhoun Rd.
New Berlin, WI 53151

Founded 1945
Total employees 200
Annual sales $30 million
Industries Holding Companies, Test and Measurement

Growth Openings in past year 50; percentage growth 33%
Contact Tim Brehm, Personnel Manager
Tel 414-786-1500
Fax 414-786-3280

Growth Openings in past year 50; percentage growth 25%
Contact Daniel Merkel, COB/CEO
Tel 414-457-5051
Fax 414-457-1485

Growth Openings in past year 25; percentage growth 9%
Contact Lowell Clapp, Personnel Manager
Tel 414-656-4011
Fax 414-656-4370

ABB Robotics, Inc.
2487 South Commerce Dr.
New Berlin, WI 53151

Founded 1984
Total employees 350
Annual sales $54 million
Industry Factory Automation
Growth Openings in past year 49; percentage growth 16%
Contact Ms. Sue Palace, Personnel Manager
Tel 414-785-3400
Fax 414-784-9779

Banner Welder, Inc.
North 117 West 18200 Fulton Dr.
Germantown, WI 53022

Founded 1949
Total employees 115
Annual sales $14 million
Industry Factory Automation
Growth Openings in past year 15; percentage growth 15%
Contact Robert Thome, President
Tel 414-253-2900
Fax 414-253-2919

Electronic Cable Specialists, Inc.
5300 West Franklin Dr.
Franklin, WI 53132

Founded 1984
Total employees 80
Annual sales $7 million
Industry Subassemblies and Components
Growth Openings in past year 24; percentage growth 42%
Contact Paul J. Smyczek, President
Tel 414-421-5300
Fax 414-421-5301

Acro Automation Systems, Inc.
2900 West Greentree Rd.
Milwaukee, WI 53209

Founded 1936
Total employees 150
Annual sales $18 million
Industry Factory Automation
Growth Openings in past year 52; percentage growth 53%
Contact Mike Puhl, VP of Finance/CFO
Tel 414-352-4540
Fax 414-352-1609

Dorner Manufacturing Corp.
580 Industrial Dr.
Hartland, WI 53029

Founded 1973
Total employees 125
Annual sales $20 million
Industries Factory Automation, Subassemblies and Components
Growth Openings in past year 15; percentage growth 13%
Contact Wolfgang Dorner, President
Tel 414-367-7600
Fax 414-367-5827

Electronic Tele-Communications, Inc.
1915 MacArthur Rd.
Waukesha, WI 53188

Founded 1980
Total employees 225
Annual sales $17.9 million
Industries Holding Companies, Telecommunications
Growth Openings in past year 65; percentage growth 40%
Contact George W. Danner, COB/CEO
Tel 414-542-5600
Fax 414-542-1524

American Orthodontics Corp.
1714 Cambridge Ave., PO Box 1048
Sheboygan, WI 53082

Founded 1968
Total employees 250
Annual sales $25 million
Industry Medical

Eaton Corp., Electric Drives Division
3122 14th Ave.
Kenosha, WI 53141

Founded 1931
Total employees 301
Annual sales $38 million
Industries Subassemblies and Components, Test and Measurement

Great Lakes Instruments, Inc.
8855 North 55th St.
Milwaukee, WI 53223

Founded 1970
Total employees 200
Annual sales $23 million
Industries Environmental, Test and Measurement

Growth Openings in past year 25; percentage growth 14%
Contact Chris Dreher, President
Tel 414-355-3601
Fax 414-355-8346

MacLean Fogg Company, Secure Medical Division
369 North Newcomb St.
Whitewater, WI 53190

Founded 1982
Total employees 50
Annual sales $5.5 million
Industries Medical, Subassemblies and Components, Test and Measurement
Growth Openings in past year 25; percentage growth 100%
Contact Tom Sabatino, President
Tel 414-473-7800

MagneTek, Inc., Drives and Systems Division
16555 West Ryerson Rd.
New Berlin, WI 53151

Founded 1901
Total employees 325
Annual sales $35 million
Industries Subassemblies and Components, Test and Measurement
Growth Openings in past year 25; percentage growth 8%
Contact John Steiner, General Manager
Tel 414-782-0200
Fax 414-782-1283

Master Appliance Corp.
2420 18th St.
Racine, WI 53403

Founded 1958
Total employees 50
Annual sales $3.8 million
Industries Factory Automation, Manufacturing Equipment

Growth Openings in past year 15; percentage growth 42%
Contact Scott Radwill, President
Tel 414-633-7791
Fax 414-633-9745

Milwaukee Gear Co.
5150 North Port Washington Rd.
Milwaukee, WI 53217

Founded 1918
Total employees 150
Industry Subassemblies and Components
Growth Openings in past year 50; percentage growth 50%
Contact Tim Sukow, Personnel Manager
Tel 414-962-3532
Fax 414-962-2774

Omega Enterprises
117 South Locust
Appleton, WI 54912

Founded 1936
Total employees 175
Annual sales $19 million
Industry Holding Companies
Growth Openings in past year 15; percentage growth 9%
Contact William R. Bassett, President
Tel 414-739-5312

Seaquist Closures
711 Fox St., PO Box 207
Mukwonago, WI 53149

Founded 1975
Total employees 350
Annual sales $44 million
Industry Factory Automation
Growth Openings in past year 23; percentage growth 7%
Contact Ms. Mary Krager, Personnel Director
Tel 414-363-3658

Strategic Data Systems, Inc.
PO Box 819
Sheboygan, WI 53082

Founded 1981
Total employees 220
Annual sales $14 million
Industry Computer Software
Growth Openings in past year 70; percentage growth 46%
Contact Stuart Warrington, COB/CEO
Tel 414-459-7999
Fax 414-459-9123

■ **608 Area Code**

Clack Corp.
4462 Duraform Ln.
Windsor, WI 53598

Founded 1950
Total employees 150
Annual sales $16 million
Industries Environmental, Manufacturing Equipment
Growth Openings in past year 20; percentage growth 15%
Contact Ms. Colleen Esch Smith, Manager of Human Resources
Tel 608-251-3010
Fax 608-846-2586

Electronic Theatre Control, Inc.
3030 Laura Ln.
Middleton, WI 53562

Founded 1975
Total employees 95
Annual sales $12 million
Industry Energy
Growth Openings in past year 15; percentage growth 18%
Contact Fred Foster, President
Tel 608-831-4116
Fax 608-836-1736

Kaul-Tronics, Inc.
1140 Sextonville Rd.
Richland Center, WI
53581

Founded 1980
Total employees 185
Industry
Telecommunications
Growth Openings in past
year 100; percentage
growth 117%
Contact John R. Kaul,
Chief Executive Officer
Tel 608-647-8902
Fax 608-647-7394

Persoft, Inc.
465 Science Dr.
Madison, WI 53711

Founded 1982
Total employees 75
Annual sales $8.7 million
Industry Computer
Software
Growth Openings in past
year 12; percentage
growth 19%
Contact Ms. Bonnie
McMullen-Lawton,
Personnel Director
Tel 608-273-6000
Fax 608-273-8227

Promega Corp.
2800 Woods Hollow Rd.
Madison, WI 53711

Founded 1977
Total employees 200
Annual sales $25 million
Industries Biotechnology,
Chemicals, Medical
Growth Openings in past
year 30; percentage
growth 17%
Contact Ralph Kauten,
Director of Finance
Tel 608-274-4330
Fax 608-273-6967

Strand Associates, Inc.
910 West Wingra Dr.
Madison, WI 53715

Founded 1946
Total employees 123
Industries Environmental,
Manufacturing
Equipment
Growth Openings in past
year 23; percentage
growth 23%
Contact Ted Richards,
President
Tel 608-251-4843
Fax 608-251-8655

Warzyn Inc.
1 Science Ct.
Madison, WI 53711

Founded 1955
Total employees 275
Annual sales $32 million
Industry Environmental
Growth Openings in past
year 25; percentage
growth 10%
Contact Ms. Veralee
Gregg,
Director of Human
Resources
Tel 608-231-4747
Fax 608-231-4777

■ 715 Area Code

Niro Hudson, Inc.
1600 County Rd. F
Hudson, WI 54016

Founded 1980
Total employees 350
Annual sales $40 million
Industries Subassemblies
and Components, Test
and Measurement
Growth Openings in past
year 134; percentage
growth 62%
Contact Ms. Bea
Simonson,
Personnel Manager
Tel 715-386-9371
Fax 715-386-9376

Rice Lake Weighing Systems, Inc.
230 West Coleman St.
Rice Lake, WI 54868

Founded 1940
Total employees 250
Industries Manufacturing
Equipment, Test and
Measurement
Growth Openings in past
year 25; percentage
growth 11%
Contact James Conn,
President
Tel 715-234-9171
Fax 715-234-6967

Video Monitors, Inc.
3833 North White Ave.
Eau Claire, WI 54703

Founded 1978
Total employees 150
Industry Computer
Hardware
Growth Openings in past
year 50; percentage
growth 50%
Contact Robert J.
Andrews,
President
Tel 715-834-7785
Fax 715-834-5672

Wyoming

■ 307 Area Code

Western Water Consultants, Inc.
611 Skyline Rd.
Laramie, WY 82070

Founded 1980
Total employees 52
Industry Manufacturing
Equipment
Growth Openings in past
year 14; percentage
growth 36%
Contact Paul Rechard,
President
Tel 307-742-0031
Fax 307-721-2913

Indexes

In the preceding part of *The Hidden Job Market 1994,* company profiles appear alphabetically within each state and telephone area code, providing a geographic directory of the fastest-growing small technology companies in the United States. To help in your search for the right job opportunity, this section features two indexes.

The first, the **Industry Index,** lists all companies in this book according to the industry or industries in which they are active, along with their state abbreviation and the page number of their detailed description. Because of the diversity of opportunities offered by high-tech companies, you might find the kind of position you are looking for in more than one area. Don't limit your possibilities!

The second index, the **Company Index,** lists all companies in *The Hidden Job Market 1994* alphabetically, giving their state abbreviation and the page number on which their description appears.

INDUSTRY INDEX

Advanced Materials

Aguirre Engineers, Inc. (CO), *63*

Alliance Pharmaceutical Corp. (CA), *45*

Allied-Signal Inc., Metglas Products Division (NJ), *155*

American Colloid Co. (IL), *89*

American Superconductor Corp. (MA), *126*

AMRESCO, Inc. (OH), *178*

Anderson Engineering, Inc. (MO), *150*

Applied Technical Services, Inc. (GA), *81*

Arlon, Inc., Adhesives & Films Division (CA), *49*

Armco, Inc., Eastern Stainless Division (MD), *114*

Aspen Systems, Inc. (MA), *118*

Auburn Foundry, Inc. (IN), *96*

Auburn Manufacturing, Inc. (ME), *107*

Barracuda Technologies, Inc. (TX), *202*

Bio-Metric Systems, Inc. (MN), *143*

Bostik, Inc. (MA), *118*

Brewer Science, Inc. (MO), *148*

Cabot Corp., Cab-O-Sil Division (IL), *86*

Carlisle Companies, Inc., Motion Control Industries, Inc. (PA), *196*

Carsonite International, Inc. (NV), *152*

Ceramic Coating Co. (KY), *104*

Chen-Northern, Inc. (CO), *63*

Continental Analytical Services, Inc. (KS), *101*

C.P. Hall Co. (IL), *88*

Creative Pultrusions, Inc. (PA), *196*

Crown International, Inc., Fabcom Division (IN), *97*

Current, Inc. (CT), *68*

Dennis Chemical Co. (MO), *149*

Dexter Corp., Dexter Electronic Materials Division (CA), *58*

Dexter Corp., Dexter Packaging Products Division (IL), *91*

Discovery Chemicals, Inc. (LA), *106*

Dixie Chemical Co., Inc. (TX), *209*

Dover Chemical Corp. (OH), *179*

Duncan Enterprises, Inc. (CA), *19*

Eaglebrook, Inc. (IN), *97*

EDO Corp., Acoustics Division (UT), *214*

EGC Corp. (TX), *210*

Elamet Technologies, Inc. (CA), *41*

Ensign-Bickford Optical Technologies, Inc. (CA), *58*

Erie Ceramic Arts Co. (PA), *196*

Fil-Tec, Inc. (MD), *110*

FMC Corp., Food Processing Systems Division (FL), *78*

FMC Corp., Lithium Division (NC), *175*

Franklin Industrial Minerals (TN), *200*

*Advanced Materials
(continued)*

Gar-Ron Plastic Corp.
(MD), *115*

Georgia Marble Co.
(GA), *83*

Goldschmidt Chemical Corp.
(VA), *222*

GTG-Fox Environmental
Services, Ltd. (CO), *64*

Hach Co. (CO), *64*

Hanson Engineers, Inc.
(IL), *87*

Harwick Chemical Corp.
(OH), *179*

Heraeus Amersil, Inc.
(GA), *83*

Hickson DanChem Corp.
(VA), *223*

High Point Chemical Corp.
(NC), *177*

Howard R. Green Co.
(IA), *100*

Howmet Corp., Dover Alloy
Division (NJ), *157*

Hybridyne, Inc. (AZ), *17*

Hydrocarbon Research, Inc.
(NJ), *160*

Industrial Dielectrics, Inc.
(IN), *98*

IRI International, Inc.
(TX), *212*

Jeneric/Pentron, Inc.
(CT), *70*

Johnson and Johnston
Associates, Inc. (NH), *154*

Johnson Matthey Electronics,
Inc. (WA), *227*

Kaneka Texas Corp.
(TX), *211*

Koppel Steel Corp.
(PA), *193*

MACSTEEL (MI), *140*

Magneco/Metrel, Inc.
(IL), *93*

Maine Poly, Inc. (ME), *107*

Martek Biosciences Corp.
(MD), *115*

McGhan NuSil Corp.
(CA), *56*

Mearl Corporation (NY), *174*

Merocel Corp. (CT), *70*

Molded Fiber Glass
Companies, Union City
Division (PA), *197*

Morganite, Inc. (NC), *177*

NEPTCO, Inc. (RI), *198*

Netra Corp. (CA), *38*

Norwood Industries, Inc.
(PA), *189*

NSA Co. (KY), *103*

Pakco Industrial Ceramics,
Inc. (PA), *193*

PCR Group, Inc. (FL), *80*

P.D. George & Co.
(MO), *149*

Pikes Peak Mining Co.
(OR), *186*

Polycast Technology Corp.
(CT), *71*

Polymetallurgical, Inc., Cooper
Wire Division (MA), *123*

Pre Finish Metals
Incorporated (IL), *94*

Reflexite Corp. (CT), *72*

Resco Products, Inc.
(PA), *190*

Sherry Laboratories
(IN), *99*

Simula, Inc. (AZ), *17*

Steward, Inc. (TN), *201*

Superior Graphite Co.
(IL), *89*

Svedala Industries, Inc.,
Grinding Division
(PA), *195*

Synthetic Products Co.
(OH), *180*

Tensar Corp. (GA), *85*

Thermedics, Inc. (MA), *136*

Thielsch Engineering
Associates, Inc. (RI), *198*

Thomas Steel Strip Corp.
(OH), *180*

Toray Plastics America, Inc.
(RI), *198*

Tuscarora Plastics, Inc.
(PA), *193*

US Rubber Reclaiming, Inc.
(MS), *148*

Venture Tape Corp.
(MA), *136*

Wahl Refractories, Inc.
(OH), *181*

Witco Corp., Chemprene
Division (NY), *174*

Zeon Chemicals Kentucky,
Inc. (KY), *103*

3M, Identification and
Converter Systems Division
(MN), *148*

Biotechnology

ABEC, Inc. (PA), *187*

Adeza Biomedical Corp.
(CA), *22*

Agouron Pharmaceuticals,
Inc. (CA), *45*

Agritope, Inc. (OR), *185*

Alltech, Inc. (KY), *104*

Alpha-Beta Technology, Inc.
(MA), *117*

American Type Culture
Collection (MD), *108*

AMRESCO, Inc. (OH), *178*

Anaquest, Inc. (NJ), *161*

Aprogenex, Inc. (TX), *208*

Becton Dickinson
Immunocytometry Systems
(CA), *24*

Becton Dickinson
Microbiology Systems
(MD), *114*

BioCryst Pharmaceuticals,
Inc. (AL), *13*

Biogen, Inc. (MA), *126*

BioGenex Laboratories, Inc.
(CA), *40*

BioKyowa, Inc. (MO), *148*

Biomatrix, Inc. (NJ), *155*

Bio-Metric Systems, Inc.
(MN), *143*

Biopure Corp. (MA), *127*

Bioqual, Inc. (MD), *109*

Boehringer Mannheim Corp.,
Biochemical Products
Division (IN), *98*

Cambridge NeuroScience,
Inc. (MA), *127*

Cell Genesys, Inc. (CA), *33*

Cellco, Inc. (MD), *109*

Cellpro, Inc. (WA), *224*

Center for Advanced
Research in Biotechnology
(MD), *109*

CeraMem Corp. (MA), *127*

CLONTECH Laboratories, Inc. (CA), *34*

Costar Corp. (MA), *128*

CryoLife, Inc. (GA), *82*

Curative Technologies, Inc. (NY), *167*

Cytel Corp. (CA), *46*

CytoTherapeutics, Inc. (RI), *197*

CytRx Corp. (GA), *82*

Cytyc Corp. (MA), *119*

Deltown Specialties (NY), *169*

EcoScience Corp. (MA), *120*

Embrex, Inc. (NC), *176*

Environmental Diagnostic, Inc. (NC), *177*

Epitope, Inc. (OR), *185*

Genencor International, Inc. (NY), *170*

Genetic Therapy, Inc. (MD), *110*

Genetics & IVF Institute (VA), *219*

Genetics Institute, Inc. (MA), *130*

Genosys Biotechnology, Inc. (TX), *210*

Genta, Inc. (CA), *47*

Gist-Brocades Food Ingredients, Inc. (PA), *188*

Hyclone Laboratories, Inc. (UT), *215*

HydroLogic, Inc. (NC), *175*

IDEXX Laboratories, Inc. (ME), *107*

Immune Response Corp. (CA), *47*

Immunex Corp. (WA), *225*

ImmunoGen, Inc. (MA), *131*

Intergen Company (NY), *174*

Jackson Laboratory (ME), *107*

Koch Membrane Systems, Inc. (MA), *122*

Lancaster Laboratories, Inc. (PA), *195*

LifeCore Biomedical, Inc. (MN), *145*

Liposome Co., Inc. (NJ), *160*

Liposome Technology, Inc. (CA), *37*

LJL Biosystems, Inc. (CA), *27*

Martek Biosciences Corp. (MD), *115*

MedImmune, Inc. (MD), *111*

Meridian Diagnostics, Inc. (OH), *182*

Midwest Grain Products, Inc. (KS), *101*

Minntech Corp. (MN), *145*

Molecular Probes, Inc. (OR), *186*

Murex Corp. (GA), *84*

National Diagnostics, Inc. (GA), *84*

National Laboratories, Inc. (IN), *99*

Neutron Products, Inc. (MD), *111*

North American Biologicals, Inc. (FL), *75*

Novo Nordisk Biochemical, Inc. (NC), *177*

Novo Nordisk Pharmaceuticals, Inc. (NJ), *160*

Nunc, Inc. (IL), *93*

Ohmicron Corp. (PA), *190*

Oncogene Science, Inc. (NY), *168*

Oncor, Inc. (MD), *112*

Oread Laboratories, Inc. (KS), *102*

Osteotech, Inc. (NJ), *162*

Otsuka Pharmaceutical Co., Ltd., Maryland Research Laboratories (MD), *112*

Pace Laboratories, Inc. (MN), *146*

PB Diagnostic Systems, Inc. (MA), *134*

Pharmingen, Inc. (CA), *48*

Promega Corp. (WI), *230*

Public Health Research Institute (NY), *165*

Repligen Corp. (MA), *135*

Research Genetics (AL), *15*

Ricerca, Inc. (OH), *180*

R.O.W. Sciences, Inc. (MD), *113*

Somatix Therapy Corporation (CA), *43*

SRA Technologies, Inc., Life Sciences Division (VA), *221*

STS Duotek, Inc. (NY), *172*

Syntex Chemicals, Inc. (CO), *66*

Tanox Biosystems, Inc. (TX), *212*

Terrapin Technologies, Inc. (CA), *30*

Thermedics, Inc. (MA), *136*

Thoren Caging Systems, Inc. (PA), *195*

Transkaryotic Therapies, Inc. (MA), *136*

Unisyn Technologies, Inc. (CA), *54*

University Hygienic Laboratory (IA), *100*

Vestar, Inc. (CA), *61*

Viagene, Inc. (CA), *49*

Chemicals

Advanced Chemical Technologies, Inc. (PA), *187*

Alco Chemical (TN), *199*

Alliance Pharmaceutical Corp. (CA), *45*

American Type Culture Collection (MD), *108*

AMRESCO, Inc. (OH), *178*

Analytical Technologies, Inc. (CA), *45*

Apollo Colors, Inc. (IL), *90*

Applied Technical Services, Inc. (GA), *81*

Avecor, Inc. (TN), *199*

Becton Dickinson Immunocytometry Systems (CA), *24*

Belmay, Inc. (NY), *173*

BioGenex Laboratories, Inc. (CA), *40*

Bio-Rad Laboratories, Inc., ECS Division (CA), *50*

Brewer Science, Inc. (MO), *148*

Cabot Corp., Cab-O-Sil Division (IL), *86*

Cedar Chemical Corp. (TN), *201*

Computer Hardware

Industry Index

Computer Software (continued)

Dataverse Corporation (NY), *174*

Dataware Technologies, Inc. (MA), *129*

Datotek, Inc. (TX), *203*

David Mitchell & Associates, Inc. (MN), *144*

Davidson & Associates, Inc. (CA), *20*

Dayna Communications, Inc. (UT), *214*

DeCarlo Paternite & Associates, Inc. (OH), *178*

Delfin Systems (CA), *25*

Delphi Information Systems, Inc. (CA), *58*

Delphi McCracken, Inc. (MA), *129*

Delta Computer Systems, Inc. (PA), *196*

Delta Research Corp. (VA), *218*

Deltek Systems, Inc. (VA), *218*

Deneba Systems, Inc. (FL), *74*

Dental Plan, Inc. (TX), *203*

Desktop Data, Inc. (MA), *129*

DHI Computing Service, Inc. (UT), *214*

Digidesign, Inc. (CA), *34*

Digimedics Corp. (CA), *26*

Digital Consulting, Inc. (MA), *119*

Digital Solutions, Inc. (MN), *144*

Digital Tools, Inc. (CA), *26*

Digitalk, Inc. (CA), *20*

DISC, Inc. (MD), *115*

DisCopyLabs, Inc. (CA), *41*

D-Link Systems, Inc. (CA), *51*

Dome Software Corp. (IN), *98*

Doradus Corp. (MN), *144*

DP Associates, Inc. (AL), *14*

Dragon Systems, Inc. (MA), *129*

DXI, Inc. (PA), *192*

Dynacs Engineering Co., Inc. (FL), *78*

Dynamac Corporation (MD), *110*

Dynamix, Inc. (OR), *185*

Dynetics, Inc. (AL), *14*

Early Cloud and Co. (RI), *197*

EAS Technologies, Inc. (KY), *102*

Easel Corp. (MA), *129*

Echelon Corp. (CA), *34*

Electronic Book Technologies, Inc. (RI), *197*

Electronic Data Systems Corp., Local Governments Division (NC), *176*

Electronic Information Systems, Inc. (CT), *69*

Electronic Systems USA, Inc. (KY), *102*

Electronics for Imaging, Inc. (CA), *34*

Engineering Design Automation (CA), *41*

ENSCO, Inc., Instrumentation Software Systems Division (NY), *169*

Ensys (PA), *192*

Enterprise Systems, Inc. (IL), *91*

Environmental Systems Research Institute, Inc. (CA), *61*

Epoch Systems, Inc. (MA), *120*

Ergo Computing, Inc. (MA), *120*

ESS Technology, Inc. (CA), *41*

Etak, Inc. (CA), *34*

Executive Software, Inc. (CA), *58*

Executive Systems, Inc. (CA), *56*

Expertware, Inc. (CA), *26*

Falcon Microsystems, Inc. (MD), *110*

Farallon Computing, Inc. (CA), *41*

FD Consulting, Inc. (NY), *164*

Fidelity Medical, Inc. (NJ), *156*

Fifth Generation Systems, Inc. (LA), *106*

Financial Data Planning Corp. (FL), *75*

First Community Services, Inc. (TX), *213*

First Data Systems, Inc. (TN), *200*

Fischer International Systems Corp. (FL), *78*

Fiserv, Inc., CBS Division (FL), *76*

Focus Enhancements (MA), *130*

FormMaker Software, Inc. (GA), *83*

FourGen Software, Inc. (WA), *225*

Frame Technology Corp. (CA), *26*

Fusion Systems Group, Inc. (NY), *164*

FutureSoft Engineering, Inc. (TX), *210*

GBS Computer Systems, Inc. (OH), *179*

GCC Technologies, Inc. (MA), *130*

GEAC Computers, Inc. (TX), *203*

Gemma International, Inc. (IL), *92*

Genelco, Inc. (MO), *149*

General Computer Corp. (OH), *179*

General Parametrics Corp. (CA), *42*

General Systems Solutions, Inc. (CT), *69*

GHG Corp. (TX), *210*

GIS/Trans, Ltd. (MA), *131*

Global Technology Corp. (MD), *110*

Global Turnkey Systems, Inc. (NJ), *157*

GMIS Inc. (PA), *188*

GO Corp. (CA), *35*

Great Plains Software (ND), *177*

Great Valley Products, Inc. (PA), *189*

Industry Index

Computer Software
(continued)

Thomas-Conrad Corp.
(TX), 208

Timberline Software Corp.
(OR), 187

Timeworks, Inc. (IL), 95

Tivoli Systems, Inc.
(TX), 208

Tone Software Corp.
(CA), 54

Traveling Software, Inc.
(WA), 227

Trident Data Systems, Inc.
(CA), 22

Tripos Associates, Inc.
(MO), 150

TRW Financial Systems, Inc.
(CA), 44

TSI International, Ltd.
(CT), 73

TSSI (OR), 187

TYBRIN Corp. (FL), 80

UIS, Inc. (MA), 136

Unifi Communications Corp.
(MA), 125

Unify Corp. (CA), 63

Unitech Systems, Inc.
(IL), 95

United States Data
Corporation (TX), 206

U.S. Robotics, Inc.
(IL), 95

Vantage Analysis Systems,
Inc. (CA), 44

Vantage Computer Systems,
Inc. (CT), 73

Verbex Voice Systems, Inc.
(NJ), 162

Verdix Corp. (VA), 222

Verity, Inc. (CA), 39

Vertex Inc. (PA), 191

V.I. Corporation (MA), 116

Viasoft, Inc. (AZ), 18

Viewlogic Systems, Inc.
(MA), 125

ViewStar Corp. (CA), 44

Virgin Games, Inc. (CA), 55

Vista Concepts, Inc.
(NY), 165

VMARK Software, Inc.
(MA), 125

Vortech Data, Inc. (TX), 206

Walker, Richer and Quinn,
Inc. (WA), 227

Wall Data, Inc. (WA), 227

W.E. Carson Associates, Inc.
(GA), 85

Wellfleet Communications,
Inc. (MA), 137

Westbrook Technologies
(CT), 74

Westcorp Software Systems,
Inc. (GA), 85

Whittaker Electronics
Systems (CA), 57

Wollongong Group, Inc.
(CA), 39

Wonderware Software
Development Corp.
(CA), 55

Workgroup Technology Corp.
(MA), 137

XATA Corp. (MN), 147

XDB Systems, Inc.
(MD), 114

Xilinx, Inc. (CA), 32

Xscribe Corp. (CA), 49

XVT Software, Inc.
(CO), 66

Zycad Corp. (CA), 44

Zymark Corp. (MA), 126

3M, Health Information
Systems Department
(UT), 216

3Net Systems, Inc.
(CA), 63

Defense

Advanced Communication
Systems, Inc. (VA), 217

Advanced Systems
Technologies, Inc.
(GA), 80

Andrulis Research Corp.
(MD), 108

Applied Research, Inc.
(AL), 13

Applied Signal Technology,
Inc. (CA), 23

California Jamar, Inc.
(CA), 46

CAS, Inc. (AL), 13

CFD Research Corp.
(AL), 13

CIC International, Inc.
(NY), 172

CMS, Inc. (FL), 77

Coleman Research Corp.
(FL), 76

Computer Sciences Corp.,
Systems Engineering
Division (MD), 114

Condor Systems, Inc.
(CA), 25

Construction Engineering
Research Laboratories
(IL), 86

Control Products Corp.
(TX), 203

DCS Corp. (VA), 218

Dynetics, Inc. (AL), 14

EDO Corp., Acoustics Division
(UT), 214

Eidetics International, Inc.
(CA), 20

EMCO, Inc. (AL), 14

EML Research, Inc.
(MA), 120

Entwistle Co. (MA), 120

Global Associates, Ltd.
(VA), 219

Group Technologies Corp.
(FL), 78

ILC Dover, Inc. (DE), 74

Information Technology and
Applications Corp.
(VA), 219

Johnson Engineering Corp.
(CO), 65

Kaiser Aerotech (CA), 42

Keller and Gannon
(CA), 36

KOR Electronics, Inc.
(CA), 51

KRUG Life Sciences Inc.,
Houston Division
(TX), 211

LB&M Associates, Inc.
(OK), 184

Logicon Eagle Technology,
Inc. (FL), 76

Logicon, Inc., Operating
Systems (VA), 220

Loral Hycor, Inc. (MA), 132

Loral Information Display
Systems (GA), 83

Energy

Environmental

Factory Automation

Holding Companies

Industry Index

Manufacturing Equipment

Pharmaceuticals

Agouron Pharmaceuticals,
Inc. (CA), *45*

Alcon Laboratories, Inc.,
Ophthalmic Division
(TX), *212*

Alliance Pharmaceutical Corp.
(CA), *45*

Alpha-Beta Technology, Inc.
(MA), *117*

Anaquest, Inc. (NJ), *161*

Arnet Pharmaceutical Corp.
(FL), *74*

Astra Pharmaceutical
Products, Inc. (MA), *118*

Athena Neurosciences, Inc.
(CA), *33*

Bausch & Lomb
Pharmaceuticals, Inc.
(FL), *77*

Biogen, Inc. (MA), *126*

Biopure Corp. (MA), *127*

Bock Pharmacal Co.
(MO), *148*

Boehringer Mannheim
Pharmaceuticals (MD), *109*

Boots Pharmaceutical, Inc.
(IL), *90*

Cambridge NeuroScience,
Inc. (MA), *127*

Center for Blood Research
(MA), *127*

Center Laboratories
(NY), *167*

ClinTrials, Inc. (KY), *104*

Colgate-Hoyt, Gel-Kam
(MA), *128*

Consolidated Technologies,
Inc. (TX), *207*

Cortech, Inc. (CO), *64*

Curative Technologies, Inc.
(NY), *167*

CytRx Corp. (GA), *82*

Danbury Pharmacal, Inc.
(NY), *173*

Dura Pharmaceuticals, Inc.
(CA), *46*

Embrex, Inc. (NC), *176*

Eon Labs Manufacturing, Inc.
(NY), *172*

Ferndale Laboratories, Inc.
(MI), *138*

FMC Corp., Lithium Division
(NC), *175*

Gensia Pharmaceuticals, Inc.
(CA), *47*

Genta, Inc. (CA), *47*

Gilead Sciences, Inc.
(CA), *35*

Gull Laboratories, Inc.
(UT), *215*

ICOS Corp. (WA), *225*

Immune Response Corp.
(CA), *47*

Intergen Company (NY), *174*

JWS Delavau Co., Inc.
(PA), *189*

K-V Pharmaceutical Co.
(MO), *149*

Lancaster Laboratories, Inc.
(PA), *195*

Lee Laboratories, Inc.
(VA), *223*

Lemmon Co. (PA), *189*

Martek Biosciences Corp.
(MD), *115*

Materials Processing
Technology, Inc. (NJ), *157*

MedImmune, Inc. (MD), *111*

Meridian Diagnostics, Inc.
(OH), *182*

Mikart, Inc. (GA), *84*

Mylan Laboratories, Inc.
(PA), *193*

National Diagnostics, Inc.
(GA), *84*

National Medical Research
Corp. (CT), *70*

National Patent Medical
(CT), *71*

Neurogen Corp. (CT), *71*

NOBL Laboratories, Inc.
(IA), *101*

Noramco, Inc. (GA), *86*

North American Biologicals,
Inc. (FL), *75*

Ohmeda, Salt Lake Division
(UT), *215*

Oread Laboratories, Inc.
(KS), *102*

Ortho Pharmaceutical Corp.,
Advanced Care Products
Division (NJ), *162*

Osteotech, Inc. (NJ), *162*

Otsuka Pharmaceutical Co.,
Ltd., Maryland Research
Laboratories (MD), *112*

PB Diagnostic Systems, Inc.
(MA), *134*

PCR Group, Inc. (FL), *80*

PharmaControl Corp.
(NJ), *158*

PharmaKinetics Laboratories,
Inc. (MD), *115*

Private Formulations, Inc.
(NJ), *162*

Regeneron Pharmaceuticals,
Inc. (NY), *174*

Repligen Corp. (MA), *135*

Roxane Laboratories, Inc.
(OH), *183*

Select Laboratories, Inc.
(GA), *85*

SoloPak Pharmaceuticals, Inc.
(IL), *94*

Steris Laboratories
(AZ), *18*

Synaptic Pharmaceutical
Corp. (NJ), *158*

Synergen, Inc. (CO), *66*

Syntex Chemicals, Inc.
(CO), *66*

Theratech, Inc. (UT), *216*

Triplex Pharmaceutical, Inc.
(TX), *212*

Univax Biologics, Inc.
(MD), *113*

U.S. Bioscience, Inc.
(PA), *191*

Vestar, Inc. (CA), *61*

Warner-Lambert Co., Warner
Chilcott Laboratories
Division (NJ), *158*

WIL Research Laboratories,
Inc. (OH), *181*

Photonics

Advanced Photonix, Inc.
(CA), *55*

Alden Electronics, Inc.
(MA), *117*

Amber Engineering, Inc.
(CA), *55*

AMP Incorporated, Kaptron
(CA), *32*

Subassemblies and Components

Vari-L Co., Inc. (CO), *66*

Verdix Corp. (VA), *222*

Vertex Communications Corp. (TX), *213*

VideoServer, Inc. (MA), *137*

VME Microsystems International Corp. (AL), *15*

VMX, Inc. (CA), *32*

VoiceCom Systems, Inc. (CA), *39*

Volpi Manufacturing USA, Inc. (NY), *166*

VTEL Corp. (TX), *208*

Wellfleet Communications, Inc. (MA), *137*

Westinghouse Electric Corp., Distribution and Control Business Unit (PA), *194*

Whittaker Electronics Systems (CA), *57*

XDB Systems, Inc. (MD), *114*

Xylogics, Inc. (MA), *137*

Test and Measurement

A&A Manufacturing Co., Inc. (WI), *227*

Acoustic Systems, Inc. (TX), *206*

Action Instruments, Inc. (CA), *44*

Alden Electronics, Inc. (MA), *117*

Alltech Associates, Inc. (IL), *89*

Amber Engineering, Inc. (CA), *55*

American Sigma, Inc. (NY), *170*

AMETEK, Inc., Mansfield and Green Division (FL), *77*

AMP Incorporated, Kaptron (CA), *32*

Amring, Inc. (CT), *68*

AMSCO Scientific (NC), *176*

Andrulis Research Corp. (MD), *108*

Anvic International (GA), *81*

Arizona Instrument Corp. (AZ), *16*

Array Analysis, Inc. (NY), *169*

Astro International Corp. (TX), *208*

Autoclave Engineers, Inc. (PA), *195*

Bacharach, Inc. (PA), *191*

Baker Co. (ME), *107*

Balluff, Inc. (KY), *104*

Becton Dickinson Microbiology Systems (MD), *114*

Beede Electrical Instrument Co., Inc. (NH), *153*

Bicron Corp. (OH), *178*

Binax, Inc. (ME), *107*

Biosystems, Inc. (CT), *68*

Bio-Tek Instruments, Inc. (VT), *216*

Bliss-Salem, Inc. (OH), *178*

Bohlin Instruments, Inc. (NJ), *159*

Bran and Luebbe, Inc. (IL), *90*

Brewer Science, Inc. (MO), *148*

Carl Zeiss, Inc. (NY), *173*

Carsonite International, Inc. (NV), *152*

CBS Scientific Co. (CA), *46*

Cell Robotics, Inc. (NM), *163*

CeraMem Corp. (MA), *127*

CI Systems, Inc. (CA), *57*

Cincinnati Sub-Zero Products, Inc. (OH), *181*

Clestra Cleanroom Technology (NY), *165*

Clif Mock Co., Inc. (TX), *206*

Columbia Scientific Industries Corp. (TX), *207*

Compressor Controls Corp. (IA), *101*

Computational Systems, Inc. (TN), *199*

Conveyor Components Co. (MI), *138*

Costar Corp. (MA), *128*

C-Power Companies, Inc. (TX), *203*

Crompton Modutec, Inc. (NH), *153*

Cuda Products Corp. (FL), *80*

DAI Technologies, Inc. (IL), *91*

Daktronics, Inc. (SD), *199*

Davis Liquid Crystals, Inc. (CA), *41*

Delavan Process Instrumentation (IL), *96*

Denver Instrument Co. (CO), *64*

Develco, Inc. (TX), *209*

Digital Products Corp. (FL), *75*

Dolan-Jenner Industries, Inc. (MA), *129*

Drexelbrook Engineering Co. (PA), *188*

DSP Technology Inc. (CA), *41*

Dwyer Instruments, Inc. (IN), *97*

Eaton Corp., Controls Division (AL), *14*

Eaton Corp., Electric Drives Division (WI), *228*

Eaton Corp., Lebow Products Division (MI), *138*

EDO Corp., Acoustics Division (UT), *214*

Electronic Associates, Inc. (NJ), *161*

Electronic Controls Co. (ID), *86*

Electronic Specialty Corp. (WA), *225*

Emerson Electric Co., Rosemount Analytical Division (CA), *26*

Endress & Hauser, Inc. (IN), *98*

Environmental Diagnostic, Inc. (NC), *177*

EPE Technologies, Inc. (CA), *51*

ETL Testing Laboratories, Inc. (NY), *169*

Fairchild Corporation, Camloc Products Division (NJ), *156*

Transportation

Industry Index

Structured Technology Corp.
(CT), *72*

Syracuse Research Corp.
(NY), *166*

TANO Automation, Inc.
(LA), *106*

V, G Systems, Inc.
(MN), *147*

VDO-Yazaki Corp. (VA), *222*

Western Filter Corp.
(CA), *57*

Wilcox Electric, Inc.
(MO), *152*

COMPANY INDEX

A

A&A Manufacturing Co., Inc.
(WI), *227*

ABB Robotics, Inc.
(WI), *228*

ABB Traction, Inc. (NY), *169*

ABEC, Inc. (PA), *187*

Abra Cadabra Software, Inc.
(FL), *77*

Academic Press, Inc.
(CA), *44*

Access Health Marketing, Inc.
(CA), *62*

ACCO USA (IL), *89*

Accolade, Inc. (CA), *22*

Accurate Electronics, Inc.
(CT), *67*

Accu-Therm, Inc. (MO), *148*

Accutron, Inc. (CT), *67*

Accu-Weather, Inc.
(PA), *195*

Acheson Industries, Inc.
(MI), *137*

Acoustic Systems, Inc.
(TX), *206*

Acro Automation Systems,
Inc. (WI), *228*

Acromed Corp. (OH), *178*

ACTEL Corp. (CA), *22*

Action Instruments, Inc.
(CA), *44*

Action Technologies, Inc.
(CA), *40*

Activision, Inc. (CA), *19*

ADAC Laboratories
(CA), *22*

Adeza Biomedical Corp.
(CA), *22*

ADI Systems, Inc. (CA), *22*

Adobe Systems, Inc.
(CA), *32*

ADRA Systems, Inc.
(MA), *116*

Adroit Systems, Inc.
(VA), *216*

Adtran, Inc. (AL), *13*

Advance Machine Technology
(OR), *184*

Advanced Assembly
Automation, Inc. (OH), *181*

Advanced Cable
Technologies, Inc.
(MA), *116*

Advanced Chemical
Technologies, Inc.
(PA), *187*

Advanced Communication
Systems, Inc. (VA), *217*

Advanced Compression
Technology, Inc. (CA), *55*

Advanced Flex, Inc.
(MN), *142*

Advanced Input Devices
(ID), *86*

Advanced Medical Systems,
Inc. (CT), *67*

Advanced NMR Systems, Inc.
(MA), *116*

Advanced Photonix, Inc.
(CA), *55*

Advanced Power Technology,
Inc. (OR), *184*

Advanced Processing
Laboratories (CA), *44*

Advanced Production
Systems, Inc. (KY), *102*

Advanced Semiconductor
Materials America, Inc.
(AZ), *15*

Advanced Systems
Technologies, Inc.
(GA), *80*

Advanced Technology
Systems, Inc. (VA), *217*

Advanced Tissue Sciences,
Inc. (CA), *45*

Advent Software, Inc.
(CA), *32*

Aegis, Inc. (MA), *117*

Aehr Test Systems
(CA), *32*

Aero Corp. (FL), *79*

Aero Plastics, Inc. (MA), *117*

AG Associates (CA), *22*

AGE Logic, Inc. (CA), *45*

Agency Management
Services, Inc. (MA), *126*

AGIE USA, Ltd. (NC), *175*

Agouron Pharmaceuticals,
Inc. (CA), *45*

Agris Corp. (GA), *80*

Agritope, Inc. (OR), *185*

Aguirre Engineers, Inc.
(CO), *63*

AIM, Inc. (MD), *114*

Aitech International Corp.
(CA), *23*

A.J. Sackett & Sons Co.
(MD), *114*

Akashic Memories
Corporation (CA), *23*

Alacrity Systems, Inc.
(NJ), *160*

Alan Plummer and
Associates, Inc. (TX), *212*

Alco Chemical (TN), *199*

Alcon Laboratories, Inc.,
Ophthalmic Division
(TX), *212*

Alden Electronics, Inc.
(MA), *117*

Aldus Corp. (WA), *223*

Alexander Batteries
(IA), *100*

Alfred Benesch & Co.
(IL), *87*

Algor, Inc. (PA), *191*

Alkermes, Inc. (MA), *126*

ALLDATA Corp. (CA), *62*

Allen Communication, Inc.
(UT), *214*

Alliance Automation Systems
(NY), *170*

Alliance Pharmaceutical Corp.
(CA), *45*

Allied Data Communications
Group, Inc. (GA), *81*

Allied Telesis, Inc. (CA), *32*

Allied-Signal Inc., Metglas
Products Division
(NJ), *155*

Alltech Associates, Inc.
(IL), *89*

Alltech, Inc. (KY), *104*

Company Index

First Data Systems, Inc.
(TN), *200*

First International Computer
of America, Inc. (CA), *41*

Fischer International Systems
Corp. (FL), *78*

FIserv, Inc., CBS Division
(FL), *76*

Fisher Research Laboratory,
Inc. (CA), *19*

Fleck Co., Inc. (WA), *225*

Flight Systems, Inc.
(PA), *194*

Flojet Corp. (CA), *51*

Fluid Energy Processing and
Equipment Co. (PA), *188*

FMC Corp., Food Processing
Systems Division
(FL), *78*

FMC Corp., Lithium Division
(NC), *175*

Focus Enhancements
(MA), *130*

Focus Graphics, Inc.
(CA), *35*

Formation, Inc. (NJ), *159*

FormMaker Software, Inc.
(GA), *83*

Forster Enterprises, Inc.
(CT), *69*

FourGen Software, Inc.
(WA), *225*

Frame Technology Corp.
(CA), *26*

Franklin Industrial Minerals
(TN), *200*

Frasca International, Inc.
(IL), *87*

Fresenius U.S.A., Inc.
(CA), *42*

Fresnel Optics, Inc.
(NY), *170*

Freudenberg-NOK, Plastic
Products Division
(NH), *154*

Friden Neopost (CA), *42*

FSI International, Inc.
(MN), *144*

FSSL, Inc. (TX), *210*

Fugro-McClelland
(Environmental), Inc.
(TX), *210*

Fujinon, Inc. (NJ), *156*

Fusion Systems Group, Inc.
(NY), *164*

FutureSoft Engineering, Inc.
(TX), *210*

FWT, Inc. (TX), *213*

G

G&E Engineering, Inc.
(LA), *106*

GAI Consultants, Inc.
(PA), *192*

Gaiser Tool Co. (CA), *56*

Gar-Ron Plastic Corp.
(MD), *115*

Garry Electronics (NJ), *160*

Gast Manufacturing Corp.
(MI), *140*

Gatan, Inc. (CA), *42*

GBS Computer Systems, Inc.
(OH), *179*

GCA Group, Inc. (KY), *102*

GCC Technologies, Inc.
(MA), *130*

GCH Systems, Inc.
(CA), *35*

GEAC Computers, Inc.
(TX), *203*

Gemma International, Inc.
(IL), *92*

Genelco, Inc. (MO), *149*

Genencor International, Inc.
(NY), *170*

General Computer Corp.
(OH), *179*

General Devices Co., Inc.
(IN), *98*

General Metal Finishing Co.,
Inc. (MA), *120*

General Parametrics Corp.
(CA), *42*

General Physics Corp.
(MD), *110*

General Systems Solutions,
Inc. (CT), *69*

Genetic Therapy, Inc.
(MD), *110*

Genetics & IVF Institute
(VA), *219*

Genetics Institute, Inc.
(MA), *130*

GENE-TRAK Systems Corp.
(MA), *120*

Genosys Biotechnology, Inc.
(TX), *210*

Gen-Probe, Inc. (CA), *47*

Gensia Pharmaceuticals, Inc.
(CA), *47*

Genta, Inc. (CA), *47*

Gentex Corp. (MI), *141*

Gentner Communications
Corp. (UT), *214*

Geomet Technologies, Inc.
(MD), *110*

George Risk Industries, Inc.
(NE), *152*

Georgens Industries, Inc.
(CA), *47*

Georgia Marble Co.
(GA), *83*

GeoTek Industries, Inc.
(NJ), *156*

GHG Corp. (TX), *210*

Giga-tronics, Inc. (CA), *42*

Gilead Sciences, Inc.
(CA), *35*

Gist-Brocades Food
Ingredients, Inc. (PA), *188*

GIS/Trans, Ltd. (MA), *131*

Glenair, Inc. (CA), *58*

Global Associates, Ltd.
(VA), *219*

Global Technology Corp.
(MD), *110*

Global Turnkey Systems, Inc.
(NJ), *157*

Global Village
Communications, Inc.
(CA), *35*

Globe Manufacturing Sales,
Inc. (NJ), *162*

Globe Motors (OH), *182*

GMIS Inc. (PA), *188*

GO Corp. (CA), *35*

Goldschmidt Chemical Corp.
(VA), *222*

Goodpasture, Inc. (TX), *212*

Gotham Ink & Color Co., Inc.
(NY), *174*

Gougler Industries, Inc.
(OH), *179*

Governair (OK), *184*

Graham Magnetics, Inc.
(TX), *213*

Graham Manufacturing Co.,
Inc. (NY), *170*

Grand Haven Stamped
Products Co. (MI), *141*
Granite Communications, Inc.
(NH), *154*
Graphnet, Inc. (NJ), *157*
Graseby Electro-Optics, Inc.
(FL), *76*
Great Lakes Instruments, Inc.
(WI), *228*
Great Plains Software
(ND), *177*
Great Valley Products, Inc.
(PA), *189*
Green Manufacturing, Inc.
(OH), *181*
Greenbrier & Russel, Inc.
(IL), *92*
Grote Industries, Inc.
(IN), *99*
Group Technologies Corp.
(FL), *78*
GSI (PA), *192*
GTE Health Systems
(AZ), *16*
GTE Industry Products and
Services, Inc. (FL), *78*
GTG-Fox Environmental
Services, Ltd. (CO), *64*
Guided Wave, Inc. (CA), *62*
Gull Laboratories, Inc.
(UT), *215*
Gupta Technologies, Inc.
(CA), *35*
G.W. Lisk Co., Inc.
(NY), *165*
GynoPharma, Inc. (NJ), *162*
GZA GeoEnvironmental, Inc.
(MA), *131*
GZA GeoEnvironmental
Technologies, Inc.
(MA), *131*

H

Hach Co. (CO), *64*
Hague International
(ME), *107*
Hallmark Circuits, Inc.
(CA), *47*
Hampshire Instruments, Inc.
(NY), *170*
Hanna Instruments
(RI), *197*

Hanson Engineers, Inc.
(IL), *87*
Harbor Electronics, Inc.
(CT), *69*
Harbor Software, Inc.
(MA), *121*
Harmon Industries, Inc.
(MO), *151*
Harris Corp., Digital
Telephone Systems Division
(CA), *35*
Harsco Corp., Sherwood
Division (NY), *171*
Hartley Courseware
(MI), *140*
Harwick Chemical Corp.
(OH), *179*
Hathaway Corp. (CO), *64*
Hauser Chemical Research,
Inc. (CO), *64*
Hazmat Environmental Group,
Inc. (NY), *171*
HBM, Inc. (MA), *121*
HCIA (MI), *138*
Healthwatch, Inc., Cambridge
Medical Division (CO), *65*
Healthy Buildings
International, Inc.
(VA), *219*
HEI, Inc. (MN), *144*
Henley International, Inc.
(TX), *210*
Heraeus Amersil, Inc.
(GA), *83*
Heraeus Electro-Nite Co.
(PA), *189*
Herbert Friedman &
Associates, Inc. (IL), *92*
Hewlett-Packard Co.,
Spokane Division
(WA), *227*
HGM Medical Laser Systems,
Inc. (UT), *215*
Hickson DanChem Corp.
(VA), *223*
High Point Chemical Corp.
(NC), *177*
Highland Laboratories, Inc.
(MA), *121*
Hilliard Corp. (NY), *170*
Hillmann Environmental Co.
(NJ), *162*

Hobart Airport Systems
(FL), *75*
Hogan Systems, Inc.
(TX), *204*
Hologic, Inc. (MA), *131*
Homaco, Inc. (IL), *88*
Homisco, Inc. (MA), *131*
Hotsy Corp. (CO), *65*
Howard R. Green Co.
(IA), *100*
Howmet Corp., Dover Alloy
Division (NJ), *157*
Hoya Electronics Corp.
(CA), *26*
HSQ Technology (CA), *35*
HTI Voice Solutions, Inc.
(MA), *121*
Hughes Display Products
Corp. (KY), *105*
Huntington Laboratories, Inc.
(IN), *97*
HWS Engineering, Inc.
(NE), *152*
Hybridyne, Inc. (AZ), *17*
Hyclone Laboratories, Inc.
(UT), *215*
Hydrocarbon Research, Inc.
(NJ), *160*
HydroLogic, Inc. (NC), *175*
HyperDesk Corp. (MA), *121*

I

I-Bus PC Technologies
(CA), *47*
IC Designs (WA), *225*
ICOM Simulations, Inc.
(IL), *92*
Iconics, Inc. (MA), *121*
ICOS Corp. (WA), *225*
IDB Communications Group,
Inc. (CA), *19*
Ideal Learning, Inc.
(TX), *204*
IDEXX Laboratories, Inc.
(ME), *107*
IDX Systems Corp.
(VT), *216*
IDX Systems Corp., Systems
Division (VT), *216*
IEC Electronics Corp.
(NY), *165*
IGEN, Inc. (MD), *110*

Company Index

Sierracin Corp., Harrison Division (CA), *59*

Sigmatech, Inc. (AL), *15*

Signal Technology Corporation (MA), *135*

Simon Hydro-Search, Inc. (CA), *53*

Simons Conkey, Inc. (MN), *146*

Simplimatic Engineering Co. (VA), *223*

Simpson Industries, Inc., Troy Operations (OH), *182*

Simula, Inc. (AZ), *17*

Simulation Sciences Inc. (CA), *53*

Skelly and Loy, Inc. (PA), *195*

SL Montevideo Technology, Inc. (MN), *146*

Slate Corp. (AZ), *17*

Smith & Nephew Dyonics (MA), *124*

Smith Micro Software, Inc. (CA), *53*

Smoot Co. (KS), *102*

S-MOS Systems, Inc. (CA), *30*

SMT East Corp. (MA), *124*

SMTEK, Inc. (CA), *56*

SofNet, Inc. (GA), *85*

Softdesk, Inc. (NH), *155*

SoftSolutions Technology Corp. (UT), *216*

Software Artistry, Inc. (IN), *99*

Software Engineering of America, Inc. (NY), *168*

Software of the Future, Inc. (TX), *205*

Software Quality Automation (MA), *135*

Software Technology, Inc. (FL), *77*

Software Toolworks, Inc. (CA), *39*

Solitec, Inc. (CA), *30*

SoloPak Pharmaceuticals, Inc. (IL), *94*

Somanetics Corp. (MI), *139*

Somatix Therapy Corporation (CA), *43*

Sonalysts, Inc. (CT), *72*

Source Data Systems, Inc. (IA), *100*

Southington Tool & Manufacturing Corp. (CT), *72*

Southwest Network Services, Inc. (TX), *207*

Spar Communications Group (CA), *57*

Sparton Technology, Inc. (NM), *163*

Special Resource Management, Inc. (MT), *152*

Spectra-Physics, Inc., Construction & Agricultural Division (OH), *182*

Spectrolab, Inc. (CA), *60*

Spectrum Control, Inc. (PA), *197*

Spectrum Human Resources Systems Corp. (CO), *66*

Spectrum Plastics Molding Resources, Inc. (CT), *72*

Spellman High Voltage Electronics Corp. (NY), *168*

Spinnaker Software Corp. (MA), *135*

Spry, Inc. (WA), *227*

SPSS, Inc. (IL), *89*

SRA Technologies, Inc. (VA), *221*

SRA Technologies, Inc., Life Sciences Division (VA), *221*

SSI, Photo I.D. (OK), *184*

Stac Electronics, Inc. (CA), *48*

Stamped Products, Inc. (AL), *15*

Star Cutter Co. (MI), *139*

State Of The Art, Inc. (CA), *54*

Statistica, Inc. (MD), *113*

Stauff Corp. (NJ), *158*

Steinbrecher Corp. (MA), *135*

Stephens Engineering Co., Inc. (MD), *113*

Steris Corp. (OH), *180*

Steris Laboratories (AZ), *18*

Sterling Electronics Corporation (TX), *211*

Sterling Information Group, Inc. (TX), *208*

Sterling Software, Inc., Directions Division (TX), *205*

Sterling Software, Inc., Dylakor Division (CA), *60*

Steward, Inc. (TN), *201*

Stockholder Systems, Inc. (GA), *85*

Storz Instrument Co. (MO), *150*

Strand Associates, Inc. (WI), *230*

Strategic Data Systems, Inc. (WI), *229*

Strategic Simulations, Inc. (CA), *30*

Structural Integrity Associates, Inc. (CA), *31*

Structured Technology Corp. (CT), *72*

Struthers Electronics (NY), *168*

STS Duotek, Inc. (NY), *172*

STV Group, Inc. (PA), *190*

Summit Information Systems Corp. (OR), *187*

SunDisk Corp. (CA), *31*

SunGard Computer Services, Inc. (PA), *190*

SunGard Financial Systems, Inc. (CA), *60*

SunGard Investment Systems, Inc. (IL), *94*

Sunland Fabricators, Inc. (LA), *106*

Sunquest Information Systems, Inc. (AZ), *18*

Sunrise Medical Inc., Quickie Designs (CA), *19*

SunSoft, Inc. (CA), *39*

Superior Graphite Co. (IL), *89*

Supra Corp. (OR), *187*

Surgimach Corp. (GA), *86*

Surya Electronics, Inc. (IL), *94*

Sutter Corporation (CA), *49*

Suttle Apparatus Corp. (MN), *146*